VIZ GRAPHIC NOVEL

From Far Away™

vol. 5

Story and Art by

Kyoko Hikawa

CONTENTS

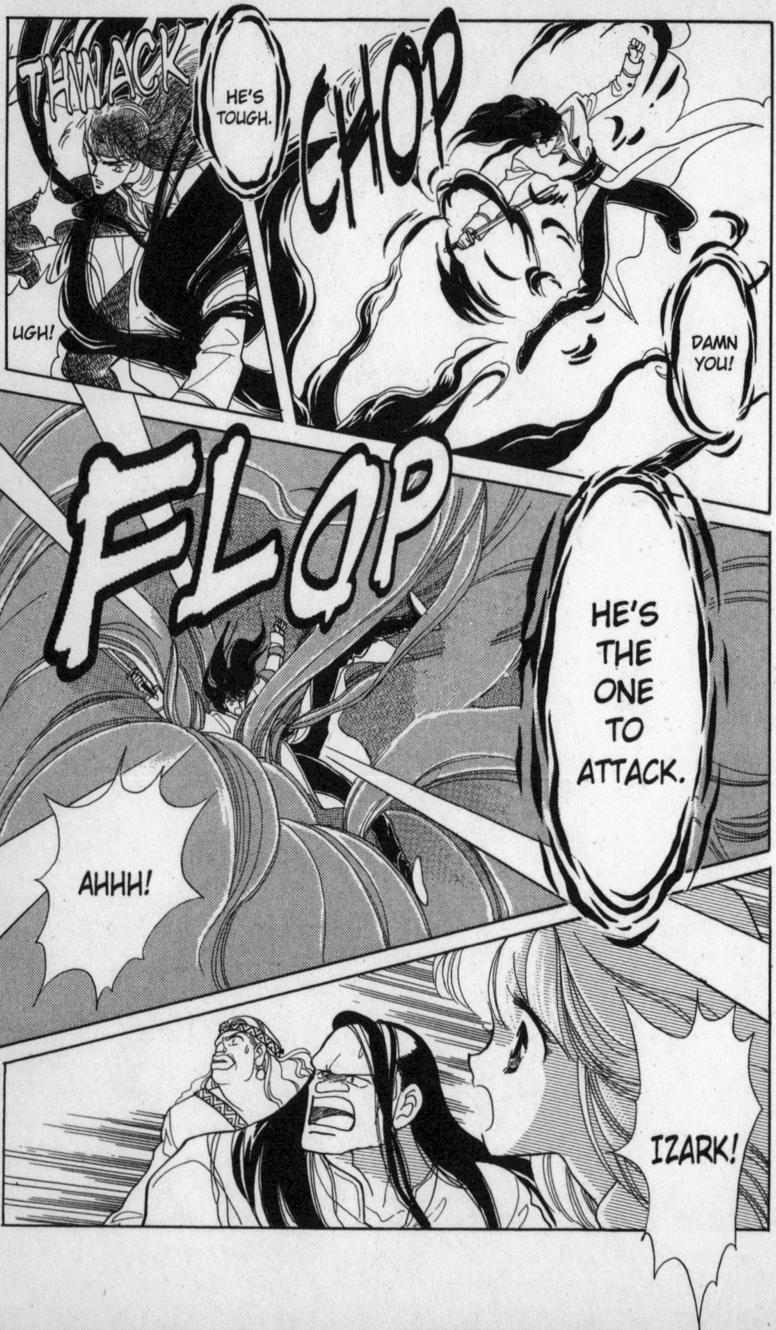
CHOP
DAMN YOU!
HE'S TOUGH.
THWACK
UGH!
HE'S THE ONE TO ATTACK.
FLOP
AHHH!
IZARK!

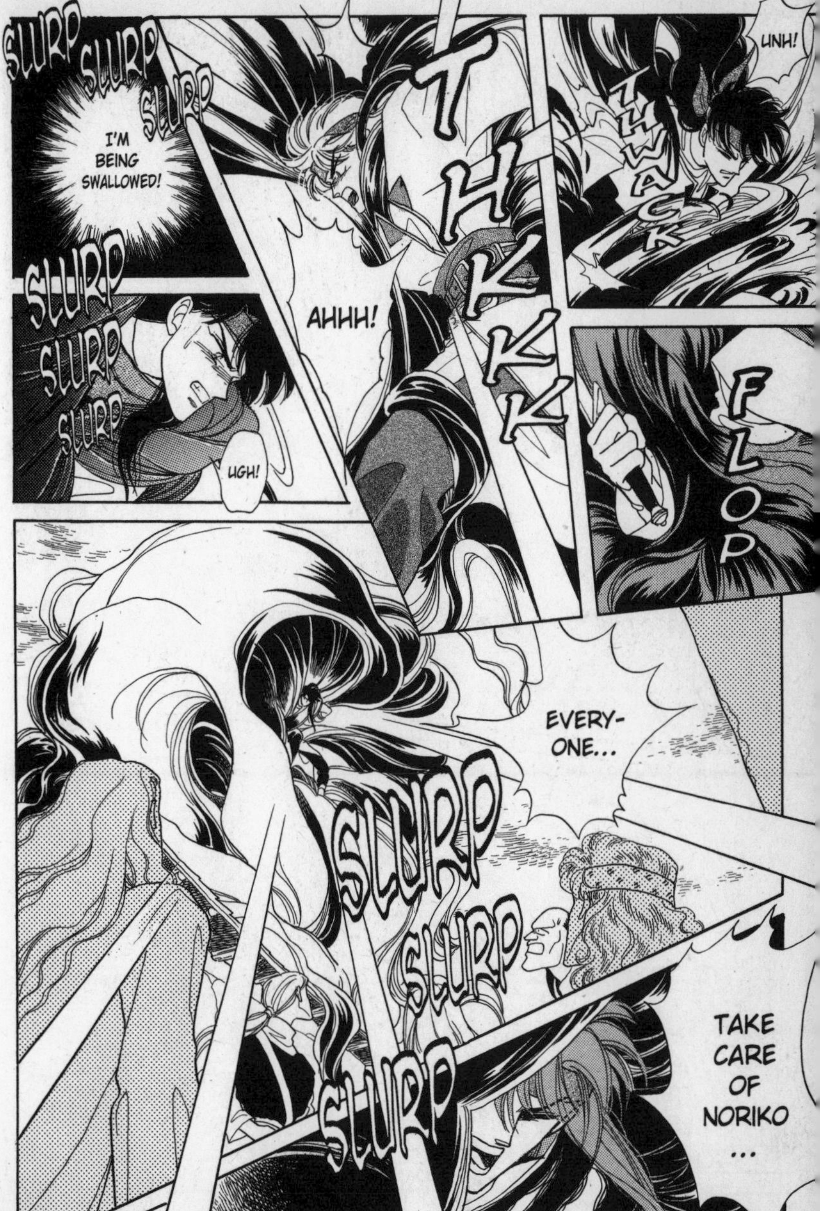
UNH!
THWACK
FLOP
THKKK
AHHH!
SLURP SLURP SLURP
I'M BEING SWALLOWED!
SLURP SLURP SLURP
UGH!
EVERY-ONE...
SLURP SLURP SLURP
TAKE CARE OF NORIKO ...

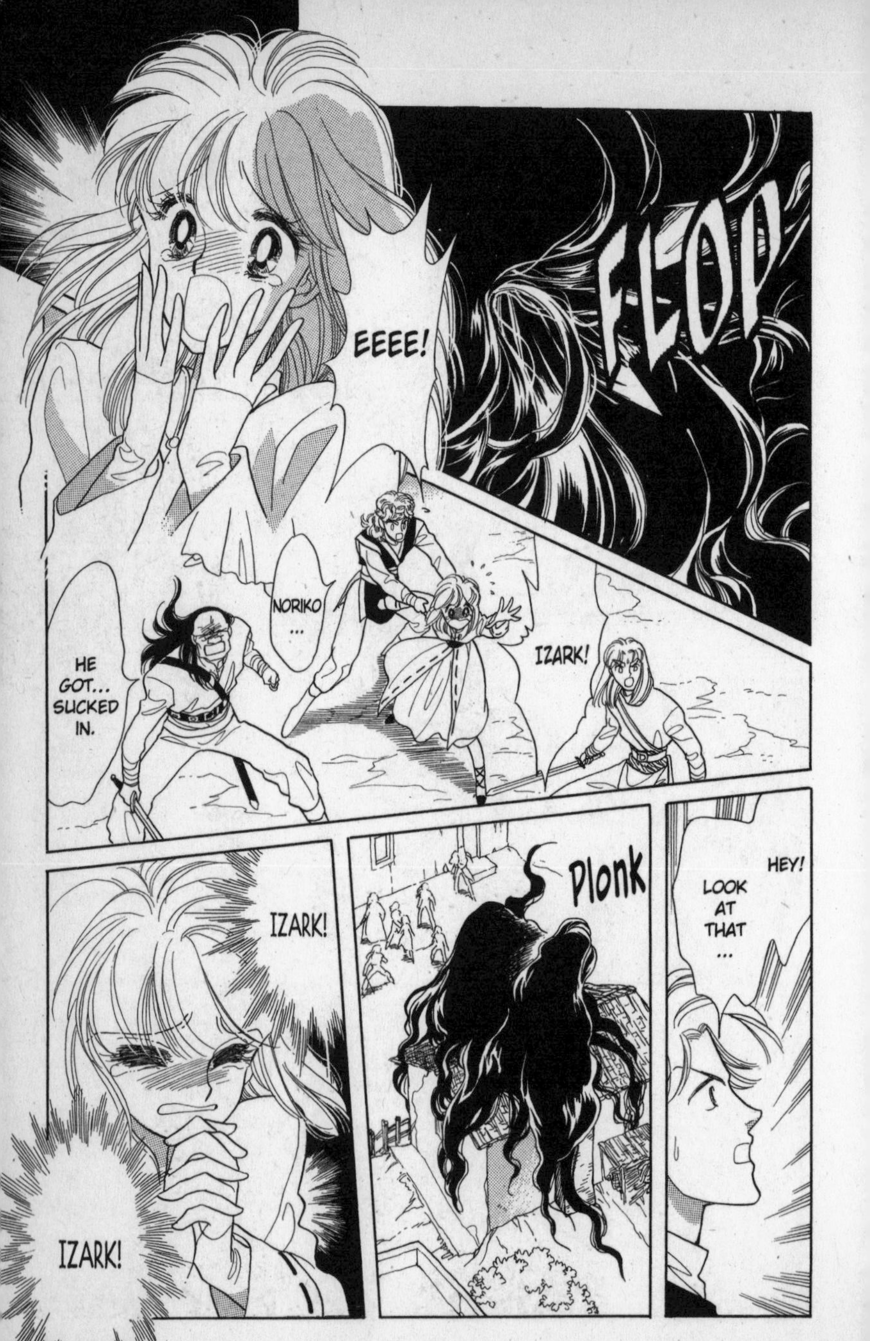
FLOP
EEEE!
IZARK!
NORIKO ...
HE GOT... SUCKED IN.
HEY!
LOOK AT THAT ...
Plonk
IZARK!
IZARK!

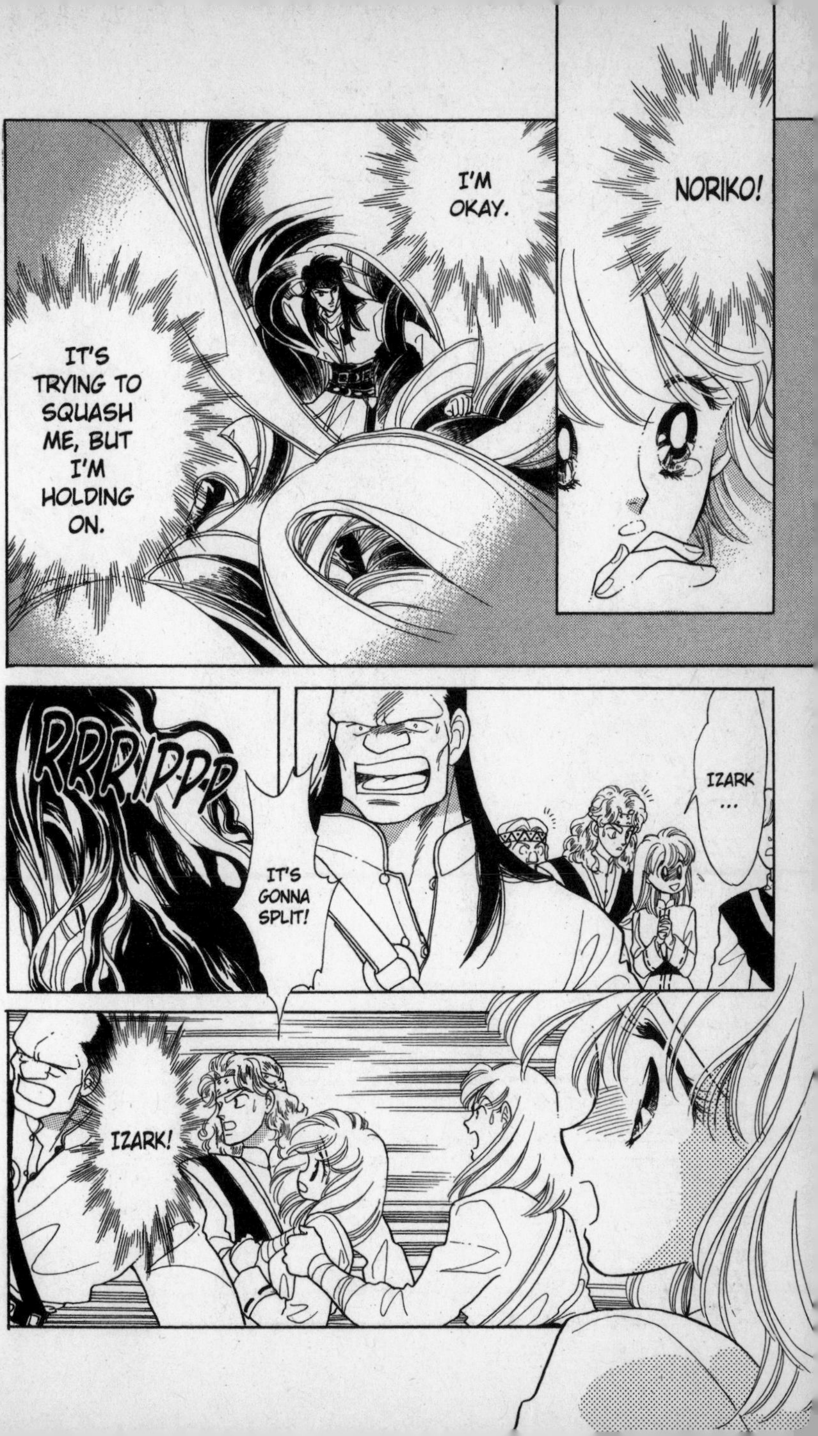
NORIKO!
I'M OKAY.
IT'S TRYING TO SQUASH ME, BUT I'M HOLDING ON.
IZARK ...
IT'S GONNA SPLIT!
RRRIP-P-P
IZARK!

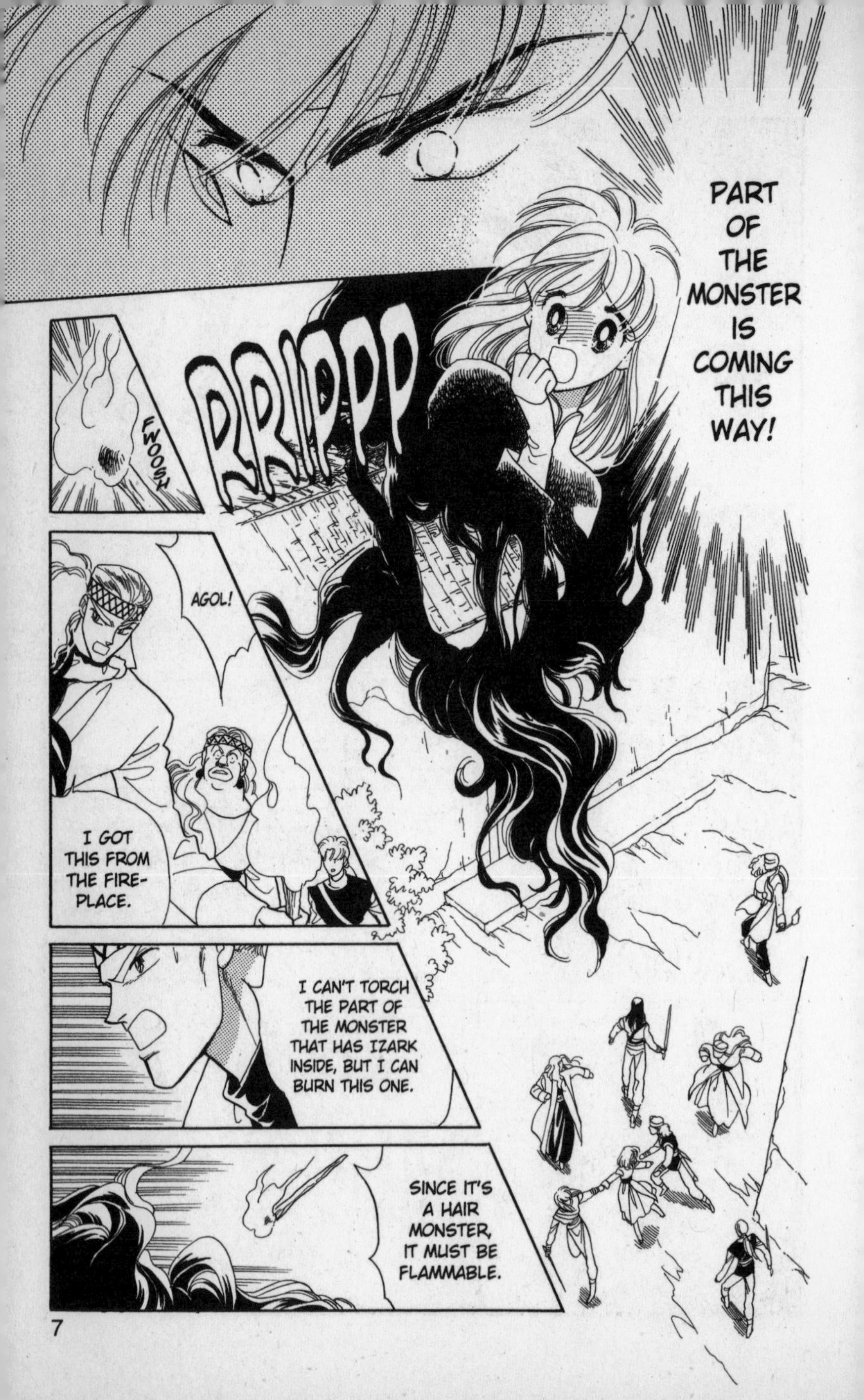
PART OF THE MONSTER IS COMING THIS WAY!
RRIPPP
FWOOSH
AGOL!
I GOT THIS FROM THE FIRE-PLACE.
I CAN'T TORCH THE PART OF THE MONSTER THAT HAS IZARK INSIDE, BUT I CAN BURN THIS ONE.
SINCE IT'S A HAIR MONSTER, IT MUST BE FLAMMABLE.

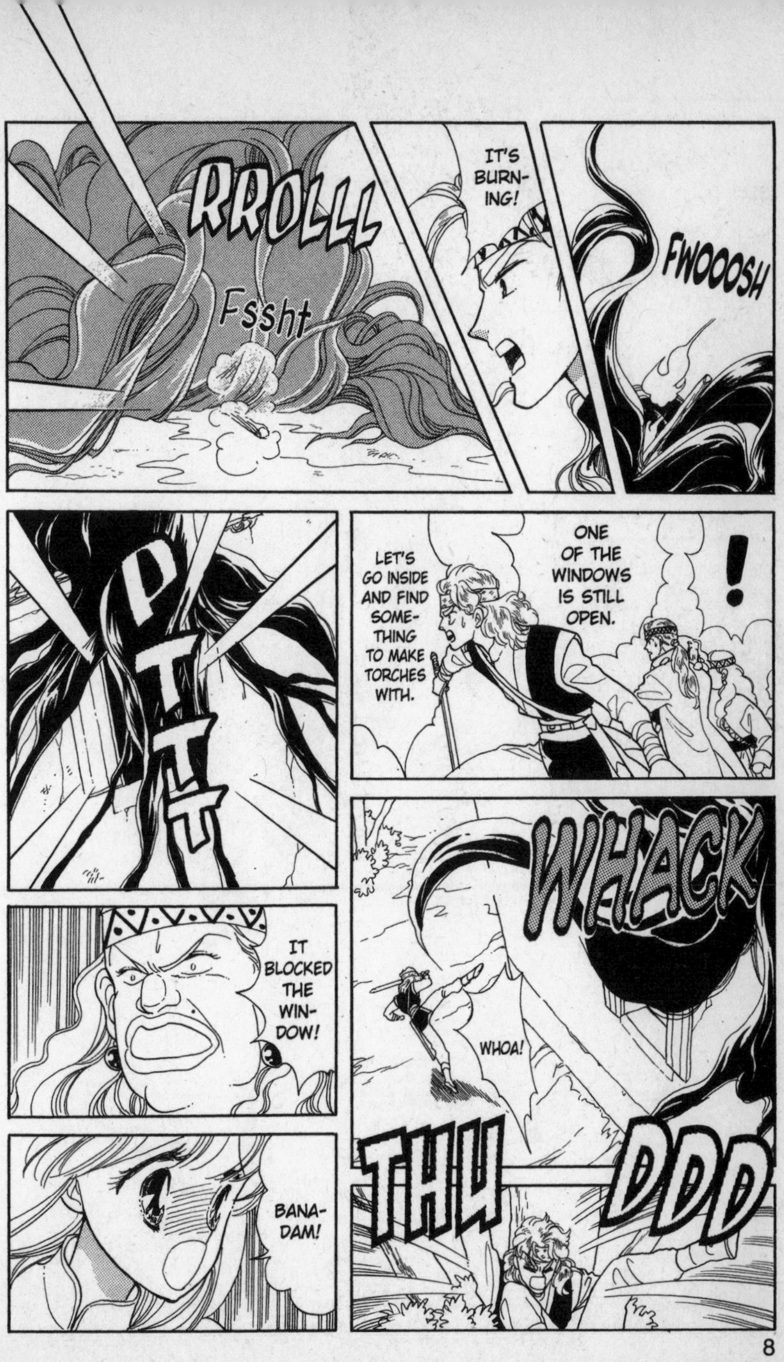
FWOOOSH
IT'S BURNING!
RROLLL
Fssht
!
ONE OF THE WINDOWS IS STILL OPEN.
LET'S GO INSIDE AND FIND SOMETHING TO MAKE TORCHES WITH.
PTTT
WHACK
WHOA!
THUDDD
IT BLOCKED THE WINDOW!
BANADAM!

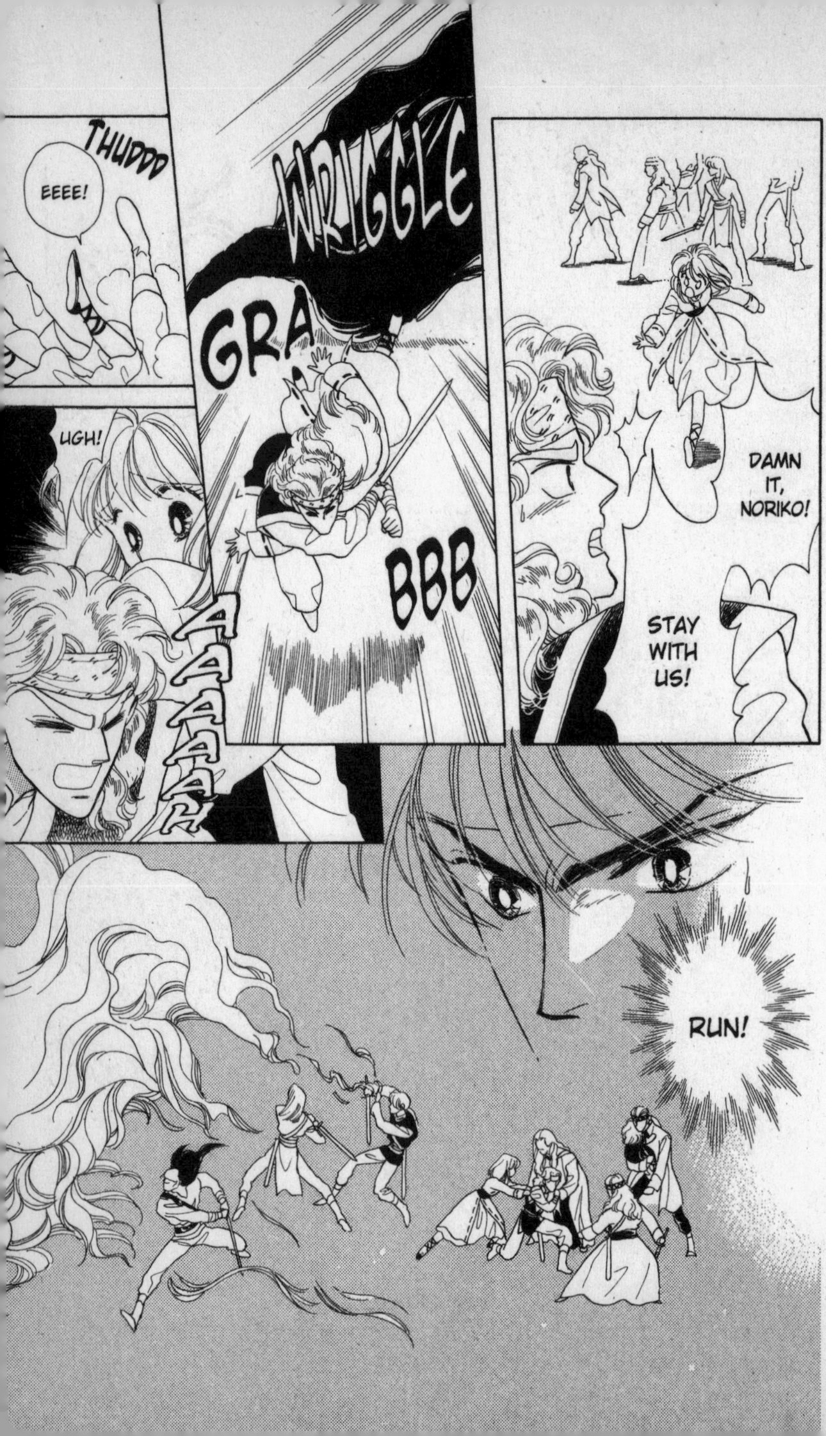
DAMN IT, NORIKO!
STAY WITH US!
WRIGGLE
GRA
BBB
THUDDD
EEEE!
UGH!
AAAAAAH
RUN!

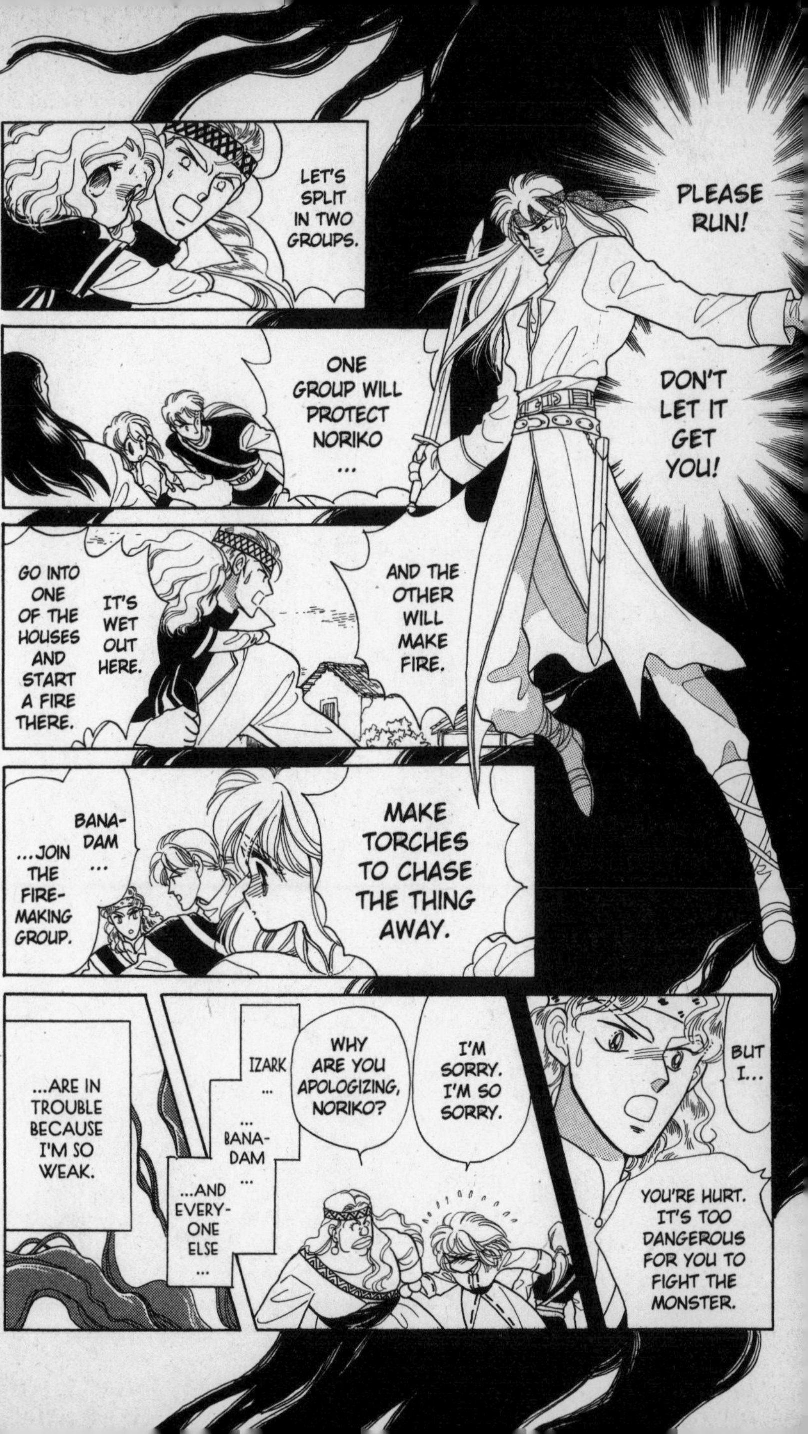

PLEASE RUN!
DON'T LET IT GET YOU!
LET'S SPLIT IN TWO GROUPS.
ONE GROUP WILL PROTECT NORIKO ...
AND THE OTHER WILL MAKE FIRE.
IT'S WET OUT HERE.
GO INTO ONE OF THE HOUSES AND START A FIRE THERE.
MAKE TORCHES TO CHASE THE THING AWAY.
BANA-DAM ...
...JOIN THE FIRE-MAKING GROUP.
BUT I...
YOU'RE HURT. IT'S TOO DANGEROUS FOR YOU TO FIGHT THE MONSTER.
I'M SORRY. I'M SO SORRY.
WHY ARE YOU APOLOGIZING, NORIKO?
IZARK ...
... BANA-DAM ...
...AND EVERY-ONE ELSE ...
...ARE IN TROUBLE BECAUSE I'M SO WEAK.

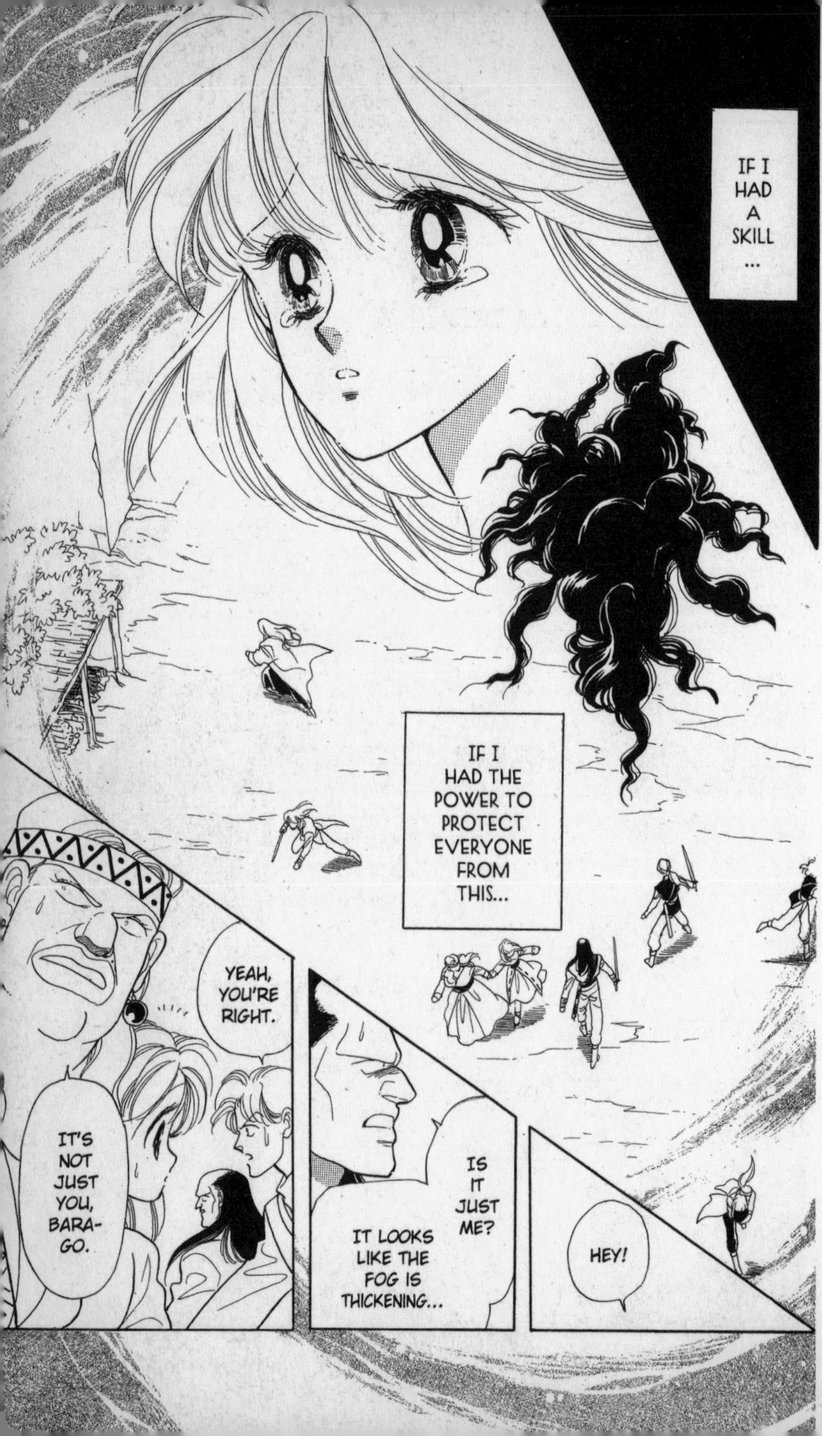
IF I HAD A SKILL...
IF I HAD THE POWER TO PROTECT EVERYONE FROM THIS...
HEY!
IS IT JUST ME?
IT LOOKS LIKE THE FOG IS THICKENING...
YEAH, YOU'RE RIGHT.
IT'S NOT JUST YOU, BARAGO.

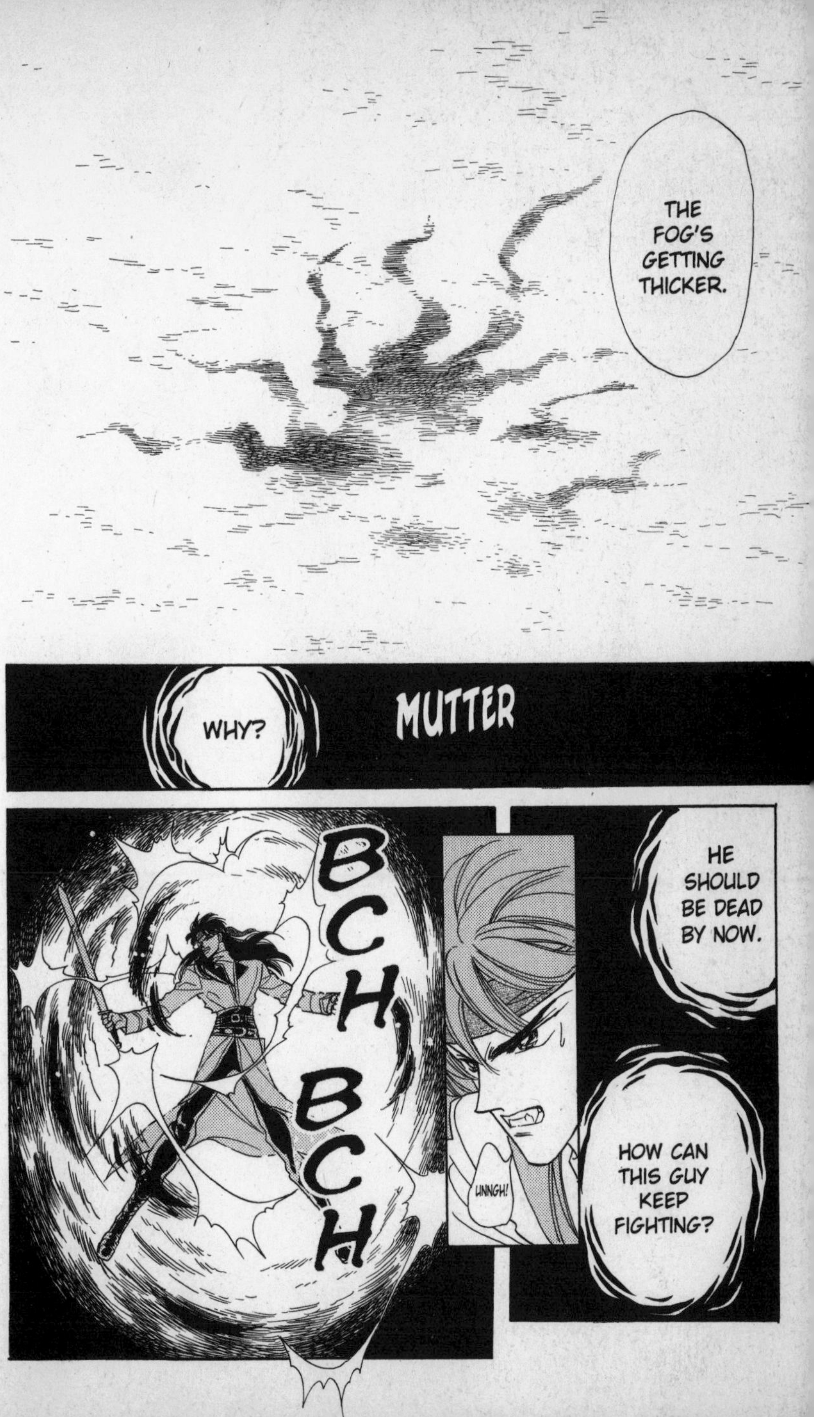
THE FOG'S GETTING THICKER.
MUTTER
WHY?
HE SHOULD BE DEAD BY NOW.
HOW CAN THIS GUY KEEP FIGHTING?
UNNGH!
BCH BCH

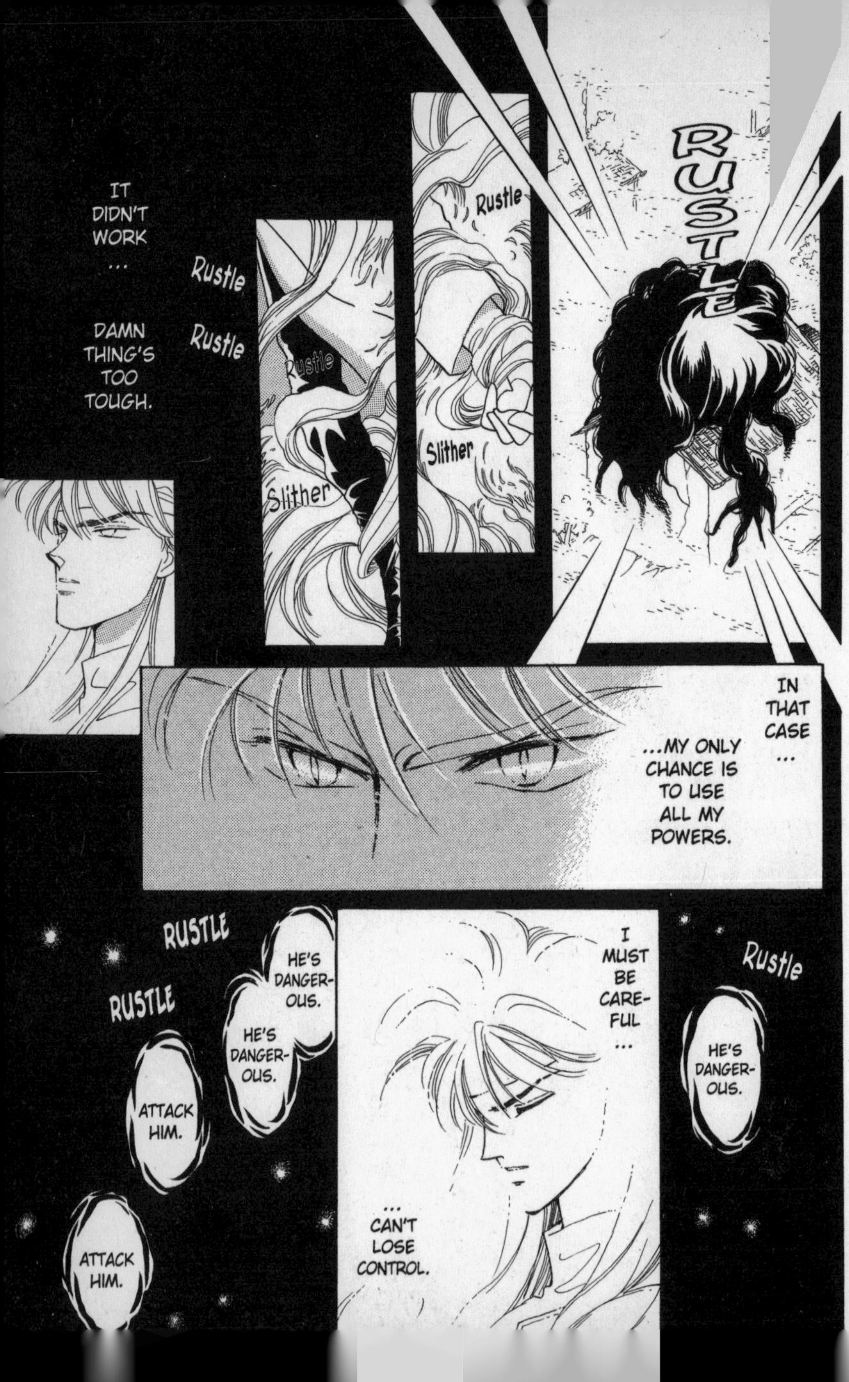
RUSTLE
Rustle
Slither
Rustle
Rustle
Rustle
Slither
IT DIDN'T WORK ...
DAMN THING'S TOO TOUGH.
IN THAT CASE ...
...MY ONLY CHANCE IS TO USE ALL MY POWERS.
Rustle
HE'S DANGER-OUS.
I MUST BE CARE-FUL ...
... CAN'T LOSE CONTROL.
HE'S DANGER-OUS.
HE'S DANGER-OUS.
RUSTLE
RUSTLE
ATTACK HIM.
ATTACK HIM.

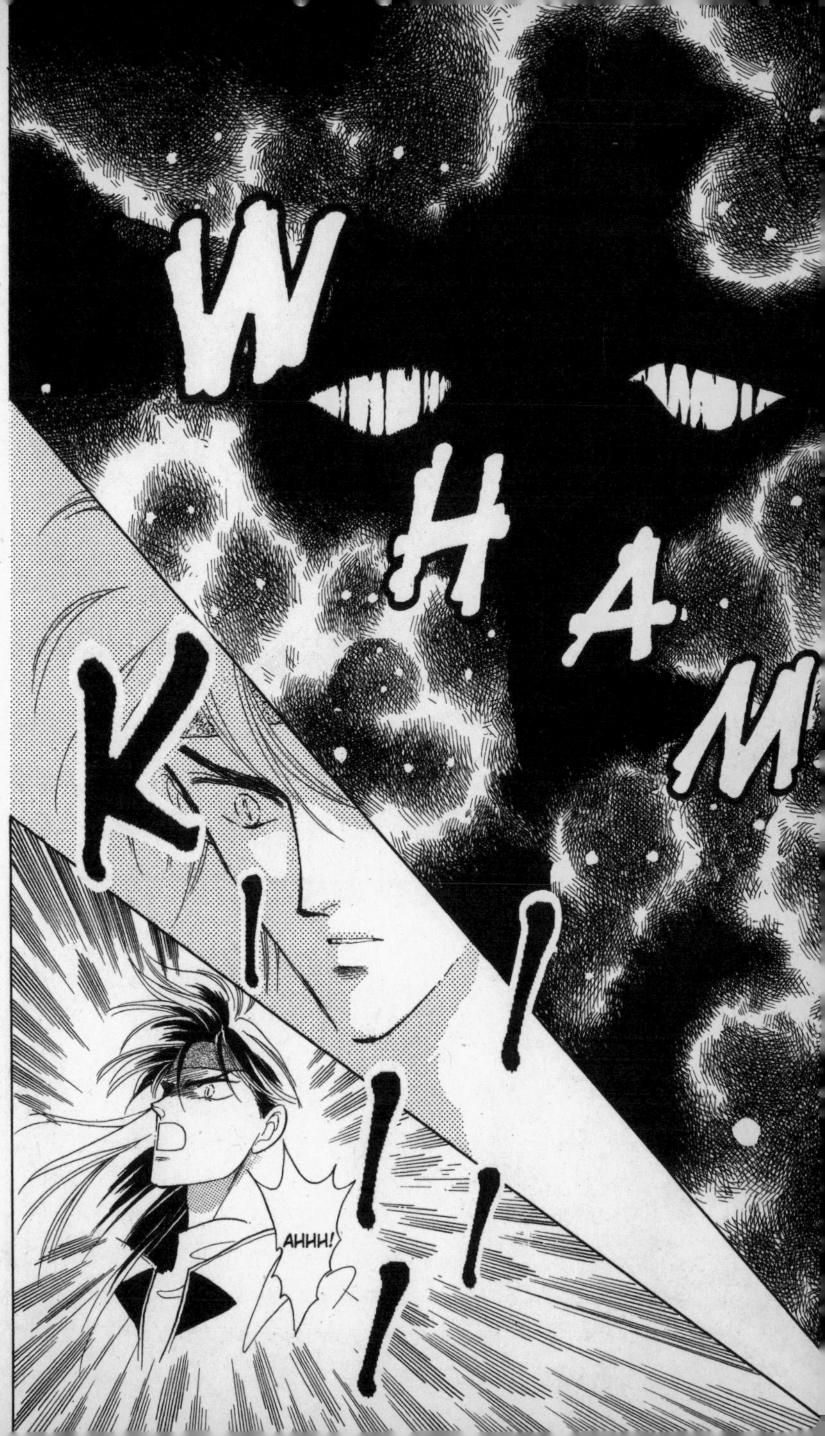
WHAM
KI!!!!!
AHHH!

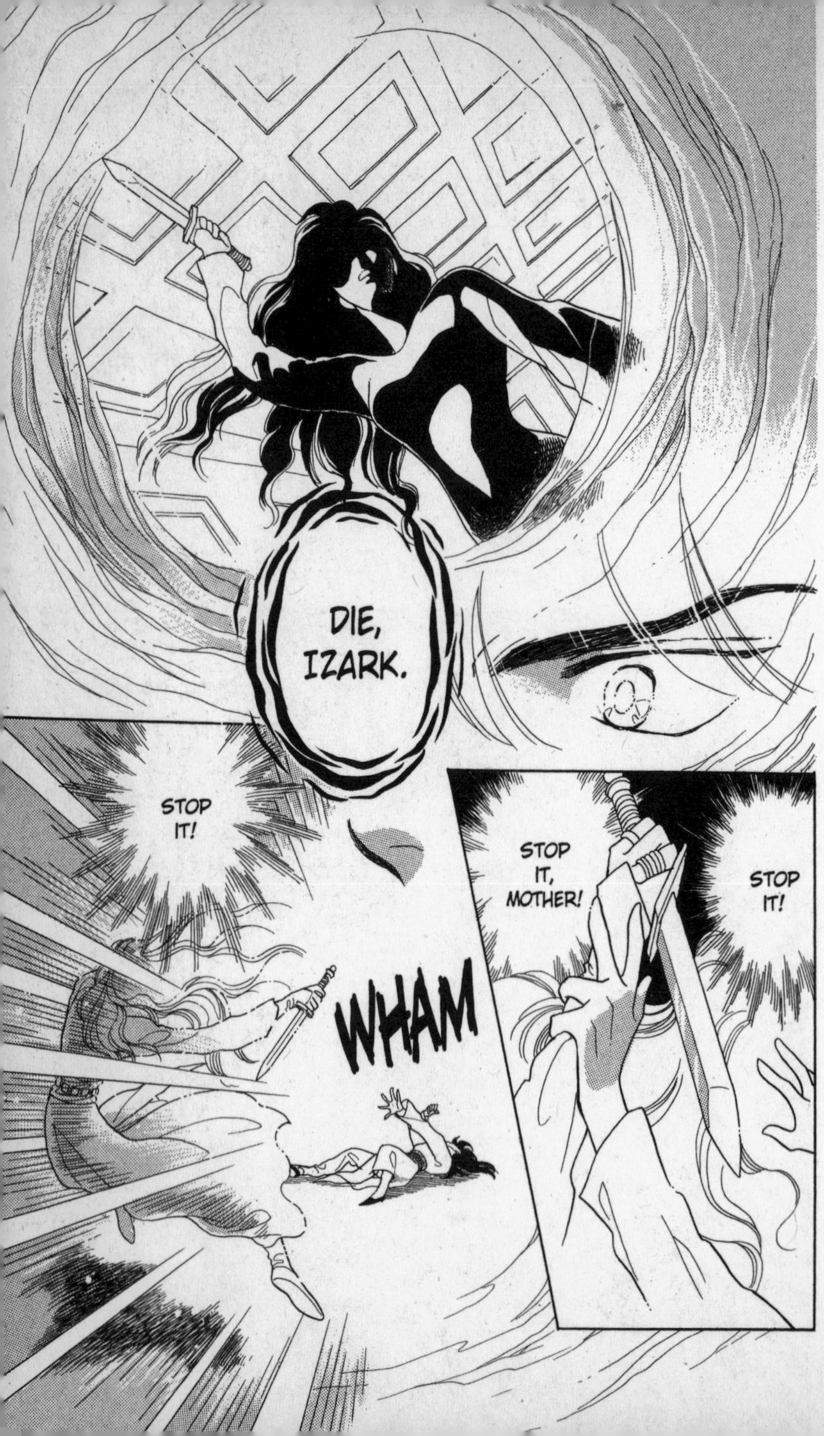
DIE, IZARK.
STOP IT!
STOP IT, MOTHER!
STOP IT!
WHAM

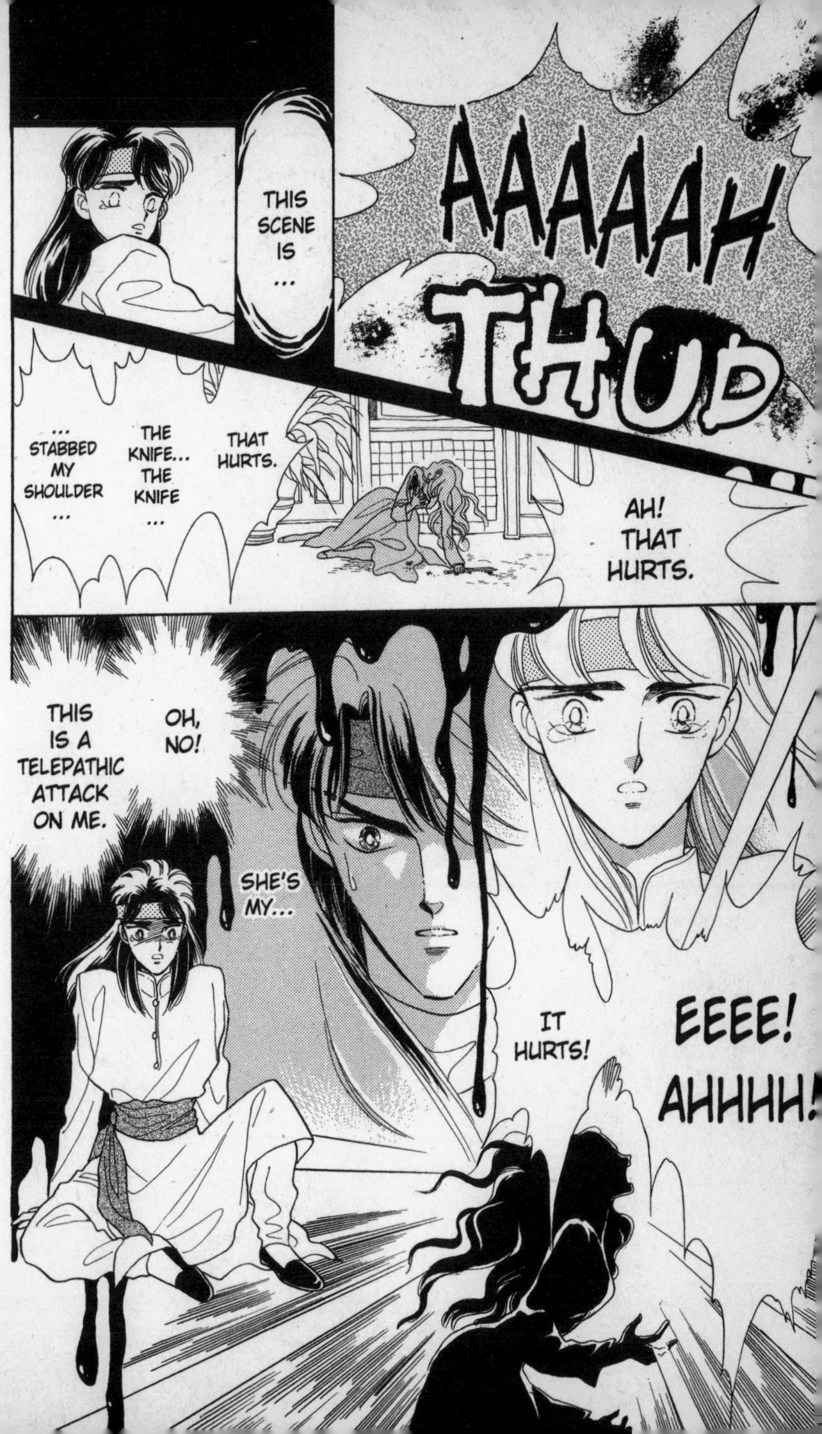
AAAAAH
THUD
THIS SCENE IS ...
AH! THAT HURTS.
THAT HURTS.
THE KNIFE... THE KNIFE ...
... STABBED MY SHOULDER ...
EEEE! AHHHH!
IT HURTS!
SHE'S MY...
OH, NO!
THIS IS A TELEPATHIC ATTACK ON ME.

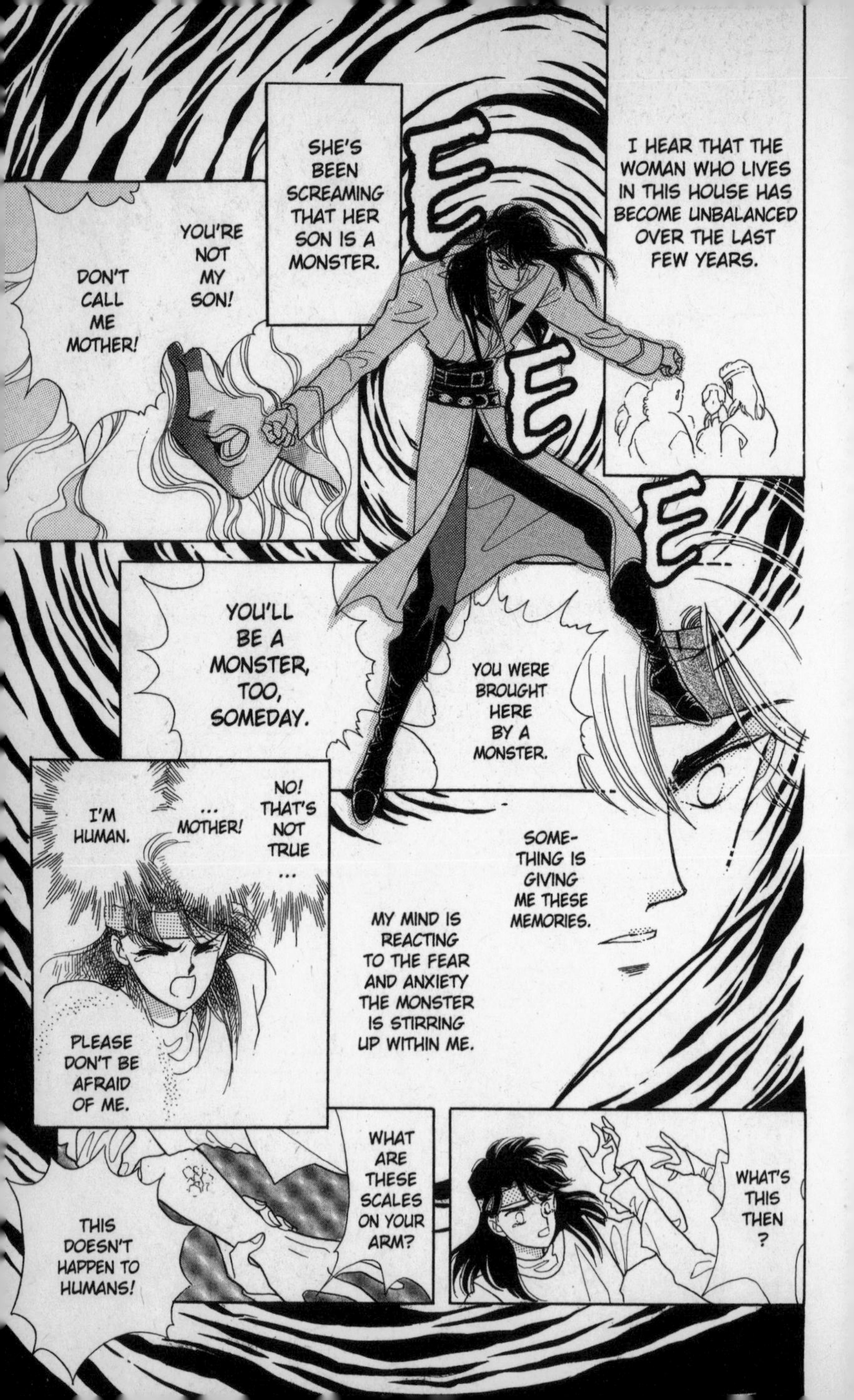
I HEAR THAT THE WOMAN WHO LIVES IN THIS HOUSE HAS BECOME UNBALANCED OVER THE LAST FEW YEARS.
SHE'S BEEN SCREAMING THAT HER SON IS A MONSTER.
YOU'RE NOT MY SON!
DON'T CALL ME MOTHER!
EEEE
YOU WERE BROUGHT HERE BY A MONSTER.
YOU'LL BE A MONSTER, TOO, SOMEDAY.
SOME-THING IS GIVING ME THESE MEMORIES.
MY MIND IS REACTING TO THE FEAR AND ANXIETY THE MONSTER IS STIRRING UP WITHIN ME.
NO! THAT'S NOT TRUE ...
... MOTHER!
I'M HUMAN.
PLEASE DON'T BE AFRAID OF ME.
WHAT'S THIS THEN ?
WHAT ARE THESE SCALES ON YOUR ARM?
THIS DOESN'T HAPPEN TO HUMANS!

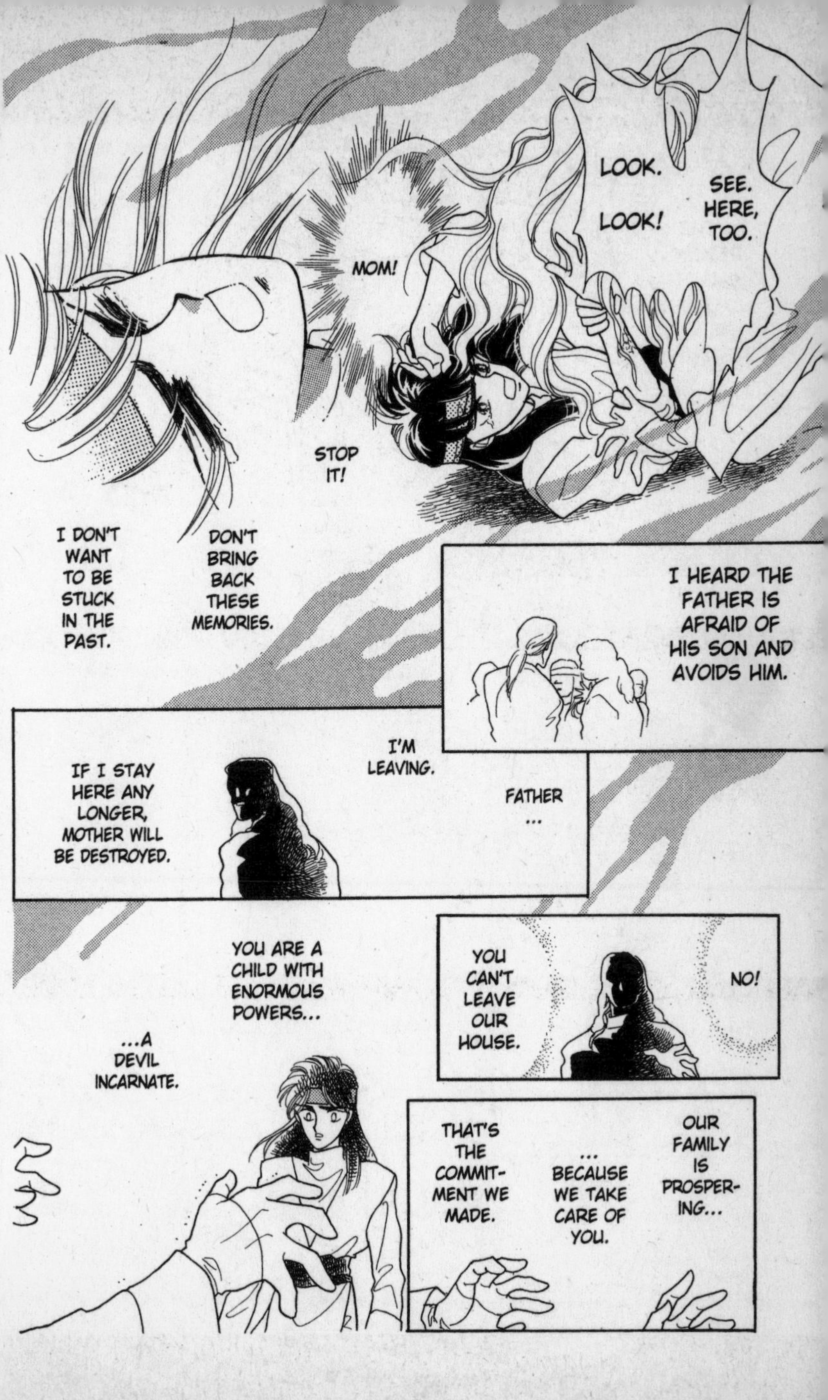
LOOK. LOOK! SEE. HERE, TOO.
MOM!
STOP IT!
DON'T BRING BACK THESE MEMORIES.
I DON'T WANT TO BE STUCK IN THE PAST.
I HEARD THE FATHER IS AFRAID OF HIS SON AND AVOIDS HIM.
FATHER ...
I'M LEAVING.
IF I STAY HERE ANY LONGER, MOTHER WILL BE DESTROYED.
NO!
YOU CAN'T LEAVE OUR HOUSE.
OUR FAMILY IS PROSPER-ING...
... BECAUSE WE TAKE CARE OF YOU.
THAT'S THE COMMIT-MENT WE MADE.
YOU ARE A CHILD WITH ENORMOUS POWERS...
...A DEVIL INCARNATE.

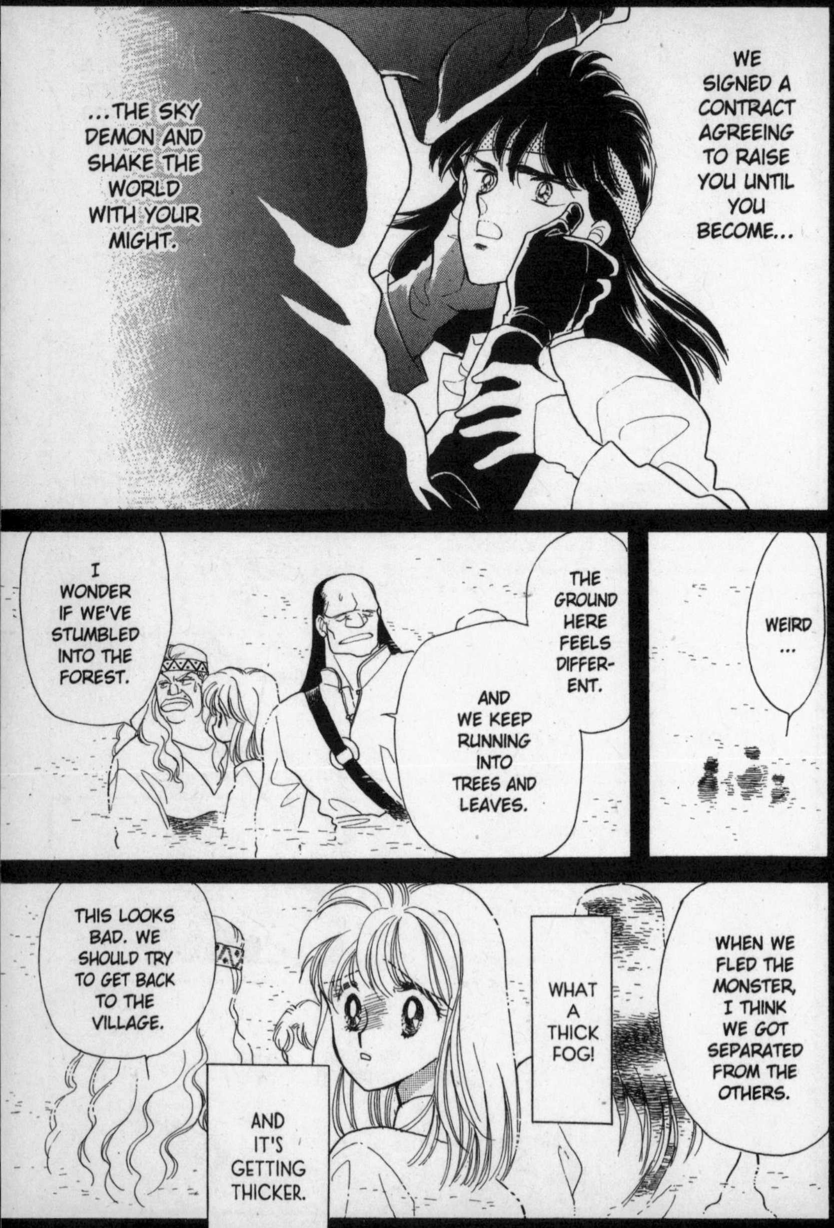
WE SIGNED A CONTRACT AGREEING TO RAISE YOU UNTIL YOU BECOME...
...THE SKY DEMON AND SHAKE THE WORLD WITH YOUR MIGHT.
WEIRD ...
THE GROUND HERE FEELS DIFFER- ENT.
AND WE KEEP RUNNING INTO TREES AND LEAVES.
I WONDER IF WE'VE STUMBLED INTO THE FOREST.
WHEN WE FLED THE MONSTER, I THINK WE GOT SEPARATED FROM THE OTHERS.
WHAT A THICK FOG!
AND IT'S GETTING THICKER.
THIS LOOKS BAD. WE SHOULD TRY TO GET BACK TO THE VILLAGE.

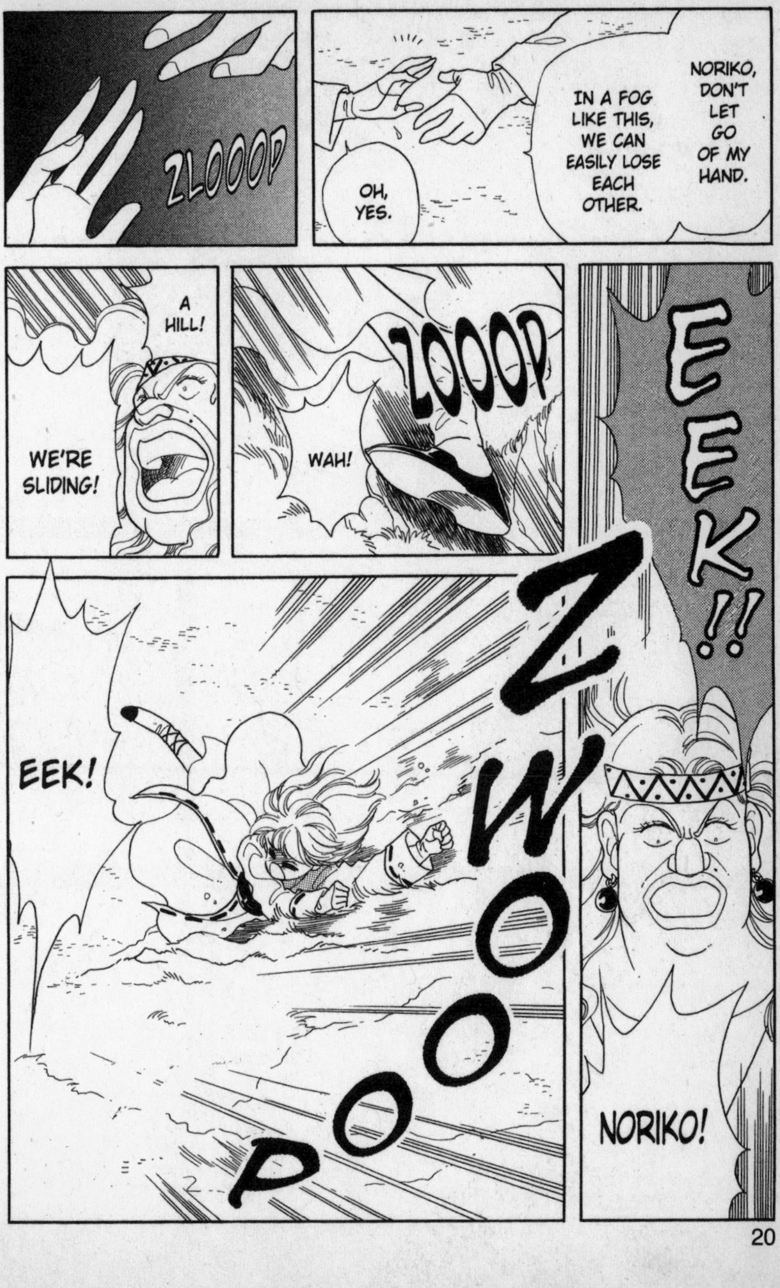
NORIKO, DON'T LET GO OF MY HAND.
IN A FOG LIKE THIS, WE CAN EASILY LOSE EACH OTHER.
OH, YES.
ZLOOOP
EEEK!!
NORIKO!
ZOOOP
WAH!
A HILL!
WE'RE SLIDING!
ZWOOOOP
EEK!

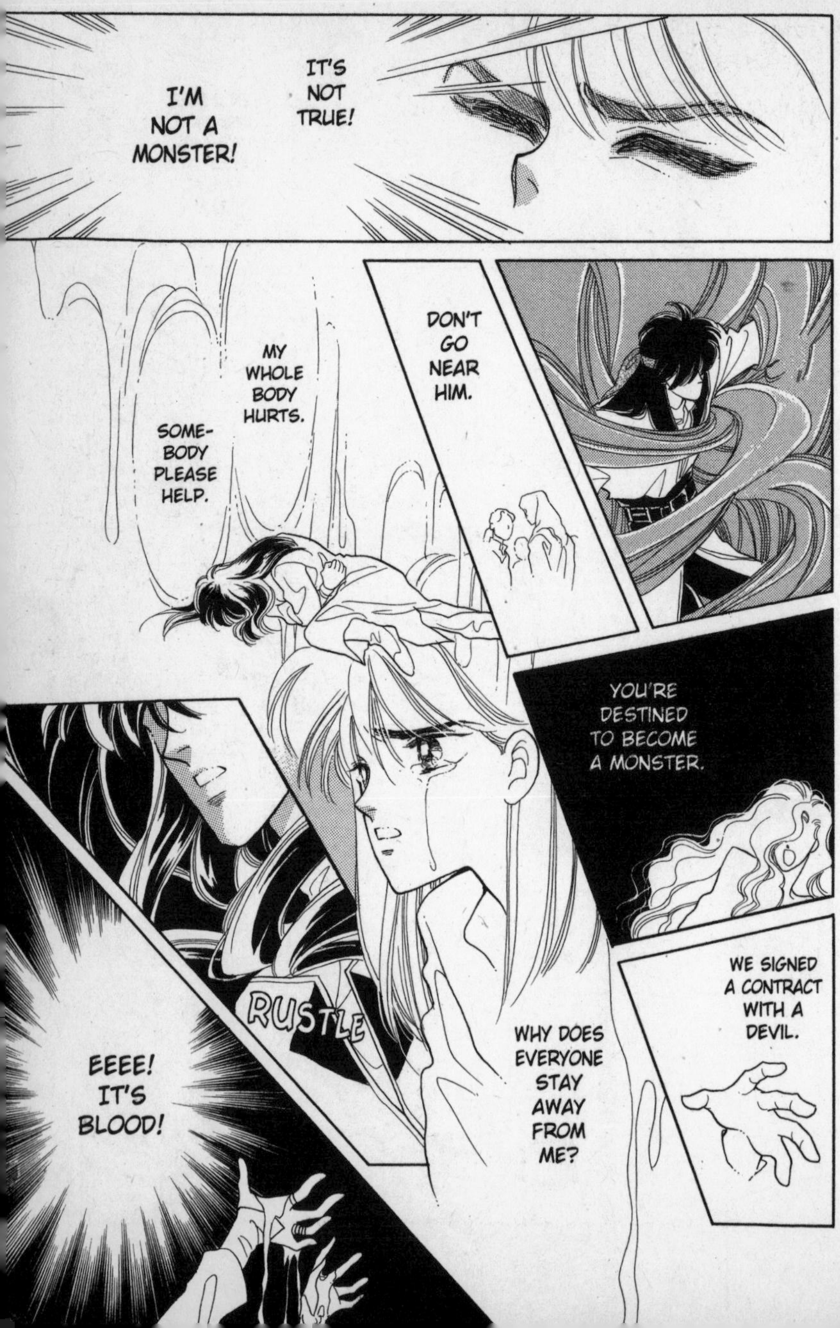
IT'S NOT TRUE!
I'M NOT A MONSTER!
DON'T GO NEAR HIM.
MY WHOLE BODY HURTS.
SOME-BODY PLEASE HELP.
YOU'RE DESTINED TO BECOME A MONSTER.
WE SIGNED A CONTRACT WITH A DEVIL.
WHY DOES EVERYONE STAY AWAY FROM ME?
RUSTLE
EEEE! IT'S BLOOD!

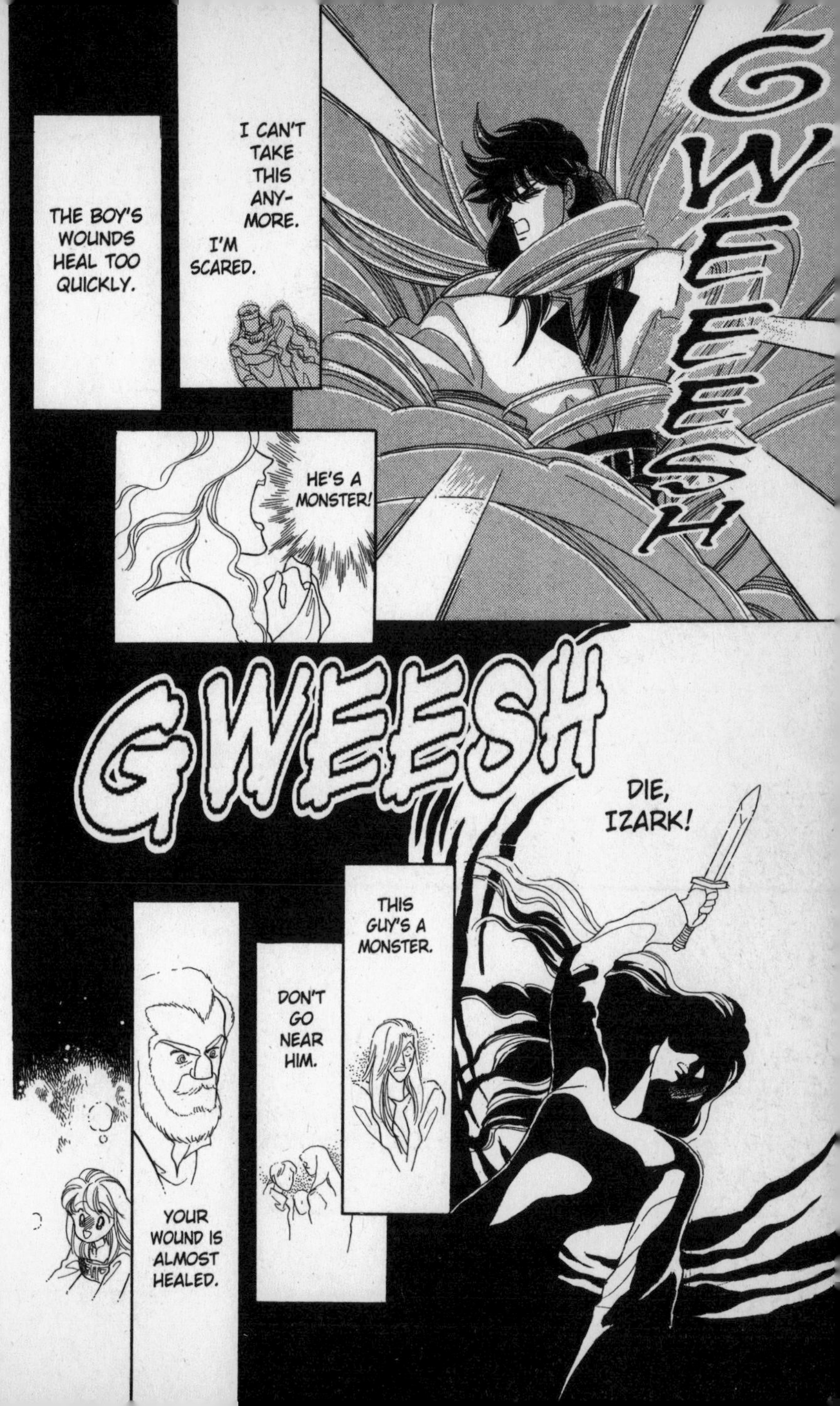
GWEEESH
I CAN'T TAKE THIS ANY-MORE.
I'M SCARED.
THE BOY'S WOUNDS HEAL TOO QUICKLY.
HE'S A MONSTER!
GWEESH
DIE, IZARK!
THIS GUY'S A MONSTER.
DON'T GO NEAR HIM.
YOUR WOUND IS ALMOST HEALED.

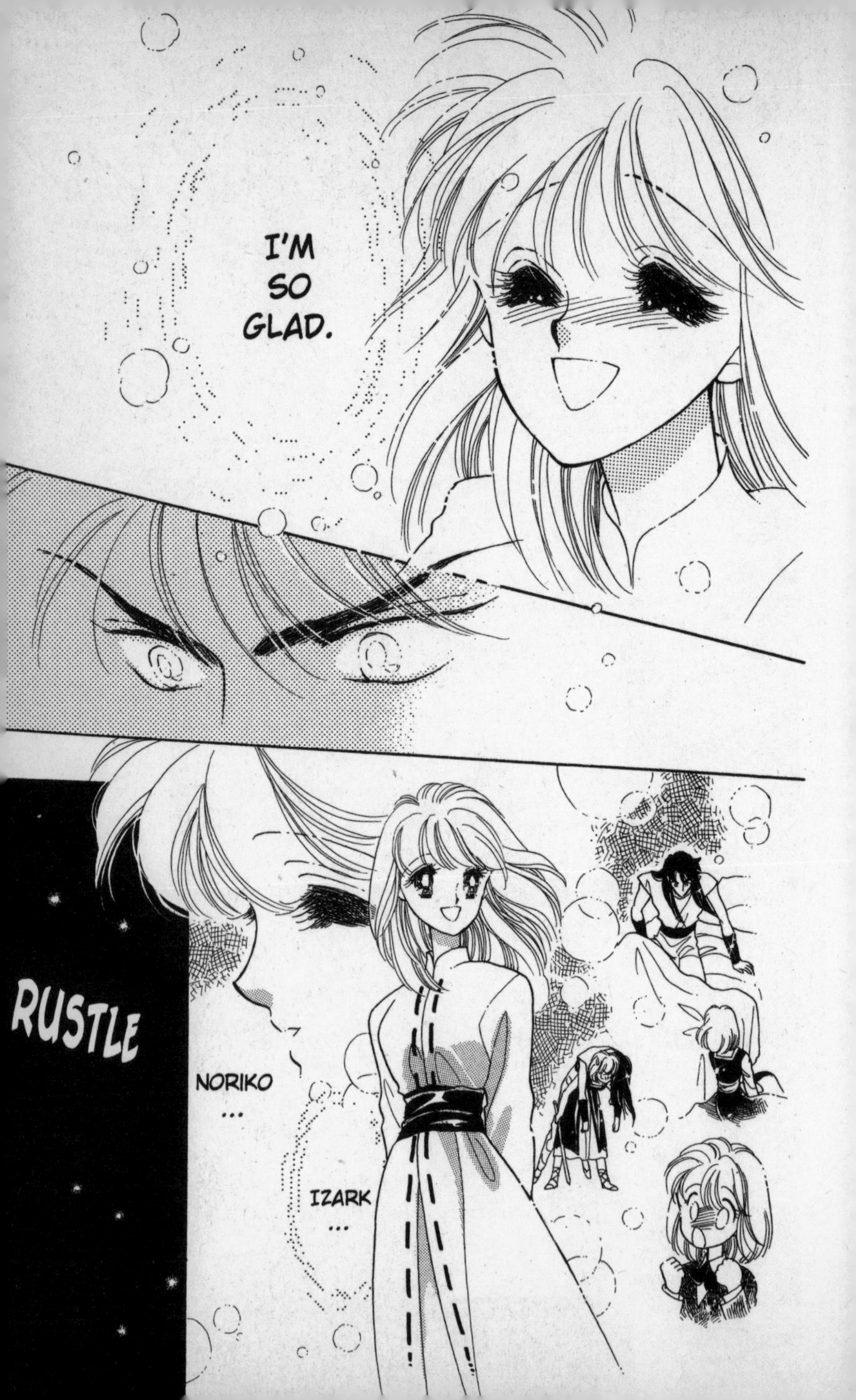
I'M SO GLAD.
NORIKO ...
IZARK ...
RUSTLE

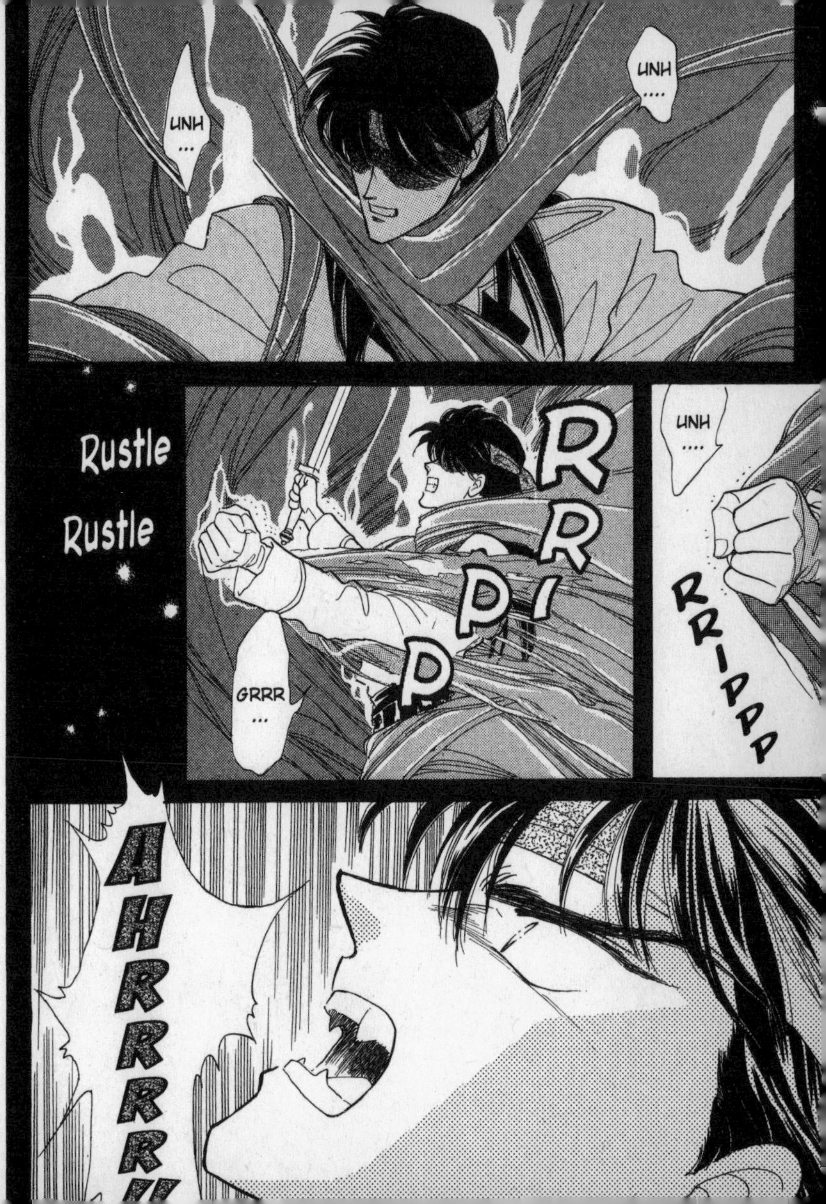
UNH ....
UNH ...
UNH ....
RRIPPP
RRIPP
GRRR ...
Rustle
Rustle
AHRRRR

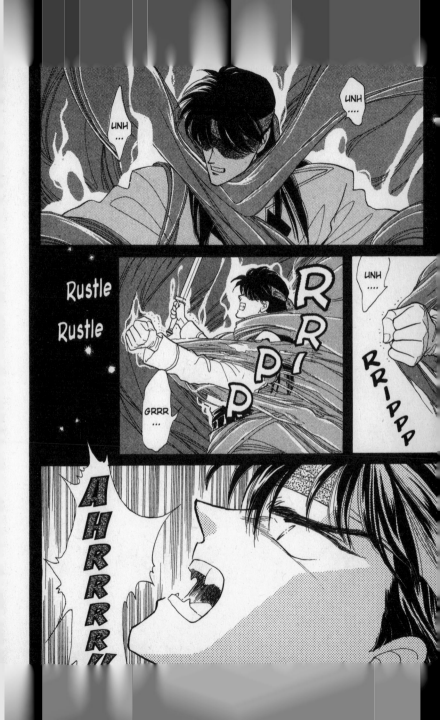

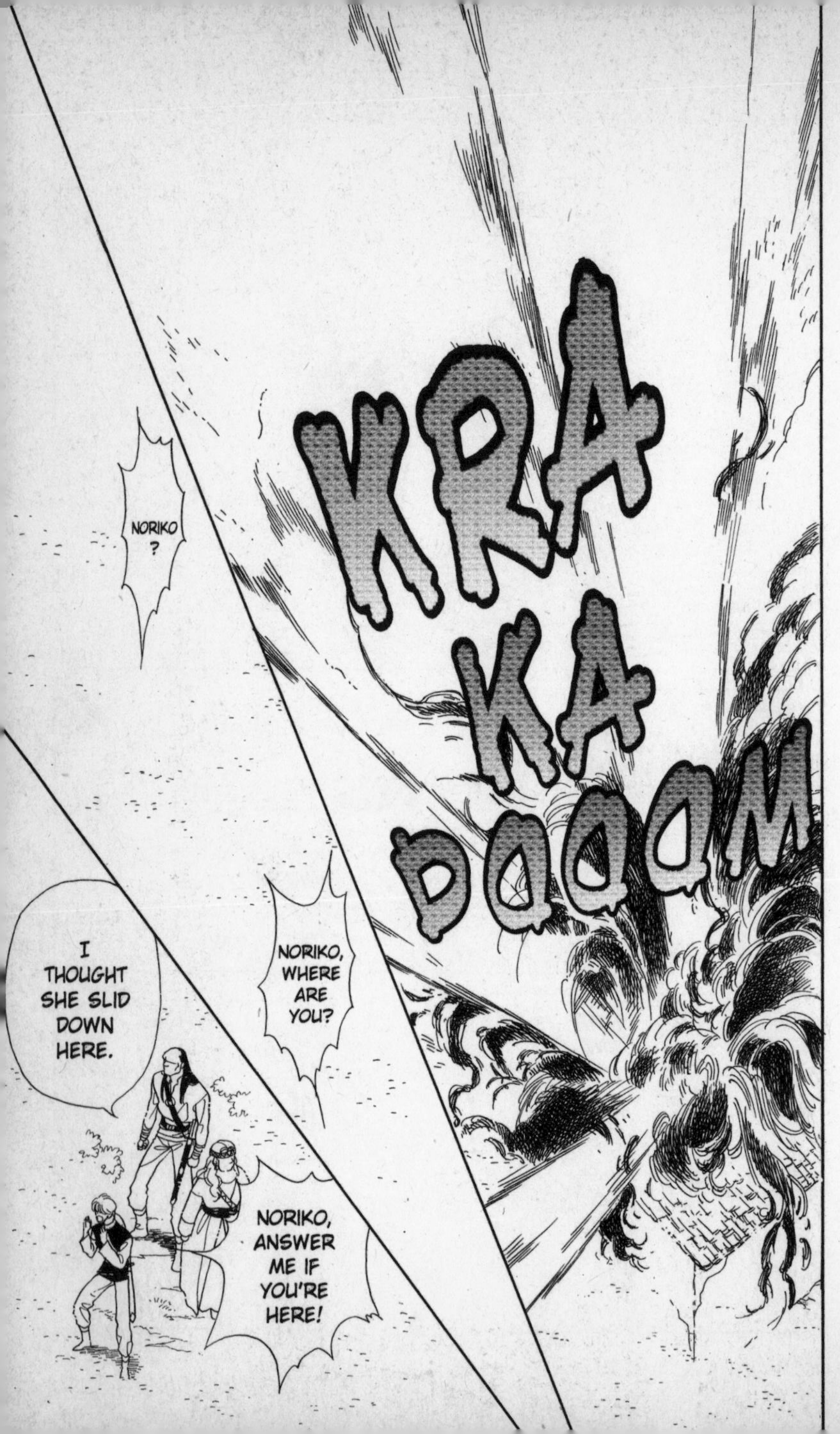
KRA KA DOOOM
NORIKO?
NORIKO, WHERE ARE YOU?
I THOUGHT SHE SLID DOWN HERE.
NORIKO, ANSWER ME IF YOU'RE HERE!

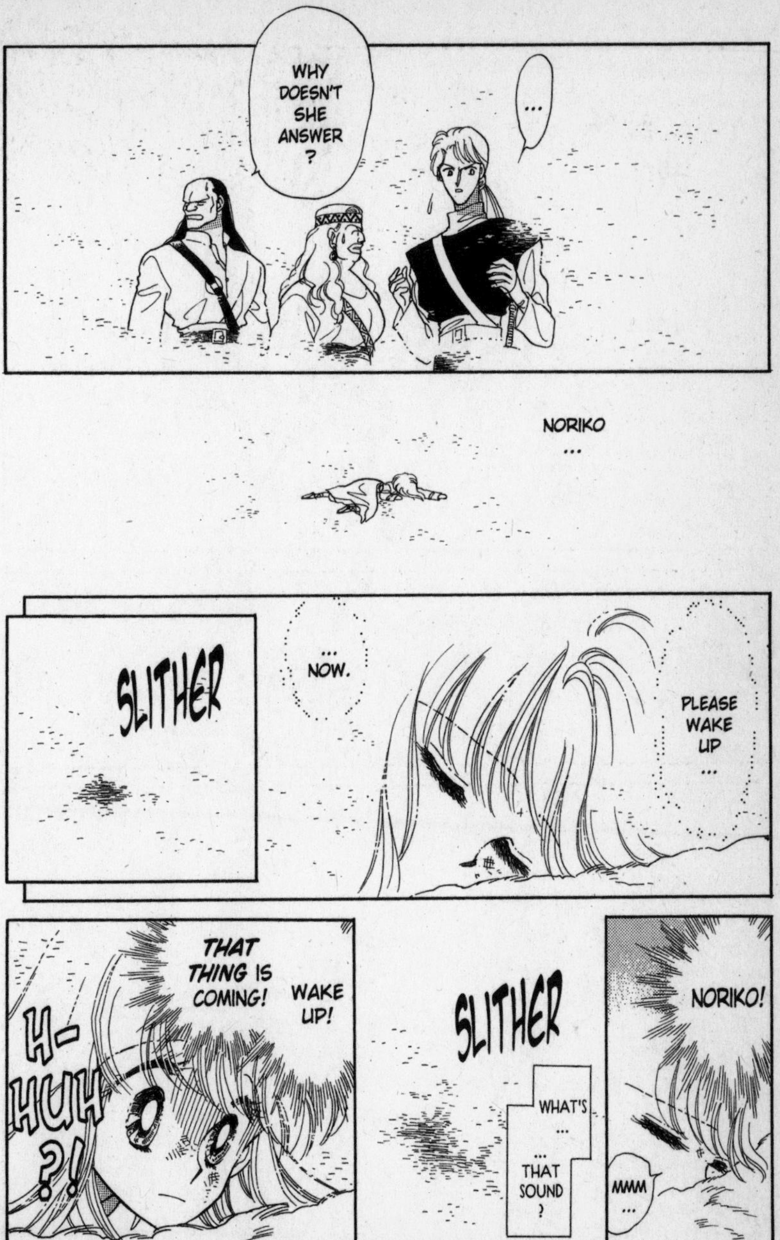
...
WHY DOESN'T SHE ANSWER?
NORIKO ...
PLEASE WAKE UP ...
... NOW.
SLITHER
NORIKO!
MMM ...
SLITHER
WHAT'S ... ... THAT SOUND ?
WAKE UP!
THAT THING IS COMING!
H-HUH ?!

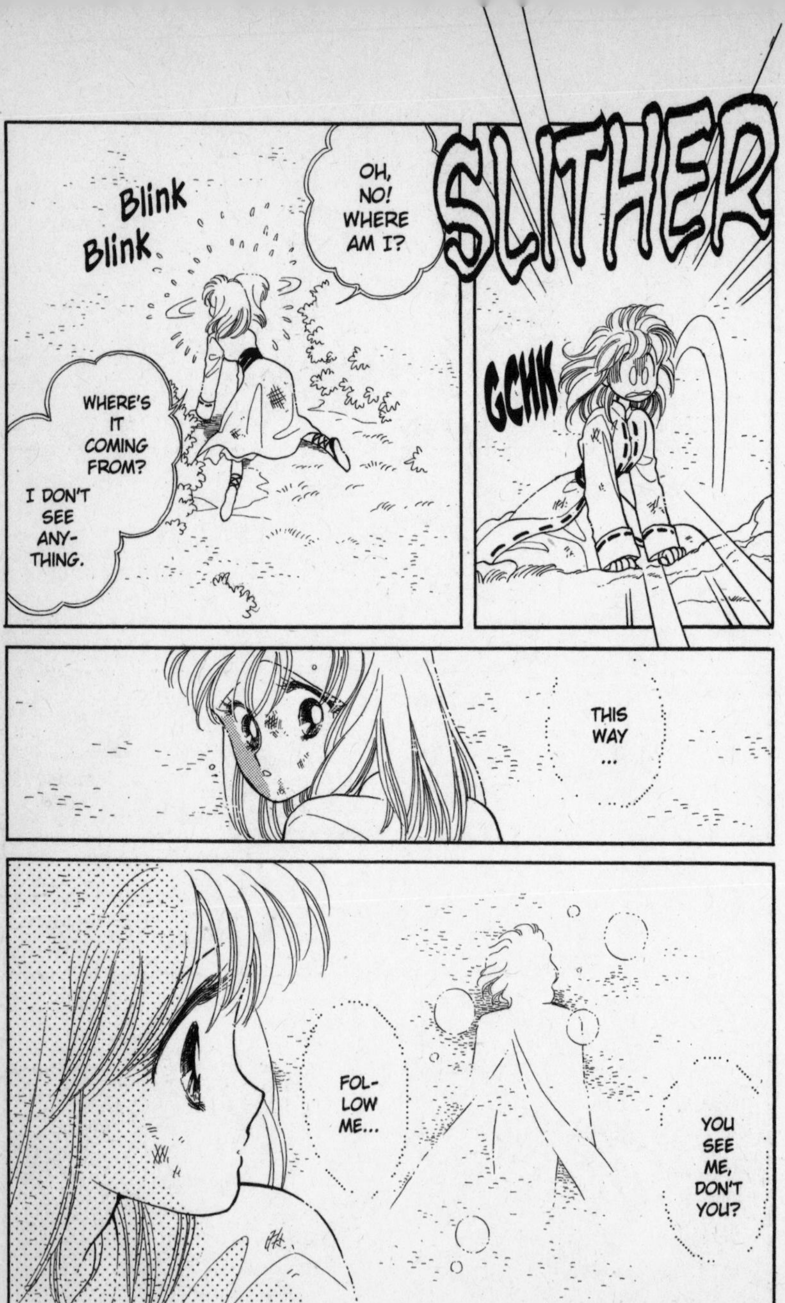
SLITHER
GCHK
OH, NO! WHERE AM I?
Blink Blink
WHERE'S IT COMING FROM?
I DON'T SEE ANY-THING.
THIS WAY ...
YOU SEE ME, DON'T YOU?
FOL-LOW ME...

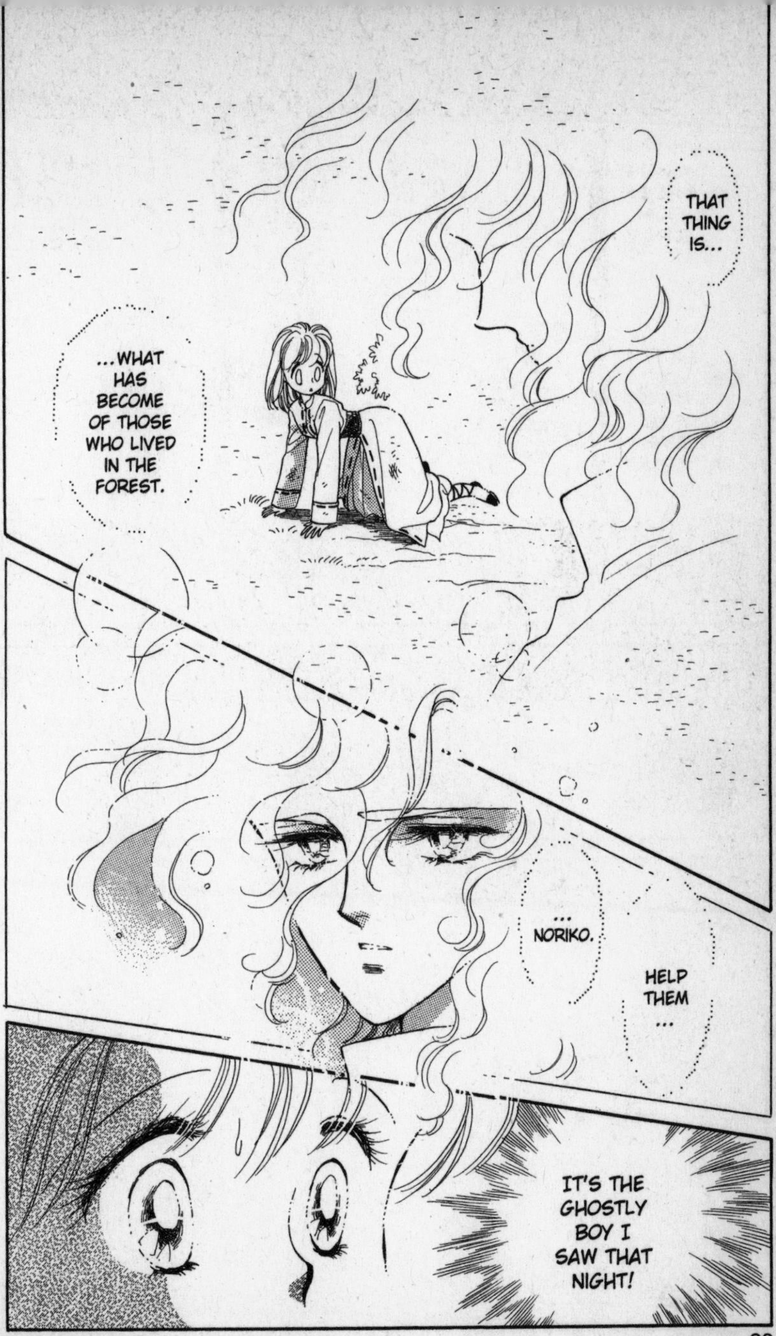
THAT THING IS...
...WHAT HAS BECOME OF THOSE WHO LIVED IN THE FOREST.
...NORIKO.
HELP THEM...
IT'S THE GHOSTLY BOY I SAW THAT NIGHT!

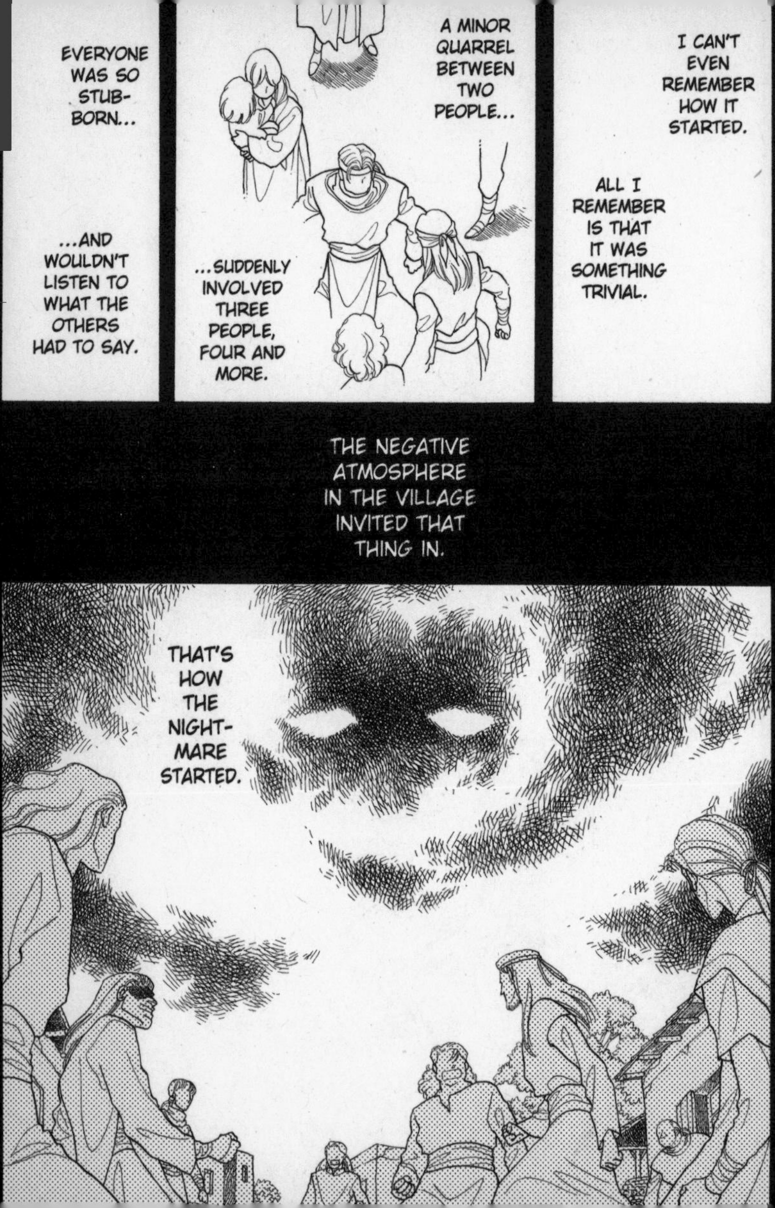
I CAN'T EVEN REMEMBER HOW IT STARTED.
ALL I REMEMBER IS THAT IT WAS SOMETHING TRIVIAL.
A MINOR QUARREL BETWEEN TWO PEOPLE...
...SUDDENLY INVOLVED THREE PEOPLE, FOUR AND MORE.
EVERYONE WAS SO STUB-BORN...
...AND WOULDN'T LISTEN TO WHAT THE OTHERS HAD TO SAY.
THE NEGATIVE ATMOSPHERE IN THE VILLAGE INVITED THAT THING IN.
THAT'S HOW THE NIGHT-MARE STARTED.

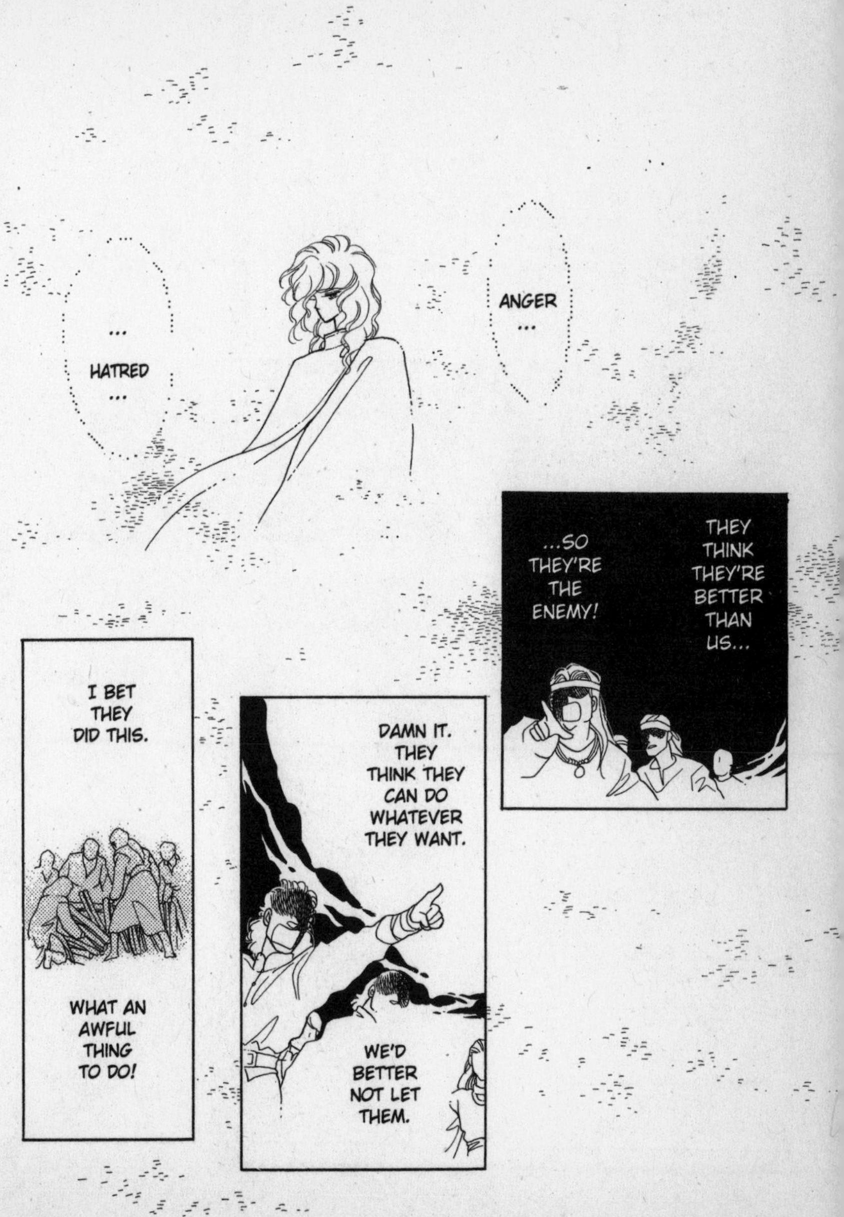
ANGER ...
... HATRED ...
THEY THINK THEY'RE BETTER THAN US...
...SO THEY'RE THE ENEMY!
DAMN IT. THEY THINK THEY CAN DO WHATEVER THEY WANT.
WE'D BETTER NOT LET THEM.
I BET THEY DID THIS.
WHAT AN AWFUL THING TO DO!

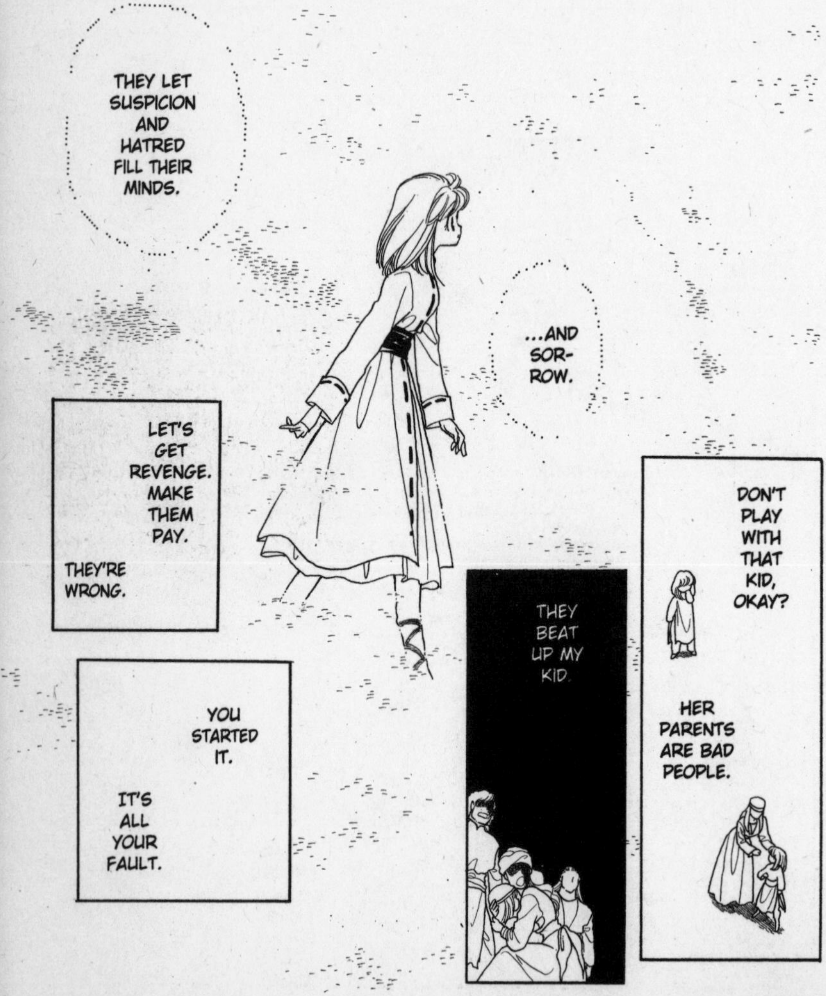
THEY LET SUSPICION AND HATRED FILL THEIR MINDS.
...AND SOR-ROW.
DON'T PLAY WITH THAT KID, OKAY?
HER PARENTS ARE BAD PEOPLE.
THEY BEAT UP MY KID.
LET'S GET REVENGE. MAKE THEM PAY.
THEY'RE WRONG.
YOU STARTED IT.
IT'S ALL YOUR FAULT.

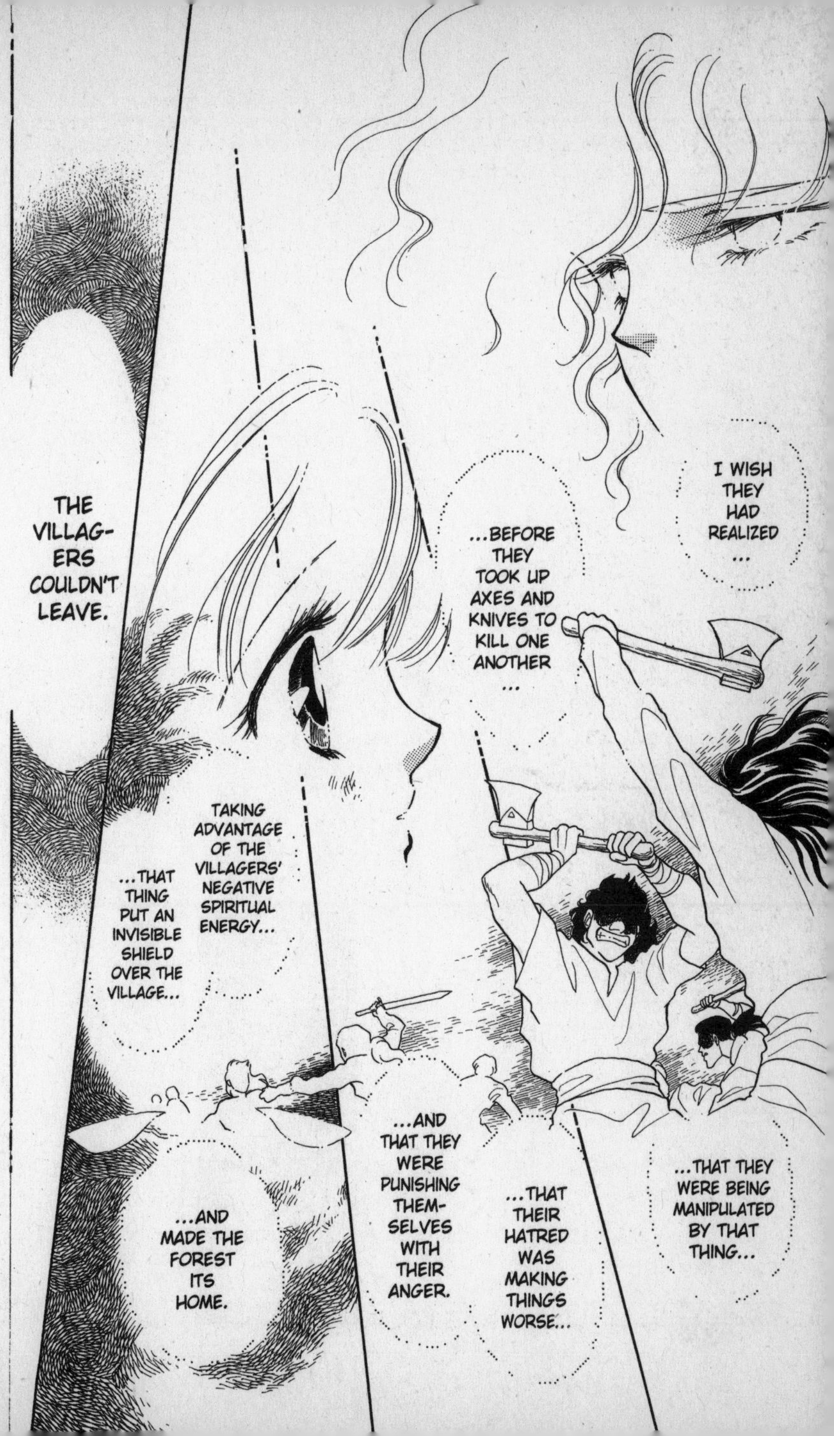
I WISH THEY HAD REALIZED...
...BEFORE THEY TOOK UP AXES AND KNIVES TO KILL ONE ANOTHER...
TAKING ADVANTAGE OF THE VILLAGERS' NEGATIVE SPIRITUAL ENERGY...
...THAT THING PUT AN INVISIBLE SHIELD OVER THE VILLAGE...
THE VILLAG-ERS COULDN'T LEAVE.
...THAT THEY WERE BEING MANIPULATED BY THAT THING...
...THAT THEIR HATRED WAS MAKING THINGS WORSE...
...AND THAT THEY WERE PUNISHING THEM-SELVES WITH THEIR ANGER.
...AND MADE THE FOREST ITS HOME.

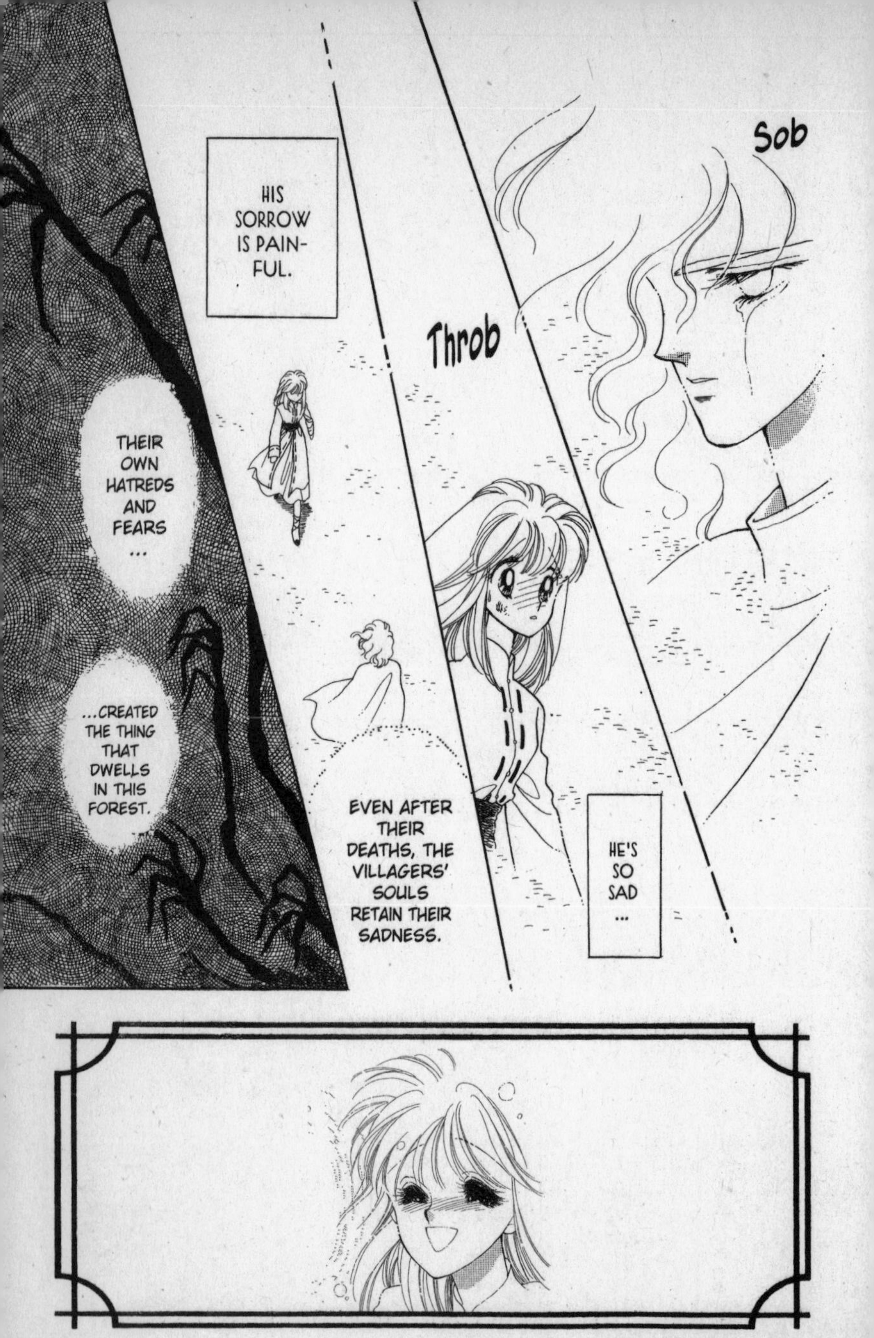
Sob
Throb
HE'S SO SAD ...
HIS SORROW IS PAIN-FUL.
EVEN AFTER THEIR DEATHS, THE VILLAGERS' SOULS RETAIN THEIR SADNESS.
THEIR OWN HATREDS AND FEARS ...
...CREATED THE THING THAT DWELLS IN THIS FOREST.

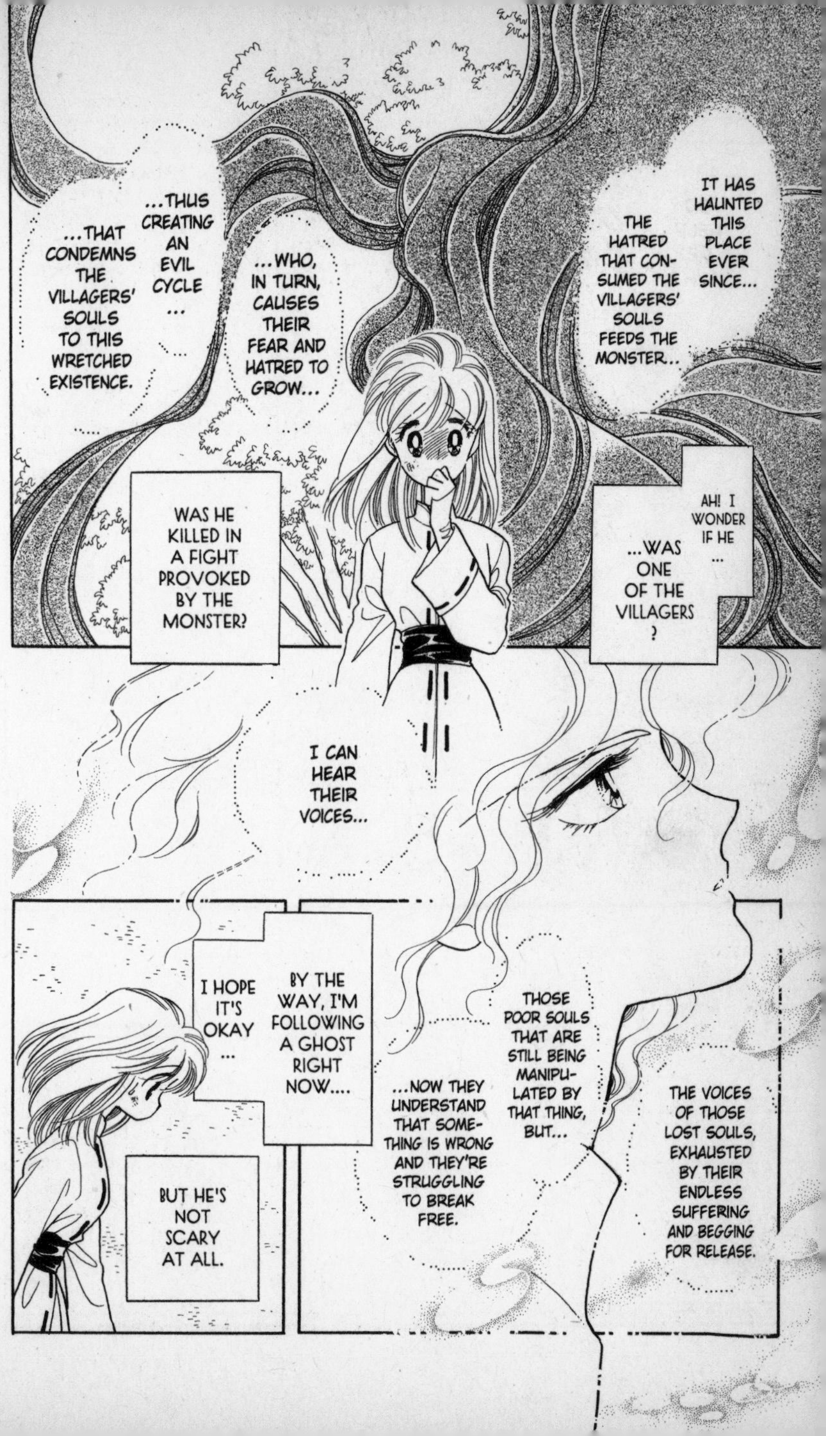
IT HAS HAUNTED THIS PLACE EVER SINCE...
THE HATRED THAT CONSUMED THE VILLAGERS' SOULS FEEDS THE MONSTER...
...WHO, IN TURN, CAUSES THEIR FEAR AND HATRED TO GROW...
...THUS CREATING AN EVIL CYCLE...
...THAT CONDEMNS THE VILLAGERS' SOULS TO THIS WRETCHED EXISTENCE.
AH! I WONDER IF HE...
...WAS ONE OF THE VILLAGERS?
WAS HE KILLED IN A FIGHT PROVOKED BY THE MONSTER?
I CAN HEAR THEIR VOICES...
THE VOICES OF THOSE LOST SOULS, EXHAUSTED BY THEIR ENDLESS SUFFERING AND BEGGING FOR RELEASE.
THOSE POOR SOULS THAT ARE STILL BEING MANIPULATED BY THAT THING, BUT...
...NOW THEY UNDERSTAND THAT SOMETHING IS WRONG AND THEY'RE STRUGGLING TO BREAK FREE.
BY THE WAY, I'M FOLLOWING A GHOST RIGHT NOW....
I HOPE IT'S OKAY...
BUT HE'S NOT SCARY AT ALL.

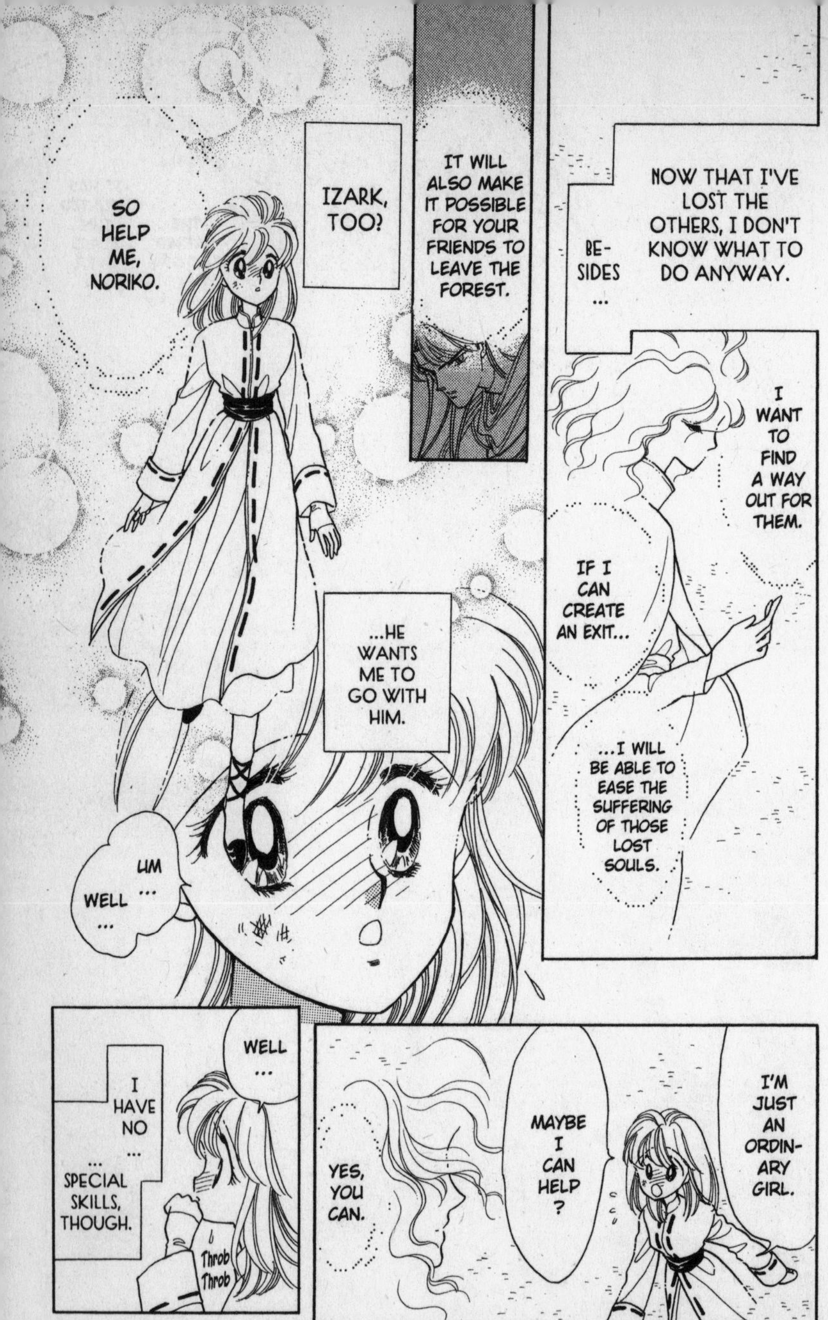
NOW THAT I'VE LOST THE OTHERS, I DON'T KNOW WHAT TO DO ANYWAY.
BE-SIDES ...
I WANT TO FIND A WAY OUT FOR THEM.
IF I CAN CREATE AN EXIT...
...I WILL BE ABLE TO EASE THE SUFFERING OF THOSE LOST SOULS.
IT WILL ALSO MAKE IT POSSIBLE FOR YOUR FRIENDS TO LEAVE THE FOREST.
IZARK, TOO?
SO HELP ME, NORIKO.
...HE WANTS ME TO GO WITH HIM.
UM ... WELL ...
I'M JUST AN ORDIN-ARY GIRL.
MAYBE I CAN HELP ?
YES, YOU CAN.
WELL ...
I HAVE NO ... SPECIAL SKILLS, THOUGH.
Throb Throb

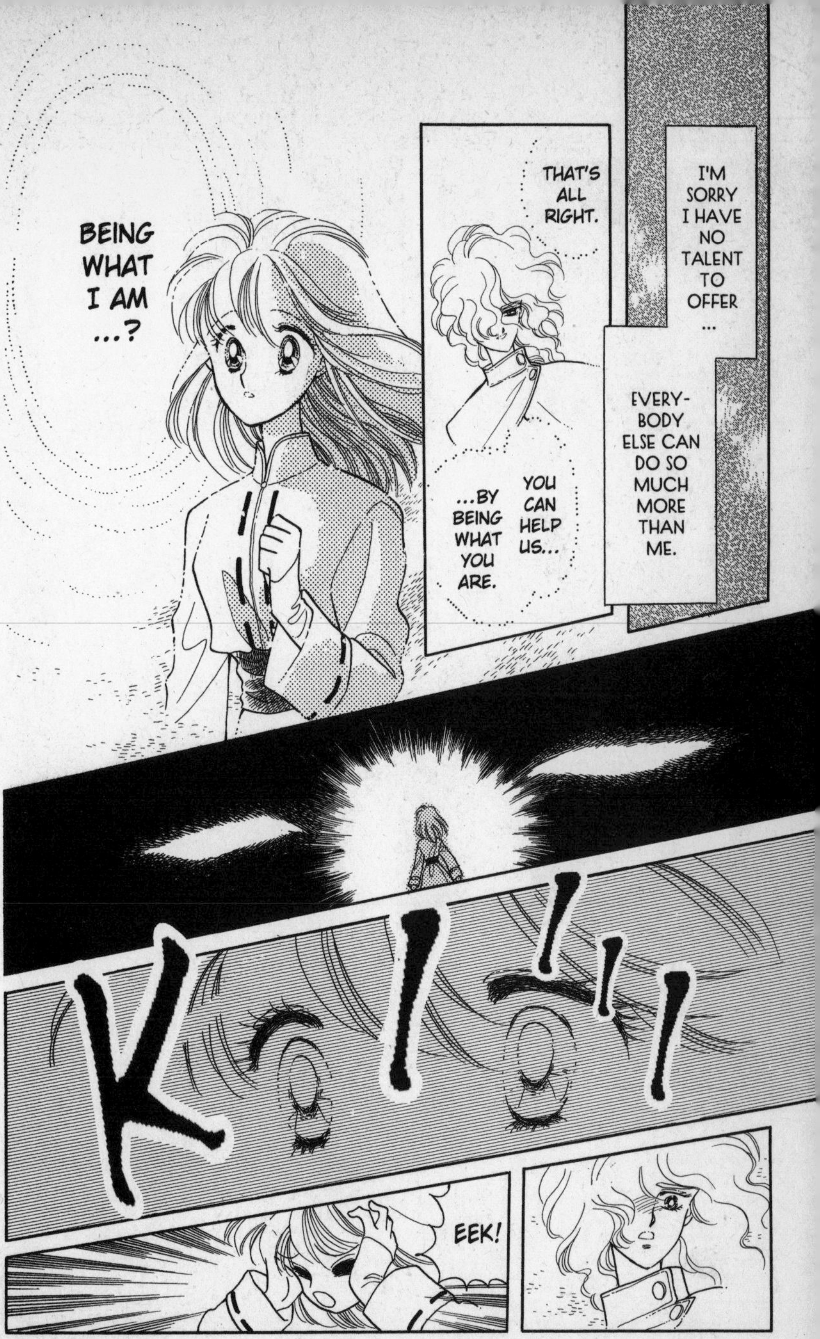
I'M SORRY I HAVE NO TALENT TO OFFER ...
EVERY-BODY ELSE CAN DO SO MUCH MORE THAN ME.
THAT'S ALL RIGHT.
YOU CAN HELP US...
...BY BEING WHAT YOU ARE.
BEING WHAT I AM ...?
K!!!!
EEK!

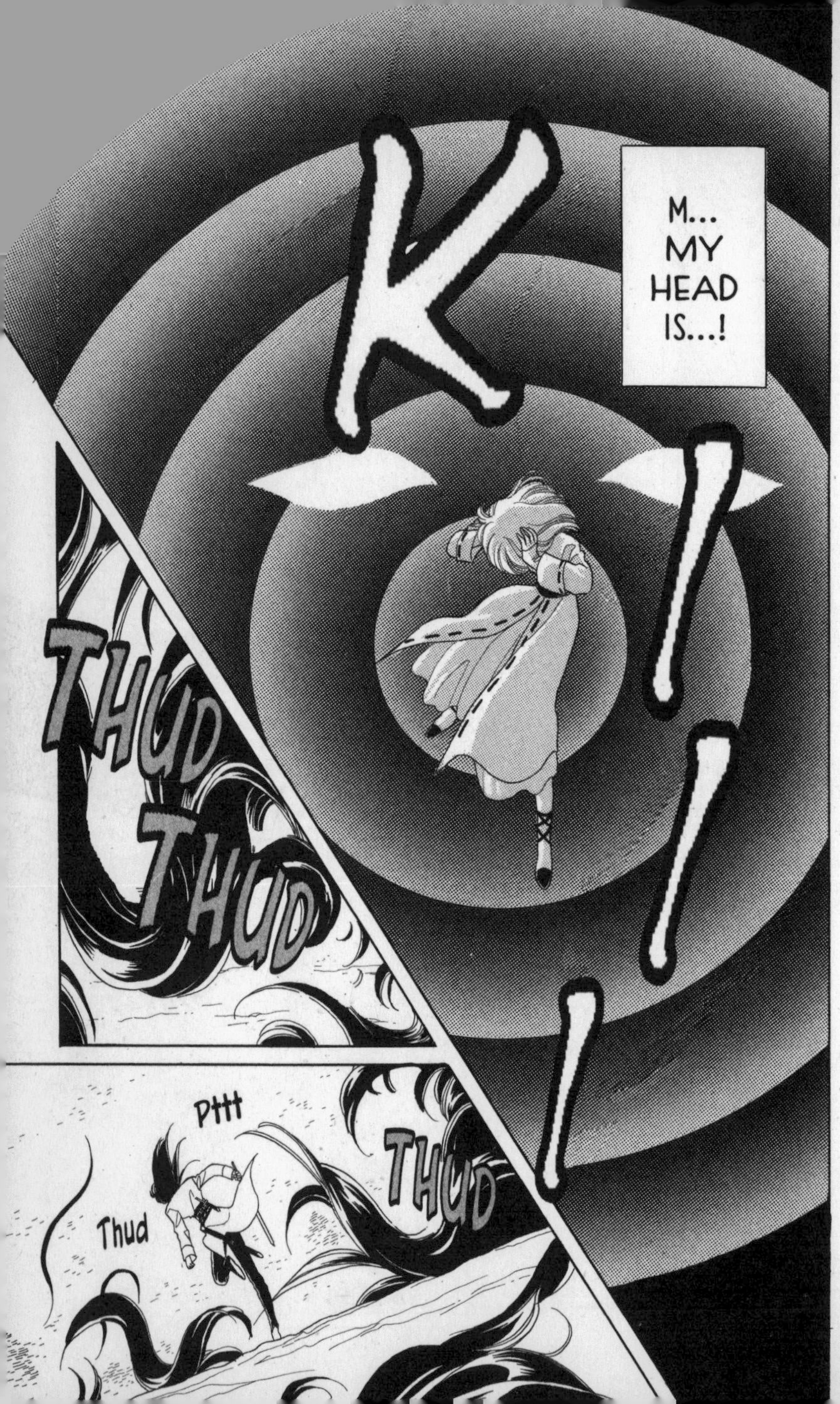
M... MY HEAD IS...!
K!!!
THUD THUD
THUD
Pttt
Thud

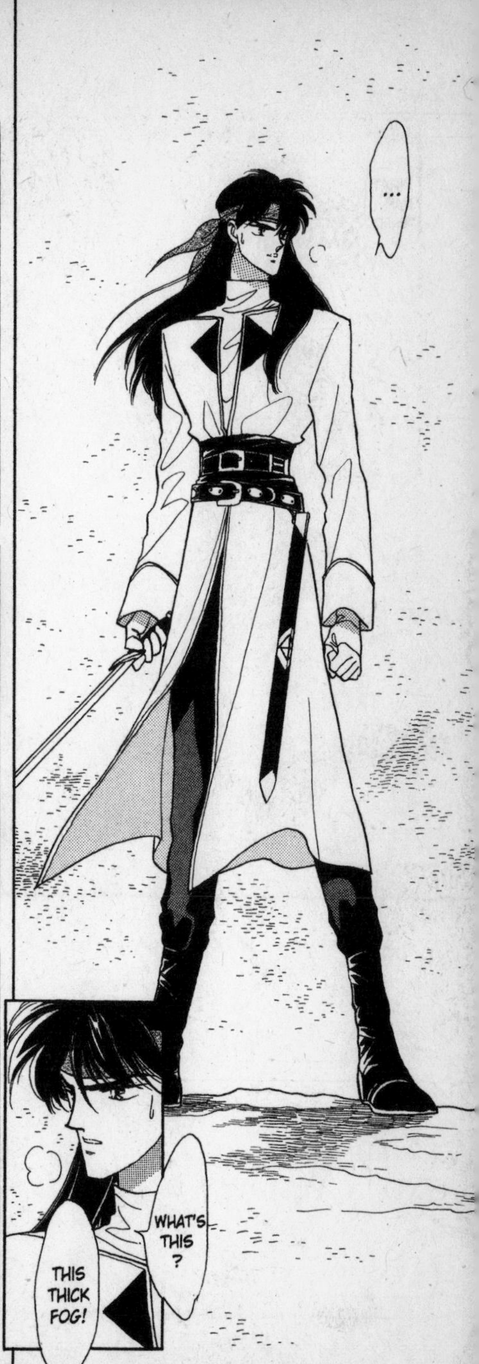
...
WHAT'S THIS?
THIS THICK FOG!
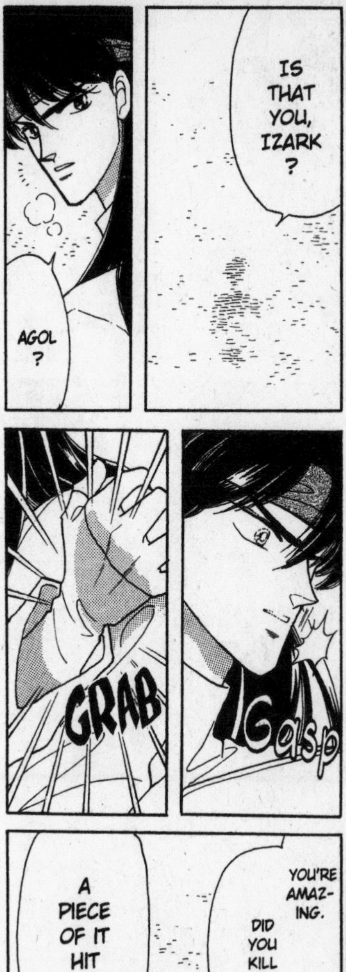
IS THAT YOU, IZARK?
AGOL?
Gasp
GRAB
YOU'RE AMAZ-ING.
DID YOU KILL THE MONSTER?
A PIECE OF IT HIT ME!

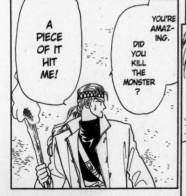

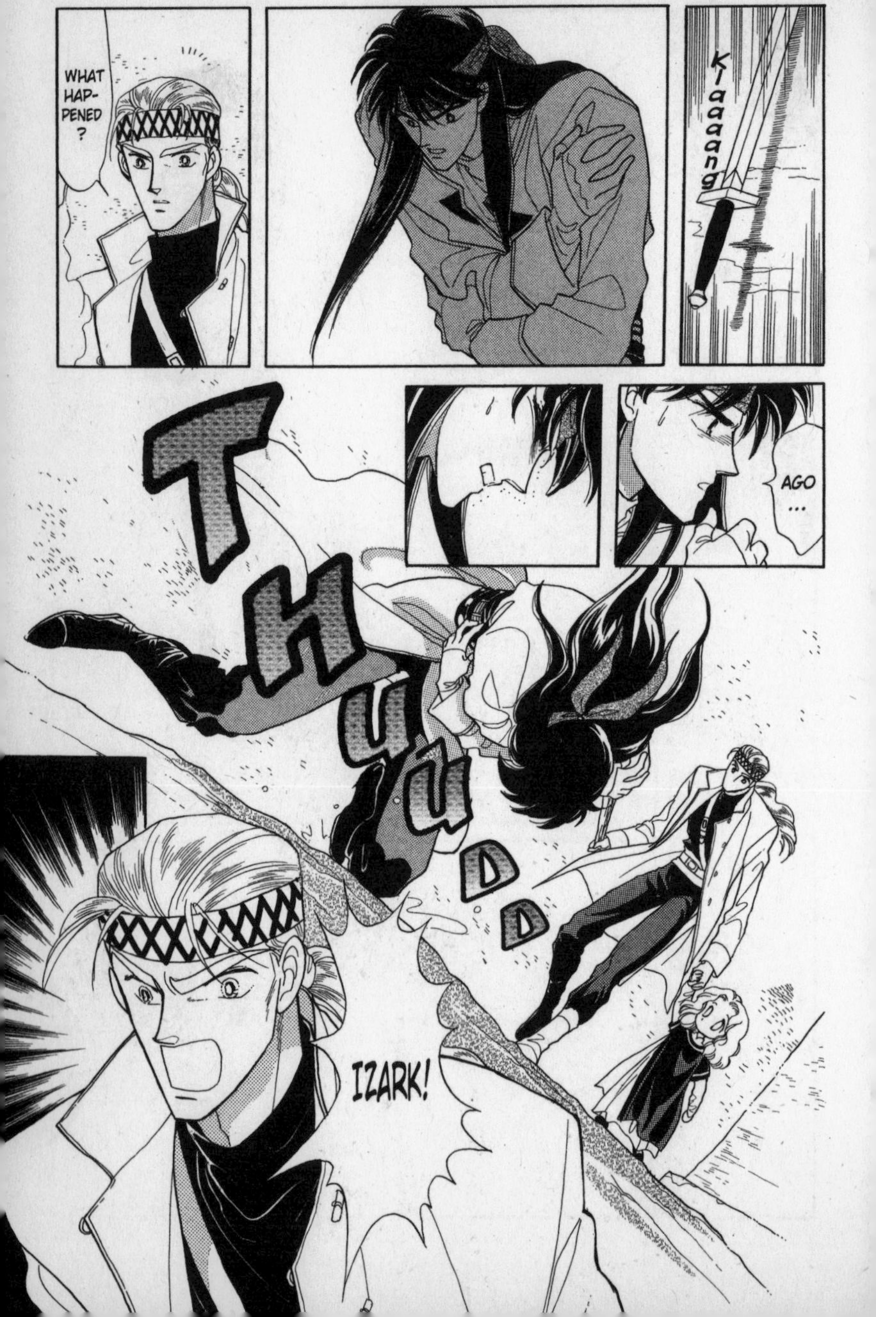
Klaaaaang!
WHAT HAP-PENED ?
AGO ...
THUUDD
IZARK!

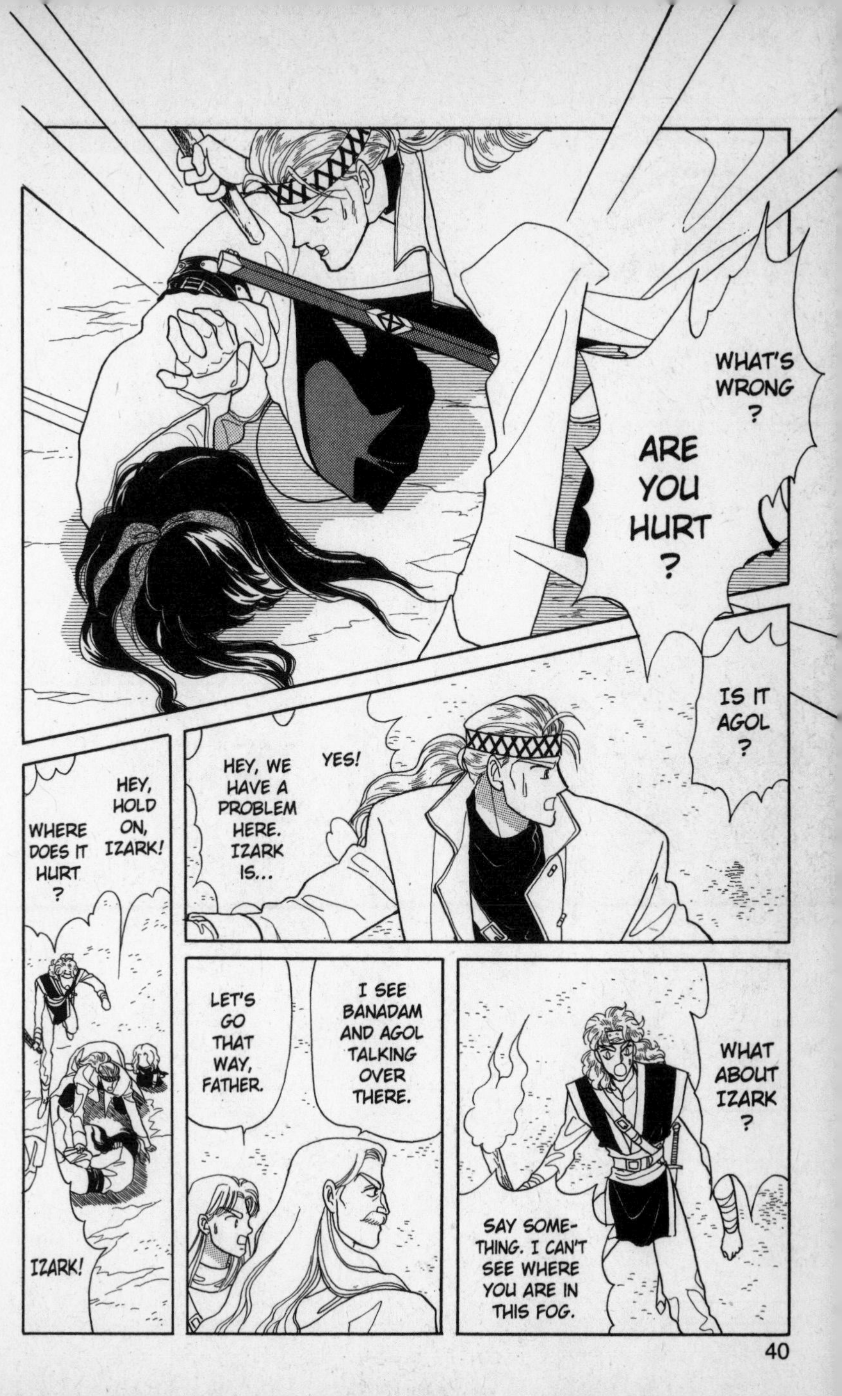
WHAT'S WRONG?
ARE YOU HURT?
IS IT AGOL?
YES!
HEY, WE HAVE A PROBLEM HERE. IZARK IS...
WHAT ABOUT IZARK?
SAY SOME-THING. I CAN'T SEE WHERE YOU ARE IN THIS FOG.
I SEE BANADAM AND AGOL TALKING OVER THERE.
LET'S GO THAT WAY, FATHER.
HEY, HOLD ON, IZARK!
WHERE DOES IT HURT?
IZARK!

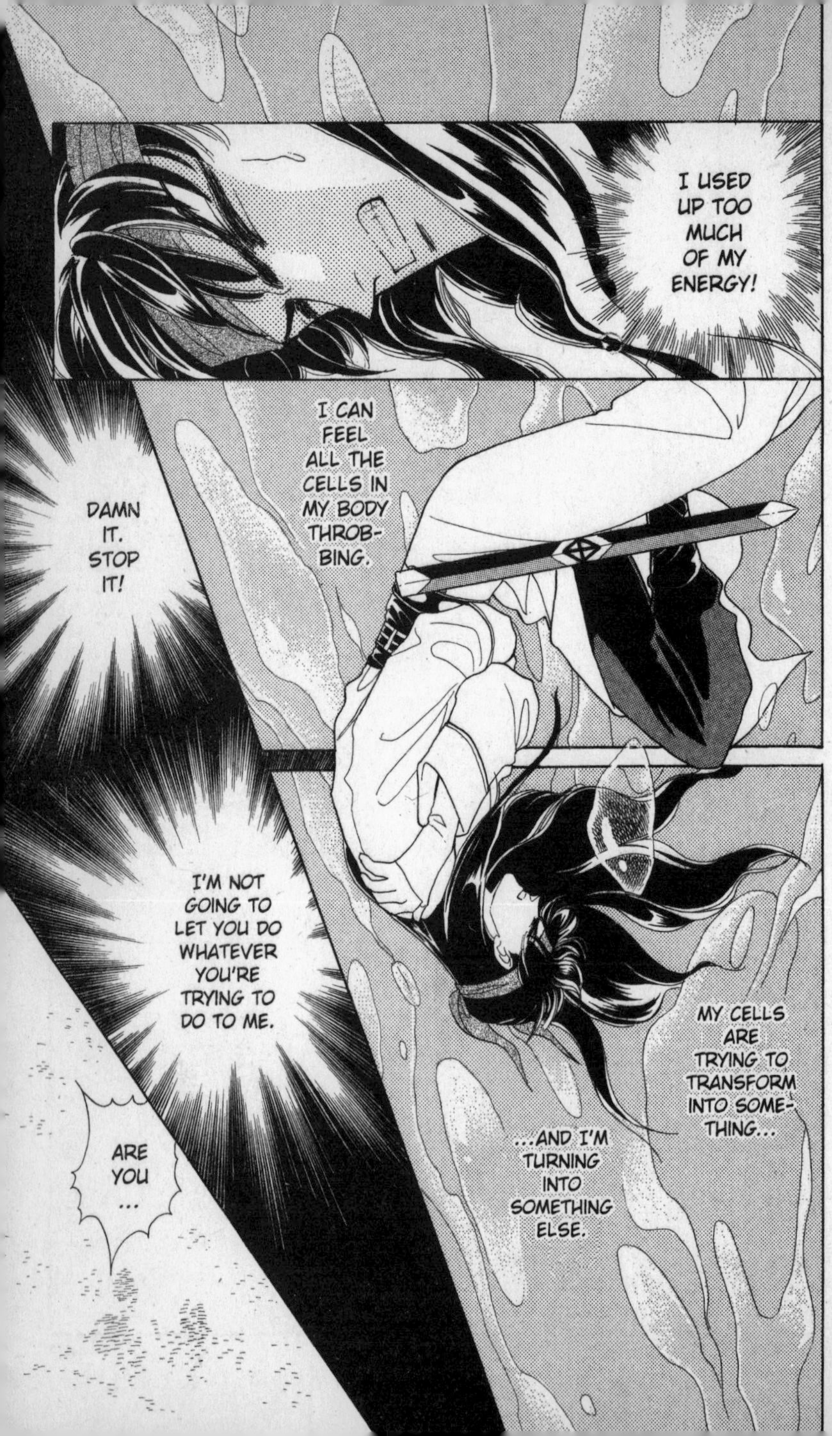
I USED UP TOO MUCH OF MY ENERGY!
I CAN FEEL ALL THE CELLS IN MY BODY THROB-BING.
MY CELLS ARE TRYING TO TRANSFORM INTO SOME-THING...
...AND I'M TURNING INTO SOMETHING ELSE.
DAMN IT. STOP IT!
I'M NOT GOING TO LET YOU DO WHATEVER YOU'RE TRYING TO DO TO ME.
ARE YOU ...

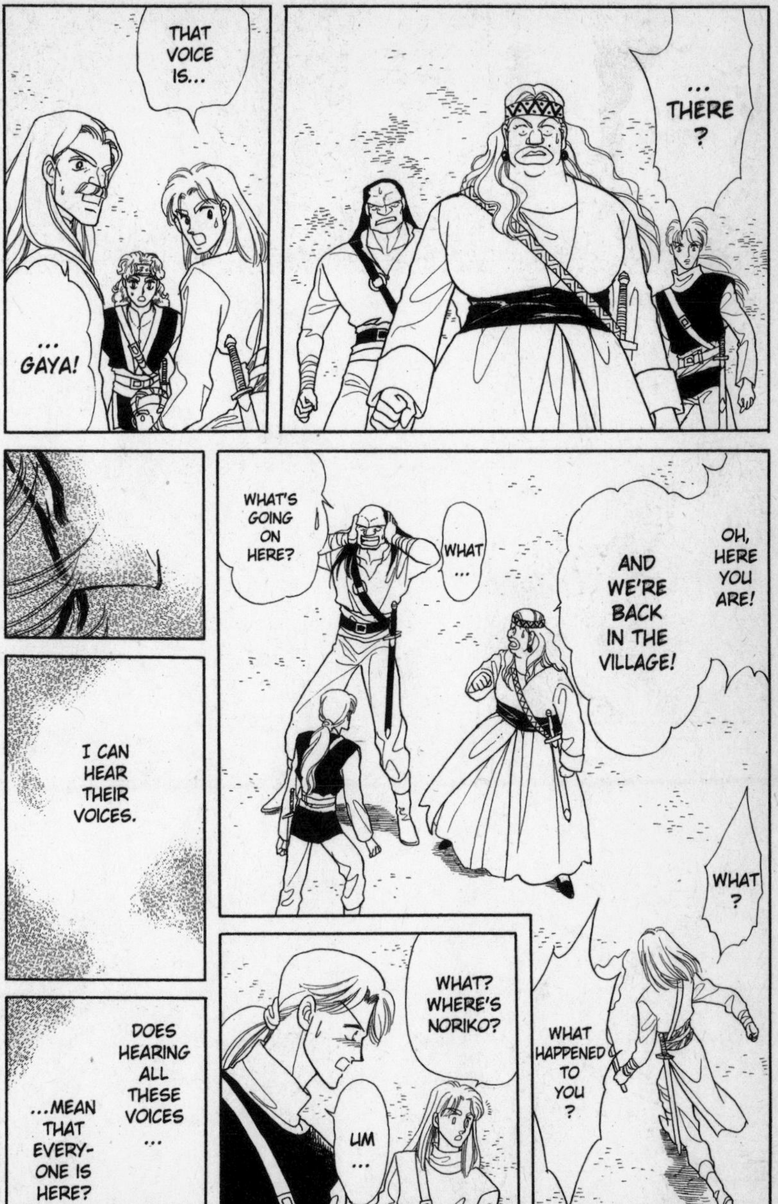

...THERE?
THAT VOICE IS...
...GAYA!
OH, HERE YOU ARE!
AND WE'RE BACK IN THE VILLAGE!
WHAT...
WHAT'S GOING ON HERE?
WHAT?
WHAT HAPPENED TO YOU?
WHAT? WHERE'S NORIKO?
UM...
I CAN HEAR THEIR VOICES.
DOES HEARING ALL THESE VOICES...
...MEAN THAT EVERY-ONE IS HERE?

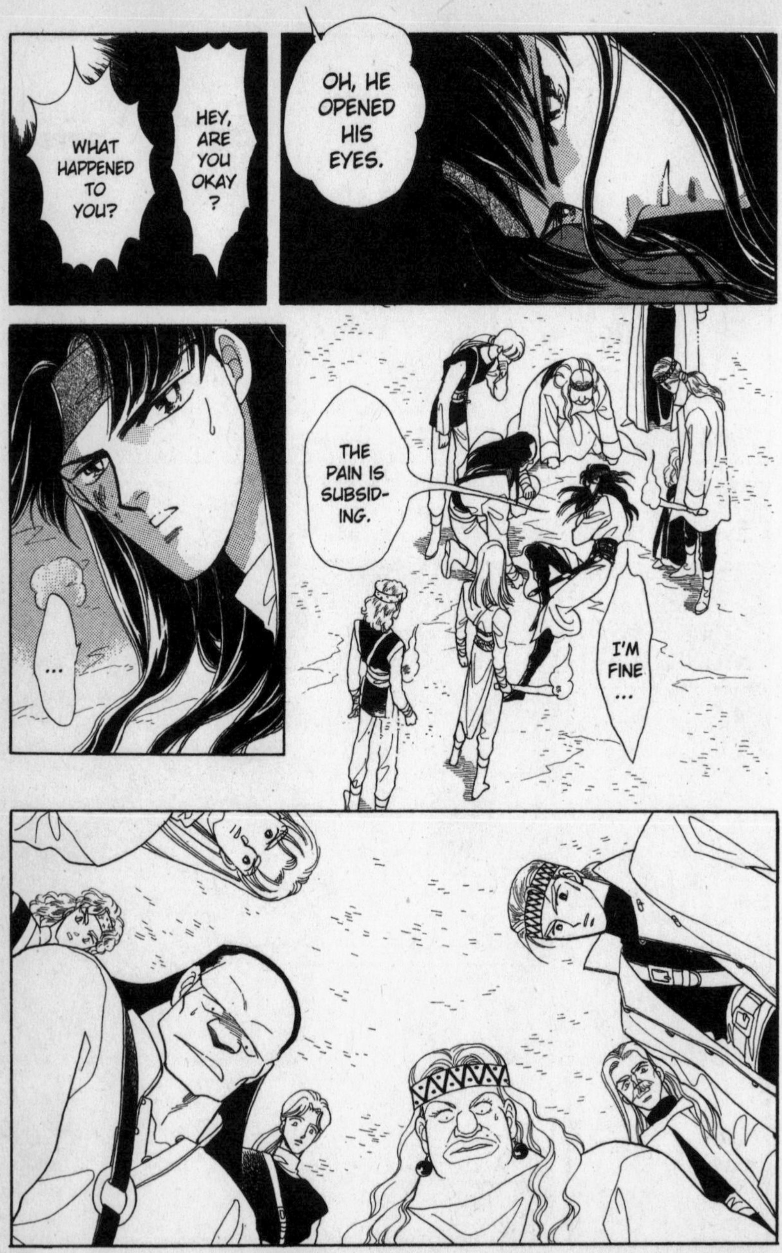
OH, HE OPENED HIS EYES.
HEY, ARE YOU OKAY?
WHAT HAPPENED TO YOU?
THE PAIN IS SUBSID-ING.
I'M FINE...
...

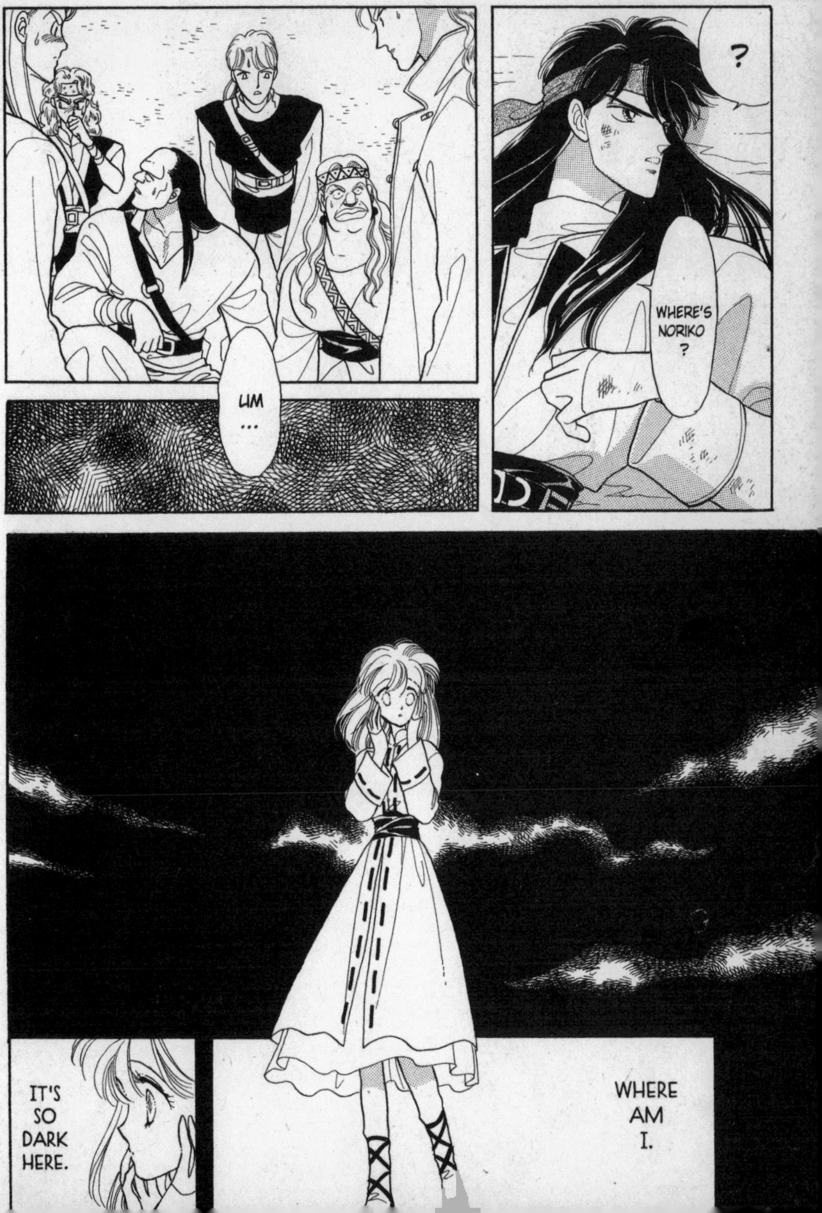
?
WHERE'S NORIKO ?
UM ...
WHERE AM I.
IT'S SO DARK HERE.

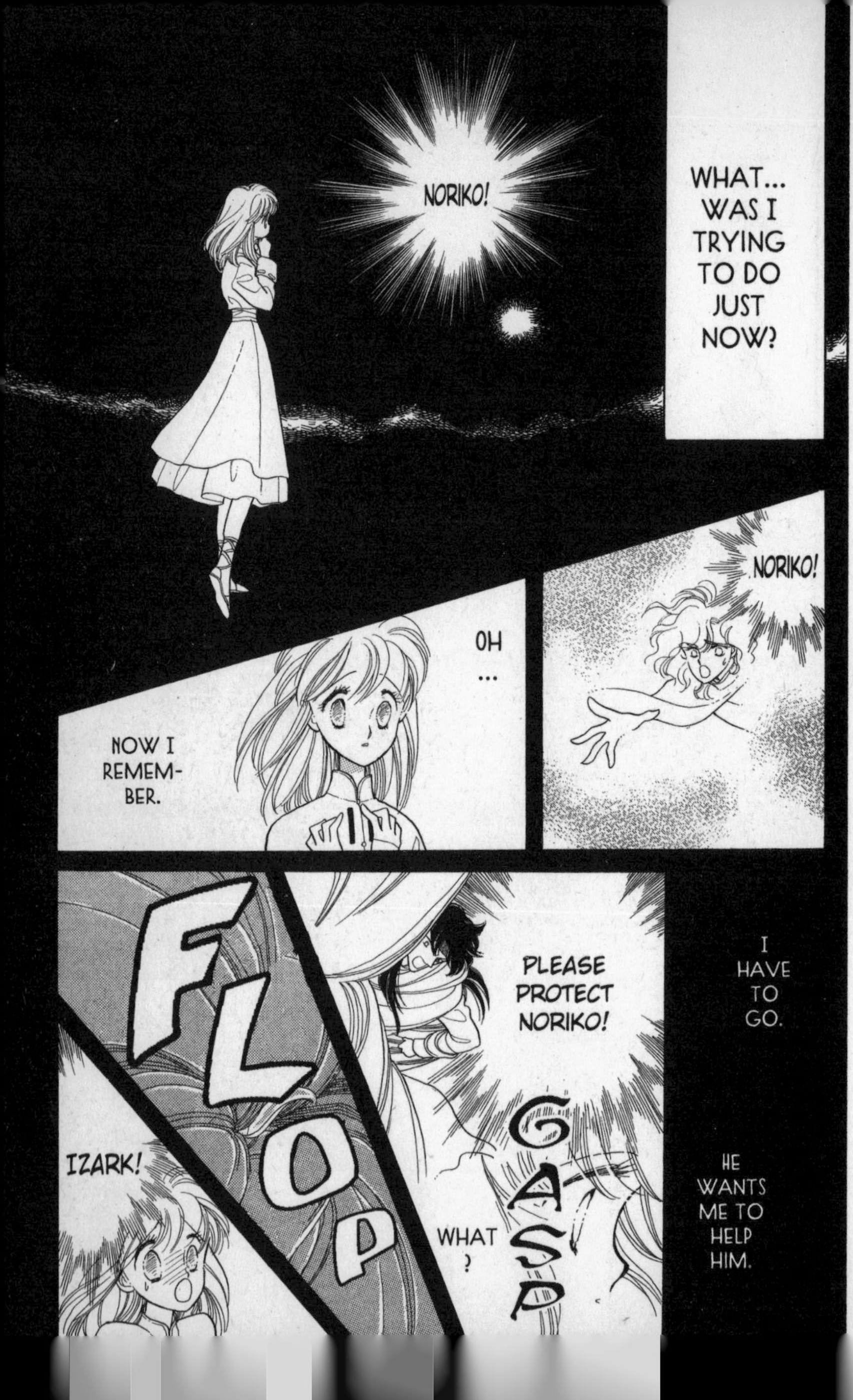
WHAT... WAS I TRYING TO DO JUST NOW?
NORIKO!
NORIKO!
OH...
NOW I REMEMBER.
I HAVE TO GO.
HE WANTS ME TO HELP HIM.
PLEASE PROTECT NORIKO!
GASP
WHAT?
FLOP
IZARK!

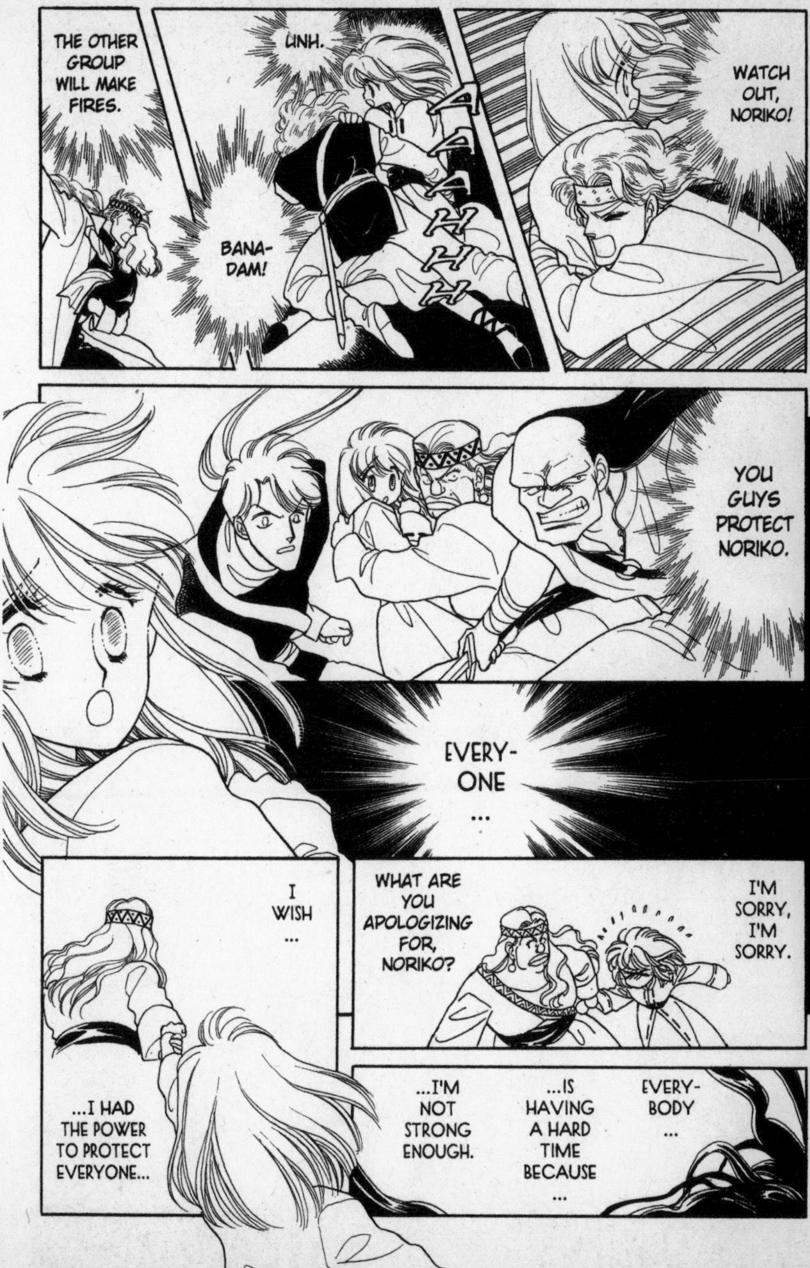
WATCH OUT, NORIKO!
UNH.
AAAHHHH
BANA-DAM!
THE OTHER GROUP WILL MAKE FIRES.
YOU GUYS PROTECT NORIKO.
EVERY-ONE ...
I'M SORRY, I'M SORRY.
WHAT ARE YOU APOLOGIZING FOR, NORIKO?
EVERY-BODY ...
...IS HAVING A HARD TIME BECAUSE ...
...I'M NOT STRONG ENOUGH.
I WISH ...
...I HAD THE POWER TO PROTECT EVERYONE...

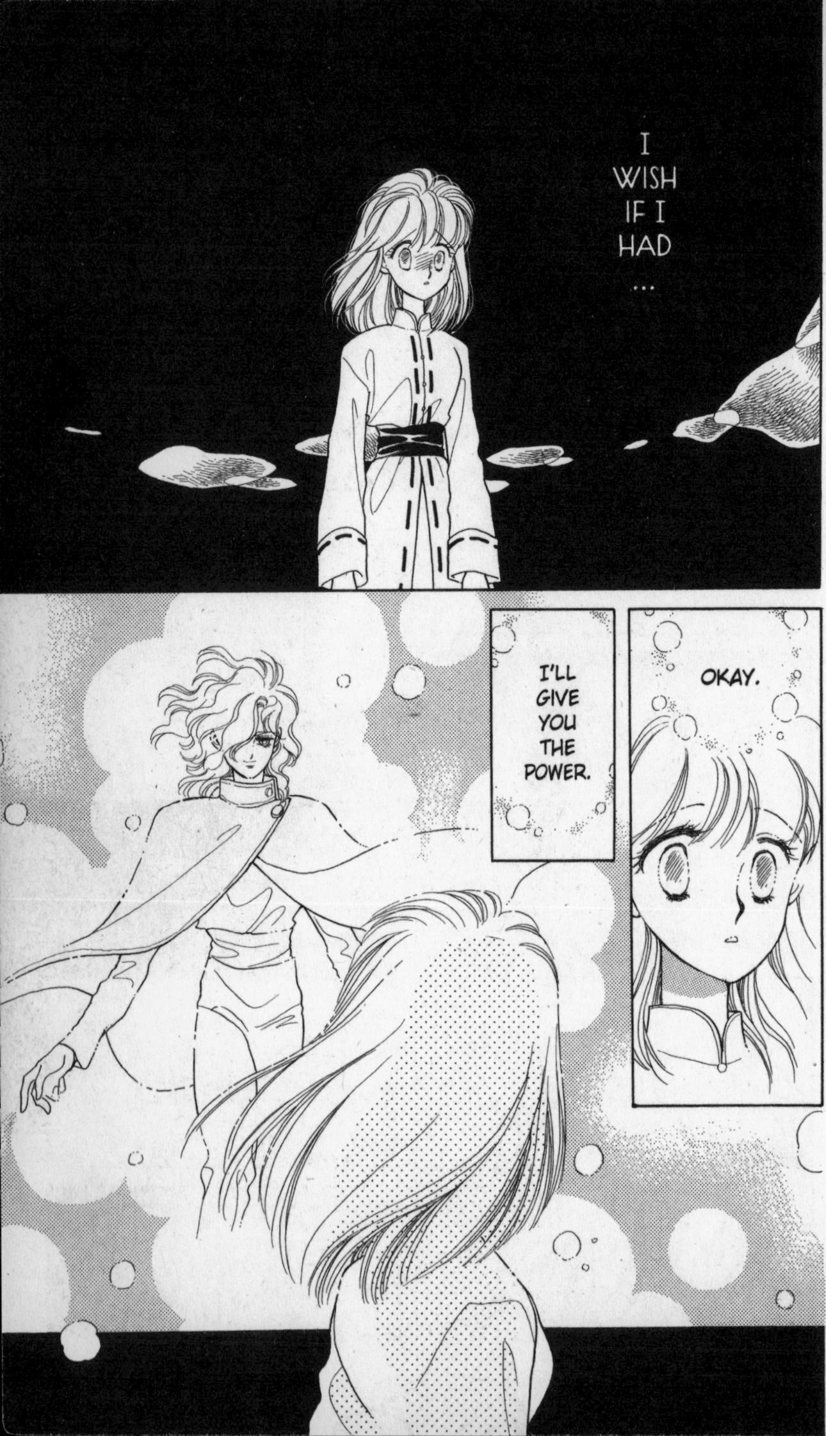
I WISH IF I HAD ...
OKAY.
I'LL GIVE YOU THE POWER.

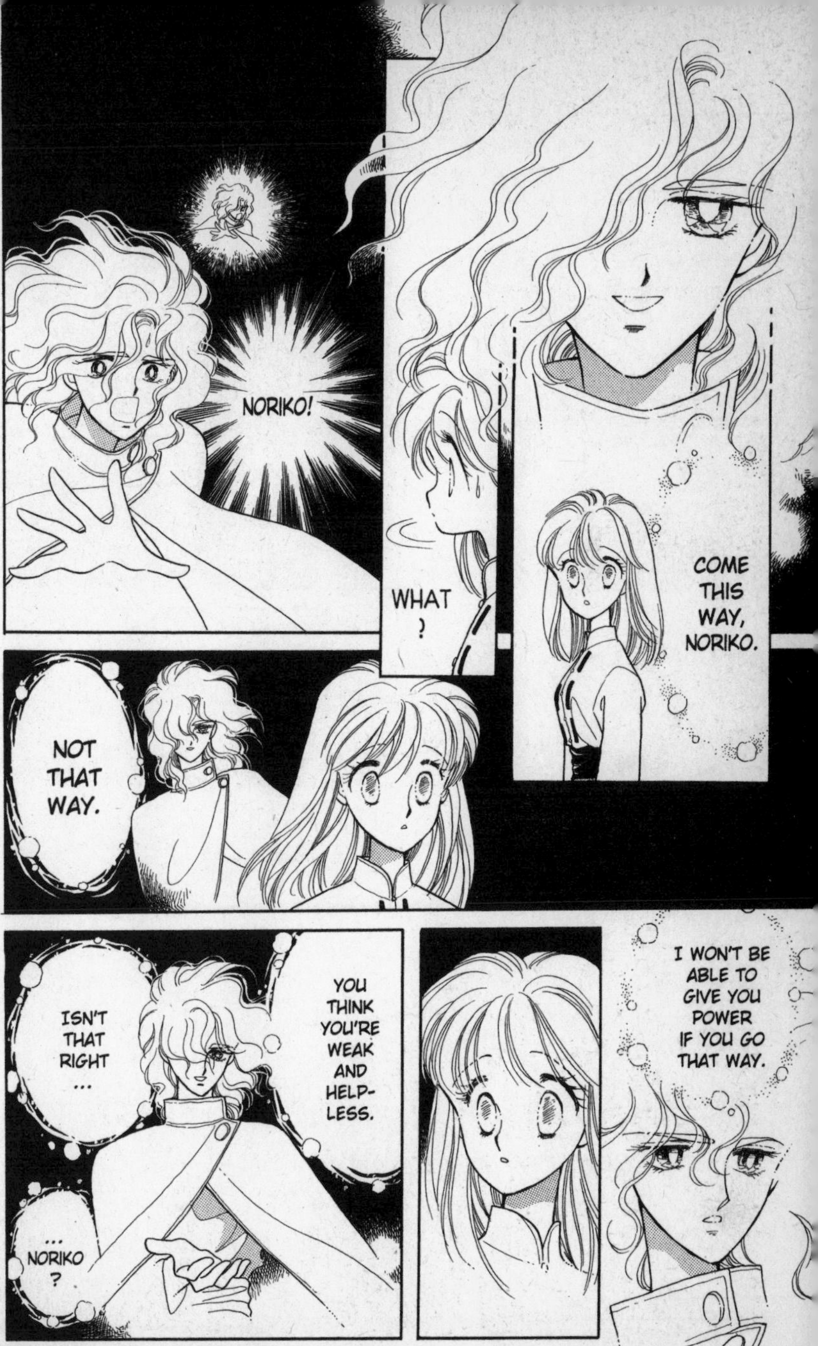
COME THIS WAY, NORIKO.
WHAT ?
NORIKO!
NOT THAT WAY.
I WON'T BE ABLE TO GIVE YOU POWER IF YOU GO THAT WAY.
YOU THINK YOU'RE WEAK AND HELP-LESS.
ISN'T THAT RIGHT ...
... NORIKO ?

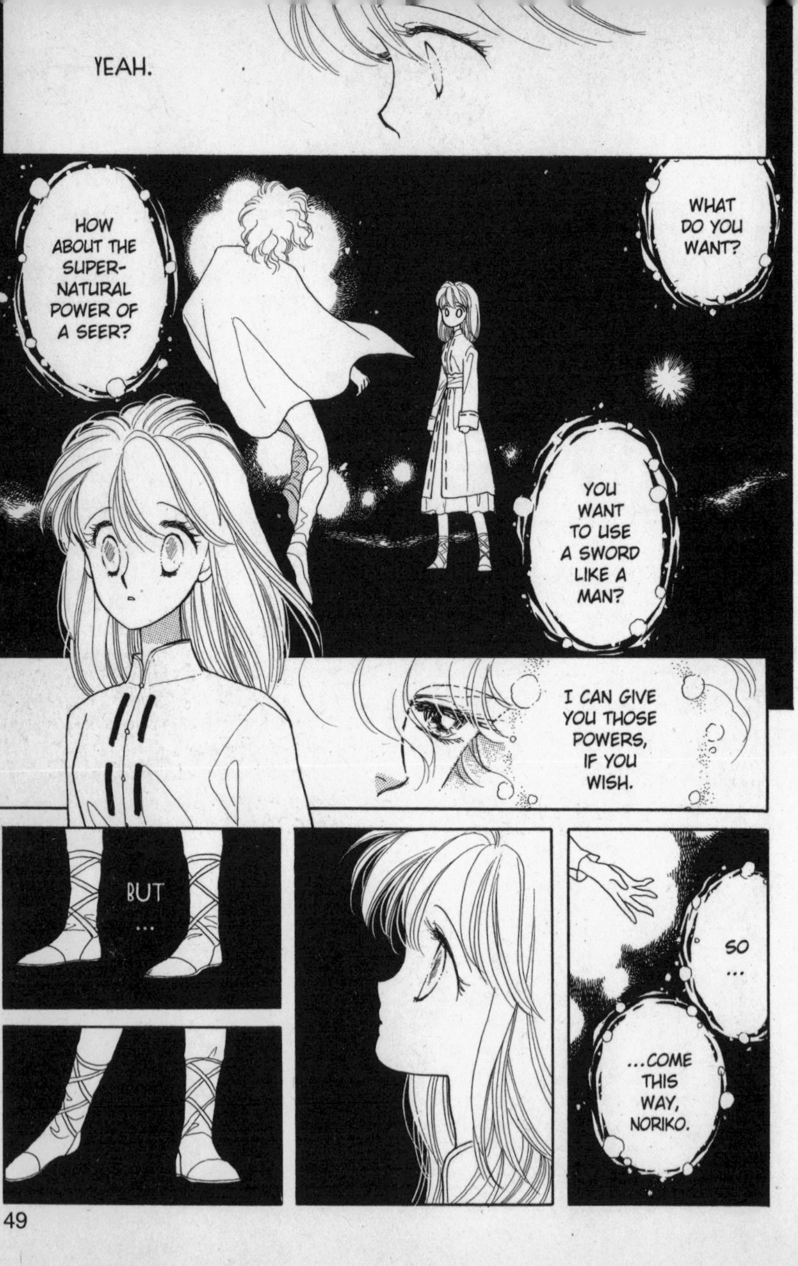
YEAH.
WHAT DO YOU WANT?
HOW ABOUT THE SUPER-NATURAL POWER OF A SEER?
YOU WANT TO USE A SWORD LIKE A MAN?
I CAN GIVE YOU THOSE POWERS, IF YOU WISH.
SO ...
...COME THIS WAY, NORIKO.
BUT ...

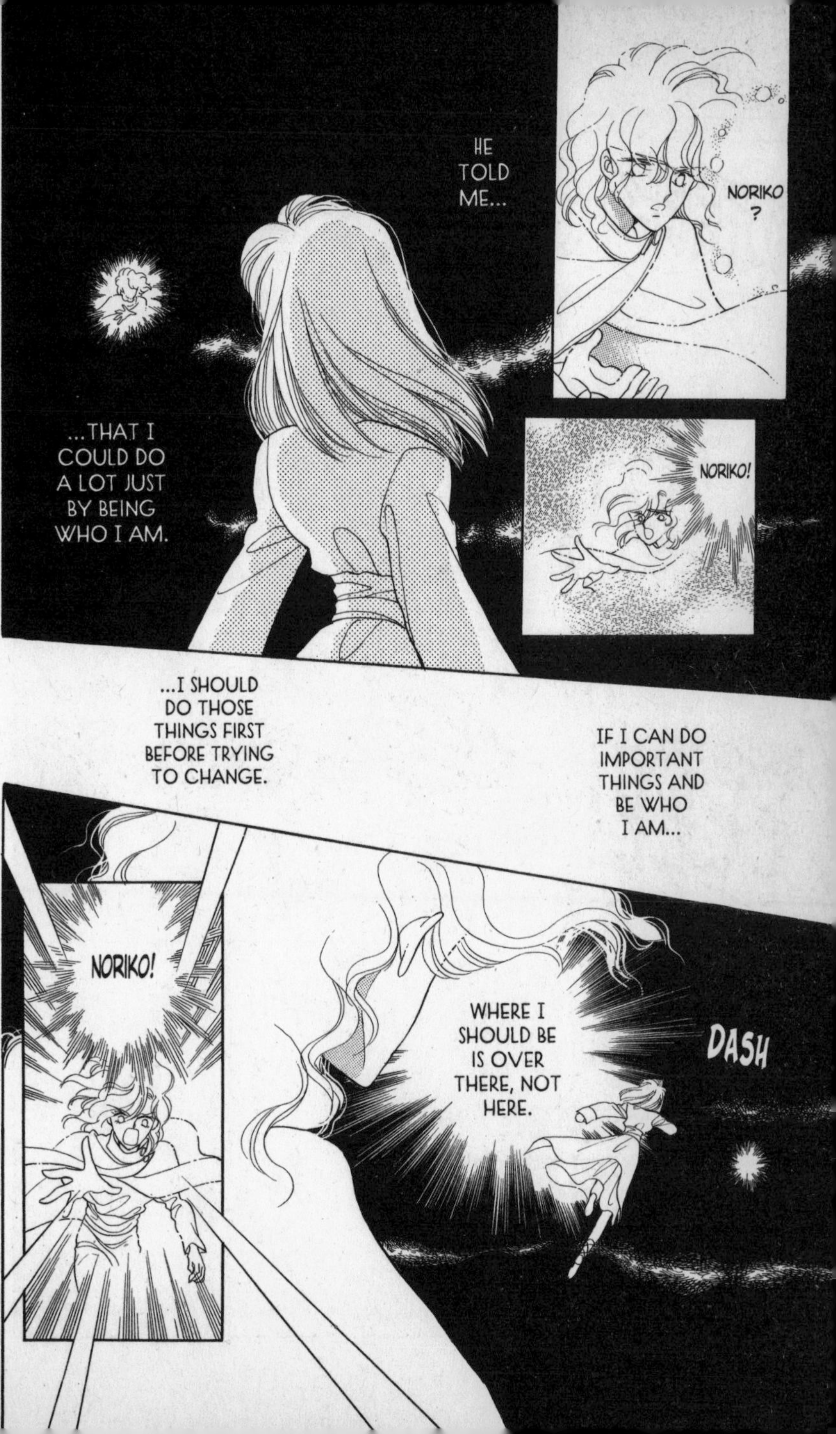
NORIKO ?
NORIKO!
HE TOLD ME...
...THAT I COULD DO A LOT JUST BY BEING WHO I AM.
IF I CAN DO IMPORTANT THINGS AND BE WHO I AM...
...I SHOULD DO THOSE THINGS FIRST BEFORE TRYING TO CHANGE.
DASH
WHERE I SHOULD BE IS OVER THERE, NOT HERE.
NORIKO!

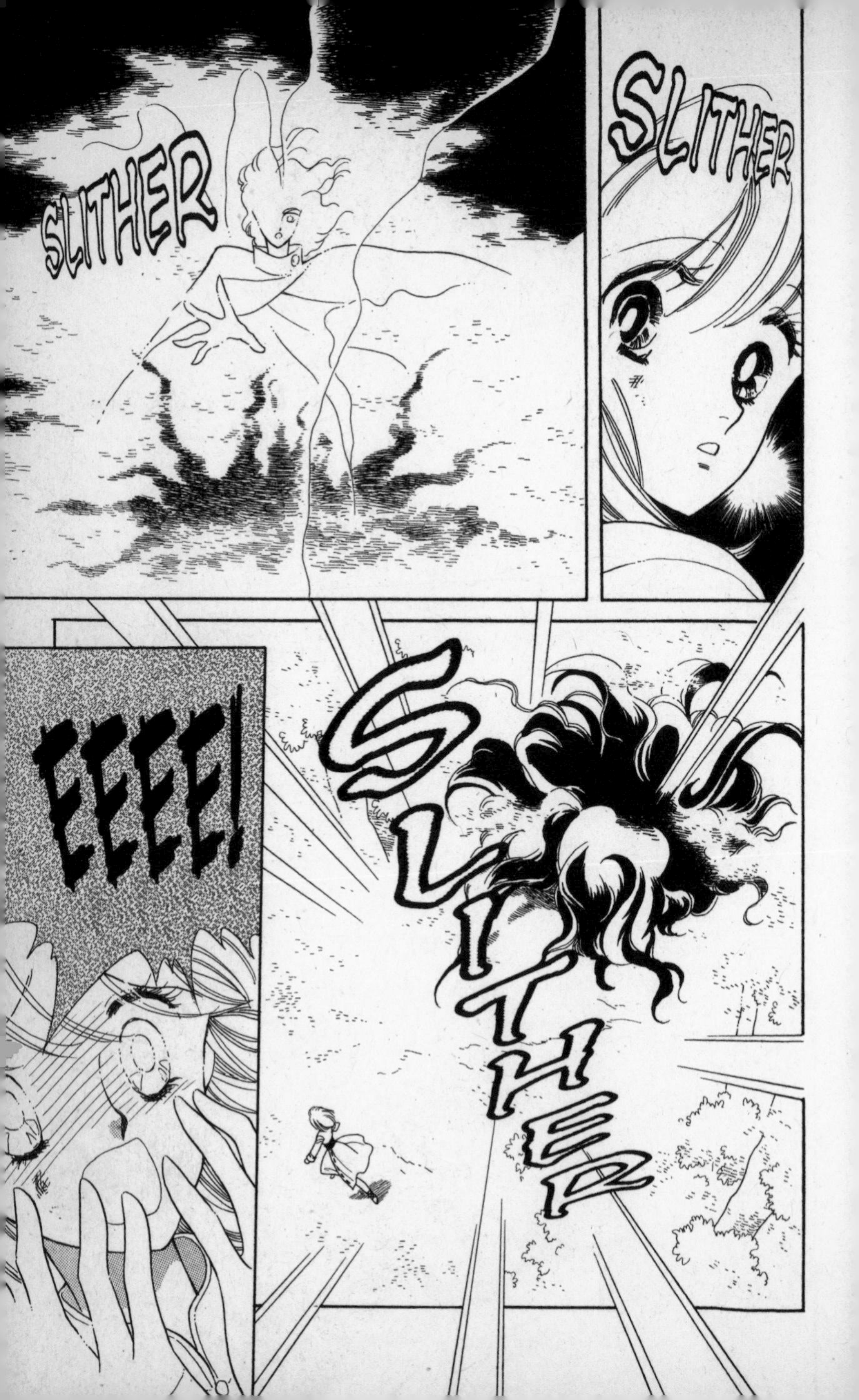
SLITHER
SLITHER
SLITHER
EEEE!

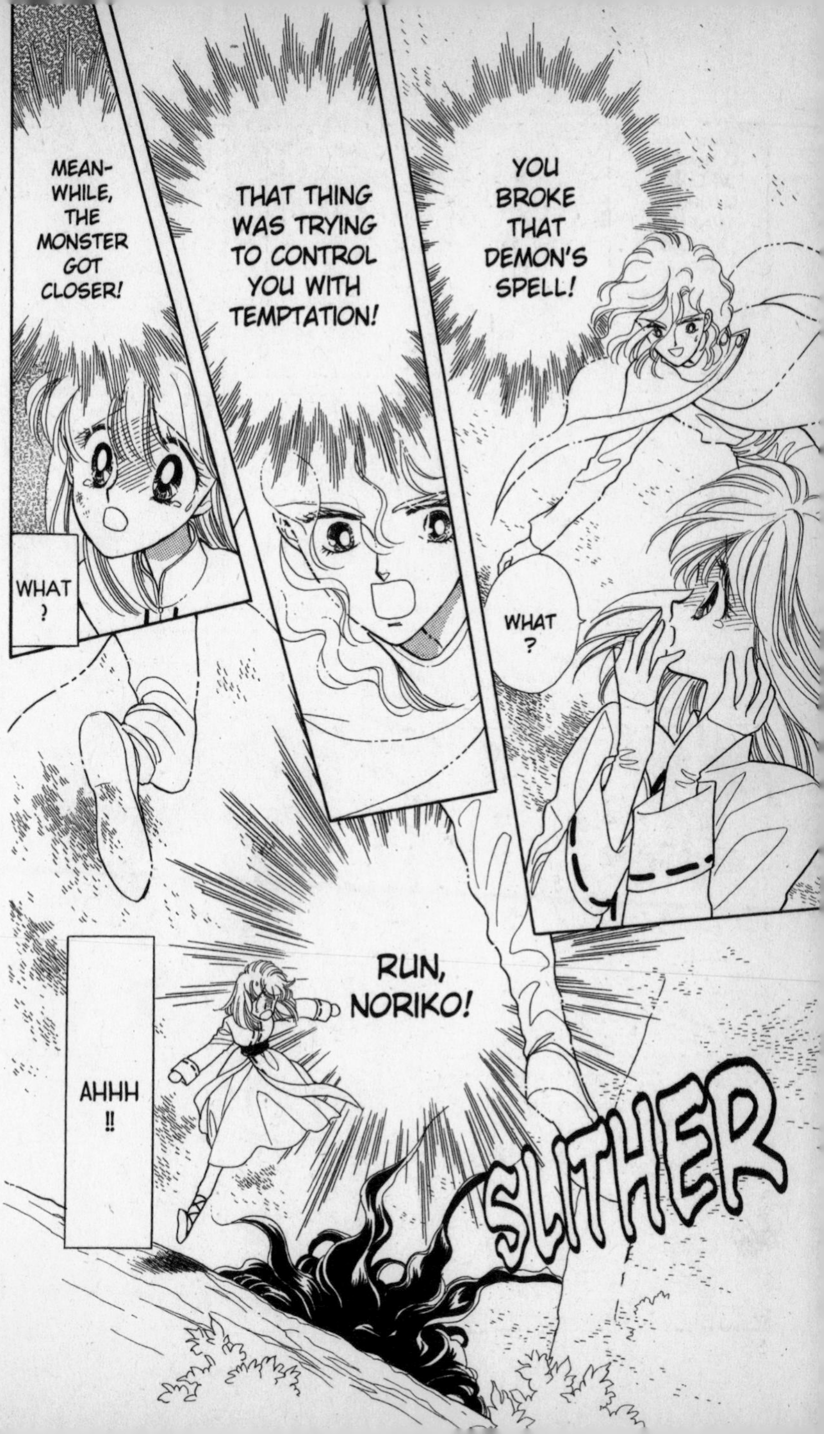
YOU BROKE THAT DEMON'S SPELL!
WHAT?
THAT THING WAS TRYING TO CONTROL YOU WITH TEMPTATION!
MEAN-WHILE, THE MONSTER GOT CLOSER!
WHAT?
RUN, NORIKO!
AHHH!!
SLITHER

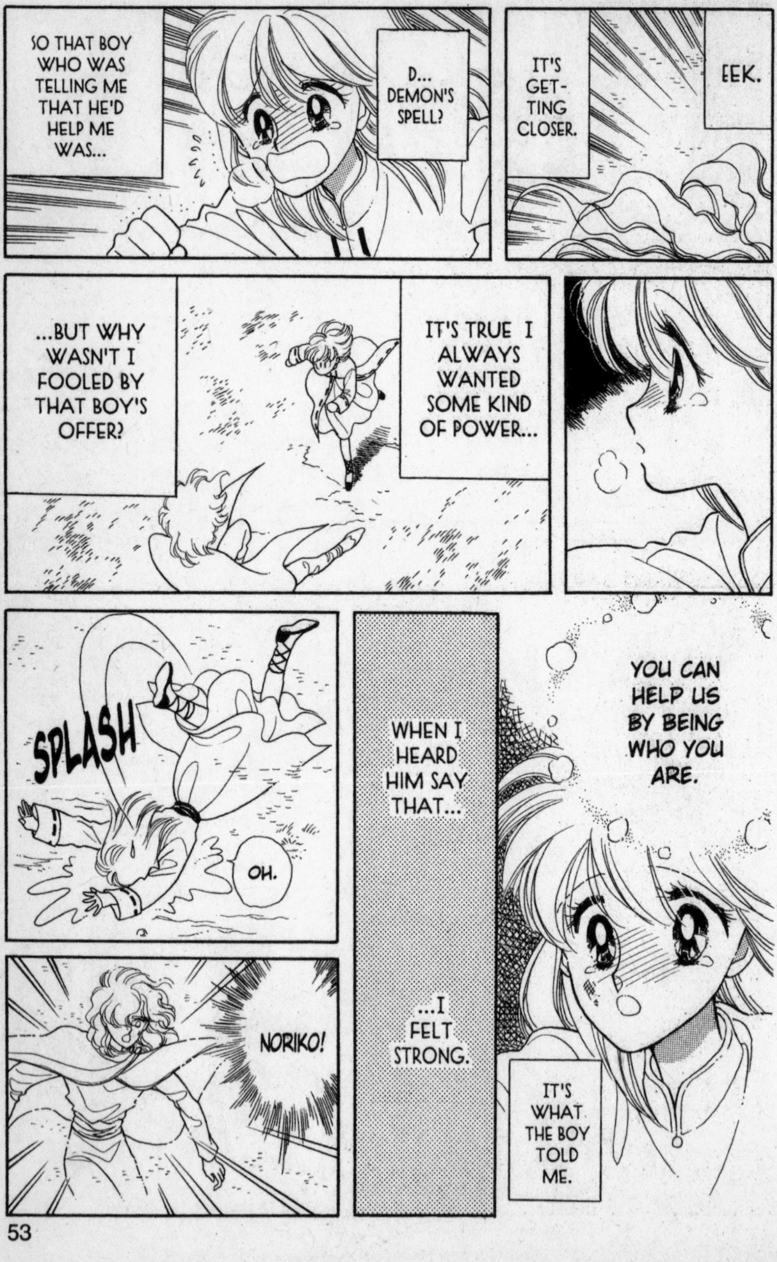
EEK.
IT'S GET-TING CLOSER.
D... DEMON'S SPELL?
SO THAT BOY WHO WAS TELLING ME THAT HE'D HELP ME WAS...
IT'S TRUE I ALWAYS WANTED SOME KIND OF POWER...
...BUT WHY WASN'T I FOOLED BY THAT BOY'S OFFER?
YOU CAN HELP US BY BEING WHO YOU ARE.
IT'S WHAT THE BOY TOLD ME.
WHEN I HEARD HIM SAY THAT...
...I FELT STRONG.
SPLASH
OH.
NORIKO!

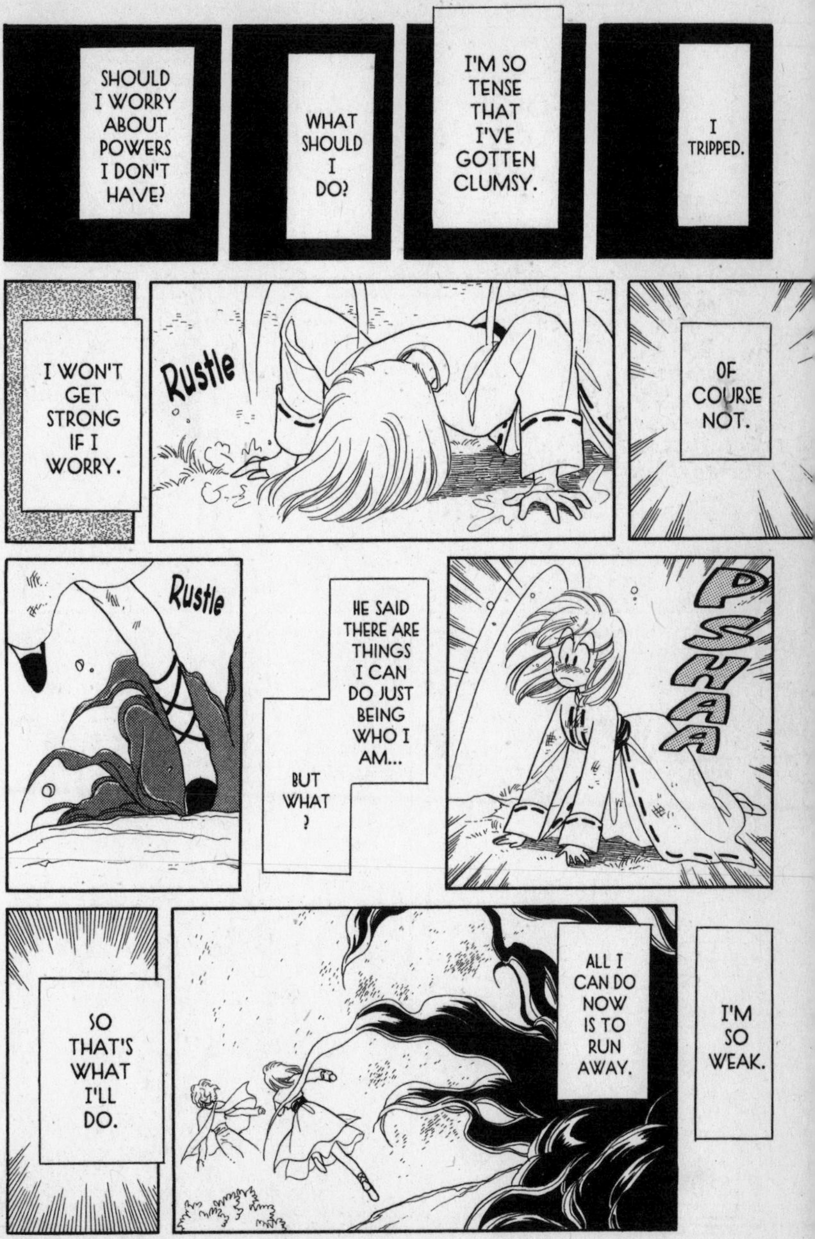
I TRIPPED.
I'M SO TENSE THAT I'VE GOTTEN CLUMSY.
WHAT SHOULD I DO?
SHOULD I WORRY ABOUT POWERS I DON'T HAVE?
OF COURSE NOT.
Rustle
I WON'T GET STRONG IF I WORRY.
PSHAA
HE SAID THERE ARE THINGS I CAN DO JUST BEING WHO I AM...
BUT WHAT?
Rustle
I'M SO WEAK.
ALL I CAN DO NOW IS TO RUN AWAY.
SO THAT'S WHAT I'LL DO.

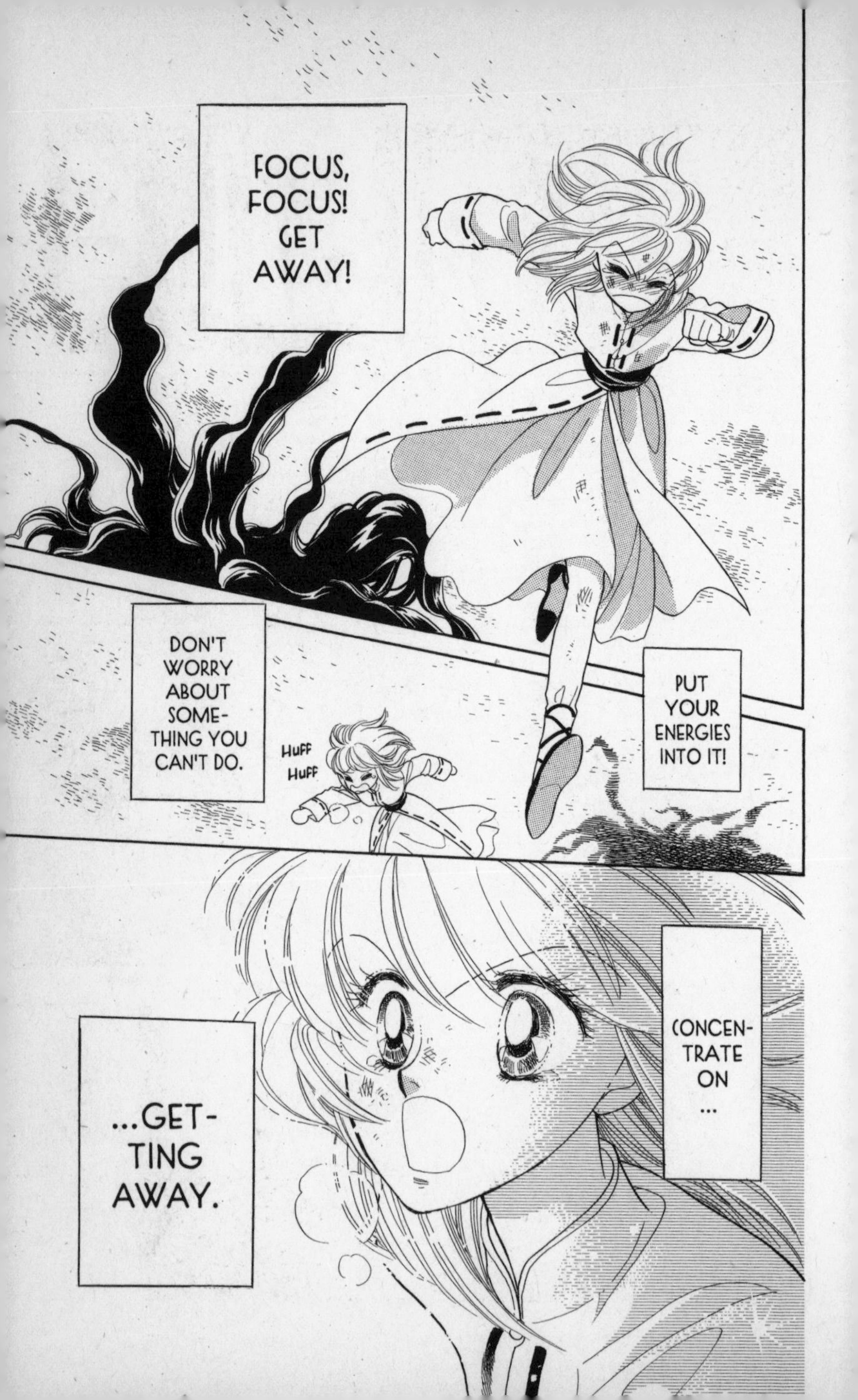
FOCUS, FOCUS! GET AWAY!
PUT YOUR ENERGIES INTO IT!
HUFF HUFF
DON'T WORRY ABOUT SOME-THING YOU CAN'T DO.
CONCEN-TRATE ON ...
...GET-TING AWAY.

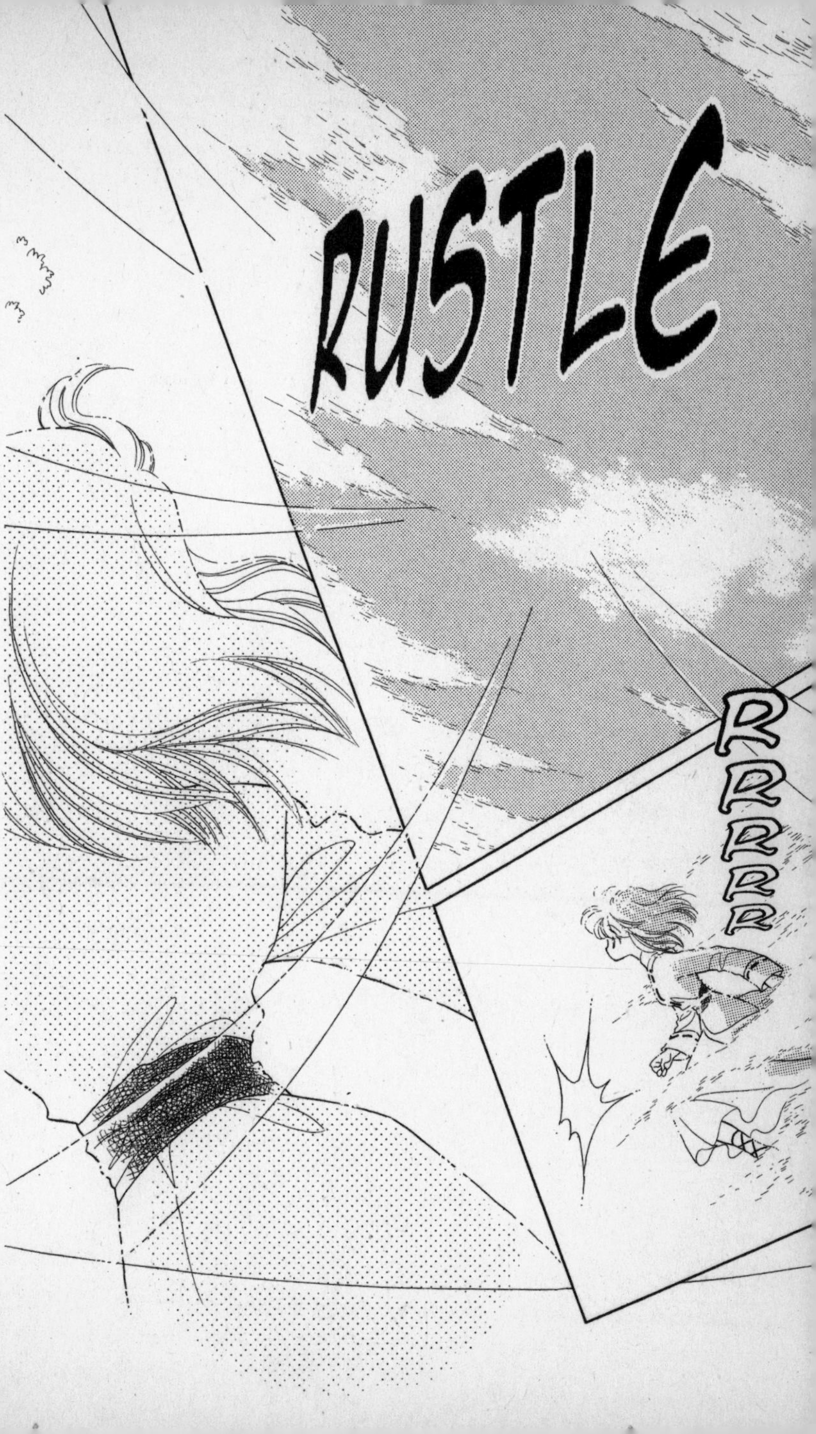
RUSTLE
RRRRRR

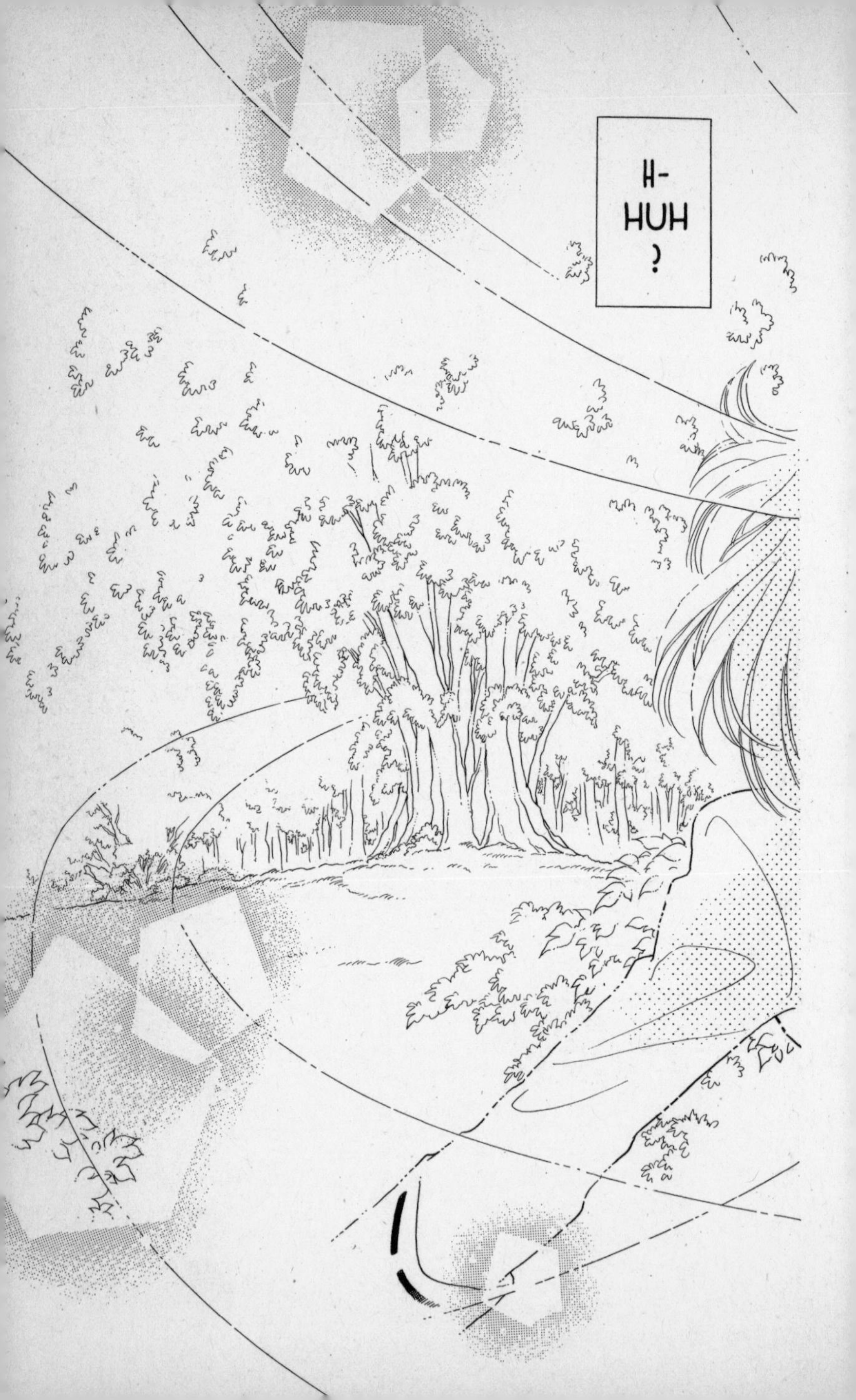
H-HUH?

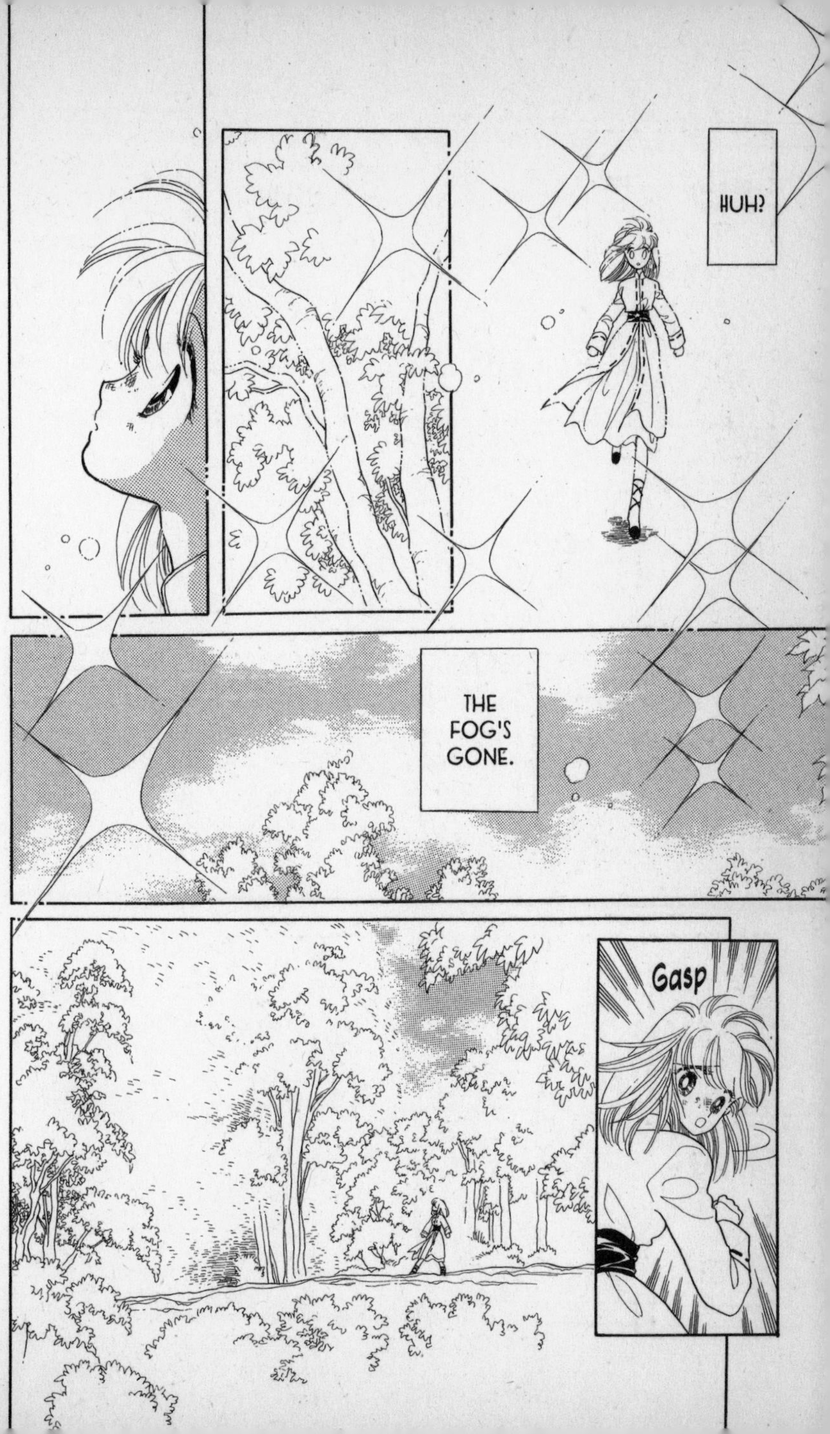
HUH?
THE FOG'S GONE.
Gasp

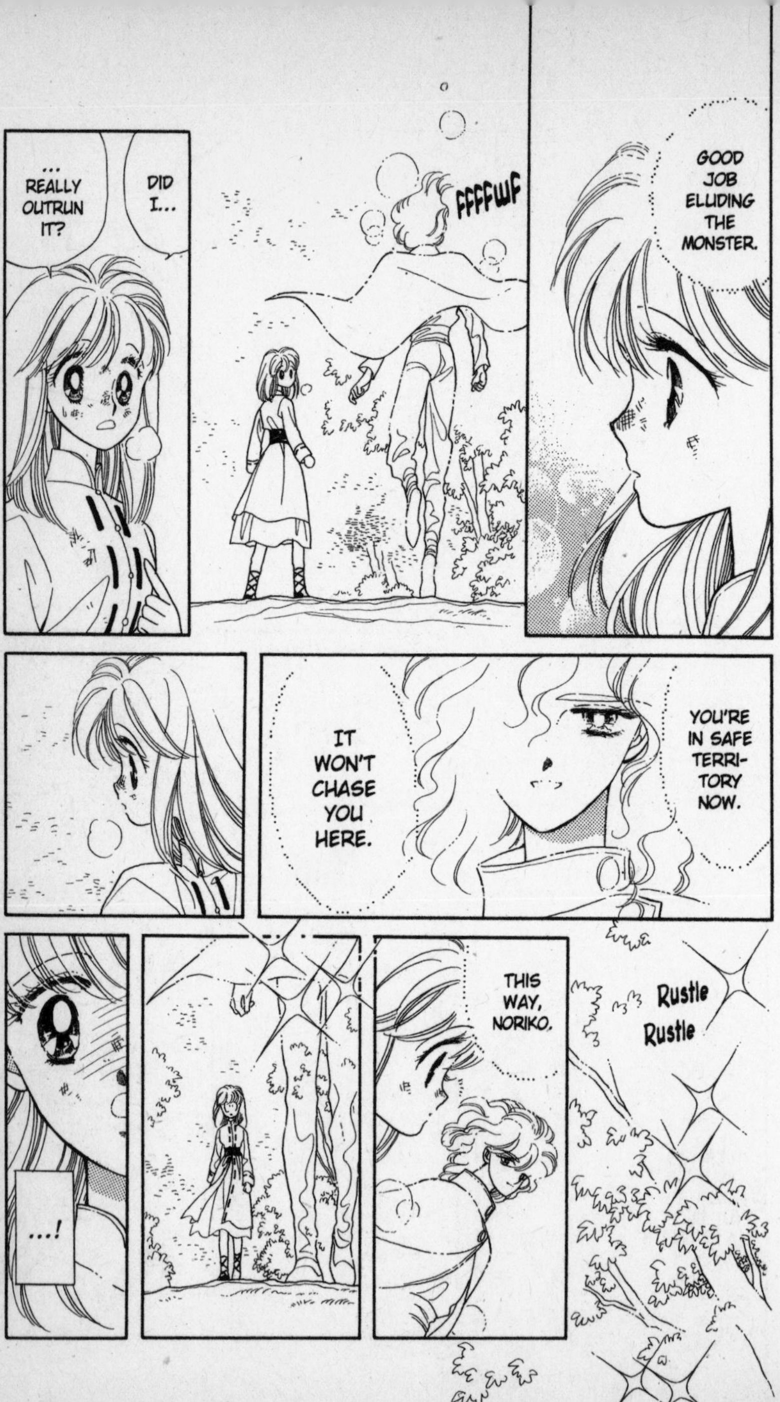
GOOD JOB ELUDING THE MONSTER.
FFFFWF
DID I...
... REALLY OUTRUN IT?
YOU'RE IN SAFE TERRI-TORY NOW.
IT WON'T CHASE YOU HERE.
Rustle Rustle
THIS WAY, NORIKO.
...!

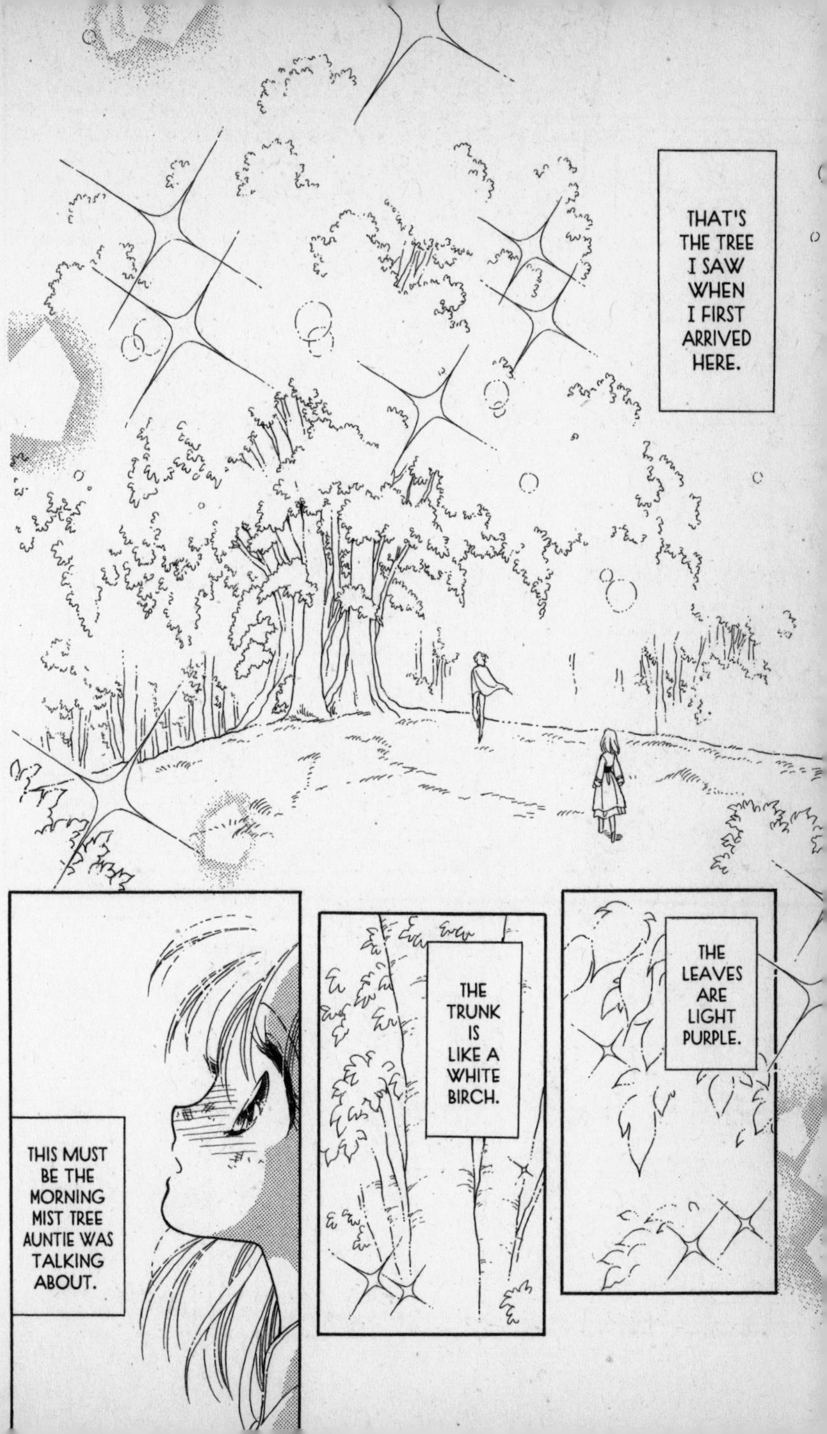
THAT'S THE TREE I SAW WHEN I FIRST ARRIVED HERE.
THE LEAVES ARE LIGHT PURPLE.
THE TRUNK IS LIKE A WHITE BIRCH.
THIS MUST BE THE MORNING MIST TREE AUNTIE WAS TALKING ABOUT.

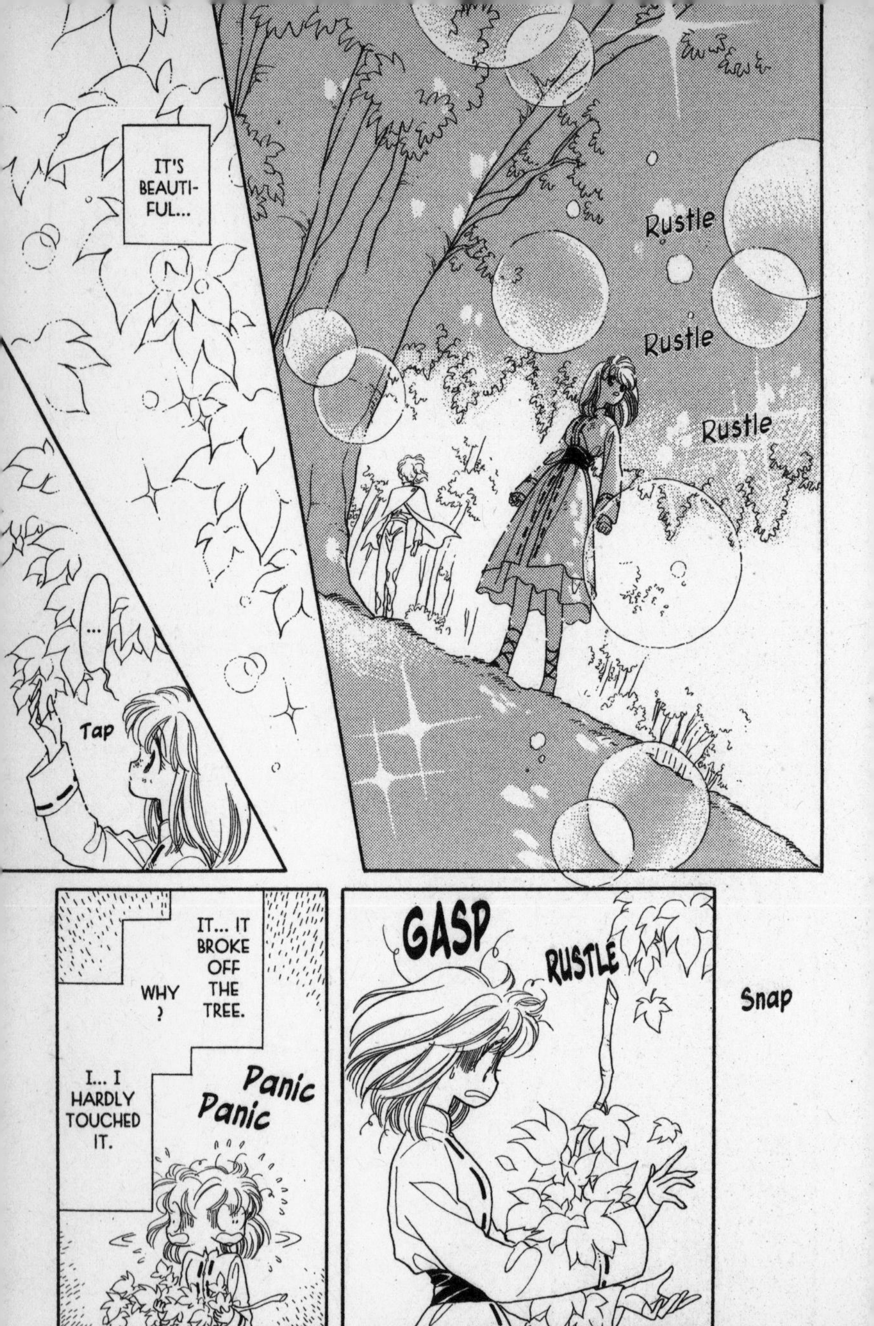
Rustle
Rustle
Rustle
IT'S BEAUTIFUL...
...
Tap
Snap
GASP
RUSTLE
IT... IT BROKE OFF THE TREE.
WHY?
I... I HARDLY TOUCHED IT.
Panic
Panic

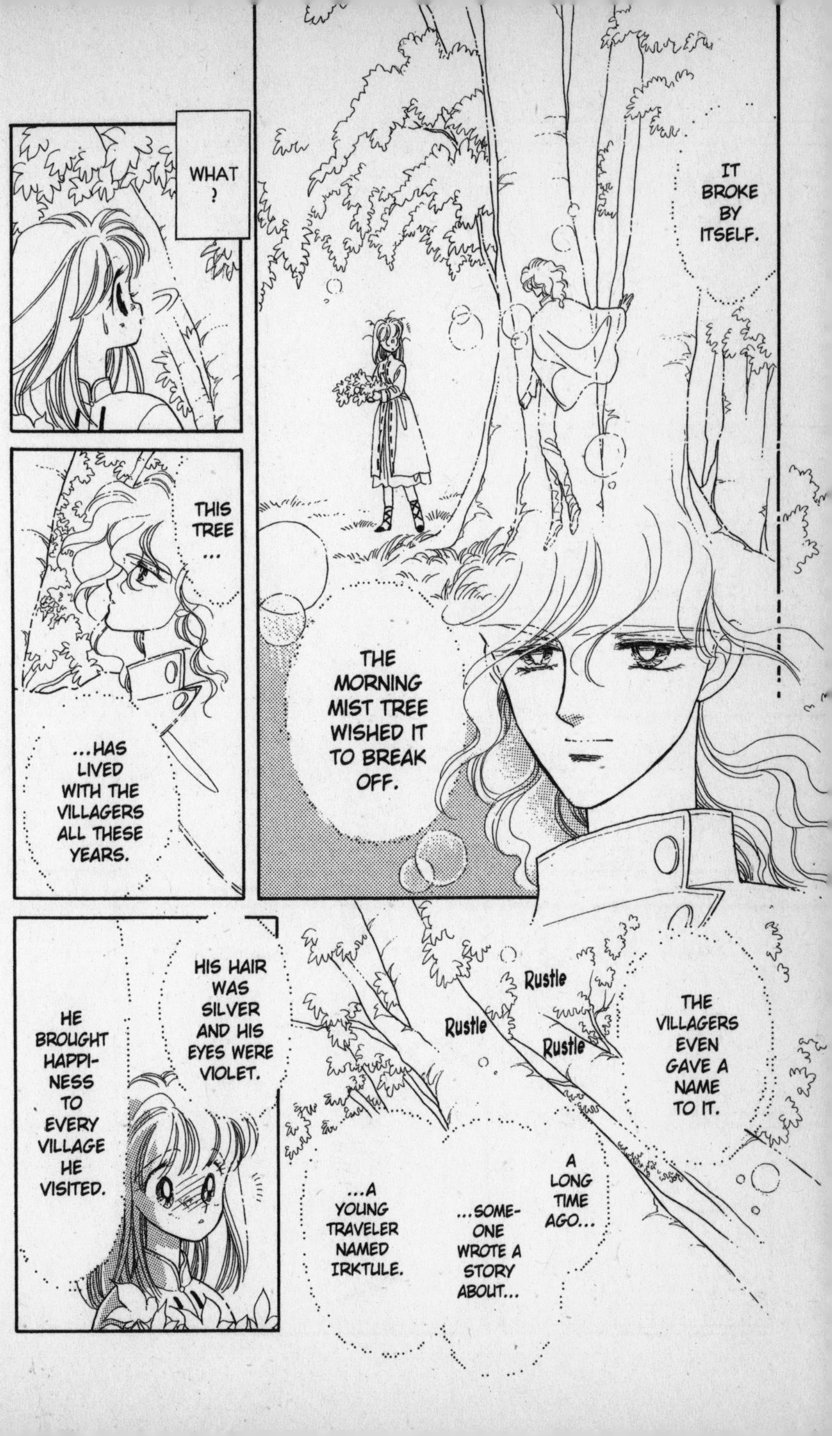
IT BROKE BY ITSELF.
THE MORNING MIST TREE WISHED IT TO BREAK OFF.
WHAT?
THIS TREE...
...HAS LIVED WITH THE VILLAGERS ALL THESE YEARS.
Rustle
Rustle
Rustle
THE VILLAGERS EVEN GAVE A NAME TO IT.
A LONG TIME AGO...
...SOME-ONE WROTE A STORY ABOUT...
...A YOUNG TRAVELER NAMED IRKTULE.
HIS HAIR WAS SILVER AND HIS EYES WERE VIOLET.
HE BROUGHT HAPPINESS TO EVERY VILLAGE HE VISITED.

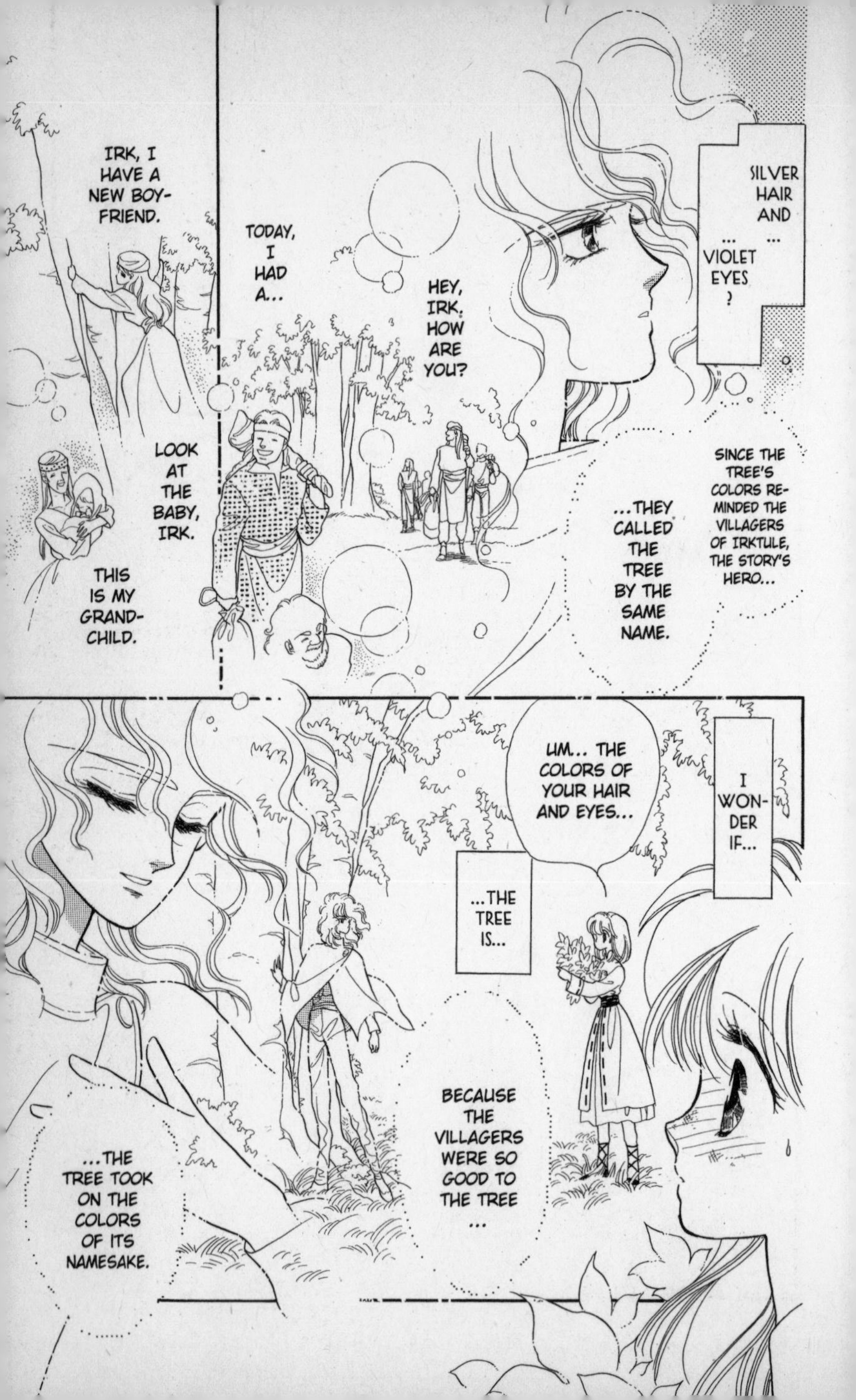
SILVER HAIR AND ... ... VIOLET EYES ?
SINCE THE TREE'S COLORS RE-MINDED THE VILLAGERS OF IRKTULE, THE STORY'S HERO...
...THEY CALLED THE TREE BY THE SAME NAME.
HEY, IRK, HOW ARE YOU?
TODAY, I HAD A...
IRK, I HAVE A NEW BOY-FRIEND.
LOOK AT THE BABY, IRK.
THIS IS MY GRAND-CHILD.
I WON-DER IF...
UM... THE COLORS OF YOUR HAIR AND EYES...
...THE TREE IS...
BECAUSE THE VILLAGERS WERE SO GOOD TO THE TREE ...
...THE TREE TOOK ON THE COLORS OF ITS NAMESAKE.

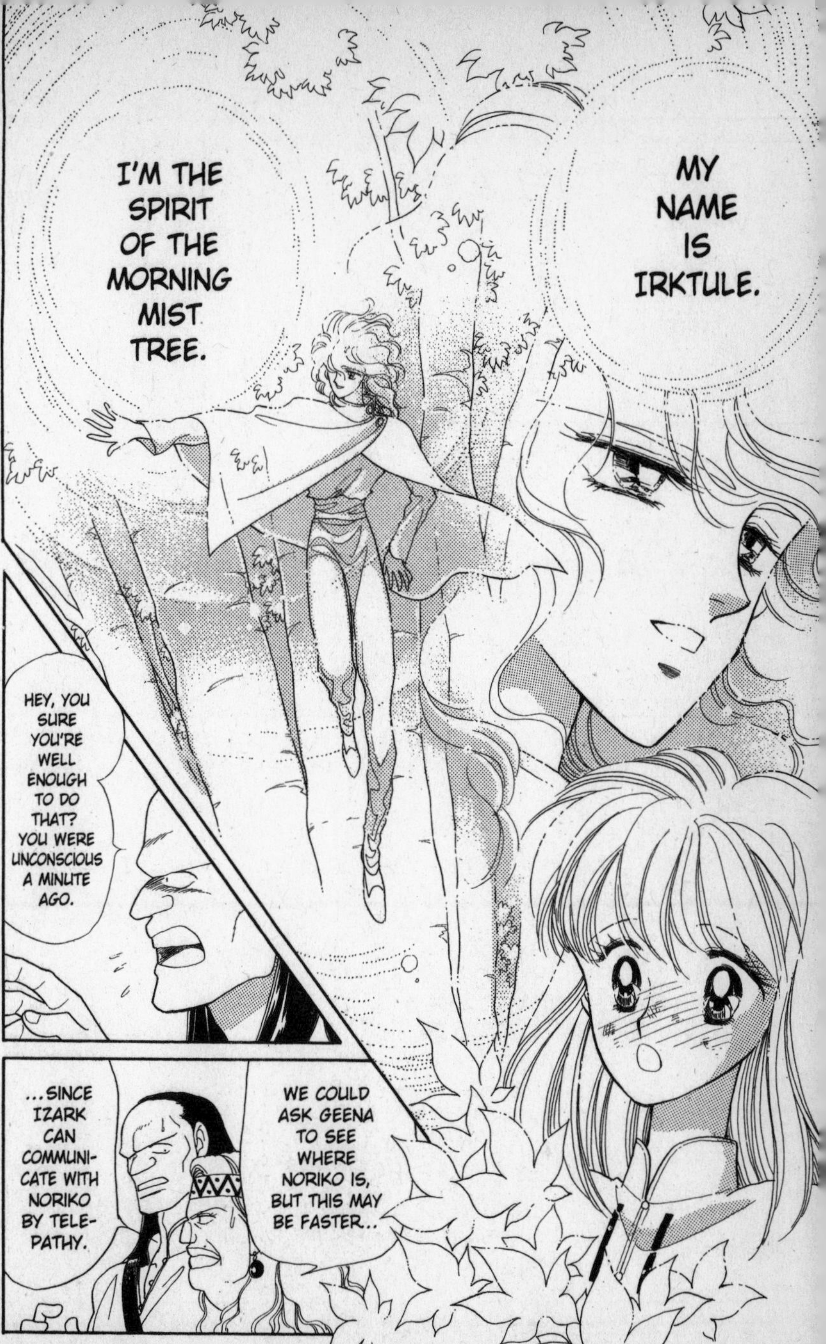
MY NAME IS IRKTULE.
I'M THE SPIRIT OF THE MORNING MIST TREE.
HEY, YOU SURE YOU'RE WELL ENOUGH TO DO THAT? YOU WERE UNCONSCIOUS A MINUTE AGO.
WE COULD ASK GEENA TO SEE WHERE NORIKO IS, BUT THIS MAY BE FASTER...
...SINCE IZARK CAN COMMUNICATE WITH NORIKO BY TELEPATHY.

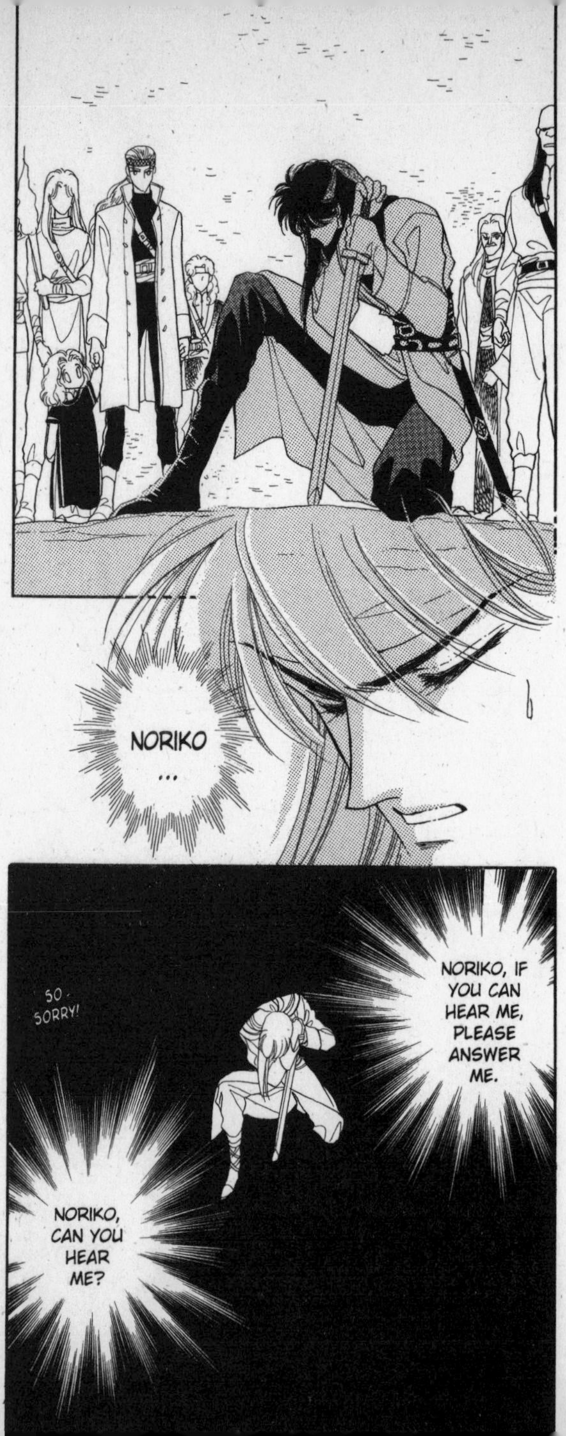
NORIKO ...
NORIKO, IF YOU CAN HEAR ME, PLEASE ANSWER ME.
SO SORRY!
NORIKO, CAN YOU HEAR ME?

It's been a while since volume four was published.

I apologize to those fans who have been waiting patiently for volume five.

Sorry I'm such a slowpoke.

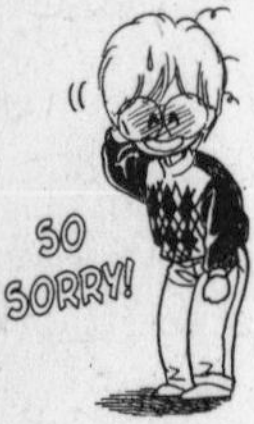
SO SORRY!

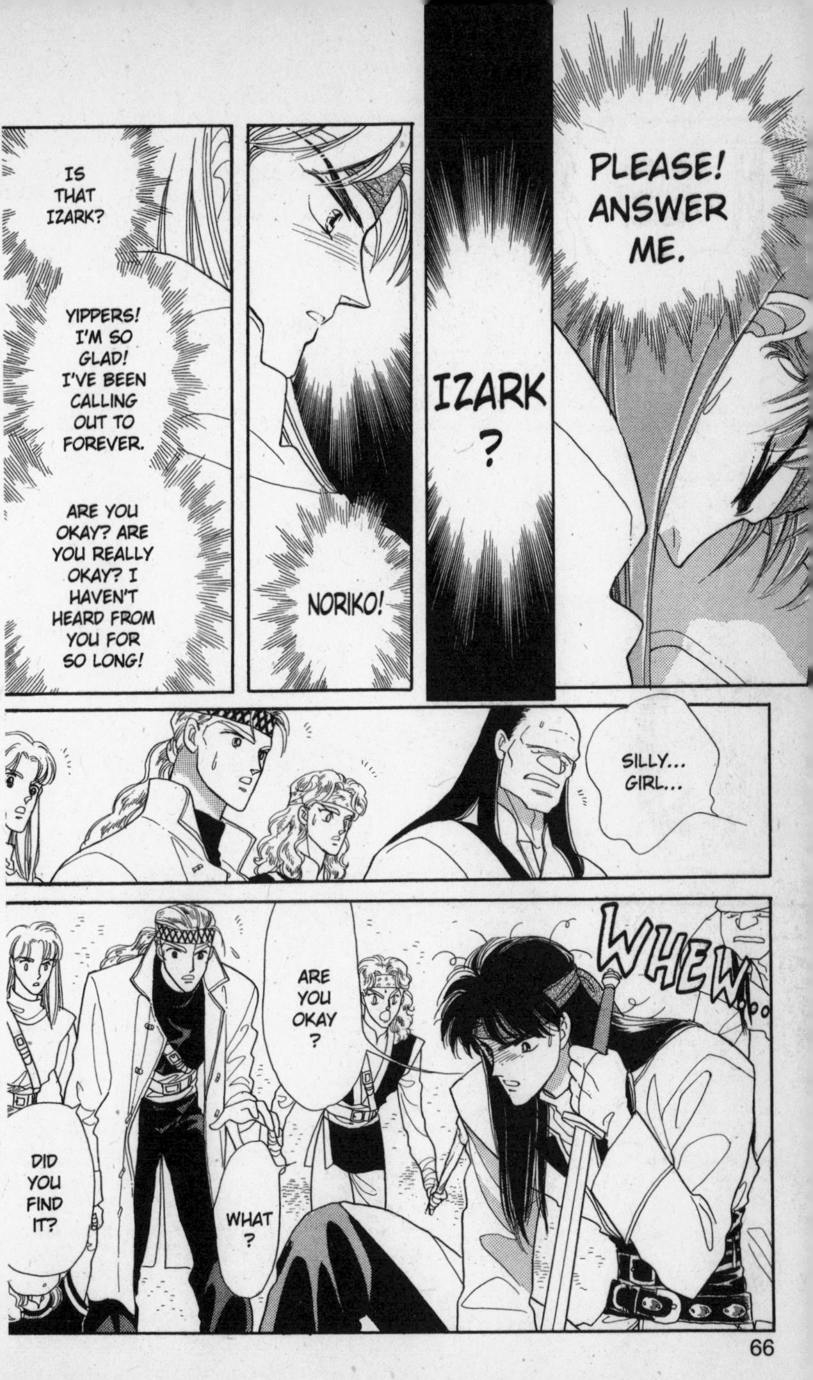
PLEASE! ANSWER ME.
IZARK ?
NORIKO!
IS THAT IZARK?
YIPPERS! I'M SO GLAD! I'VE BEEN CALLING OUT TO FOREVER.
ARE YOU OKAY? ARE YOU REALLY OKAY? I HAVEN'T HEARD FROM YOU FOR SO LONG!
SILLY... GIRL...
WHEW...
ARE YOU OKAY ?
WHAT ?
DID YOU FIND IT?

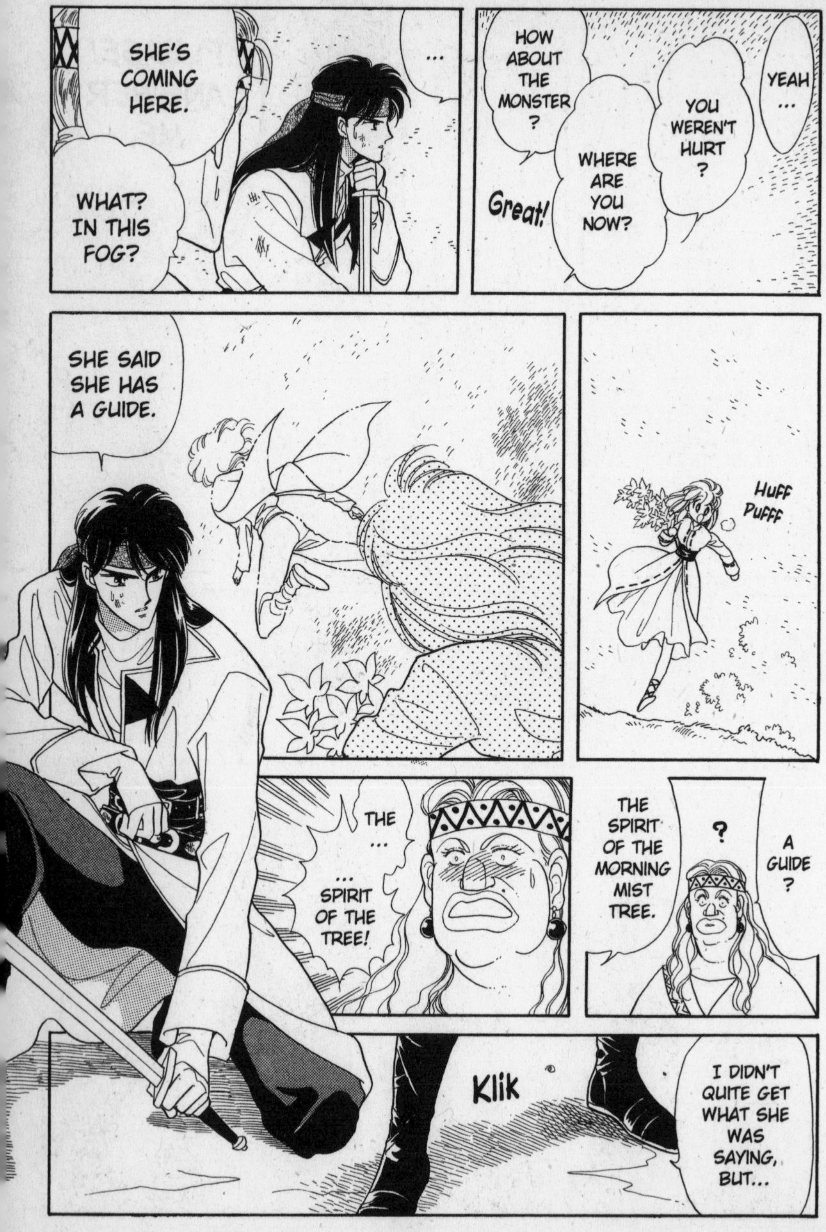
YEAH ...
YOU WEREN'T HURT?
WHERE ARE YOU NOW?
HOW ABOUT THE MONSTER?
Great!
...
SHE'S COMING HERE.
WHAT? IN THIS FOG?
Huff Pufff
SHE SAID SHE HAS A GUIDE.
A GUIDE?
?
THE SPIRIT OF THE MORNING MIST TREE.
THE ...
... SPIRIT OF THE TREE!
I DIDN'T QUITE GET WHAT SHE WAS SAYING, BUT...
Klik

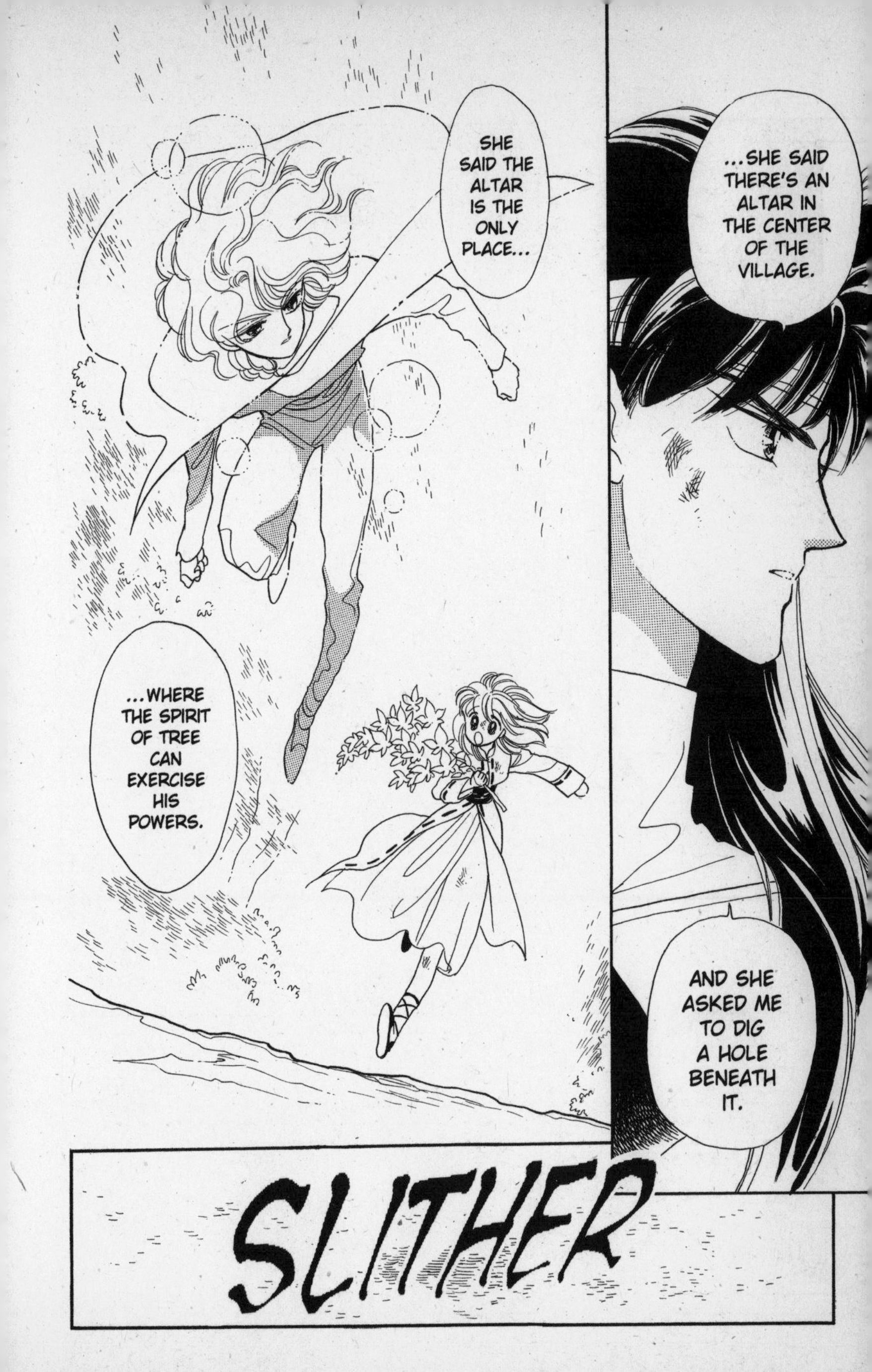
...SHE SAID THERE'S AN ALTAR IN THE CENTER OF THE VILLAGE.
AND SHE ASKED ME TO DIG A HOLE BENEATH IT.
SHE SAID THE ALTAR IS THE ONLY PLACE...
...WHERE THE SPIRIT OF TREE CAN EXERCISE HIS POWERS.
SLITHER

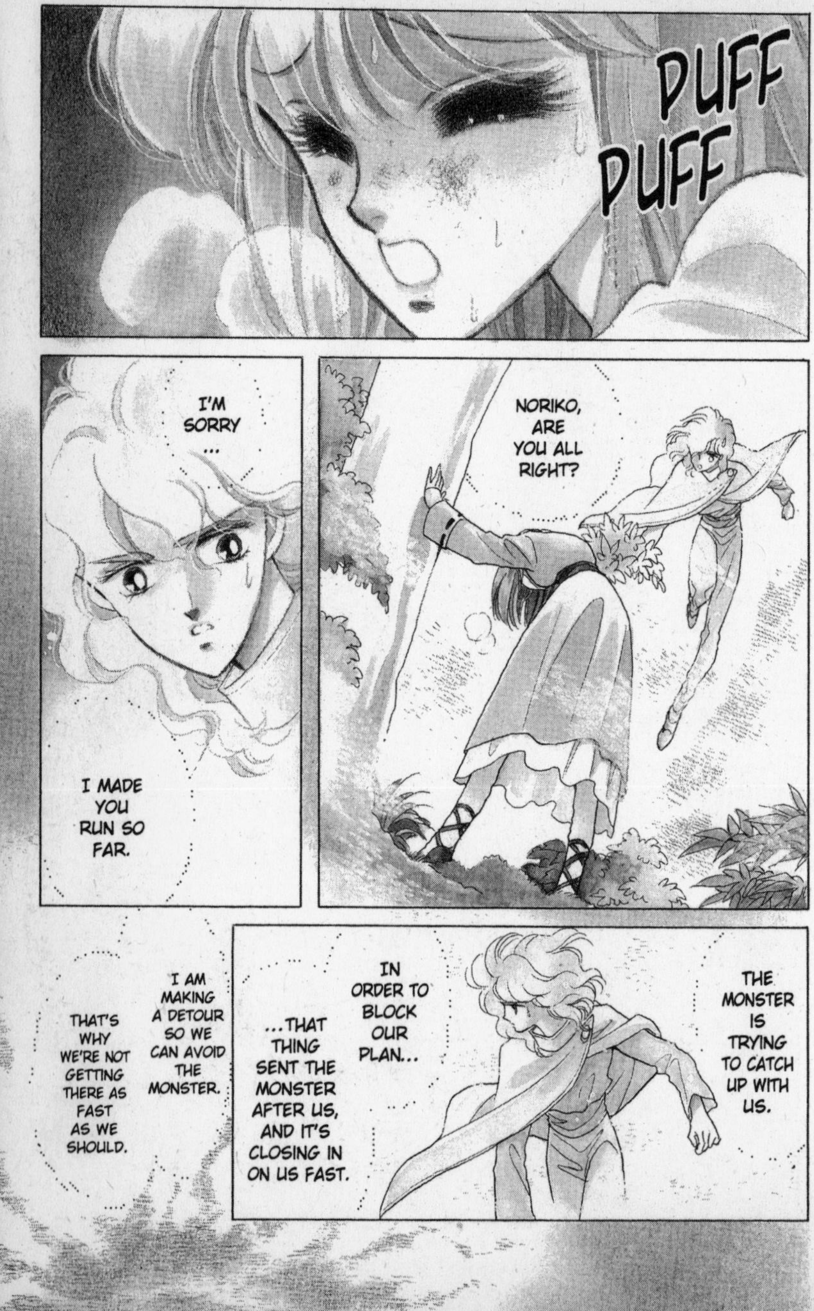
DUFF
DUFF
NORIKO, ARE YOU ALL RIGHT?
I'M SORRY ...
I MADE YOU RUN SO FAR.
THE MONSTER IS TRYING TO CATCH UP WITH US.
IN ORDER TO BLOCK OUR PLAN...
...THAT THING SENT THE MONSTER AFTER US, AND IT'S CLOSING IN ON US FAST.
I AM MAKING A DETOUR SO WE CAN AVOID THE MONSTER.
THAT'S WHY WE'RE NOT GETTING THERE AS FAST AS WE SHOULD.

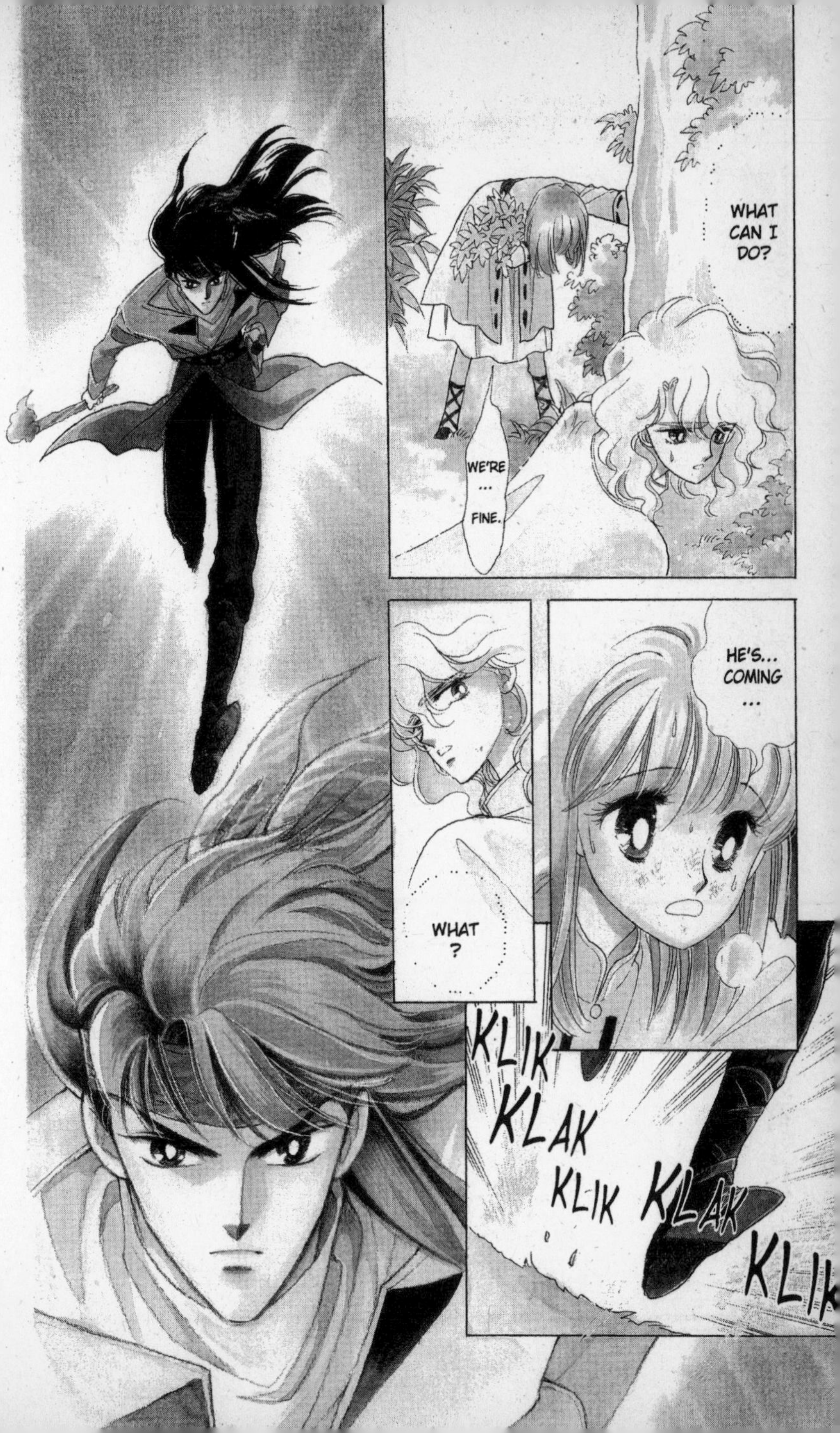
WHAT CAN I DO?
WE'RE ... FINE.
HE'S... COMING ...
WHAT ?
KLIK
KLAK
KLIK
KLAK
KLIK

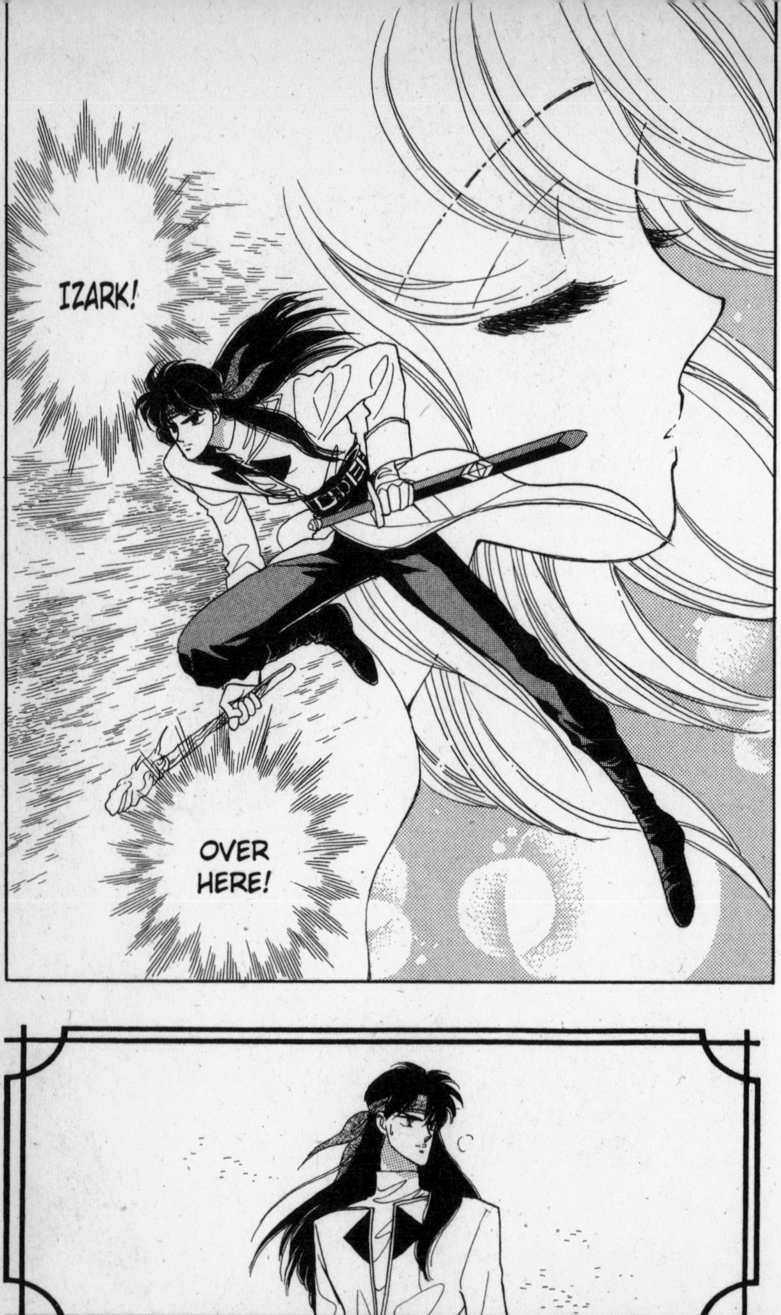
IZARK!
OVER HERE!

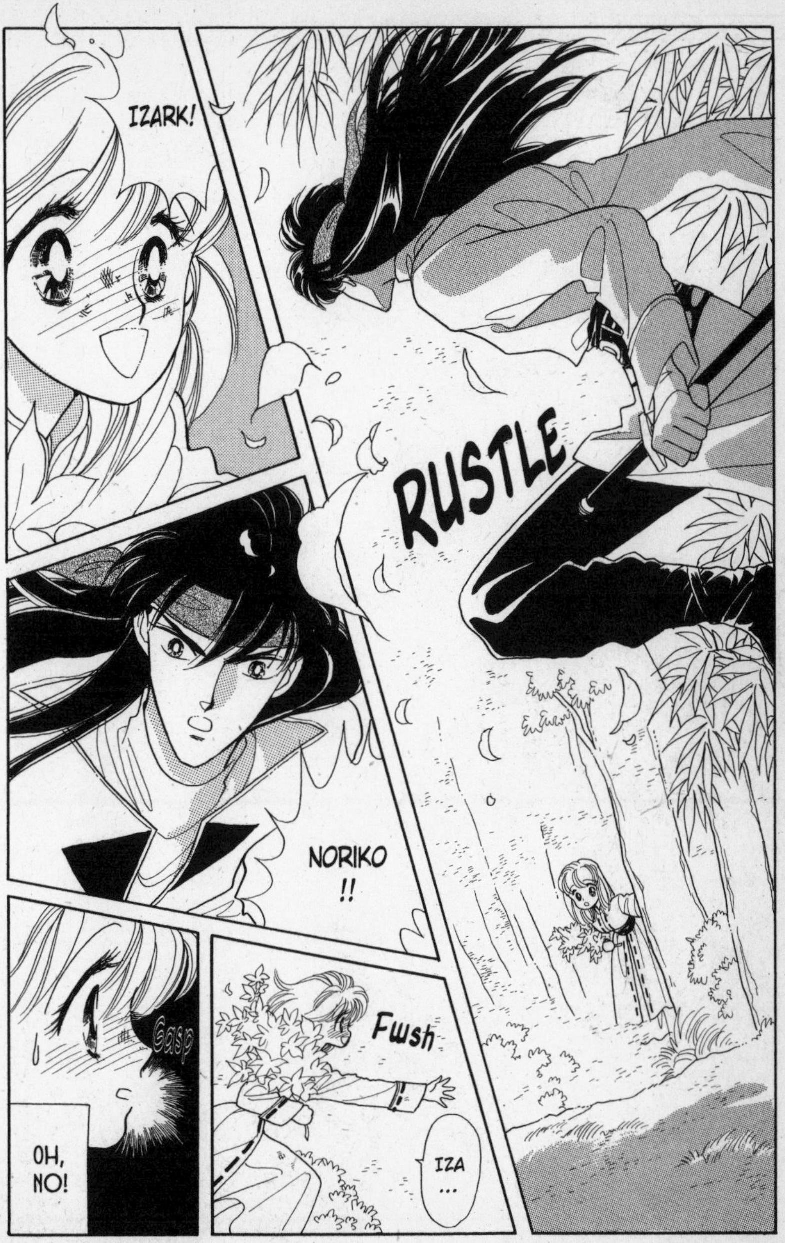
RUSTLE
IZARK!
NORIKO !!
Fwsh
IZA ...
Gasp
OH, NO!

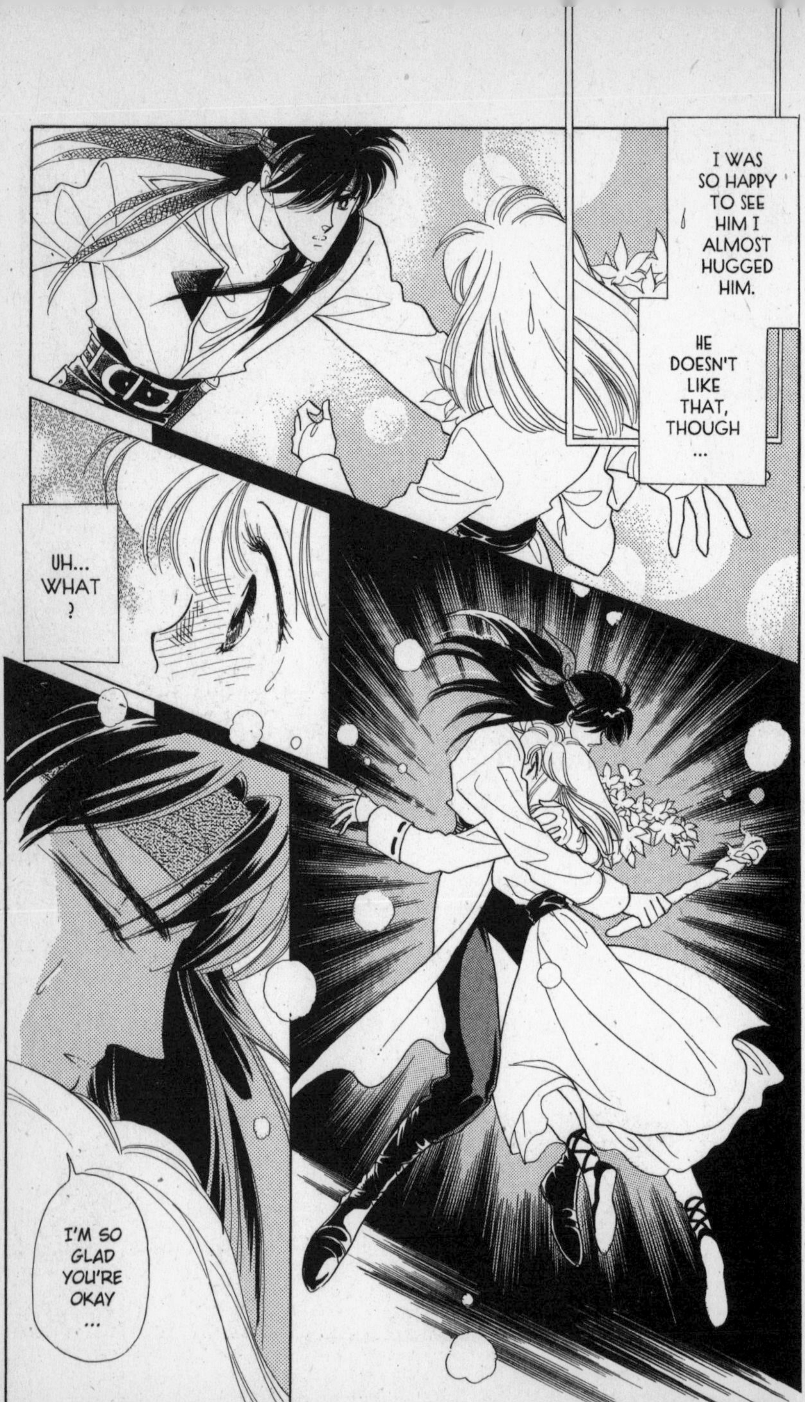
I WAS SO HAPPY TO SEE HIM I ALMOST HUGGED HIM.
HE DOESN'T LIKE THAT, THOUGH ...
UH... WHAT ?
I'M SO GLAD YOU'RE OKAY ...

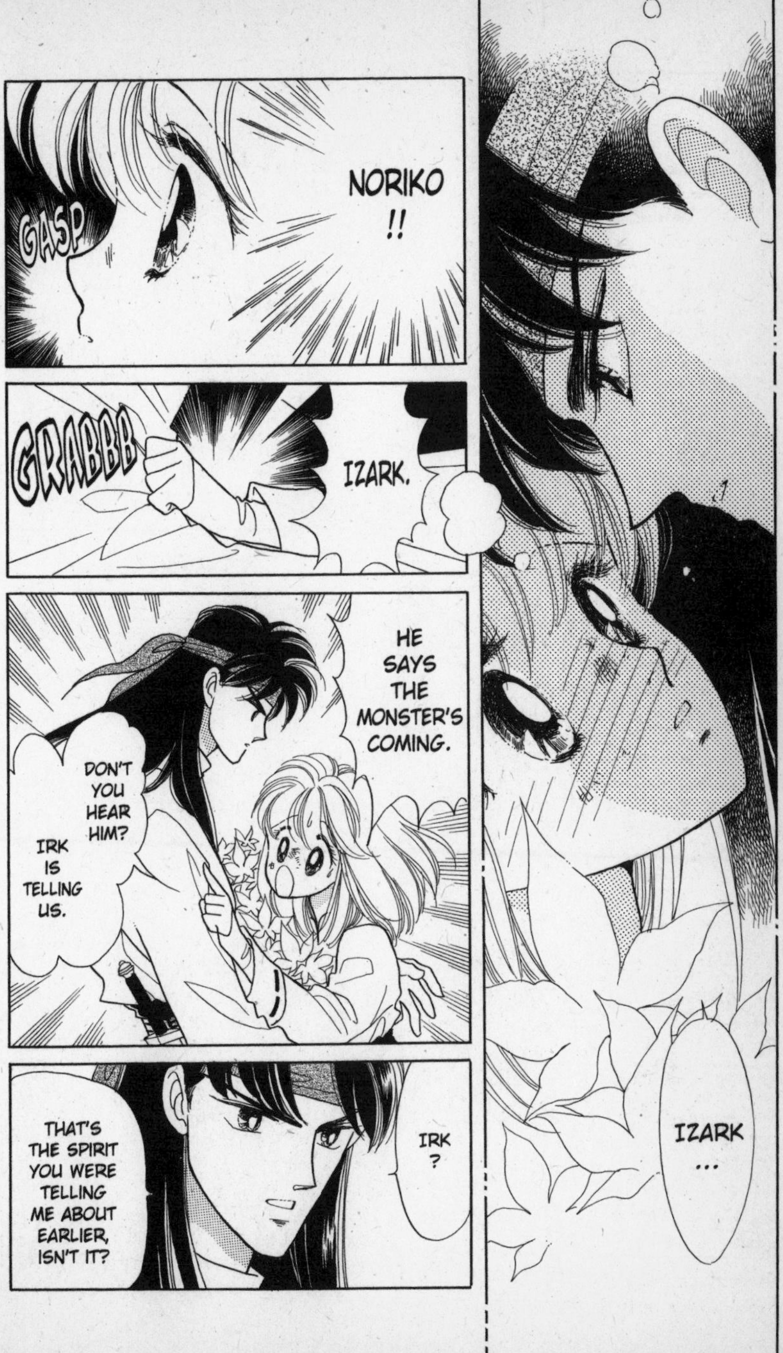
IZARK ...
NORIKO !!
GASP
IZARK.
GRABBB
HE SAYS THE MONSTER'S COMING.
DON'T YOU HEAR HIM?
IRK IS TELLING US.
IRK ?
THAT'S THE SPIRIT YOU WERE TELLING ME ABOUT EARLIER, ISN'T IT?

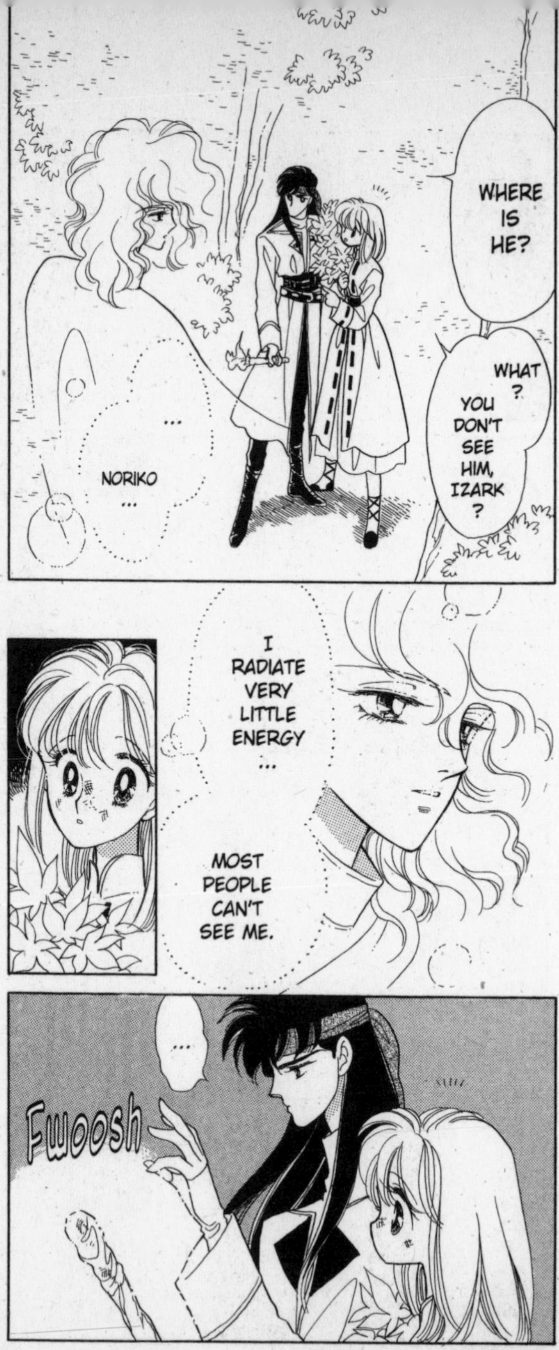
WHERE IS HE?
WHAT? YOU DON'T SEE HIM, IZARK?
...
NORIKO ...
I RADIATE VERY LITTLE ENERGY ...
MOST PEOPLE CAN'T SEE ME.
...
Fwoosh

Thank you for your fan letters. I always appreciate your writing to me. I haven't had the time to answer you, but I read all your letters. ♡♡♡

Those fans who were junior high and high school students when I started are now grownups. Time flies!

In case anyone is curious, the ages of the fans who have written to me are as follows:

Elementary school students 3%

Junior high school students 20%

High school students 30%

College students/ 20 years and over ... 30%

30 and over 15%

40 and over 3%

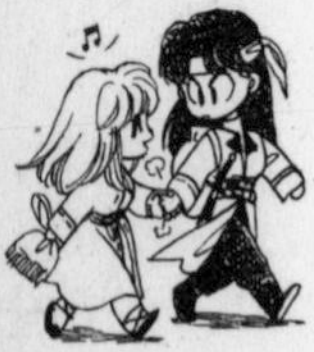

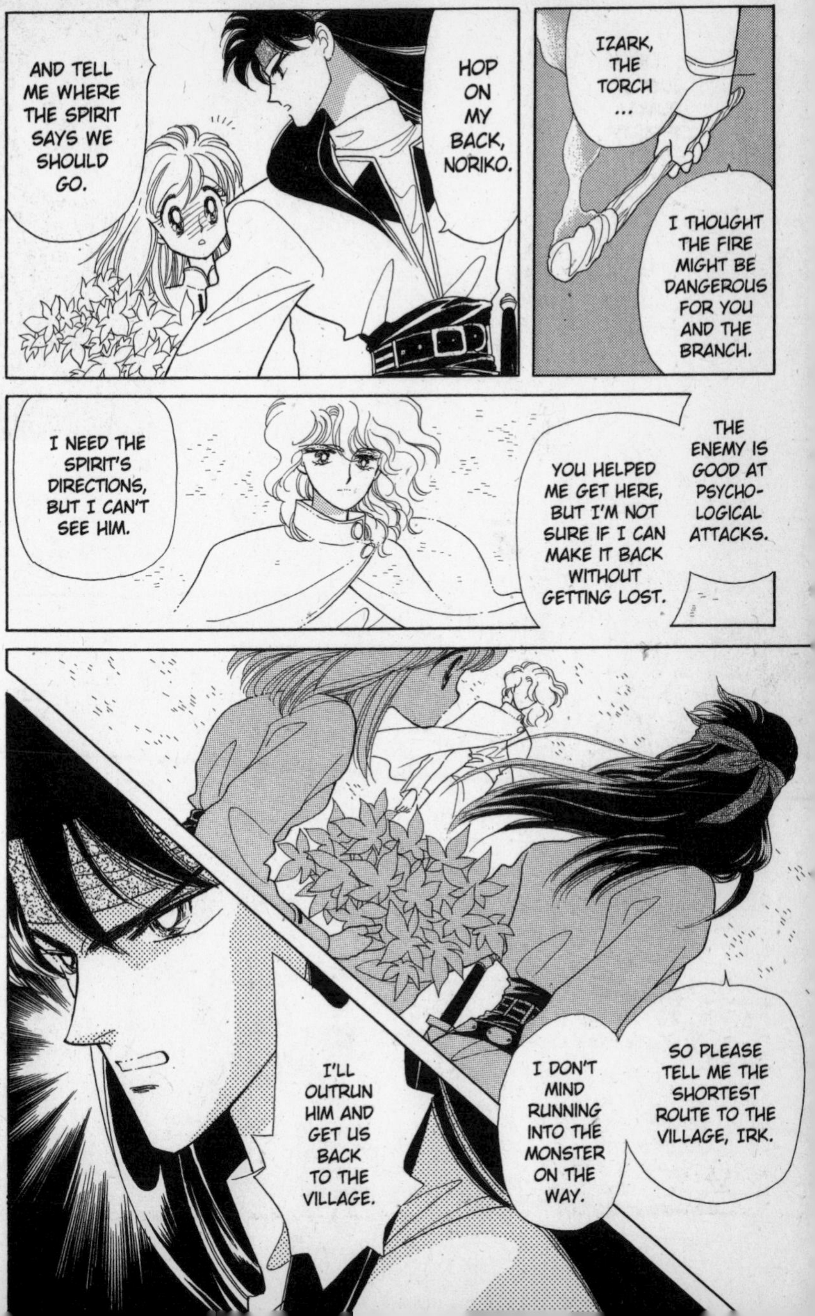
IZARK, THE TORCH ...
I THOUGHT THE FIRE MIGHT BE DANGEROUS FOR YOU AND THE BRANCH.
HOP ON MY BACK, NORIKO.
AND TELL ME WHERE THE SPIRIT SAYS WE SHOULD GO.
THE ENEMY IS GOOD AT PSYCHO-LOGICAL ATTACKS.
YOU HELPED ME GET HERE, BUT I'M NOT SURE IF I CAN MAKE IT BACK WITHOUT GETTING LOST.
I NEED THE SPIRIT'S DIRECTIONS, BUT I CAN'T SEE HIM.
SO PLEASE TELL ME THE SHORTEST ROUTE TO THE VILLAGE, IRK.
I DON'T MIND RUNNING INTO THE MONSTER ON THE WAY.
I'LL OUTRUN HIM AND GET US BACK TO THE VILLAGE.

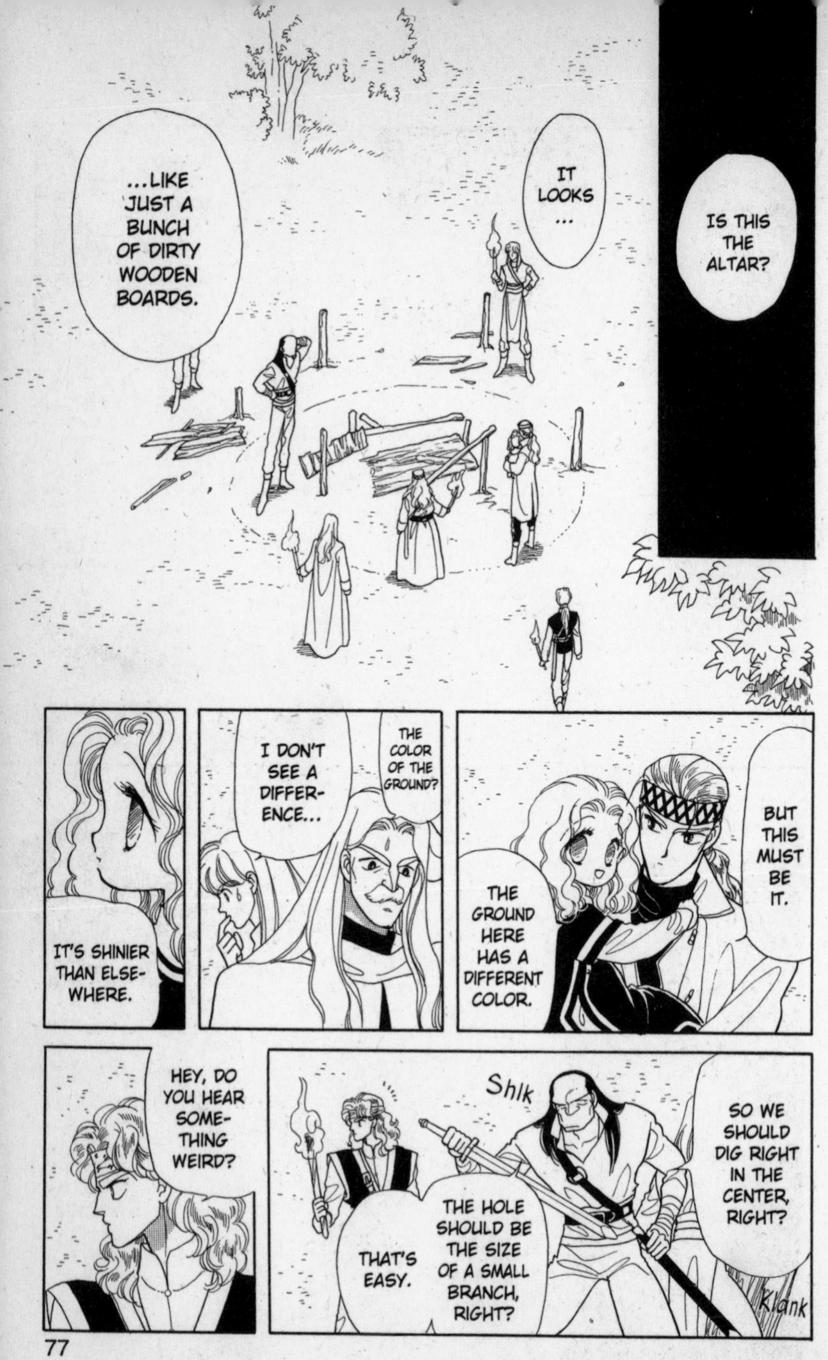
IS THIS THE ALTAR?
IT LOOKS ...
...LIKE JUST A BUNCH OF DIRTY WOODEN BOARDS.
BUT THIS MUST BE IT.
THE GROUND HERE HAS A DIFFERENT COLOR.
THE COLOR OF THE GROUND?
I DON'T SEE A DIFFER-ENCE...
IT'S SHINIER THAN ELSE-WHERE.
SO WE SHOULD DIG RIGHT IN THE CENTER, RIGHT?
Shlk
THE HOLE SHOULD BE THE SIZE OF A SMALL BRANCH, RIGHT?
THAT'S EASY.
Klank
HEY, DO YOU HEAR SOME-THING WEIRD?

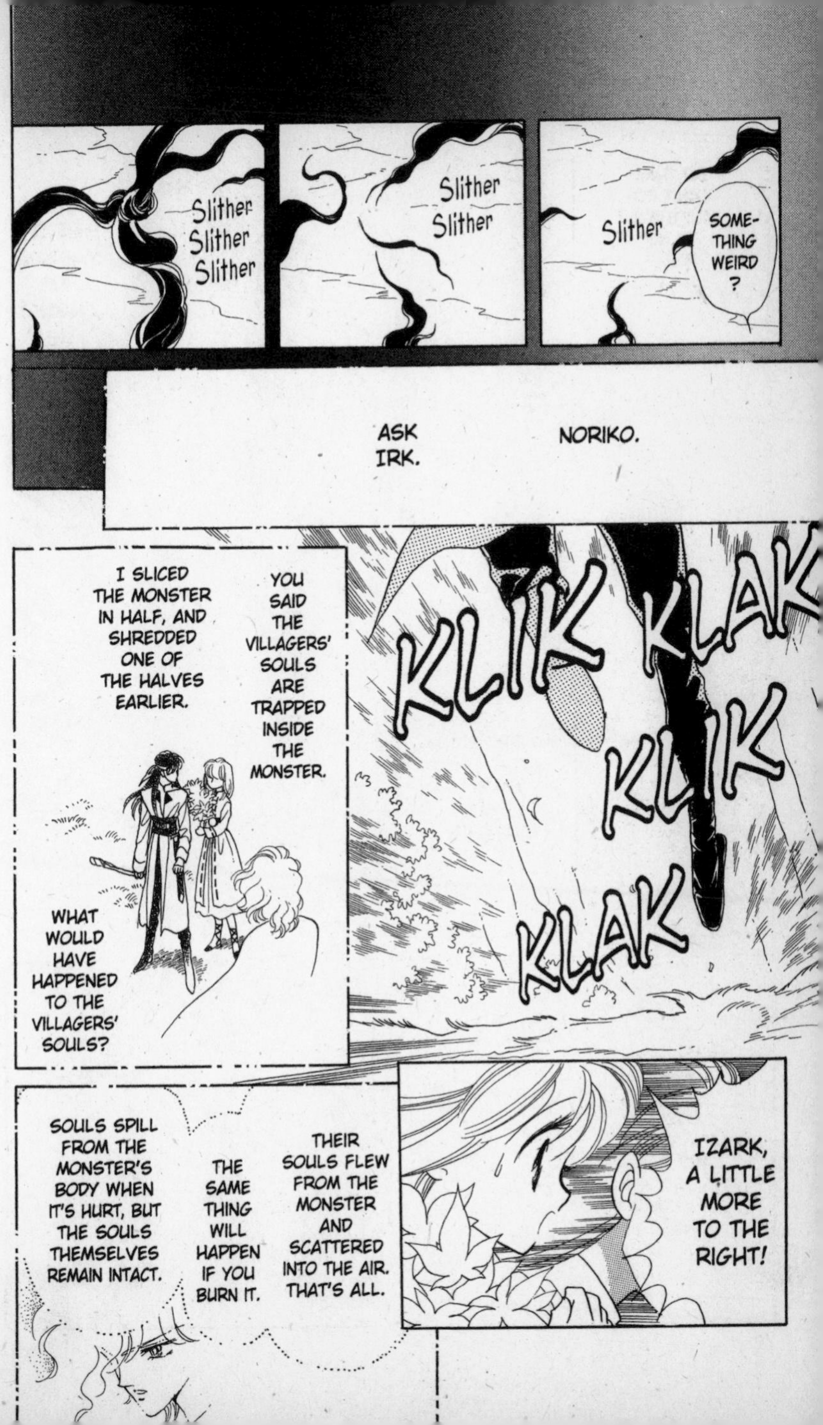
Slither
SOME-THING WEIRD ?
Slither Slither
Slither Slither Slither
NORIKO.
ASK IRK.
KLIK KLAK KLIK KLAK
YOU SAID THE VILLAGERS' SOULS ARE TRAPPED INSIDE THE MONSTER.
I SLICED THE MONSTER IN HALF, AND SHREDDED ONE OF THE HALVES EARLIER.
WHAT WOULD HAVE HAPPENED TO THE VILLAGERS' SOULS?
IZARK, A LITTLE MORE TO THE RIGHT!
THEIR SOULS FLEW FROM THE MONSTER AND SCATTERED INTO THE AIR. THAT'S ALL.
THE SAME THING WILL HAPPEN IF YOU BURN IT.
SOULS SPILL FROM THE MONSTER'S BODY WHEN IT'S HURT, BUT THE SOULS THEMSELVES REMAIN INTACT.

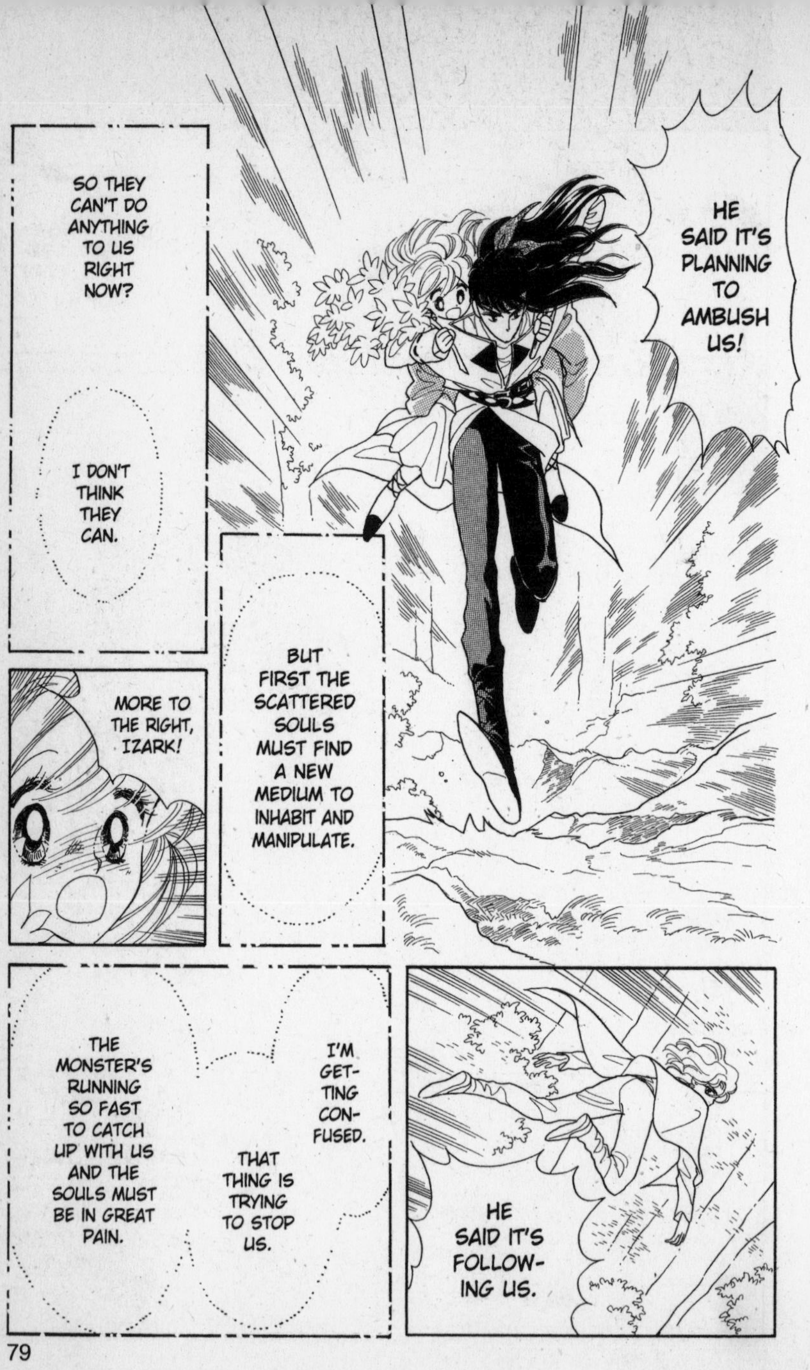
HE SAID IT'S PLANNING TO AMBUSH US!
SO THEY CAN'T DO ANYTHING TO US RIGHT NOW?
I DON'T THINK THEY CAN.
BUT FIRST THE SCATTERED SOULS MUST FIND A NEW MEDIUM TO INHABIT AND MANIPULATE.
MORE TO THE RIGHT, IZARK!
HE SAID IT'S FOLLOW-ING US.
I'M GET-TING CON-FUSED.
THAT THING IS TRYING TO STOP US.
THE MONSTER'S RUNNING SO FAST TO CATCH UP WITH US AND THE SOULS MUST BE IN GREAT PAIN.

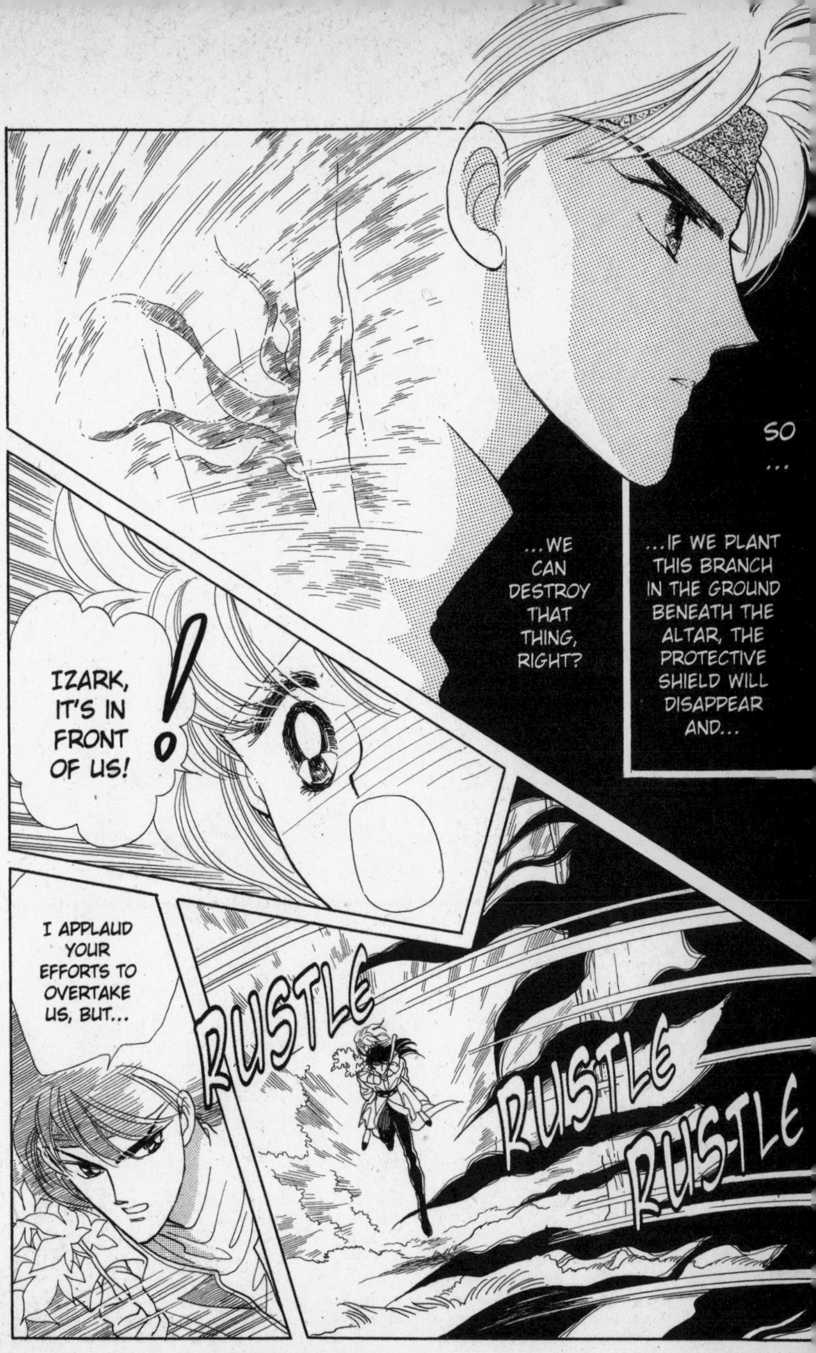
SO ...
...IF WE PLANT THIS BRANCH IN THE GROUND BENEATH THE ALTAR, THE PROTECTIVE SHIELD WILL DISAPPEAR AND...
...WE CAN DESTROY THAT THING, RIGHT?
!
IZARK, IT'S IN FRONT OF US!
RUSTLE
RUSTLE
RUSTLE
RUSTLE
I APPLAUD YOUR EFFORTS TO OVERTAKE US, BUT...

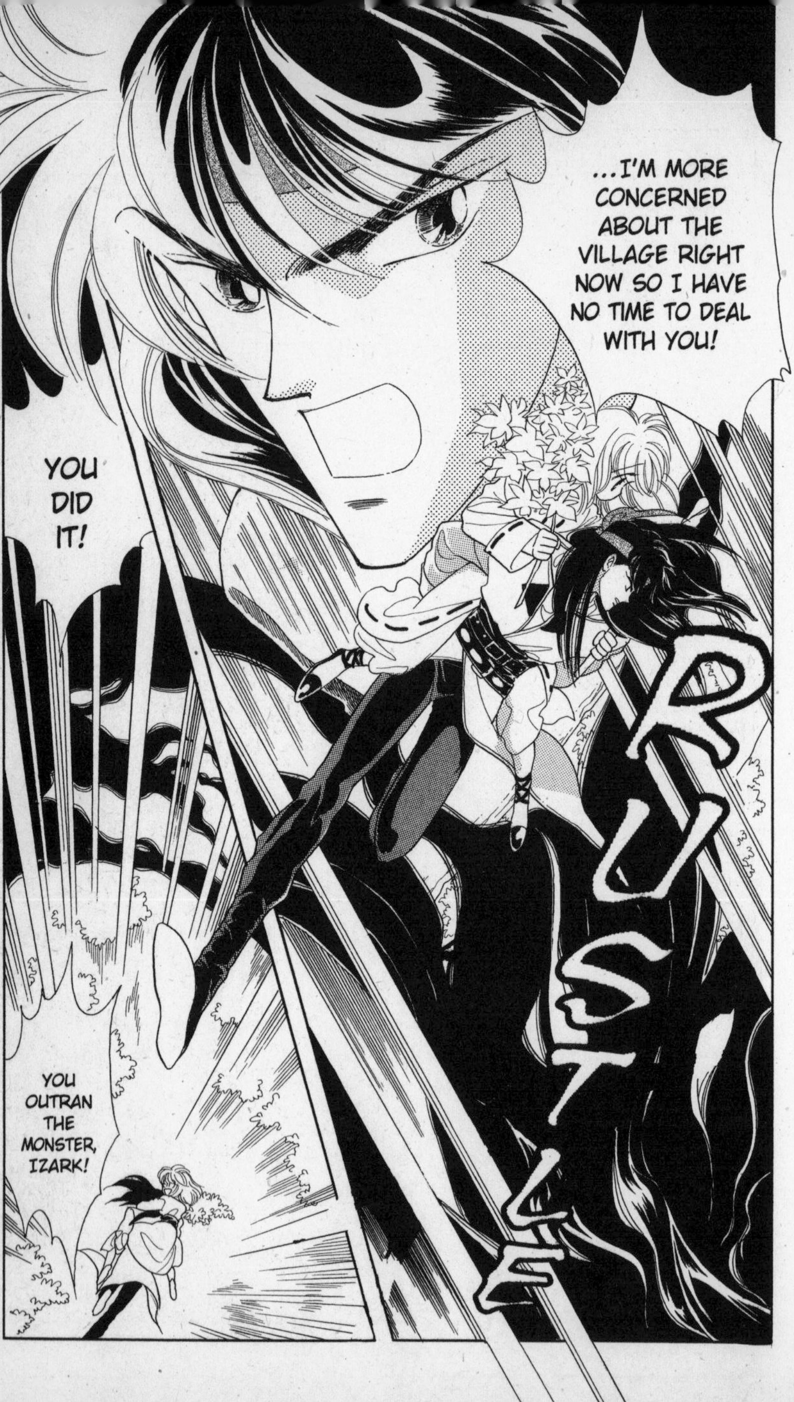
...I'M MORE CONCERNED ABOUT THE VILLAGE RIGHT NOW SO I HAVE NO TIME TO DEAL WITH YOU!
RUSTLE
YOU DID IT!
YOU OUTRAN THE MONSTER, IZARK!

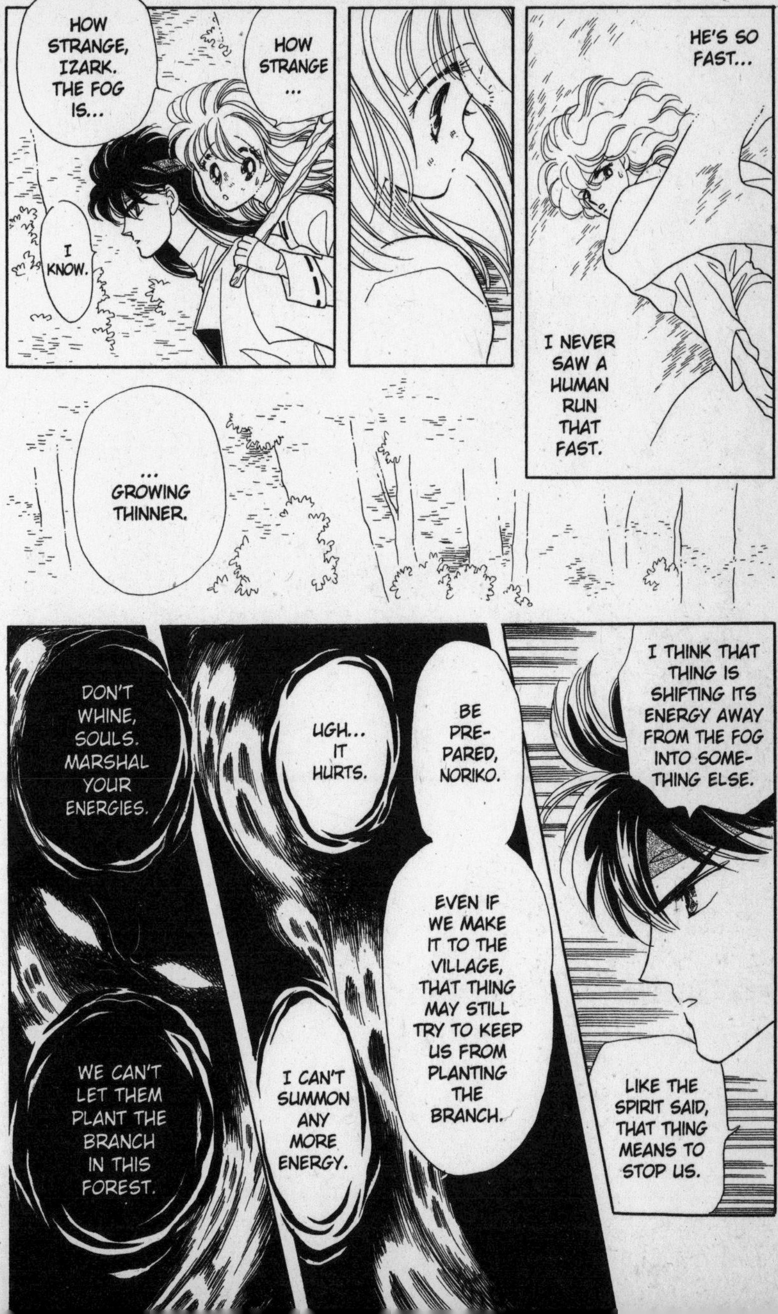
HE'S SO FAST...
I NEVER SAW A HUMAN RUN THAT FAST.
HOW STRANGE ...
HOW STRANGE, IZARK. THE FOG IS...
I KNOW.
... GROWING THINNER.
I THINK THAT THING IS SHIFTING ITS ENERGY AWAY FROM THE FOG INTO SOME-THING ELSE.
LIKE THE SPIRIT SAID, THAT THING MEANS TO STOP US.
BE PRE-PARED, NORIKO.
UGH... IT HURTS.
EVEN IF WE MAKE IT TO THE VILLAGE, THAT THING MAY STILL TRY TO KEEP US FROM PLANTING THE BRANCH.
I CAN'T SUMMON ANY MORE ENERGY.
DON'T WHINE, SOULS. MARSHAL YOUR ENERGIES.
WE CAN'T LET THEM PLANT THE BRANCH IN THIS FOREST.

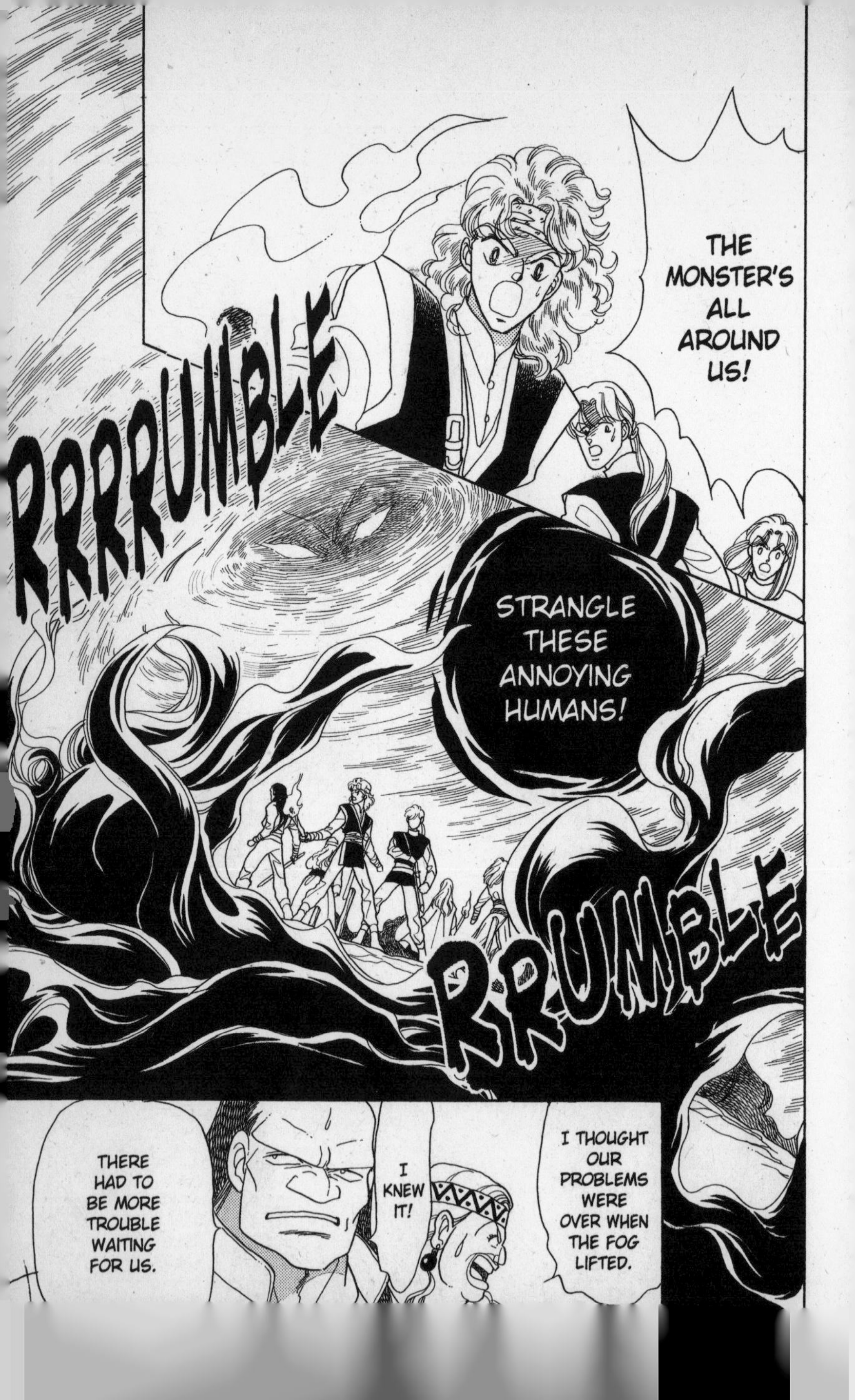
THE MONSTER'S ALL AROUND US!
RRRRUMBLE
STRANGLE THESE ANNOYING HUMANS!
RRUMBLE
I THOUGHT OUR PROBLEMS WERE OVER WHEN THE FOG LIFTED.
I KNEW IT!
THERE HAD TO BE MORE TROUBLE WAITING FOR US.

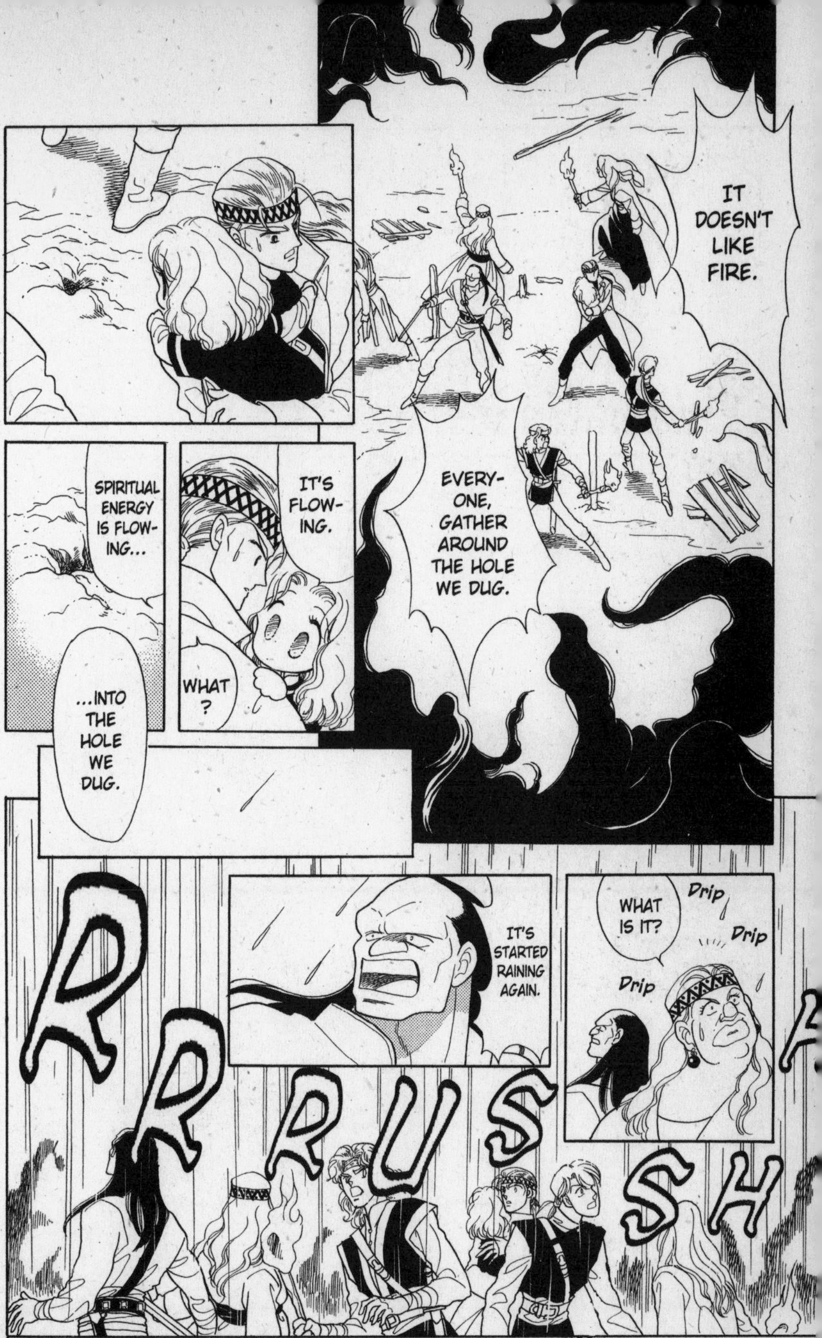
IT DOESN'T LIKE FIRE.
EVERY-ONE, GATHER AROUND THE HOLE WE DUG.
IT'S FLOW-ING.
WHAT?
SPIRITUAL ENERGY IS FLOW-ING...
...INTO THE HOLE WE DUG.
WHAT IS IT?
Drip
Drip
Drip
IT'S STARTED RAINING AGAIN.
RRRUSSH

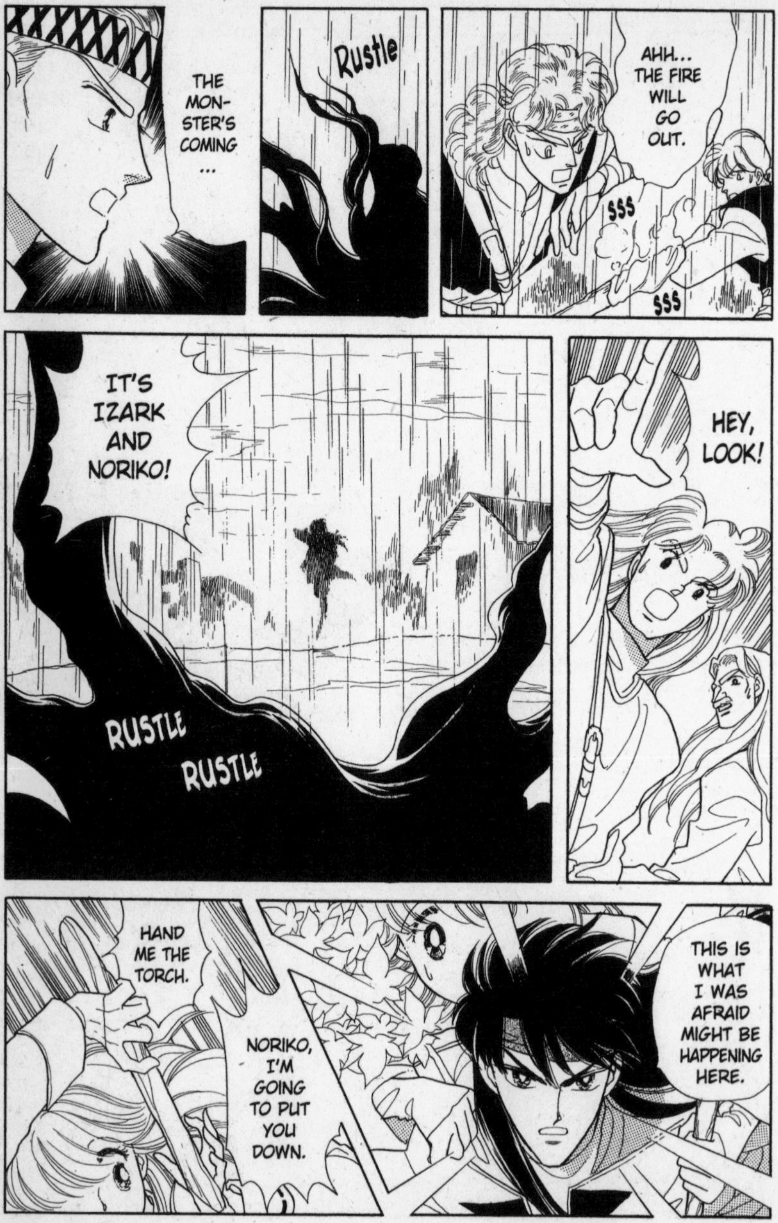
AHH... THE FIRE WILL GO OUT.
SSS
SSS
Rustle
THE MON-STER'S COMING ...
HEY, LOOK!
IT'S IZARK AND NORIKO!
RUSTLE
RUSTLE
THIS IS WHAT I WAS AFRAID MIGHT BE HAPPENING HERE.
NORIKO, I'M GOING TO PUT YOU DOWN.
HAND ME THE TORCH.

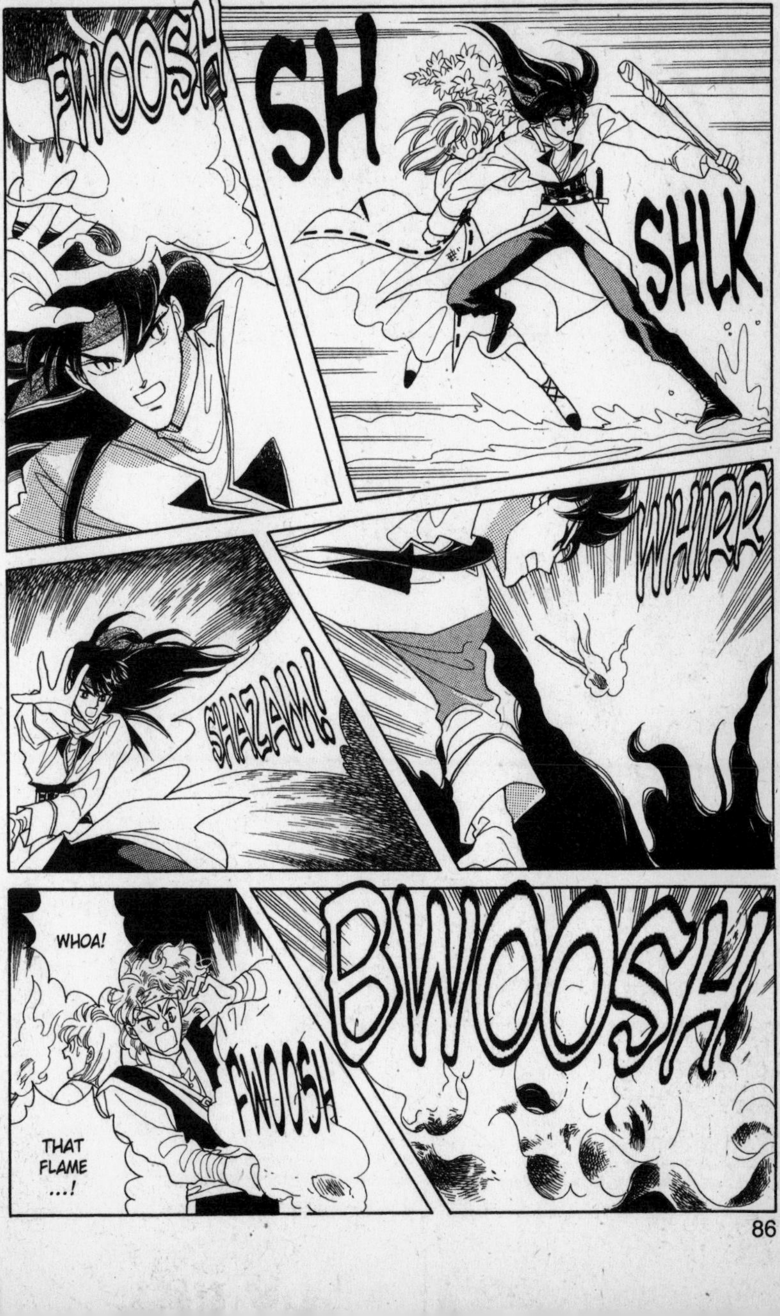
SH
SHLK
FWOOSH
WHIRR
SHAZAM!
BWOOSH
WHOA!
FWOOSH
THAT FLAME ...!

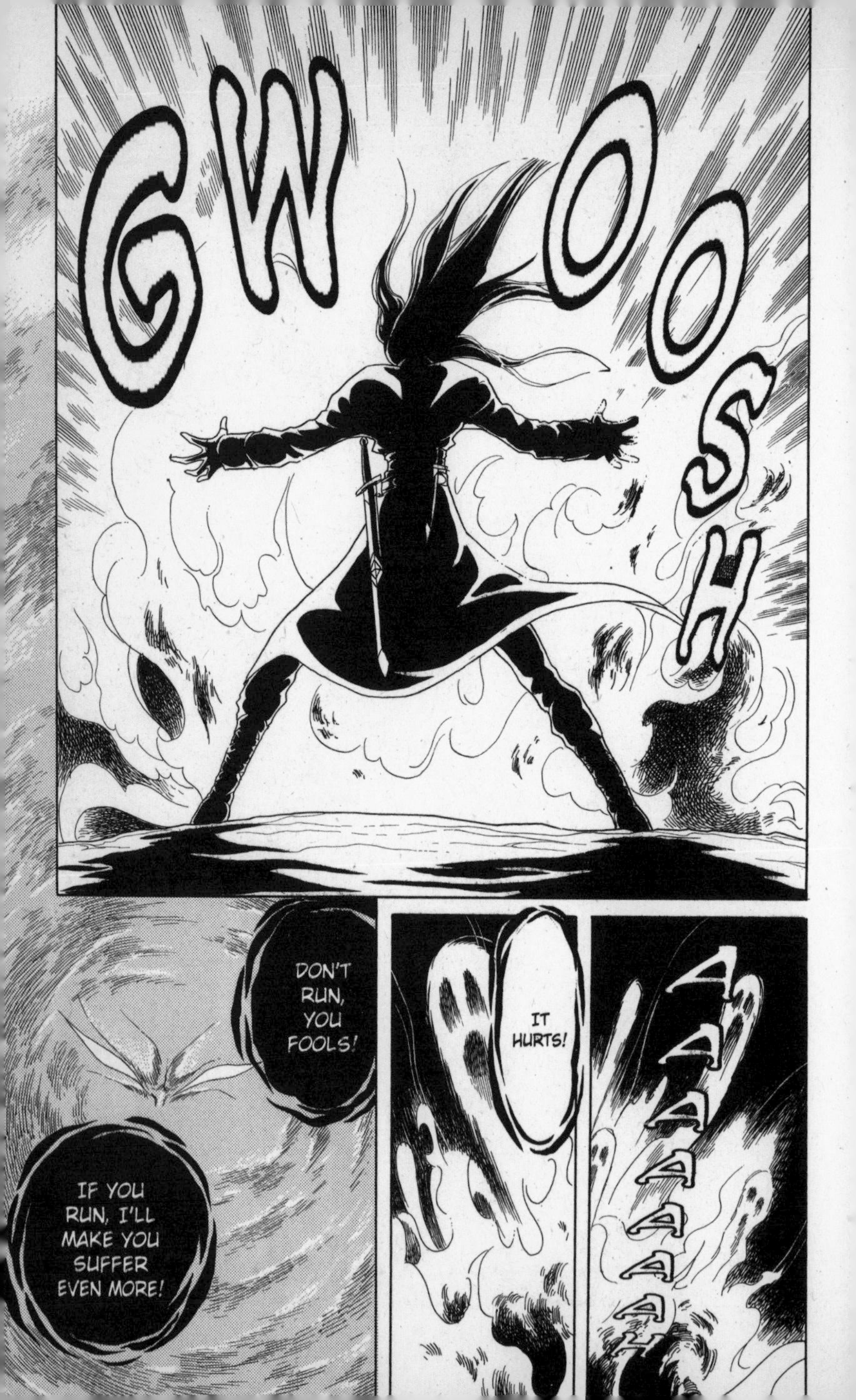
GWOOOSH
AAAAAAAH
IT HURTS!
DON'T RUN, YOU FOOLS!
IF YOU RUN, I'LL MAKE YOU SUFFER EVEN MORE!

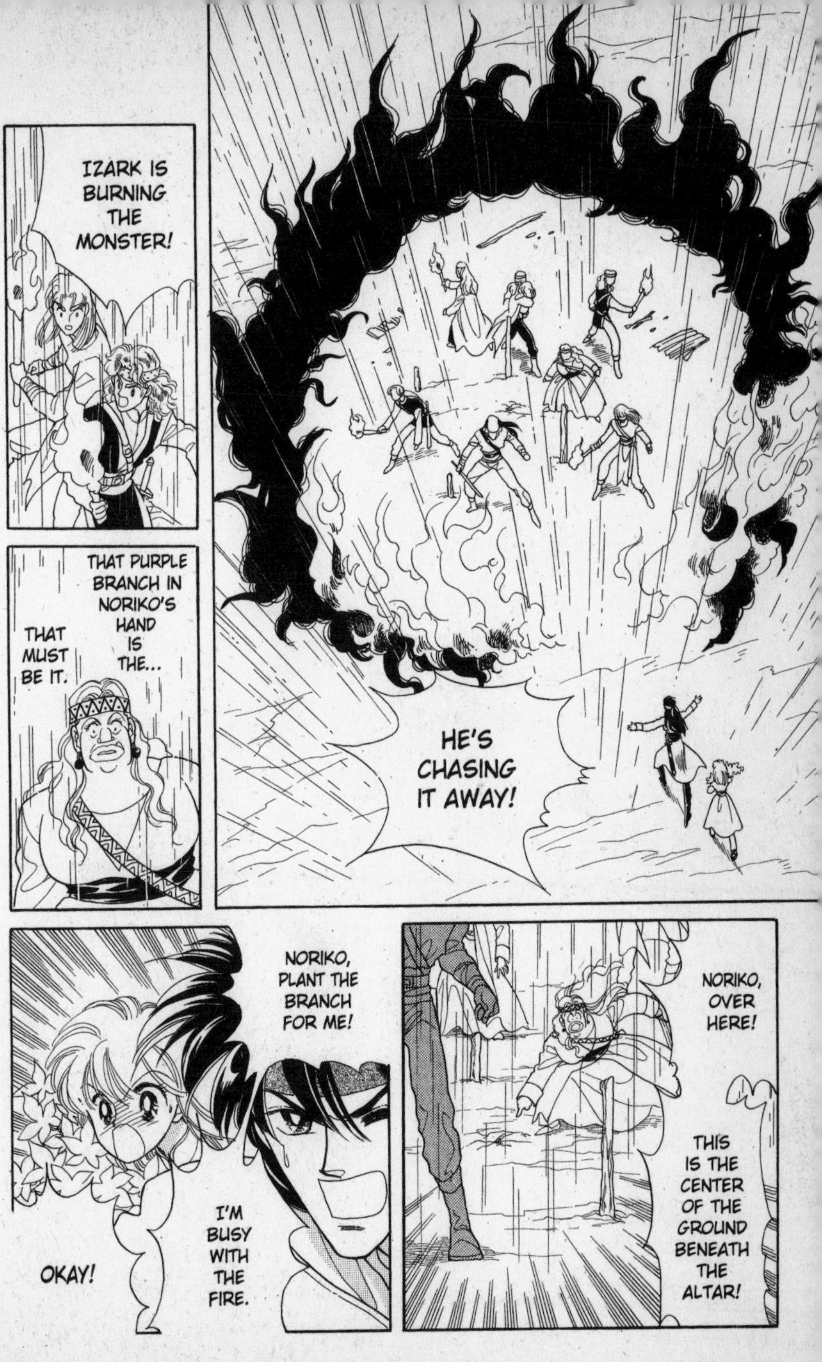
HE'S CHASING IT AWAY!
IZARK IS BURNING THE MONSTER!
THAT PURPLE BRANCH IN NORIKO'S HAND IS THE...
THAT MUST BE IT.
NORIKO, OVER HERE!
THIS IS THE CENTER OF THE GROUND BENEATH THE ALTAR!
NORIKO, PLANT THE BRANCH FOR ME!
I'M BUSY WITH THE FIRE.
OKAY!

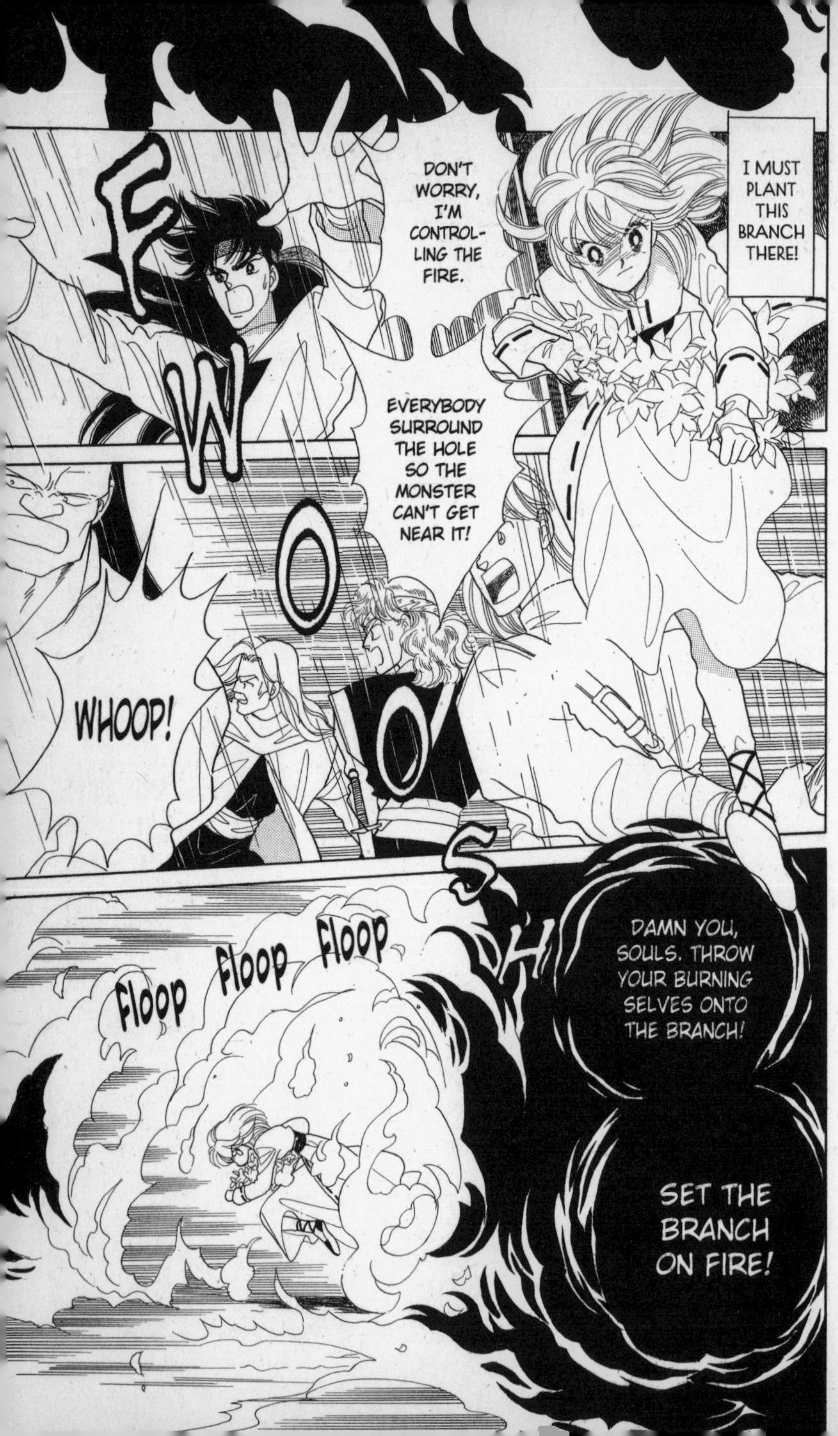
I MUST PLANT THIS BRANCH THERE!
DON'T WORRY, I'M CONTROL-LING THE FIRE.
FWOOSH
EVERYBODY SURROUND THE HOLE SO THE MONSTER CAN'T GET NEAR IT!
WHOOP!
DAMN YOU, SOULS. THROW YOUR BURNING SELVES ONTO THE BRANCH!
SET THE BRANCH ON FIRE!
Floop Floop Floop

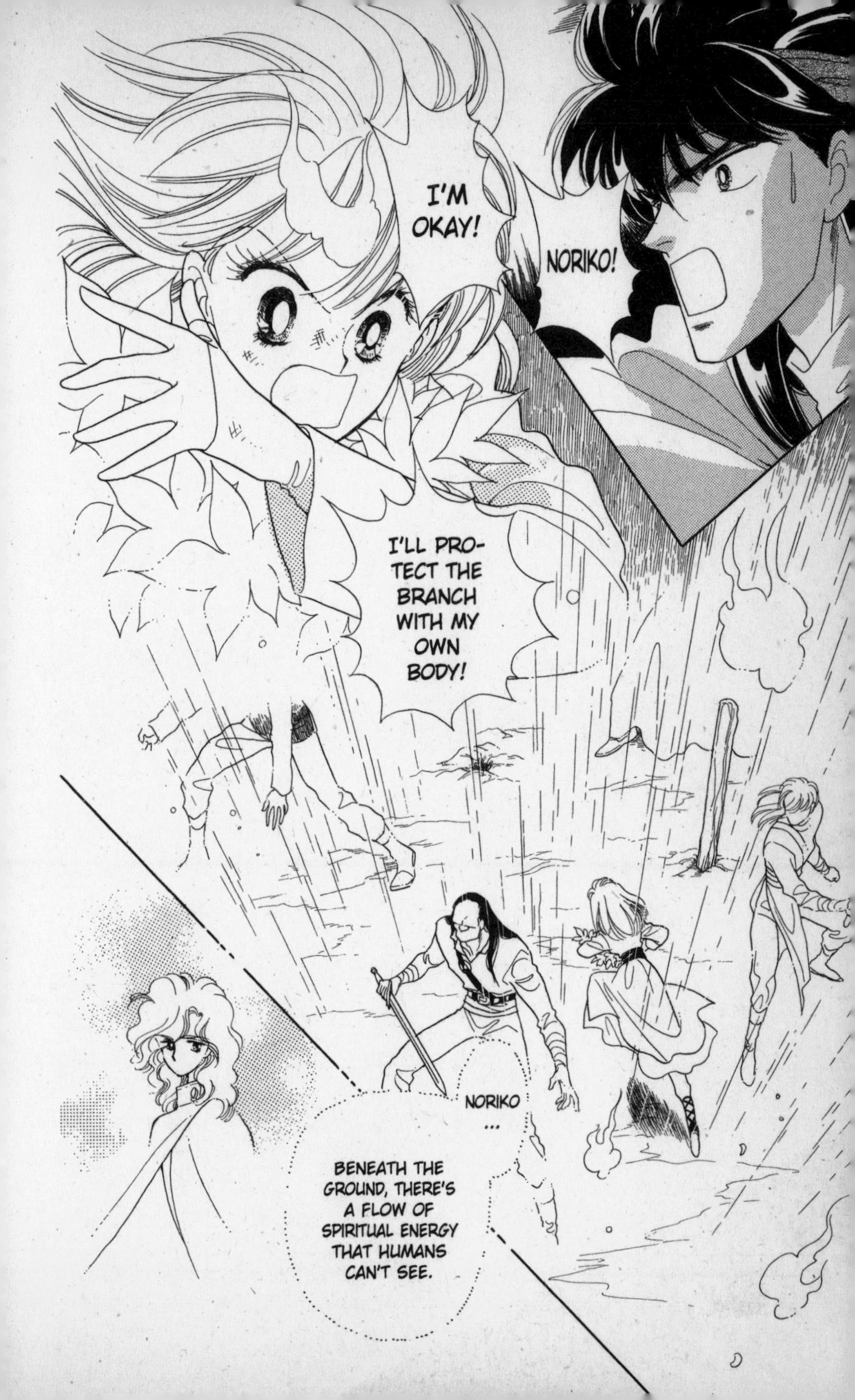
NORIKO!
I'M OKAY!
I'LL PROTECT THE BRANCH WITH MY OWN BODY!
NORIKO...
BENEATH THE GROUND, THERE'S A FLOW OF SPIRITUAL ENERGY THAT HUMANS CAN'T SEE.

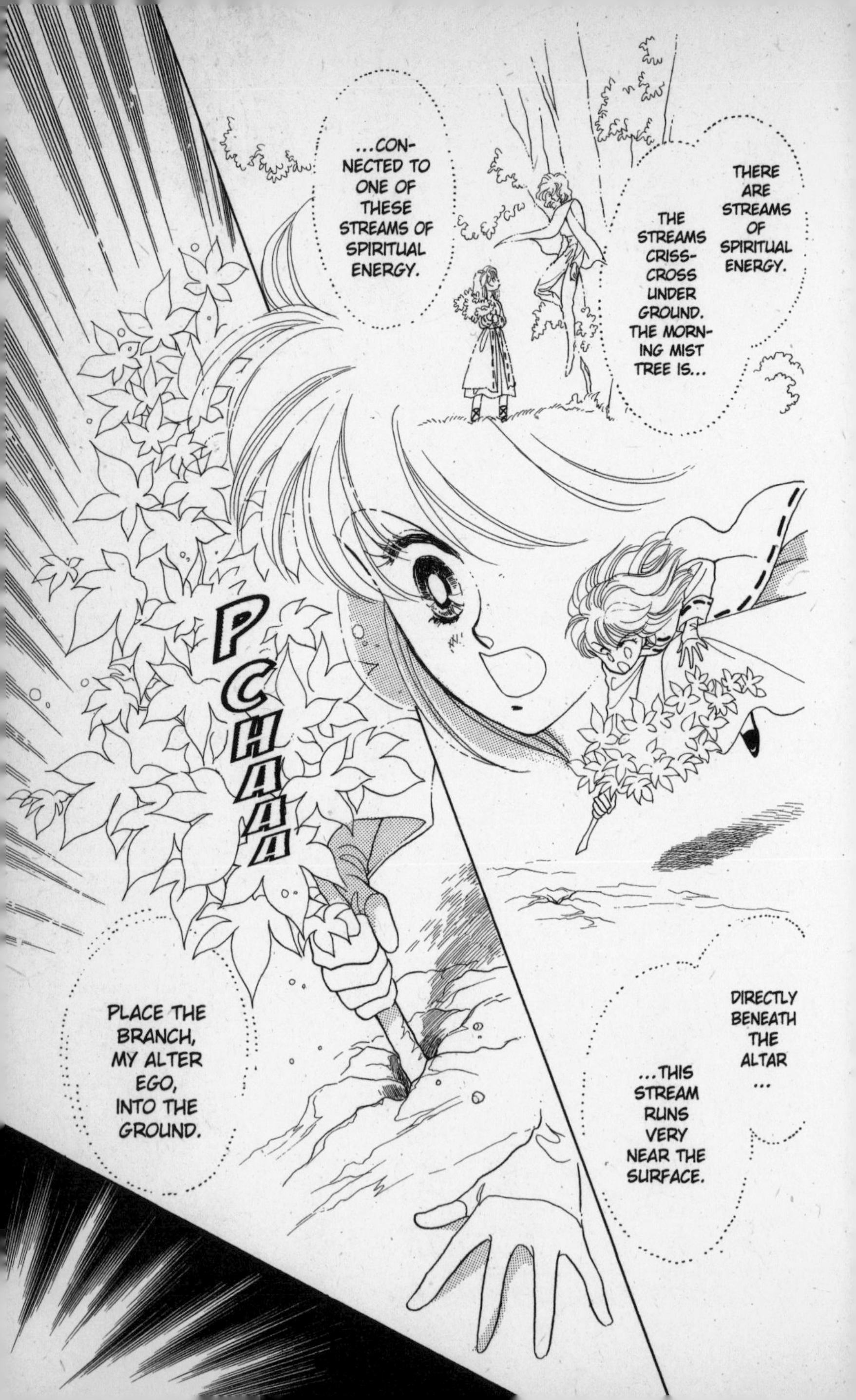
THERE ARE STREAMS OF SPIRITUAL ENERGY.
THE STREAMS CRISS-CROSS UNDER GROUND. THE MORNING MIST TREE IS...
...CONNECTED TO ONE OF THESE STREAMS OF SPIRITUAL ENERGY.
PCHAAA
DIRECTLY BENEATH THE ALTAR...
...THIS STREAM RUNS VERY NEAR THE SURFACE.
PLACE THE BRANCH, MY ALTER EGO, INTO THE GROUND.

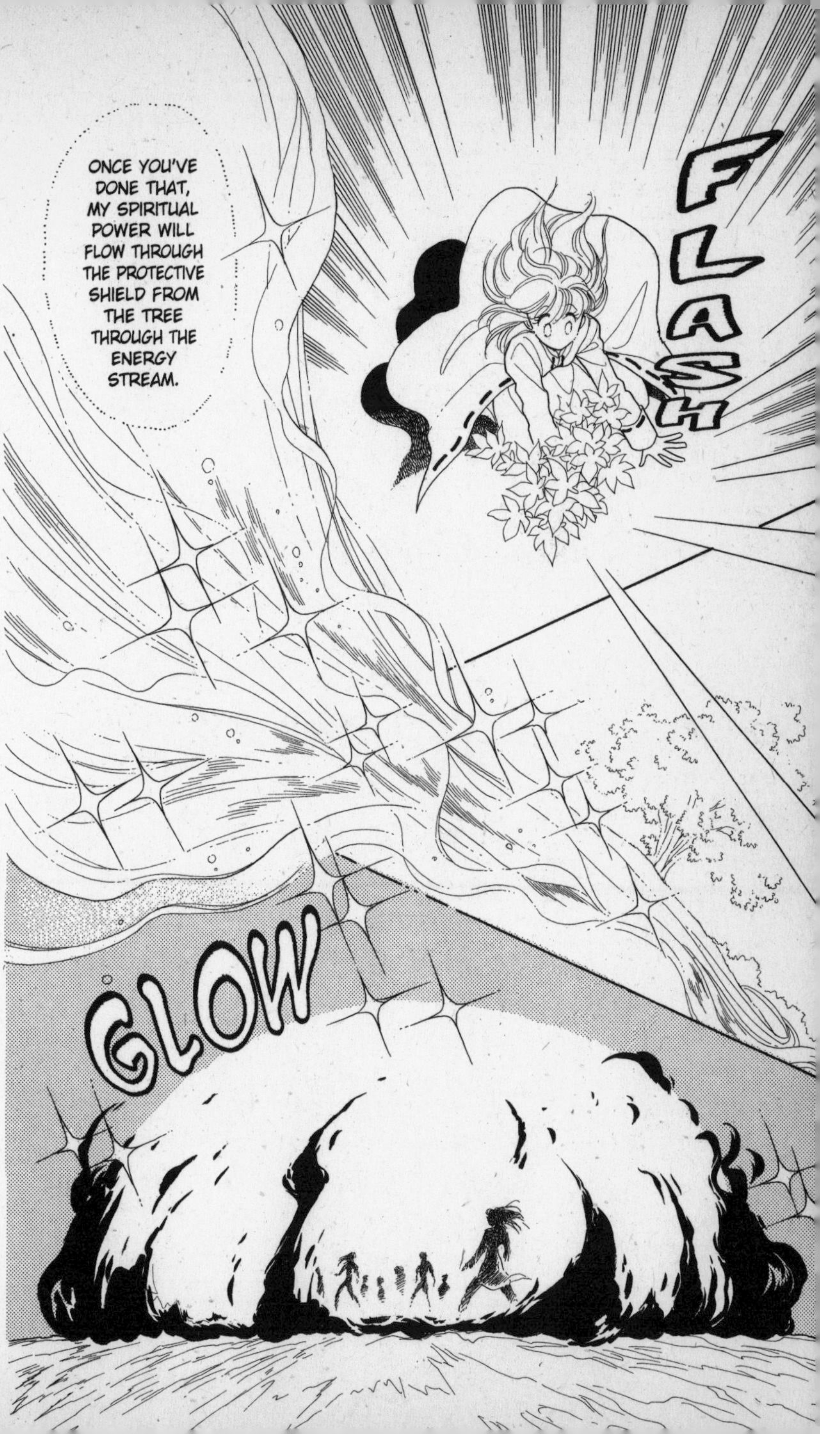
FLASH
ONCE YOU'VE DONE THAT, MY SPIRITUAL POWER WILL FLOW THROUGH THE PROTECTIVE SHIELD FROM THE TREE THROUGH THE ENERGY STREAM.
GLOW

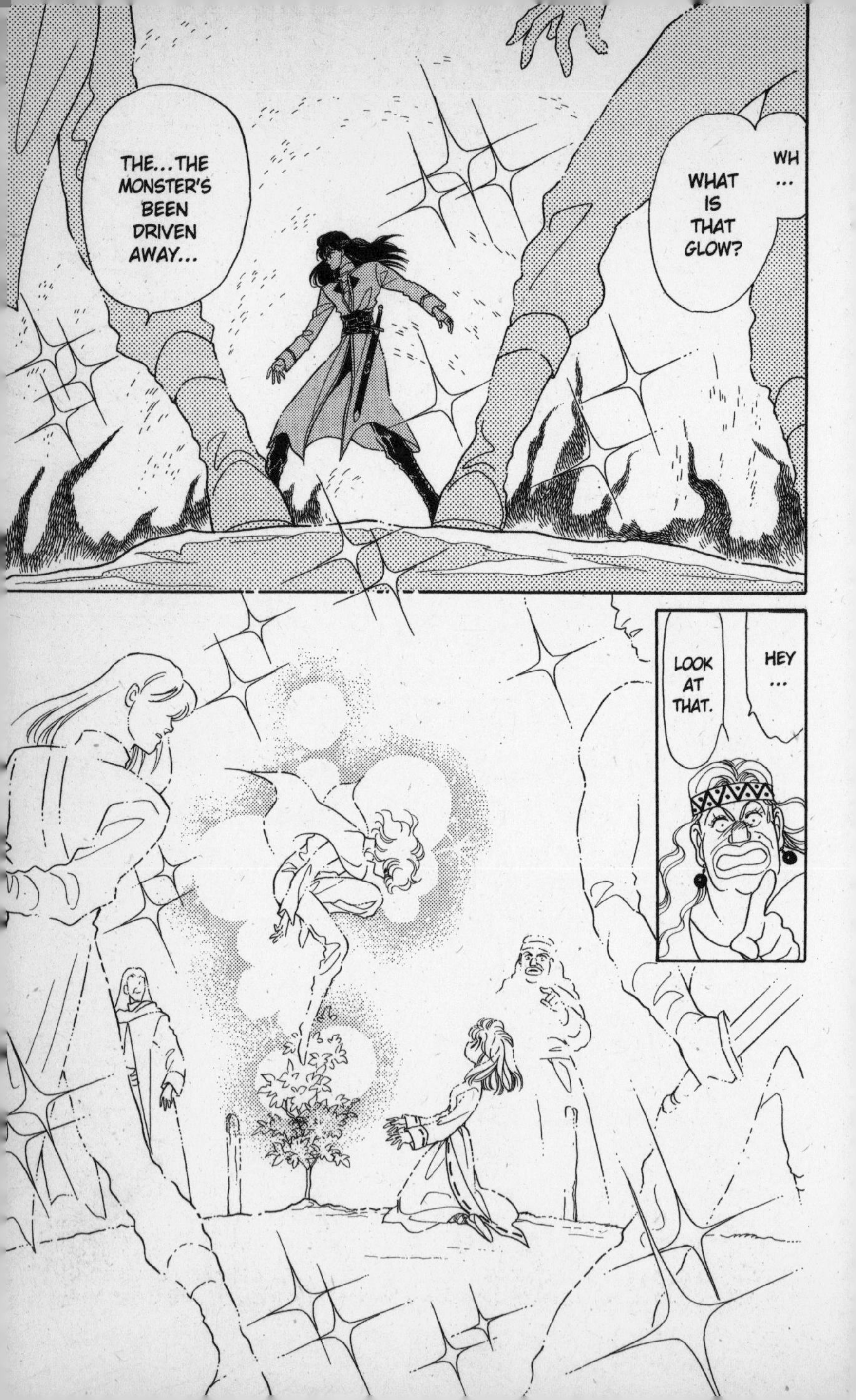
WH... WHAT IS THAT GLOW?
THE...THE MONSTER'S BEEN DRIVEN AWAY...
HEY...
LOOK AT THAT.

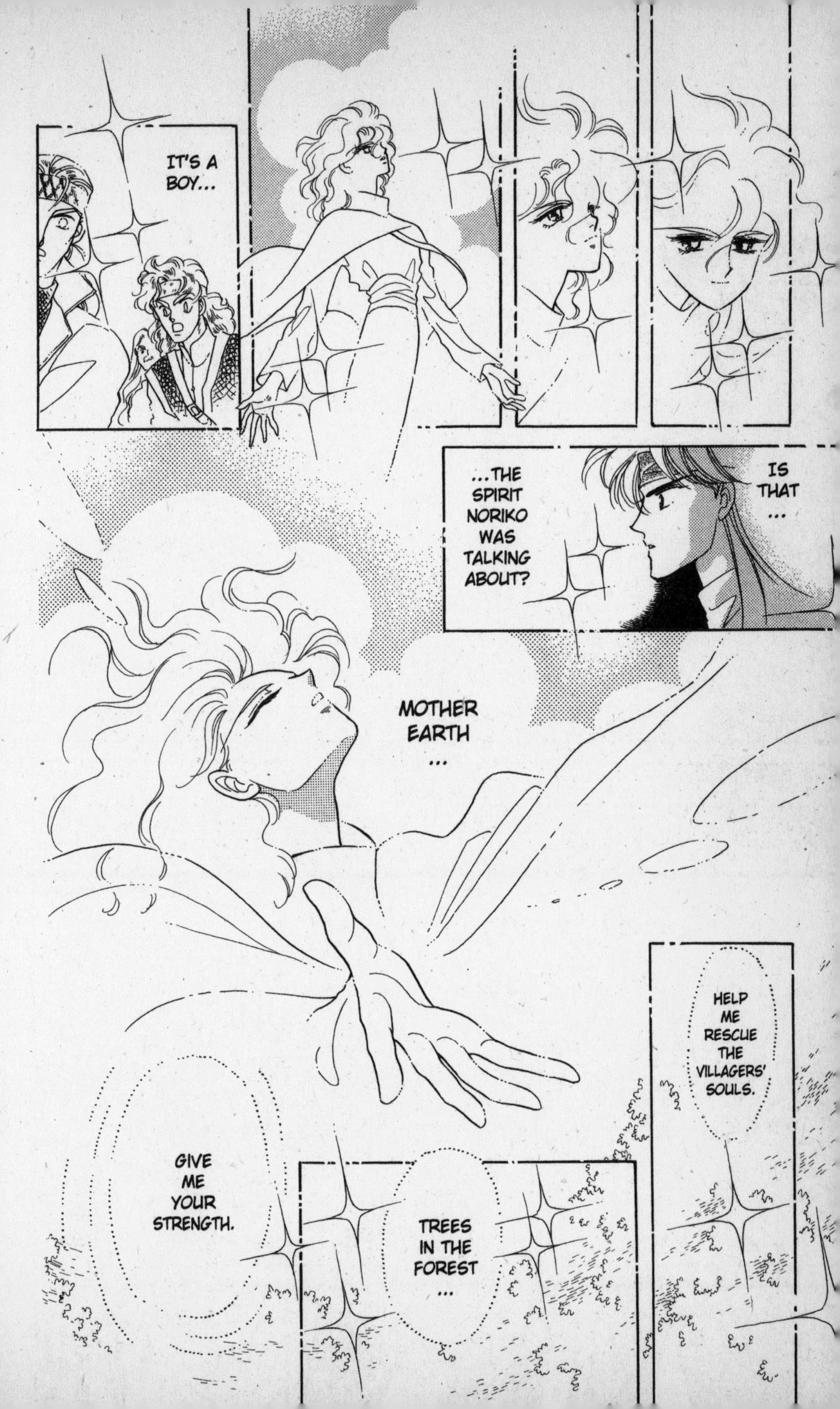
IT'S A BOY...
IS THAT ...
...THE SPIRIT NORIKO WAS TALKING ABOUT?
MOTHER EARTH ...
HELP ME RESCUE THE VILLAGERS' SOULS.
TREES IN THE FOREST ...
GIVE ME YOUR STRENGTH.

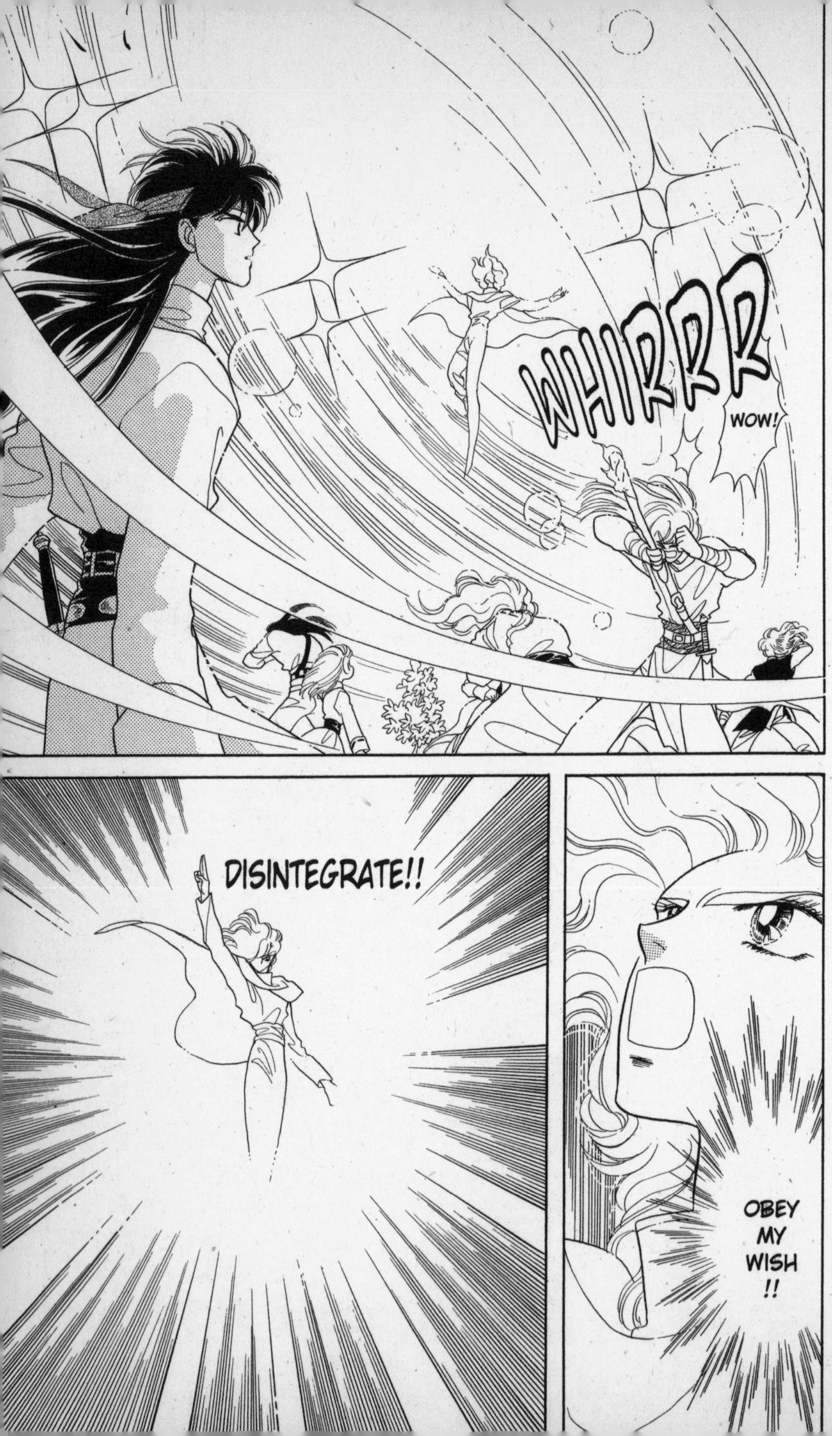
WHIRRR
WOW!
OBEY MY WISH!!
DISINTEGRATE!!

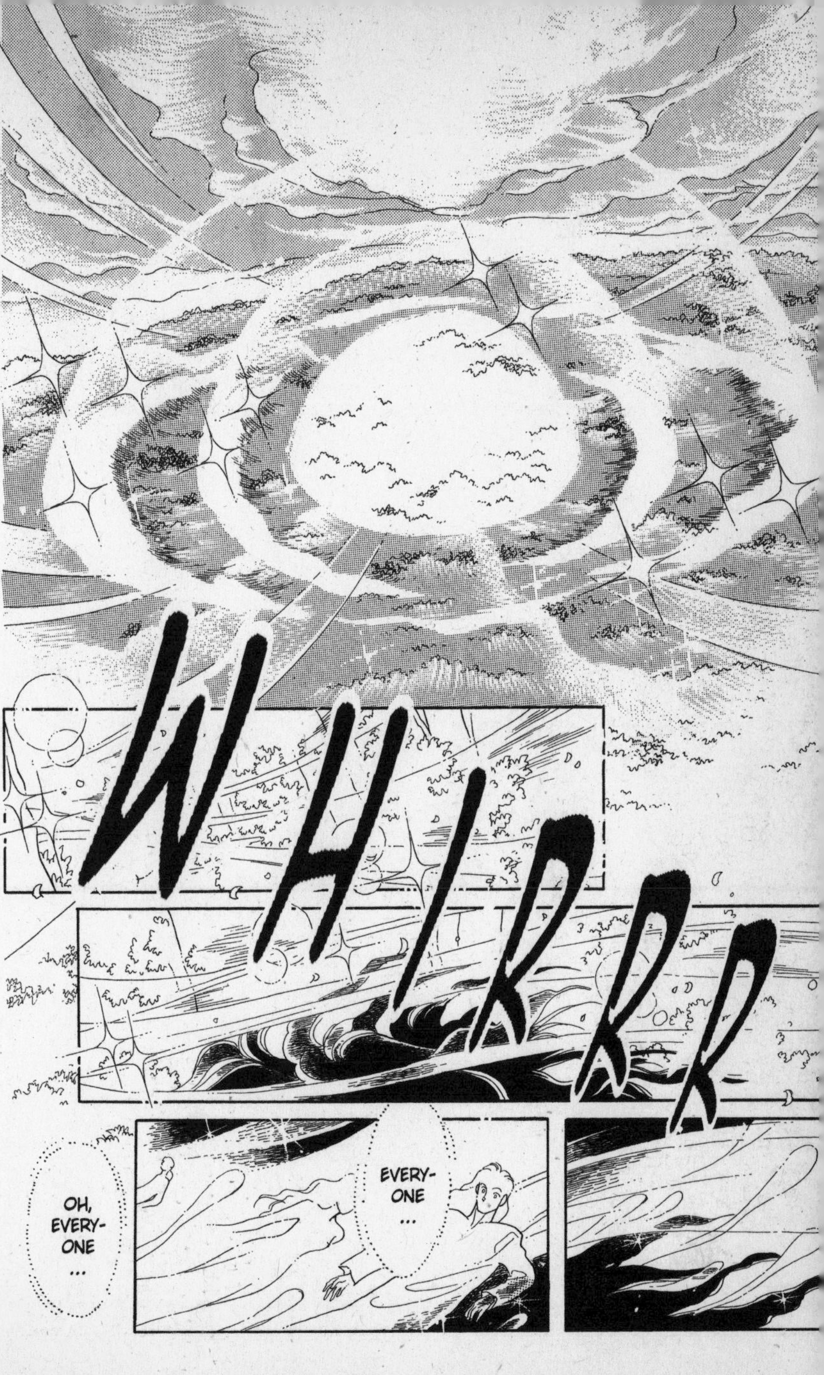
WHIRRR
EVERY-ONE...
OH, EVERY-ONE...

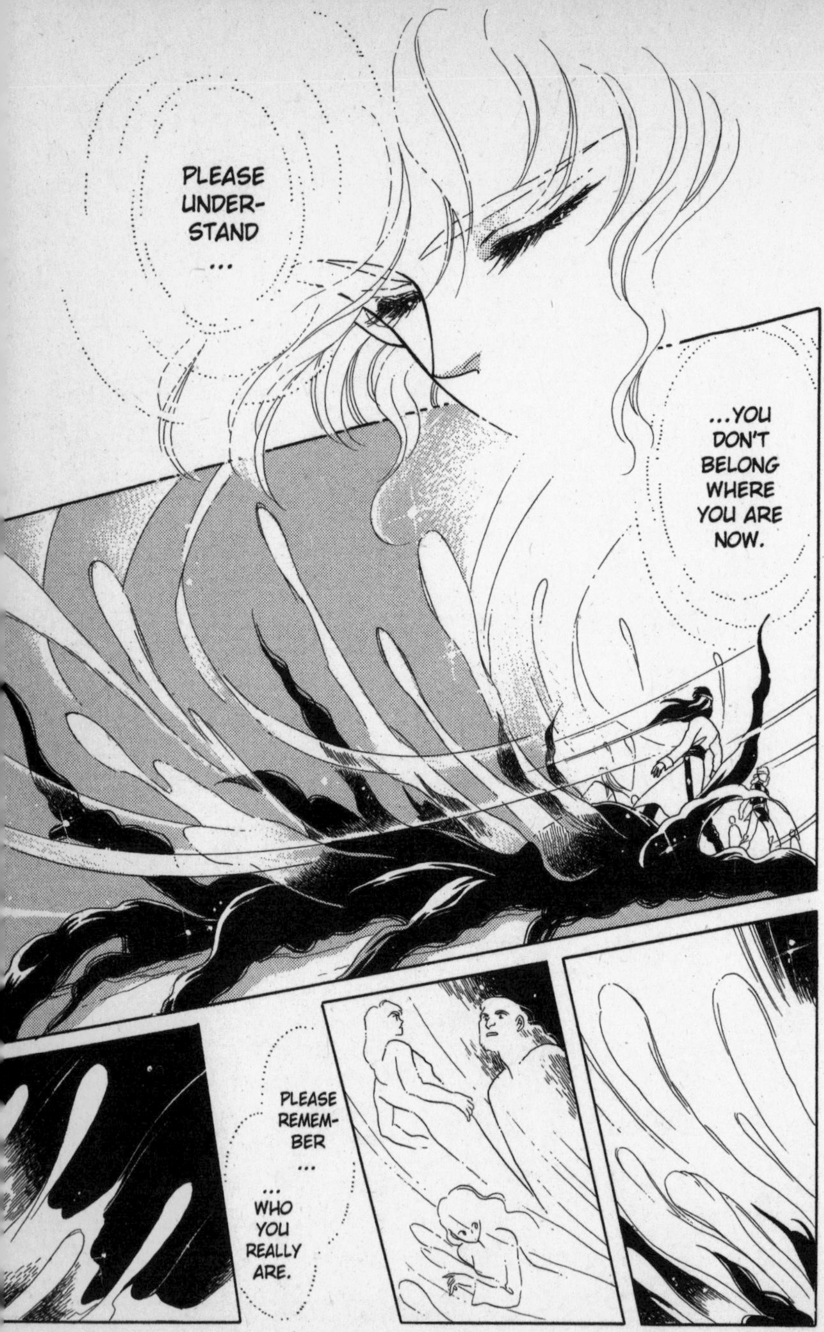
PLEASE UNDER-STAND ...
...YOU DON'T BELONG WHERE YOU ARE NOW.
PLEASE REMEM-BER ...
... WHO YOU REALLY ARE.

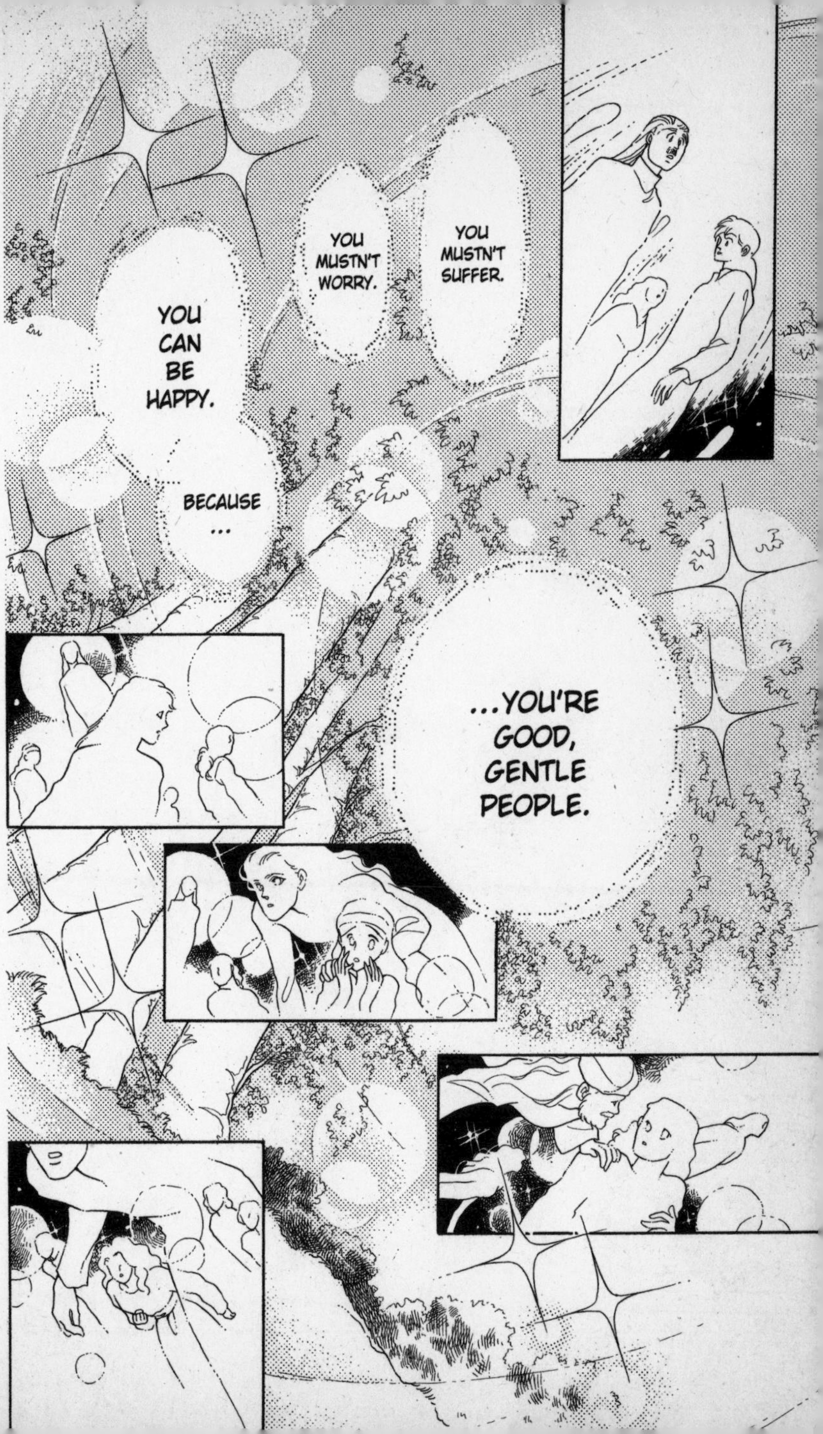
YOU MUSTN'T SUFFER.
YOU MUSTN'T WORRY.
YOU CAN BE HAPPY.
BECAUSE ...
...YOU'RE GOOD, GENTLE PEOPLE.

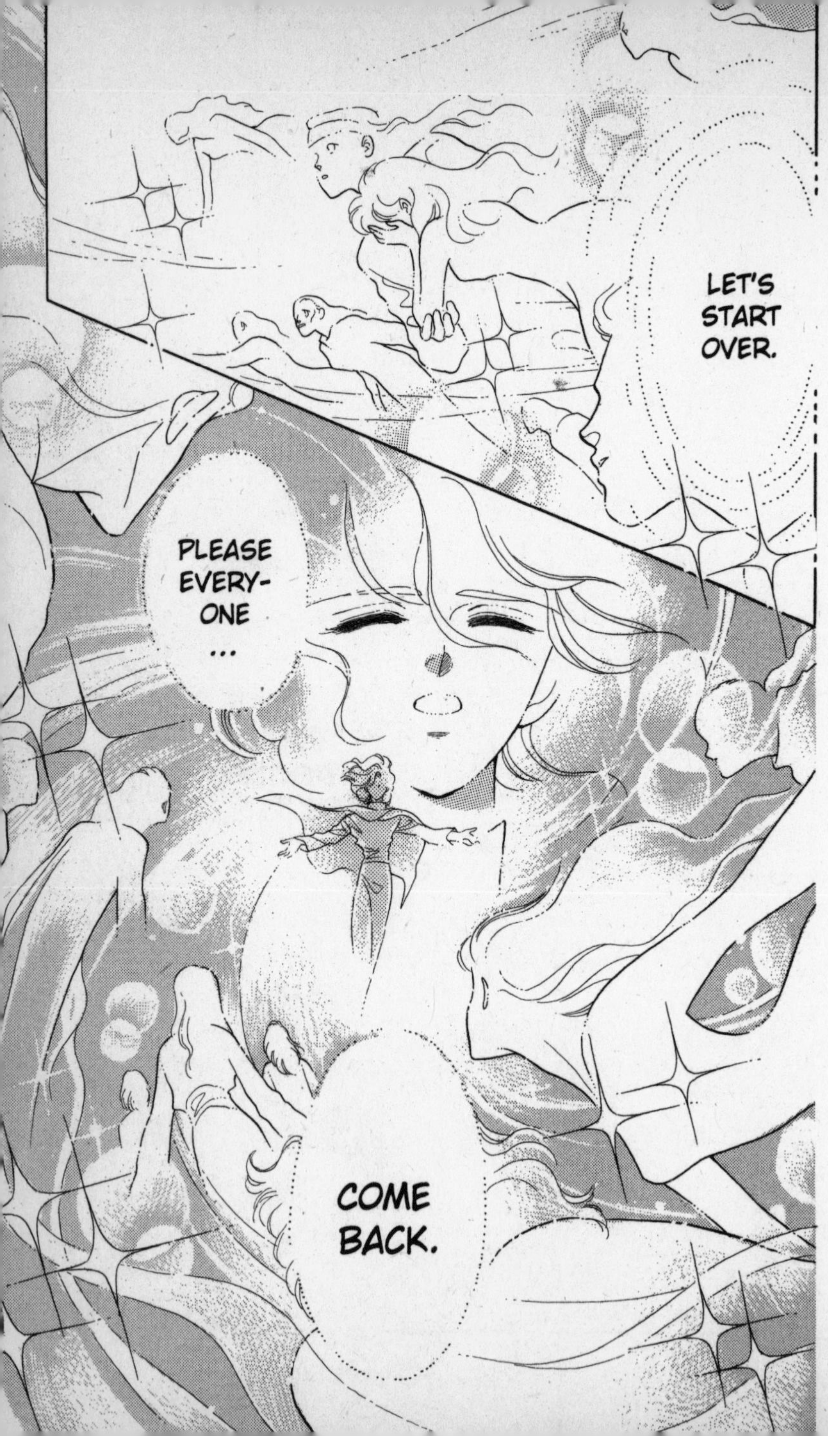
LET'S START OVER.
PLEASE EVERY-ONE ...
COME BACK.

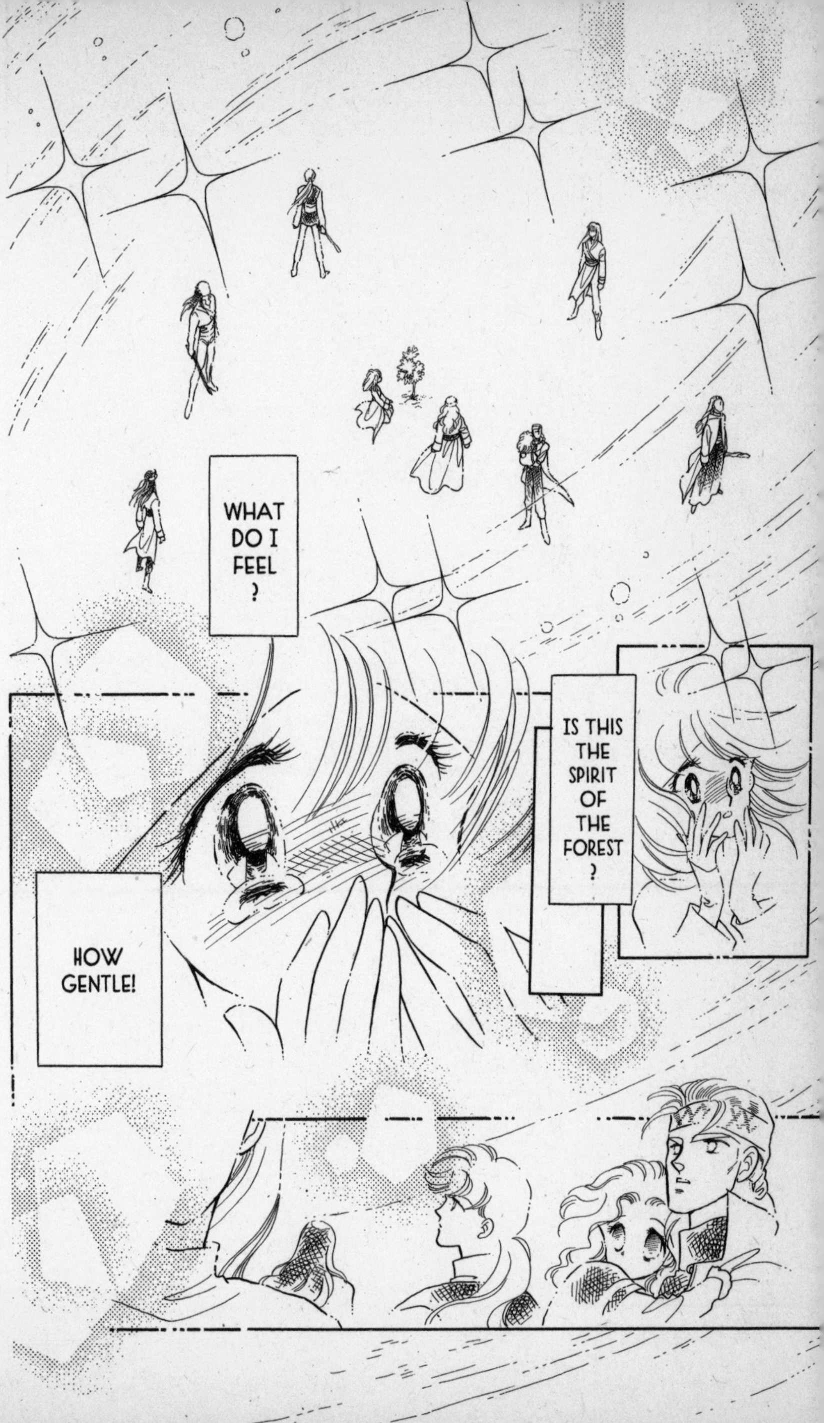
WHAT DO I FEEL?
IS THIS THE SPIRIT OF THE FOREST?
HOW GENTLE!

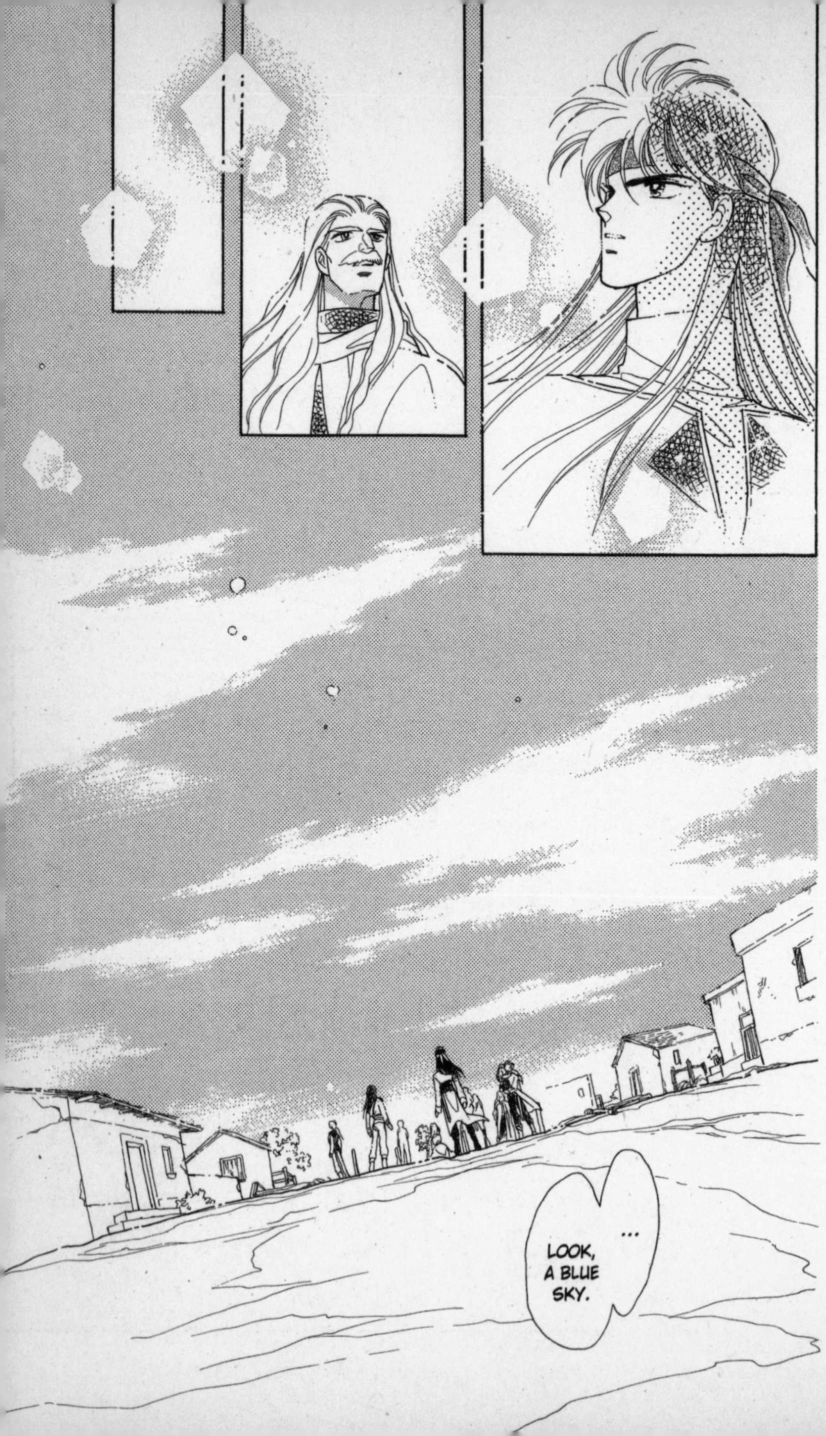
...
LOOK, A BLUE SKY.

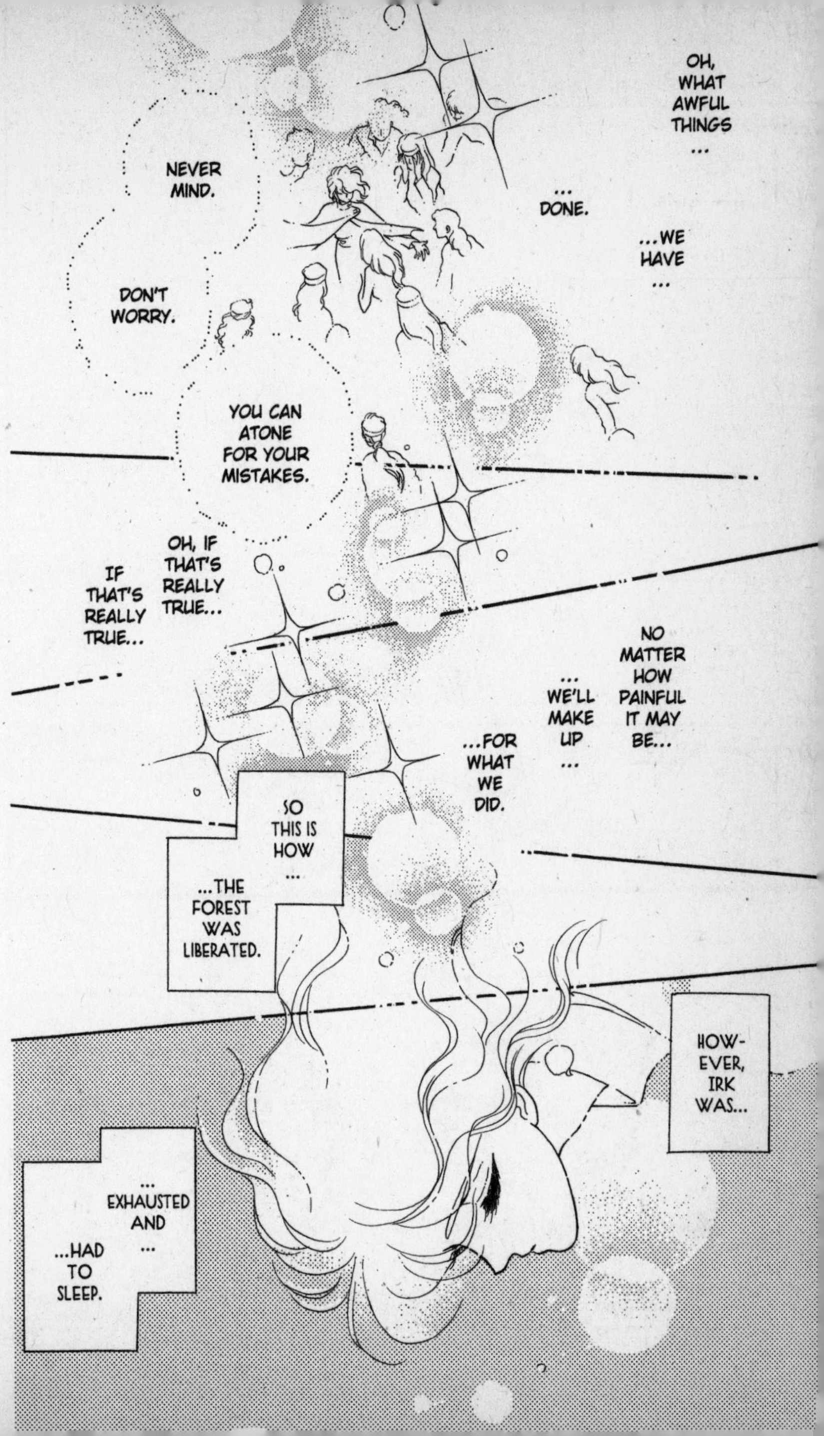
OH, WHAT AWFUL THINGS...
...WE HAVE...
...DONE.
NEVER MIND.
DON'T WORRY.
YOU CAN ATONE FOR YOUR MISTAKES.
OH, IF THAT'S REALLY TRUE...
IF THAT'S REALLY TRUE...
NO MATTER HOW PAINFUL IT MAY BE...
...WE'LL MAKE UP...
...FOR WHAT WE DID.
SO THIS IS HOW...
...THE FOREST WAS LIBERATED.
HOW-EVER, IRK WAS...
...EXHAUSTED AND...
...HAD TO SLEEP.

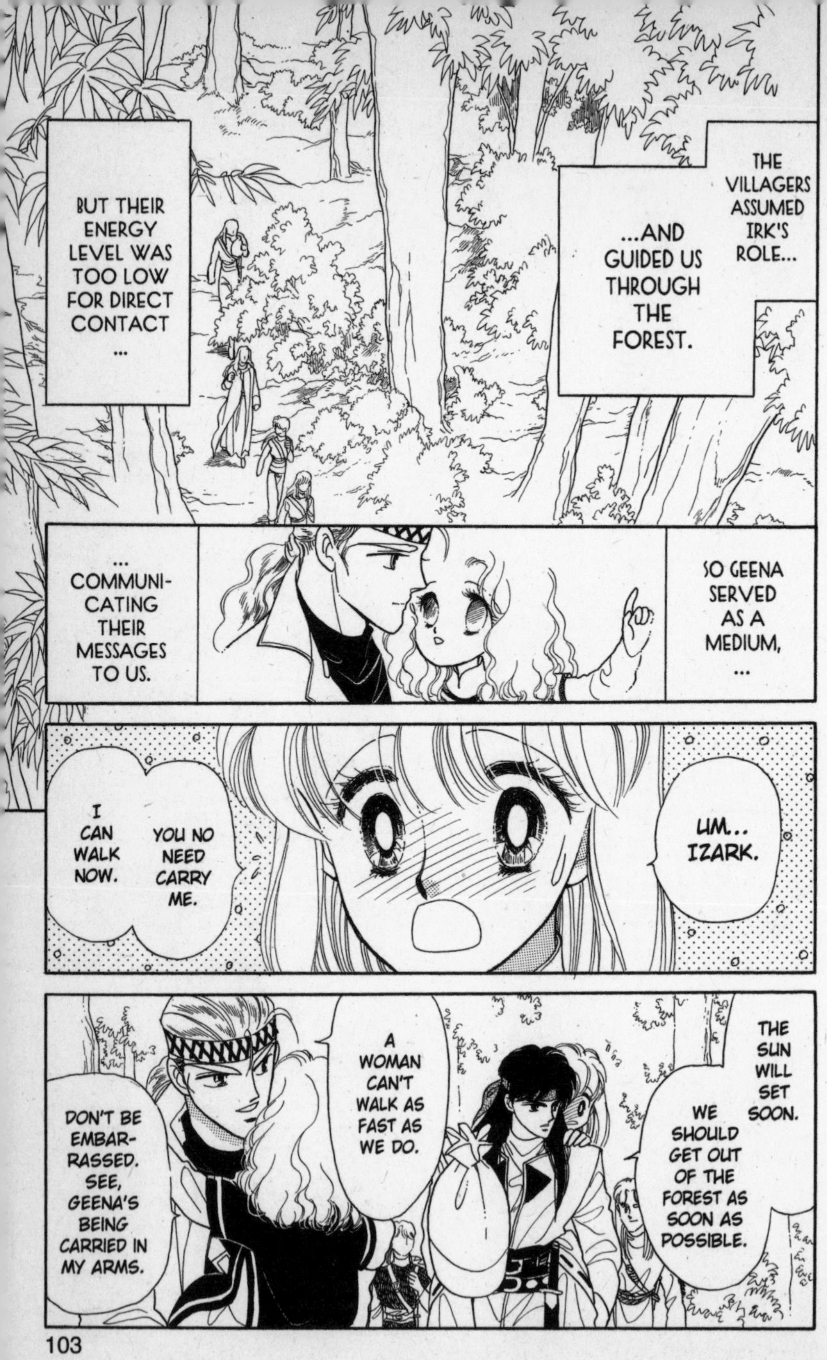
THE VILLAGERS ASSUMED IRK'S ROLE...
...AND GUIDED US THROUGH THE FOREST.
BUT THEIR ENERGY LEVEL WAS TOO LOW FOR DIRECT CONTACT ...
SO GEENA SERVED AS A MEDIUM, ...
... COMMUNICATING THEIR MESSAGES TO US.
UM... IZARK.
I CAN WALK NOW. YOU NO NEED CARRY ME.
THE SUN WILL SET SOON.
WE SHOULD GET OUT OF THE FOREST AS SOON AS POSSIBLE.
A WOMAN CAN'T WALK AS FAST AS WE DO.
DON'T BE EMBARRASSED. SEE, GEENA'S BEING CARRIED IN MY ARMS.

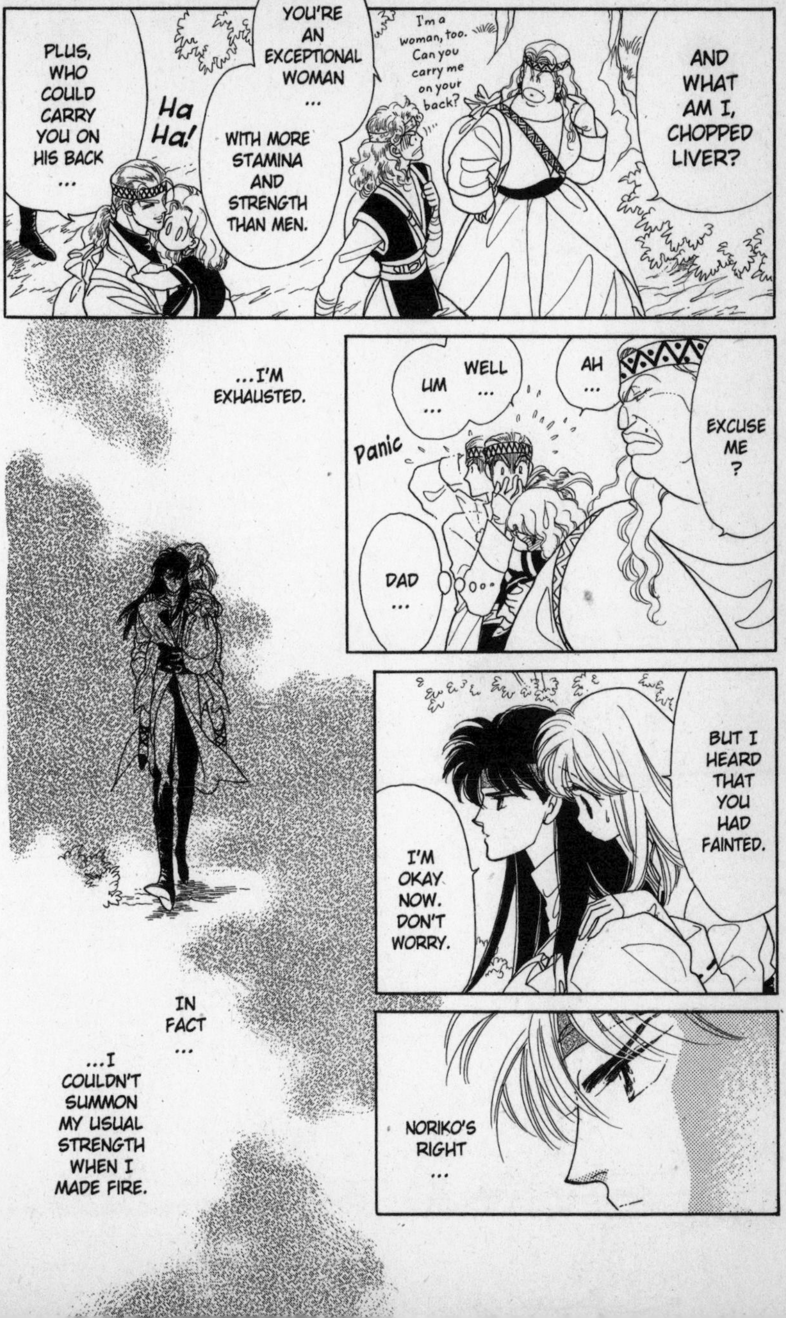
AND WHAT AM I, CHOPPED LIVER?
I'm a woman, too. Can you carry me on your back?
YOU'RE AN EXCEPTIONAL WOMAN ...
WITH MORE STAMINA AND STRENGTH THAN MEN.
Ha Ha!
PLUS, WHO COULD CARRY YOU ON HIS BACK ...
EXCUSE ME ?
AH ...
WELL ...
UM ...
Panic
DAD ...
BUT I HEARD THAT YOU HAD FAINTED.
I'M OKAY NOW. DON'T WORRY.
NORIKO'S RIGHT ...
...I'M EXHAUSTED.
IN FACT ...
...I COULDN'T SUMMON MY USUAL STRENGTH WHEN I MADE FIRE.

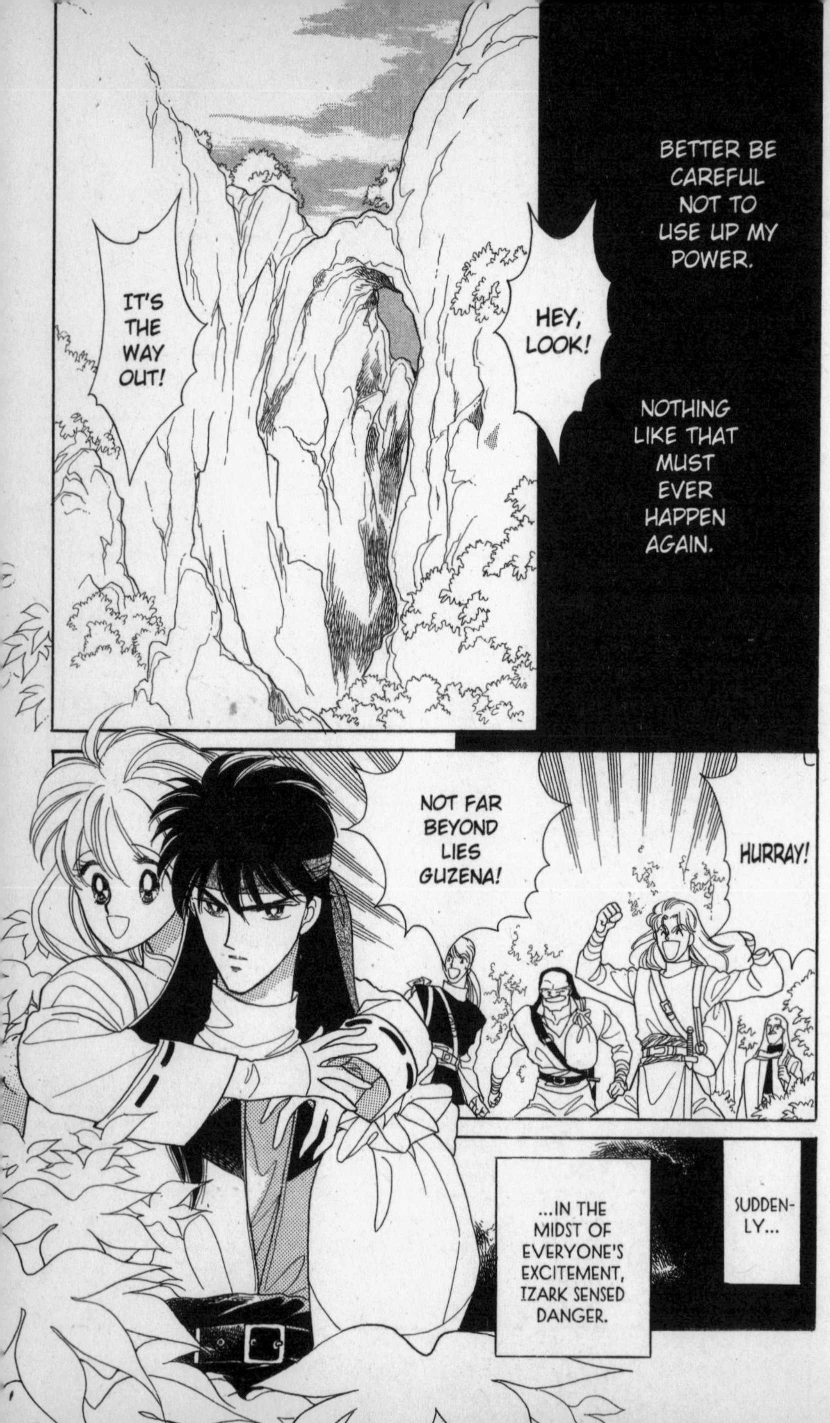
BETTER BE CAREFUL NOT TO USE UP MY POWER.
NOTHING LIKE THAT MUST EVER HAPPEN AGAIN.
HEY, LOOK!
IT'S THE WAY OUT!
NOT FAR BEYOND LIES GUZENA!
HURRAY!
SUDDEN-LY...
...IN THE MIDST OF EVERYONE'S EXCITEMENT, IZARK SENSED DANGER.

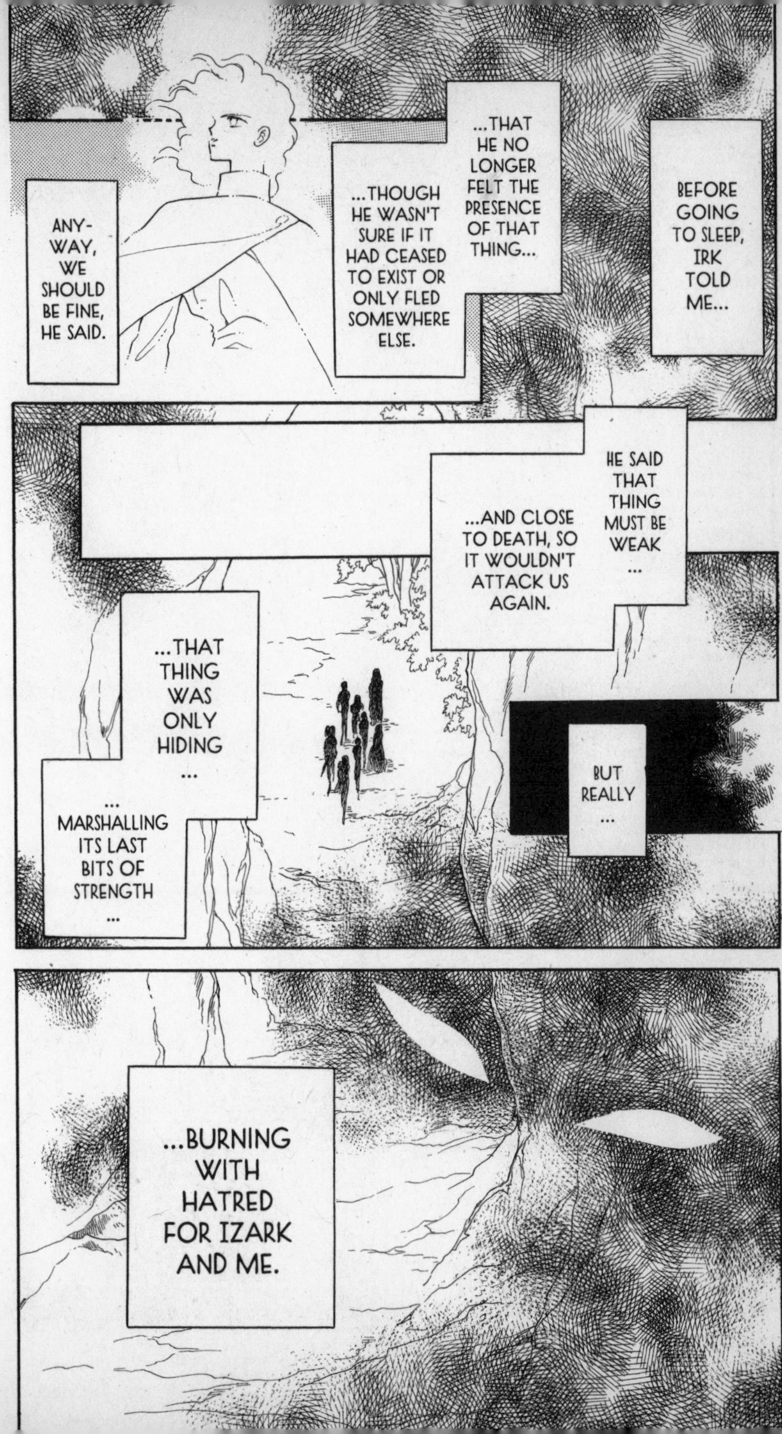
BEFORE GOING TO SLEEP, IRK TOLD ME...
...THAT HE NO LONGER FELT THE PRESENCE OF THAT THING...
...THOUGH HE WASN'T SURE IF IT HAD CEASED TO EXIST OR ONLY FLED SOMEWHERE ELSE.
ANY-WAY, WE SHOULD BE FINE, HE SAID.
HE SAID THAT THING MUST BE WEAK ...
...AND CLOSE TO DEATH, SO IT WOULDN'T ATTACK US AGAIN.
BUT REALLY ...
...THAT THING WAS ONLY HIDING ...
... MARSHALLING ITS LAST BITS OF STRENGTH ...
...BURNING WITH HATRED FOR IZARK AND ME.

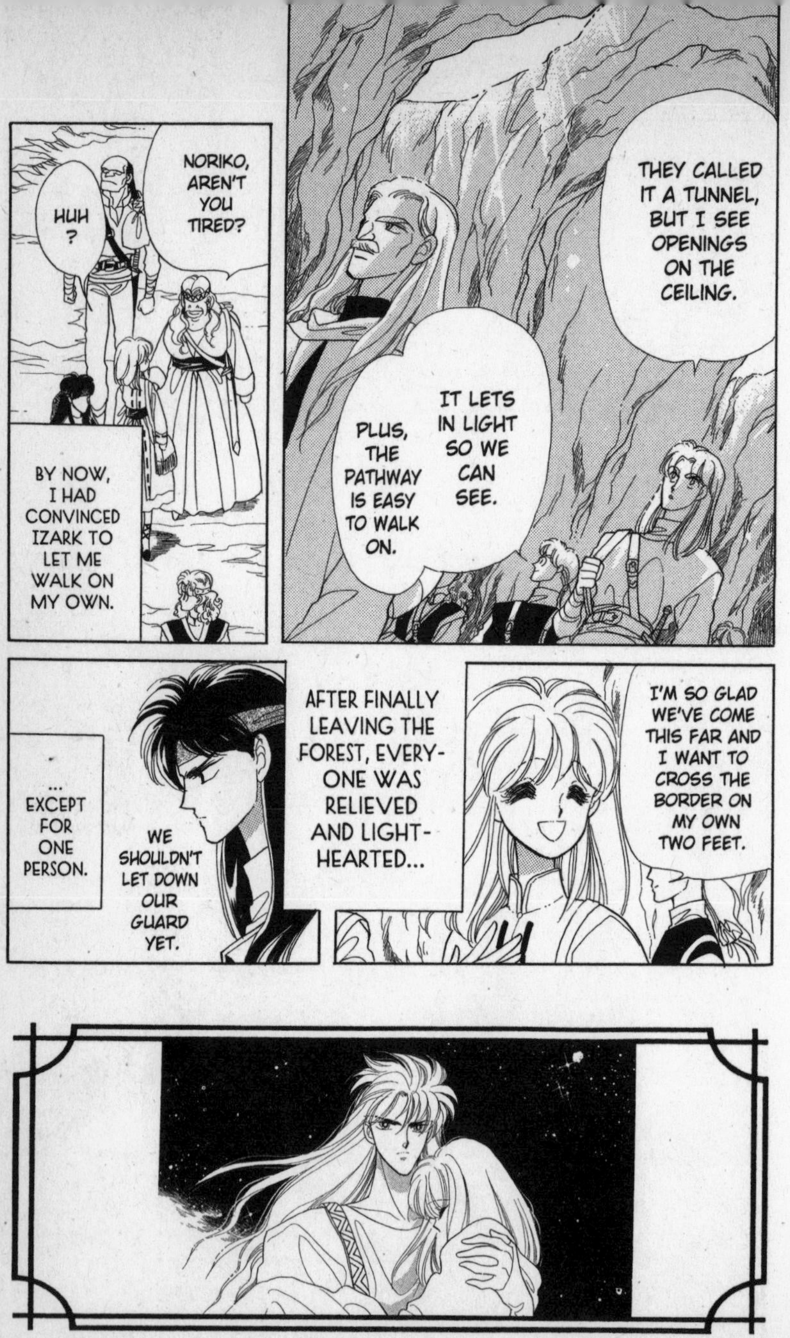
THEY CALLED IT A TUNNEL, BUT I SEE OPENINGS ON THE CEILING.
IT LETS IN LIGHT SO WE CAN SEE.
PLUS, THE PATHWAY IS EASY TO WALK ON.
NORIKO, AREN'T YOU TIRED?
HUH ?
BY NOW, I HAD CONVINCED IZARK TO LET ME WALK ON MY OWN.
I'M SO GLAD WE'VE COME THIS FAR AND I WANT TO CROSS THE BORDER ON MY OWN TWO FEET.
AFTER FINALLY LEAVING THE FOREST, EVERY-ONE WAS RELIEVED AND LIGHT-HEARTED...
WE SHOULDN'T LET DOWN OUR GUARD YET.
... EXCEPT FOR ONE PERSON.

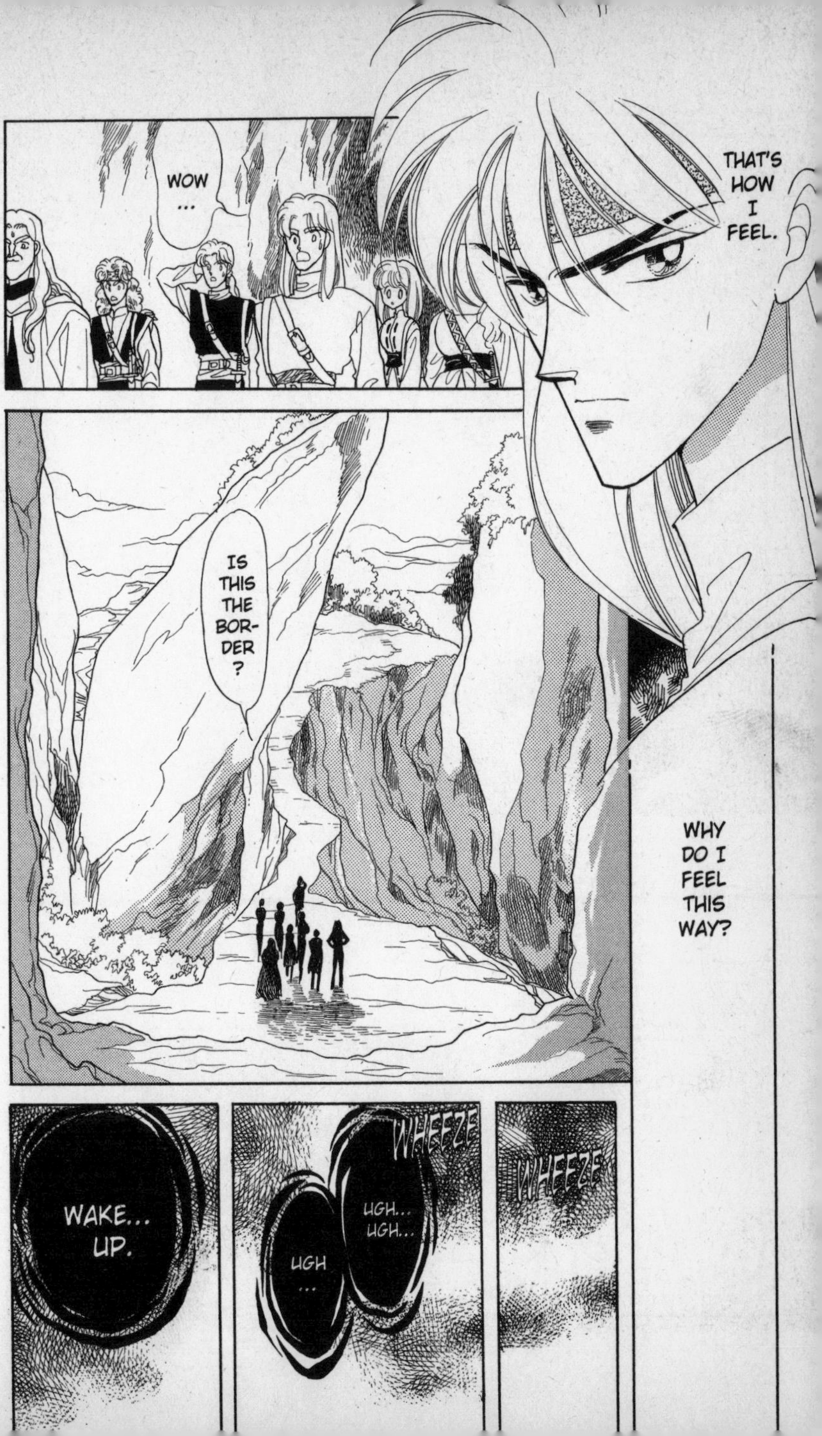
THAT'S HOW I FEEL.
WHY DO I FEEL THIS WAY?
WOW ...
IS THIS THE BOR-DER?
WHEEZE
WHEEZE
UGH... UGH...
UGH ...
WAKE... UP.

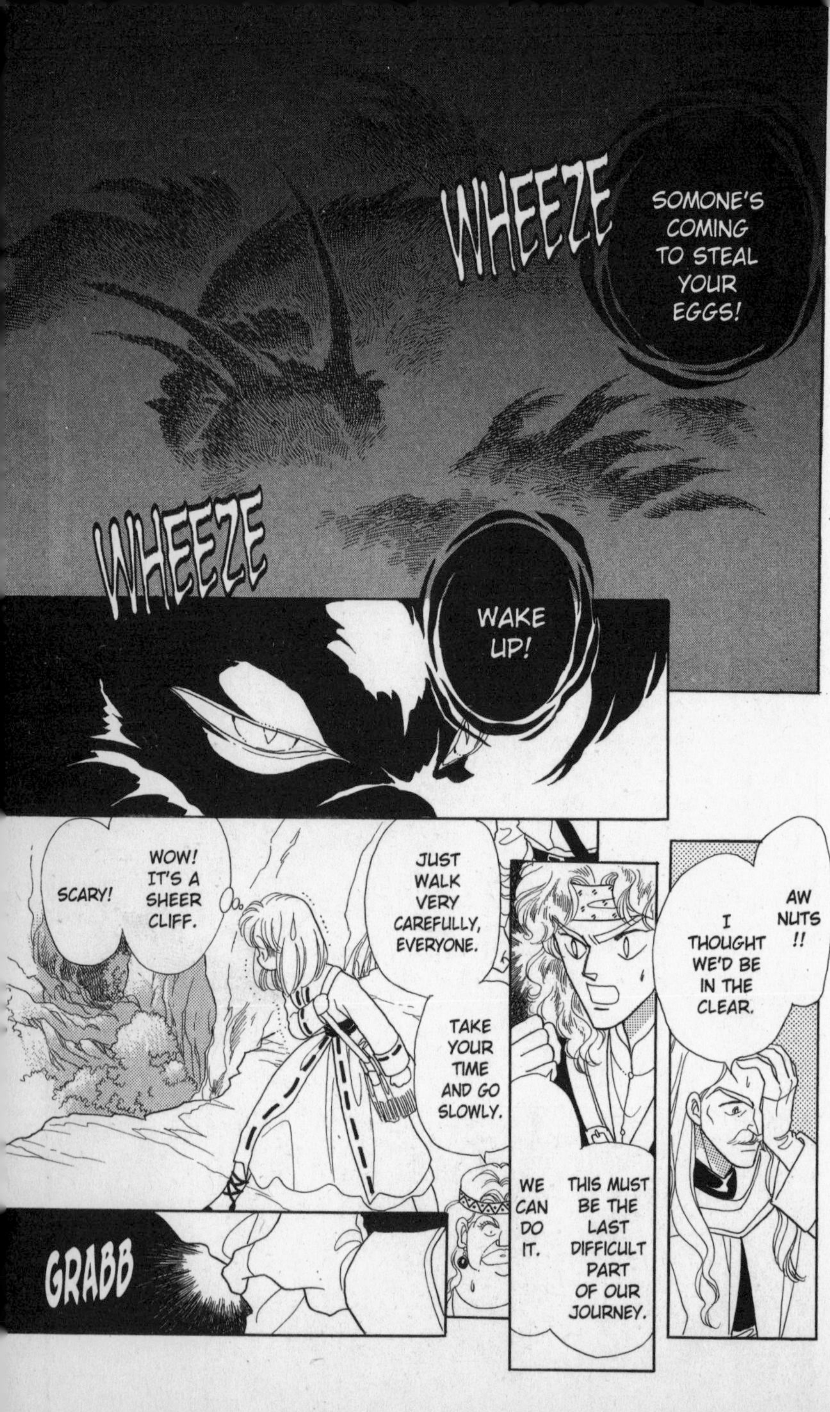
WHEEZE
SOMONE'S COMING TO STEAL YOUR EGGS!
WHEEZE
WAKE UP!
AW NUTS!!
I THOUGHT WE'D BE IN THE CLEAR.
THIS MUST BE THE LAST DIFFICULT PART OF OUR JOURNEY.
WE CAN DO IT.
JUST WALK VERY CAREFULLY, EVERYONE.
TAKE YOUR TIME AND GO SLOWLY.
WOW! IT'S A SHEER CLIFF.
SCARY!
GRABB

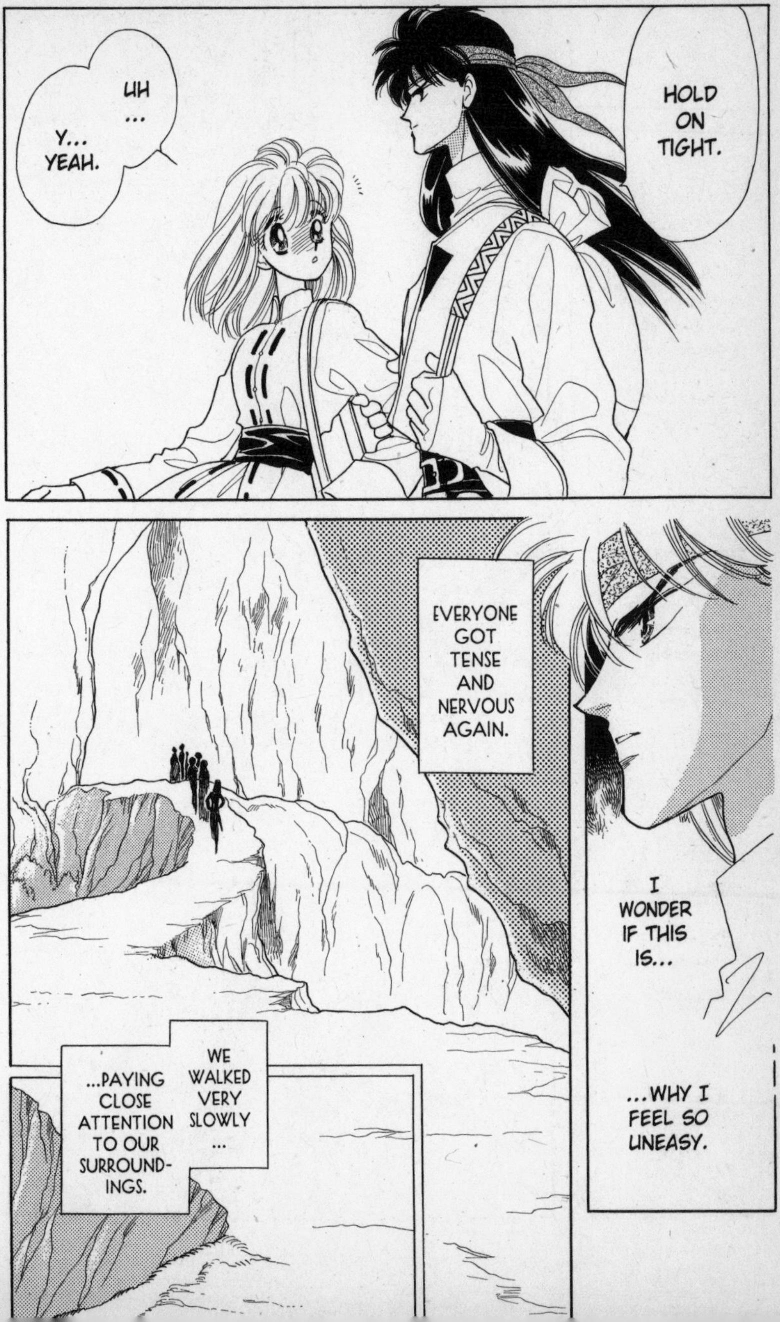
HOLD ON TIGHT.
UH ...
Y... YEAH.
I WONDER IF THIS IS...
...WHY I FEEL SO UNEASY.
EVERYONE GOT TENSE AND NERVOUS AGAIN.
WE WALKED VERY SLOWLY ...
...PAYING CLOSE ATTENTION TO OUR SURROUND-INGS.

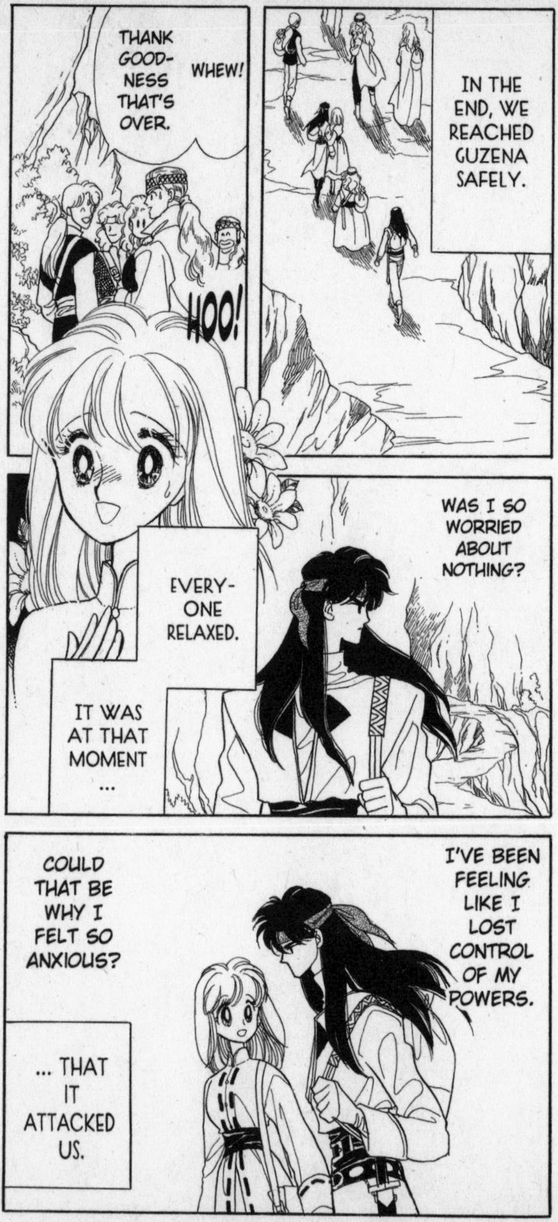
IN THE END, WE REACHED GUZENA SAFELY.
THANK GOODNESS THAT'S OVER.
WHEW!
HOO!
EVERYONE RELAXED.
WAS I SO WORRIED ABOUT NOTHING?
IT WAS AT THAT MOMENT ...
I'VE BEEN FEELING LIKE I LOST CONTROL OF MY POWERS.
COULD THAT BE WHY I FELT SO ANXIOUS?
... THAT IT ATTACKED US.

After I wrote about insects in Vol. 2, I received some letters from my readers. Here's what they wrote to me.

Most of the readers wrote that the creature was planarian.

According to one reader who went to the library and did some research, it was probably a kind of planarian called a bipaliid land planarian.

This is what the drawing in her letter looks like.

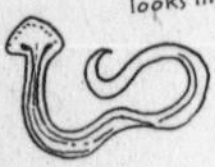

She says it eats worms and snails.

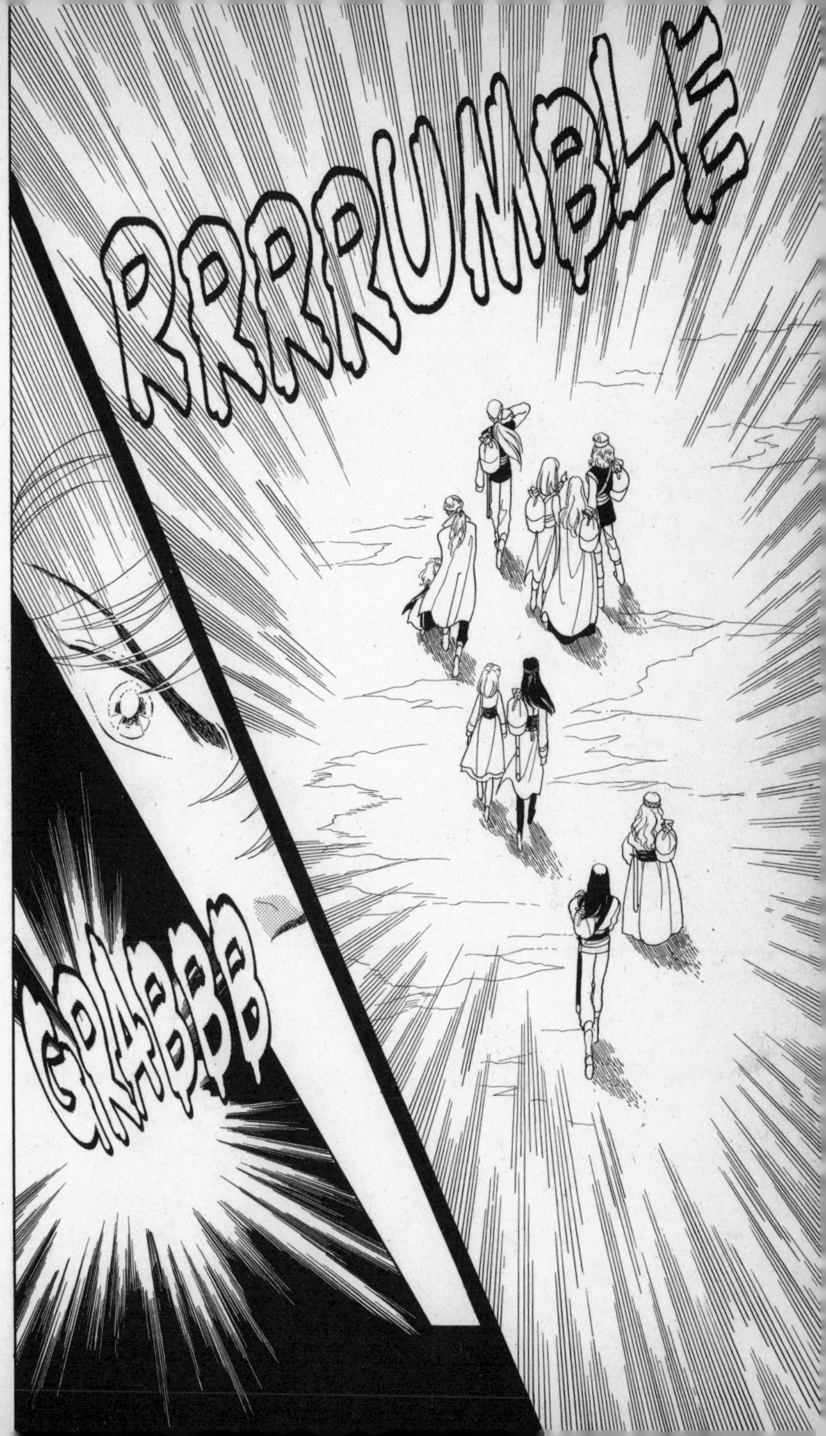
RRRRUMBLE
GRABBB

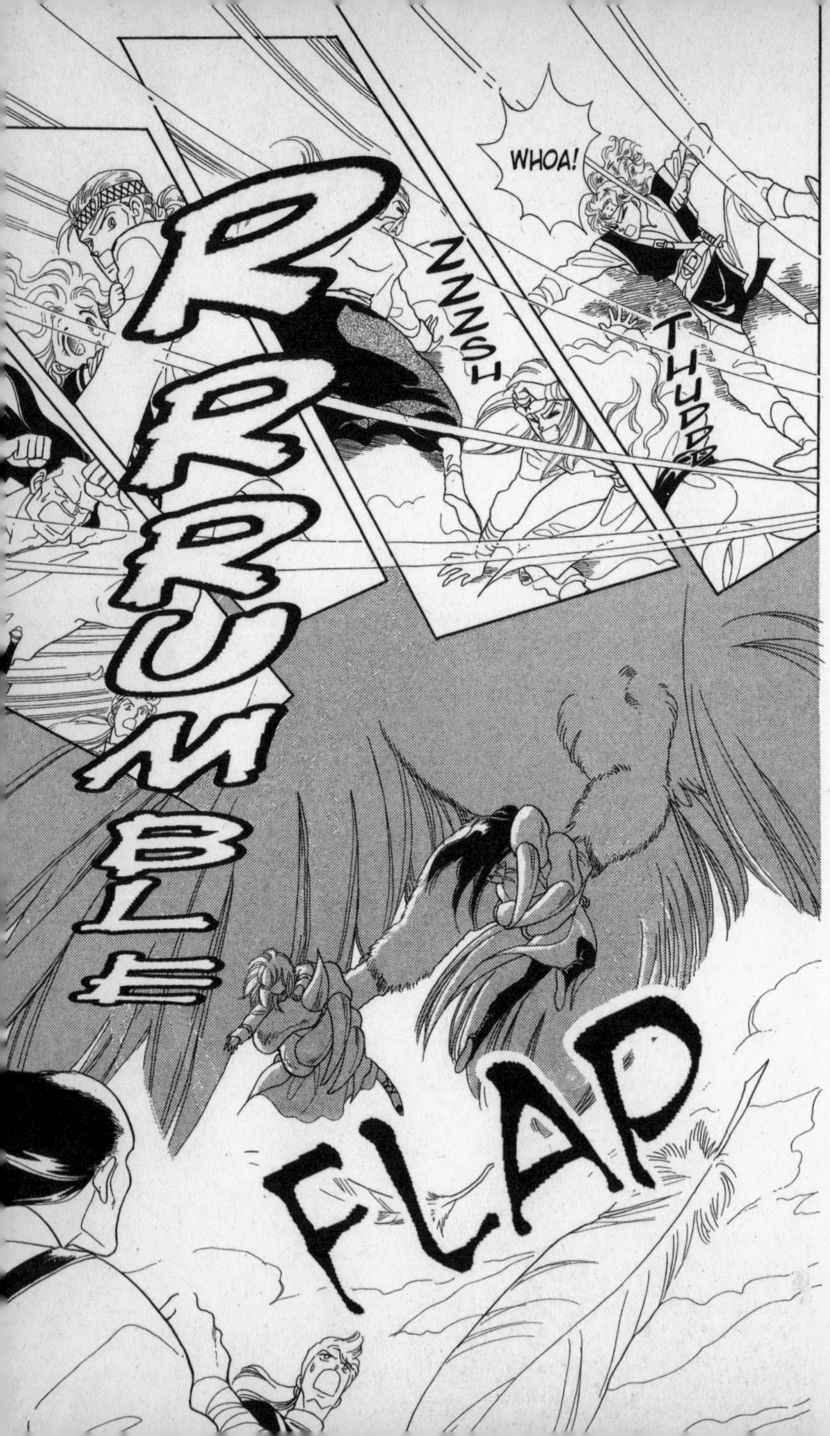
WHOA!
THUDD
ZZZZSH
RRRUMBLE
FLAP

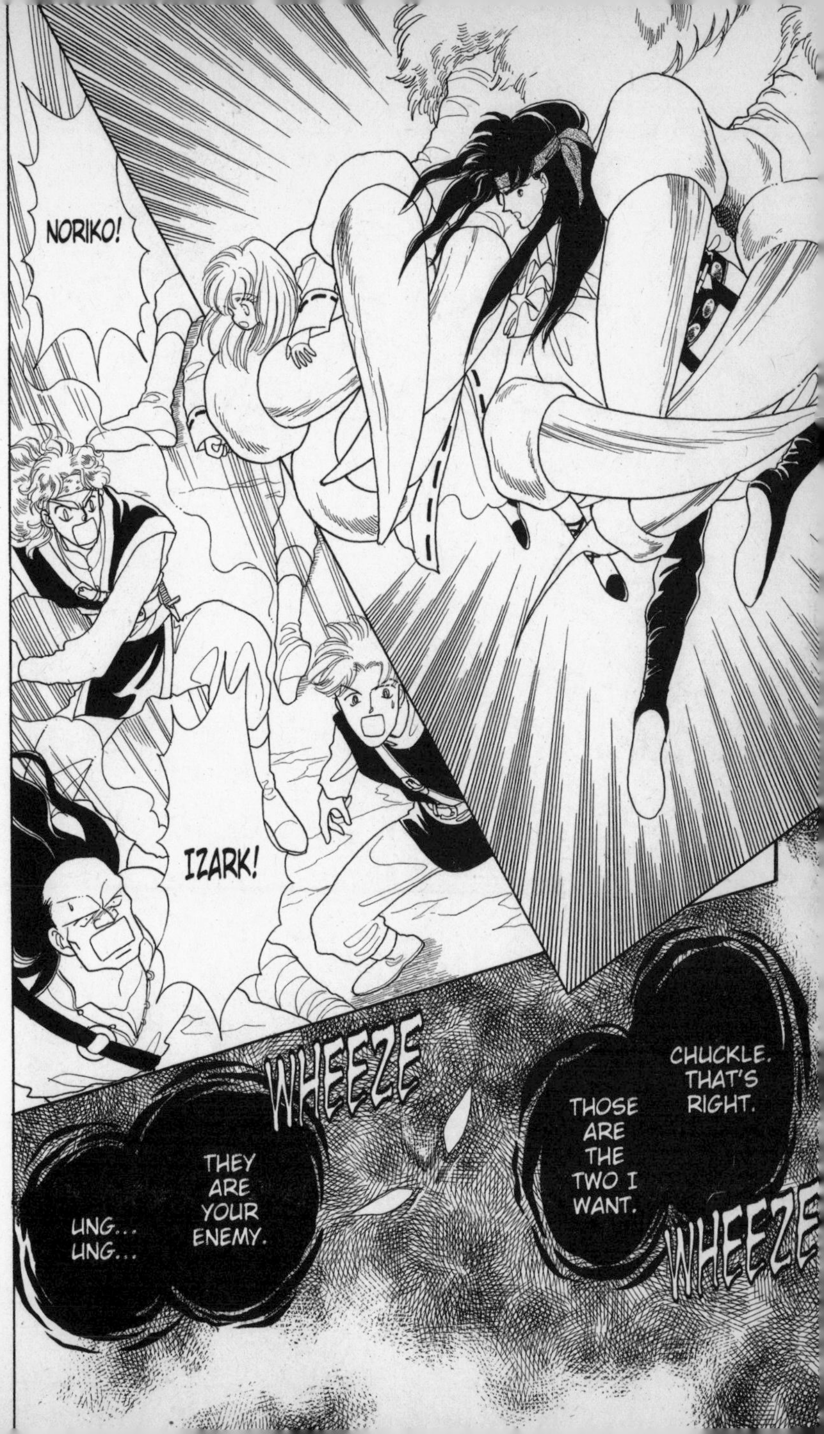
NORIKO!
IZARK!
CHUCKLE. THAT'S RIGHT.
THOSE ARE THE TWO I WANT.
WHEEZE
WHEEZE
THEY ARE YOUR ENEMY.
UNG... UNG...

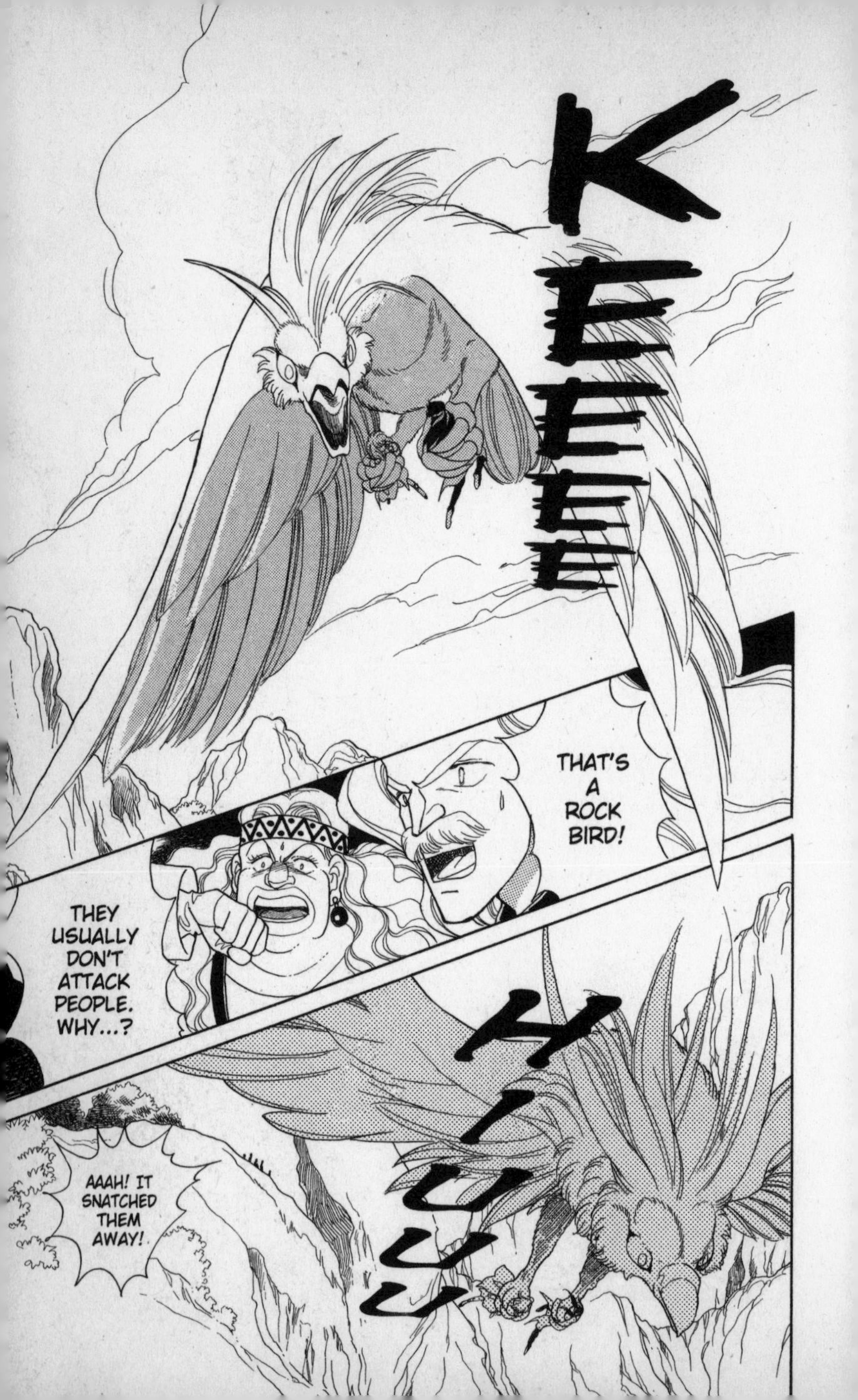
KEEEEE
THAT'S A ROCK BIRD!
THEY USUALLY DON'T ATTACK PEOPLE. WHY...?
HYUUU
AAAH! IT SNATCHED THEM AWAY!

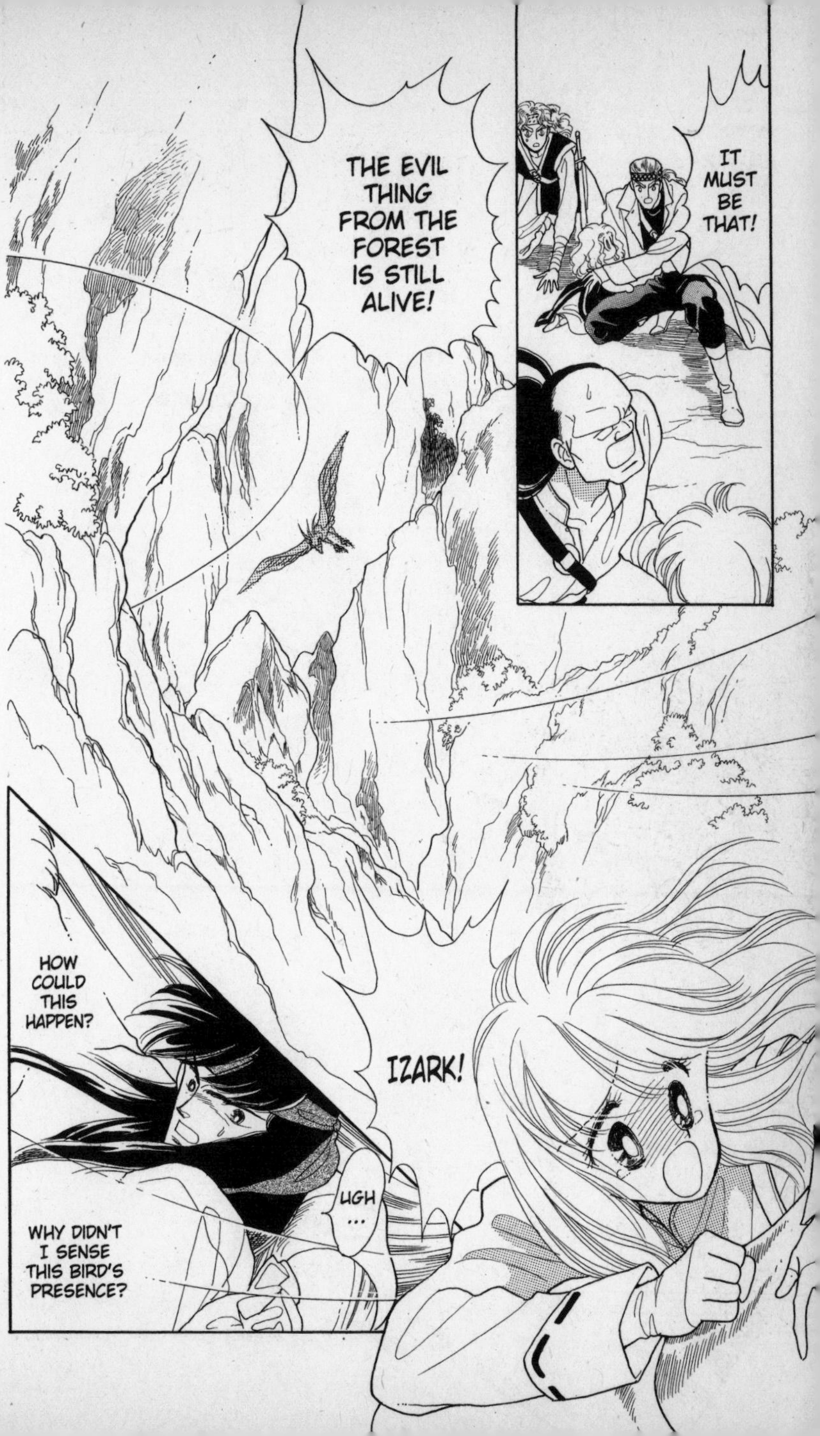
IT MUST BE THAT!
THE EVIL THING FROM THE FOREST IS STILL ALIVE!
IZARK!
HOW COULD THIS HAPPEN?
UGH ...
WHY DIDN'T I SENSE THIS BIRD'S PRESENCE?

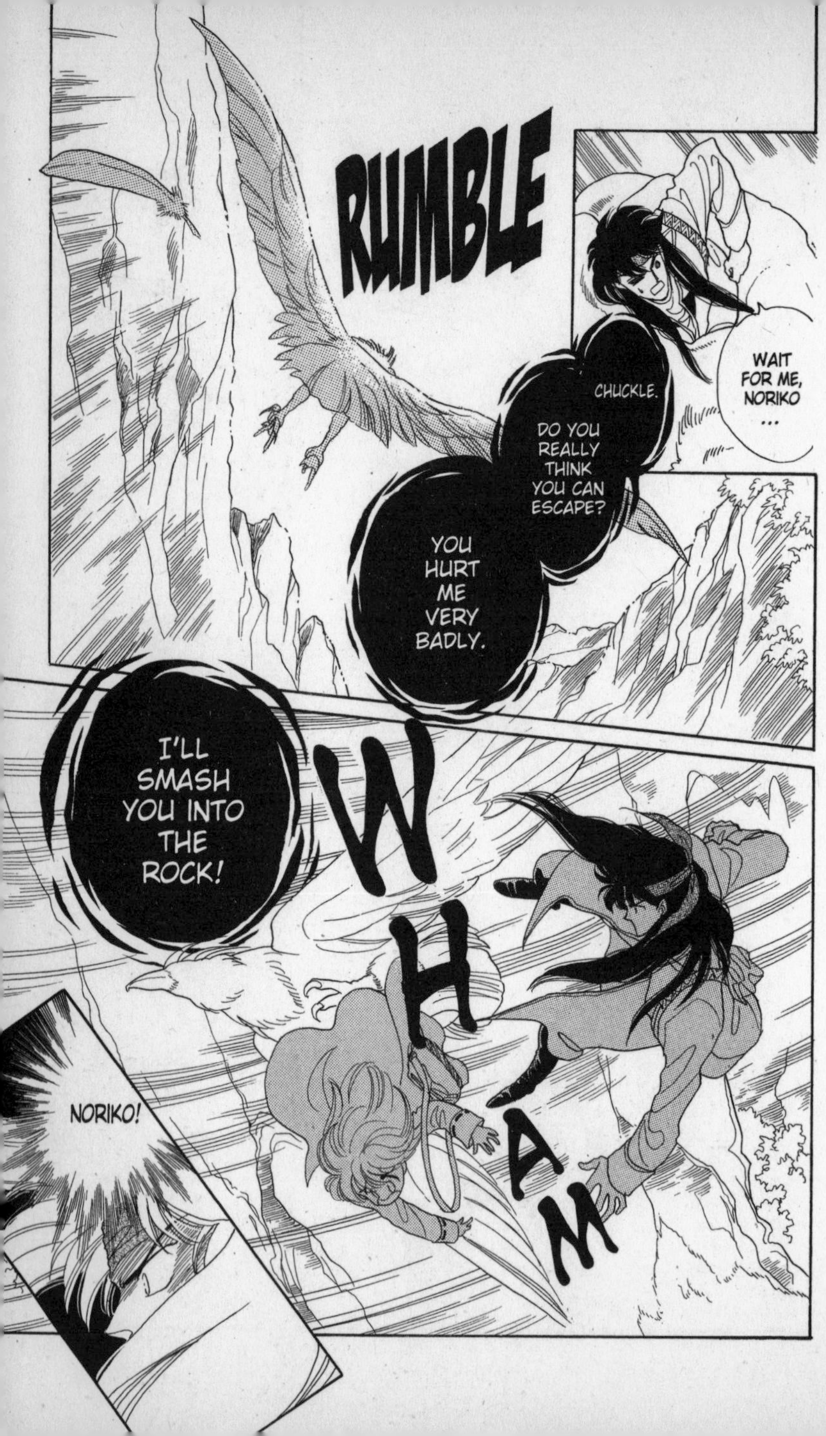
WAIT FOR ME, NORIKO ...
RUMBLE
CHUCKLE.
DO YOU REALLY THINK YOU CAN ESCAPE?
YOU HURT ME VERY BADLY.
I'LL SMASH YOU INTO THE ROCK!
WHAM
NORIKO!

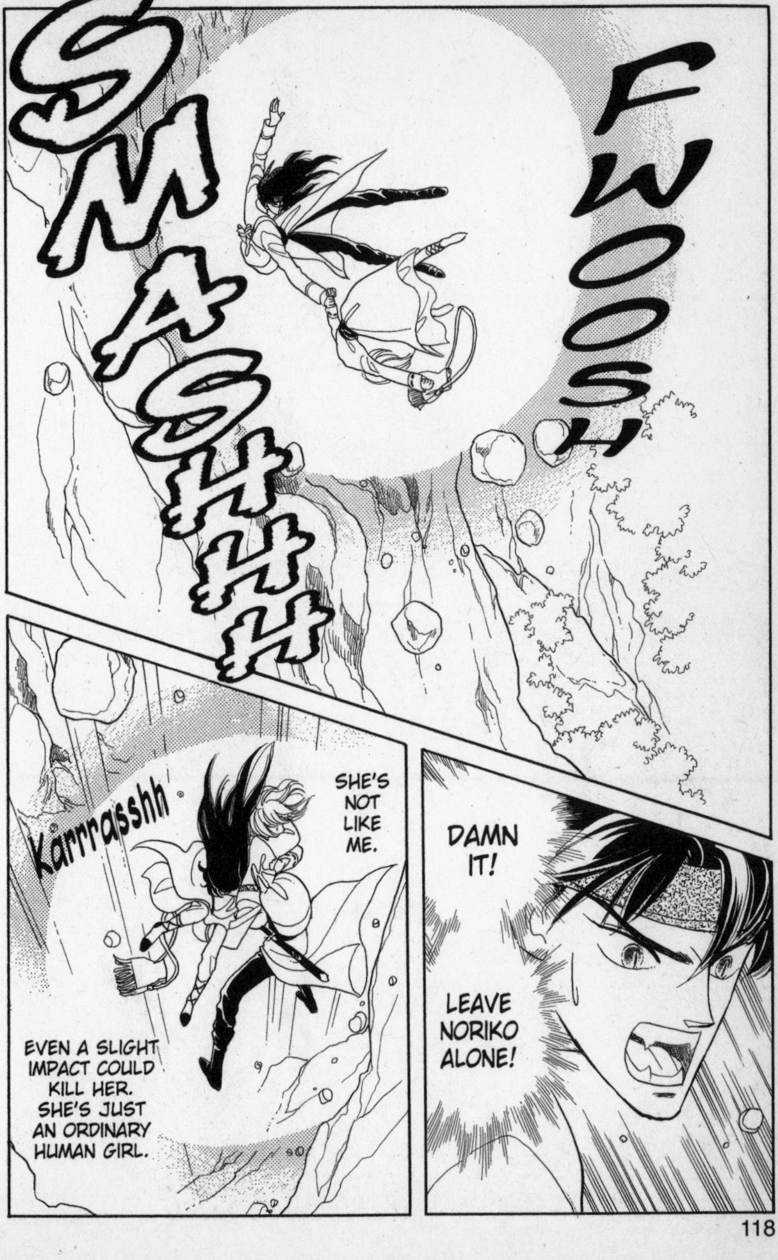
FWOOSH
SMASHHH
DAMN IT!
LEAVE NORIKO ALONE!
SHE'S NOT LIKE ME.
Karrrasshh
EVEN A SLIGHT IMPACT COULD KILL HER. SHE'S JUST AN ORDINARY HUMAN GIRL.

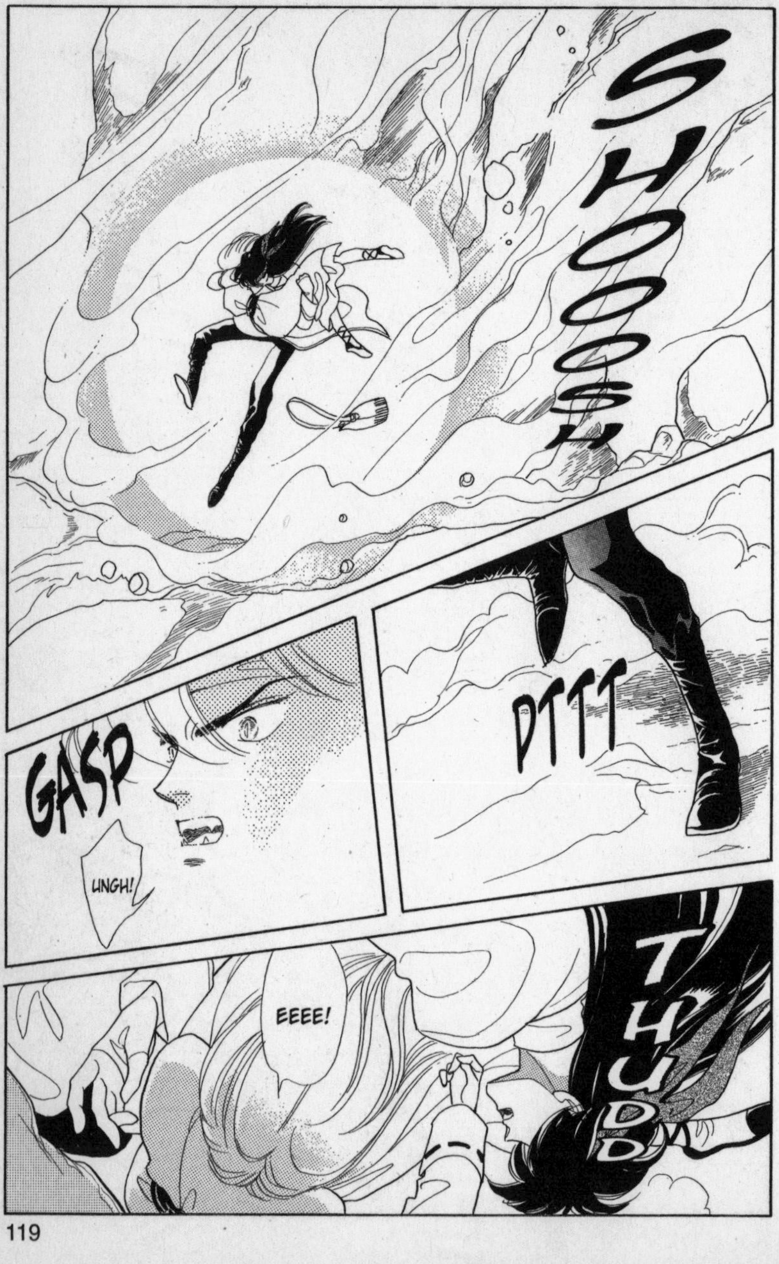
SHOOOOSH
DTTT
GASP
UNGH!
THUDD
EEEE!

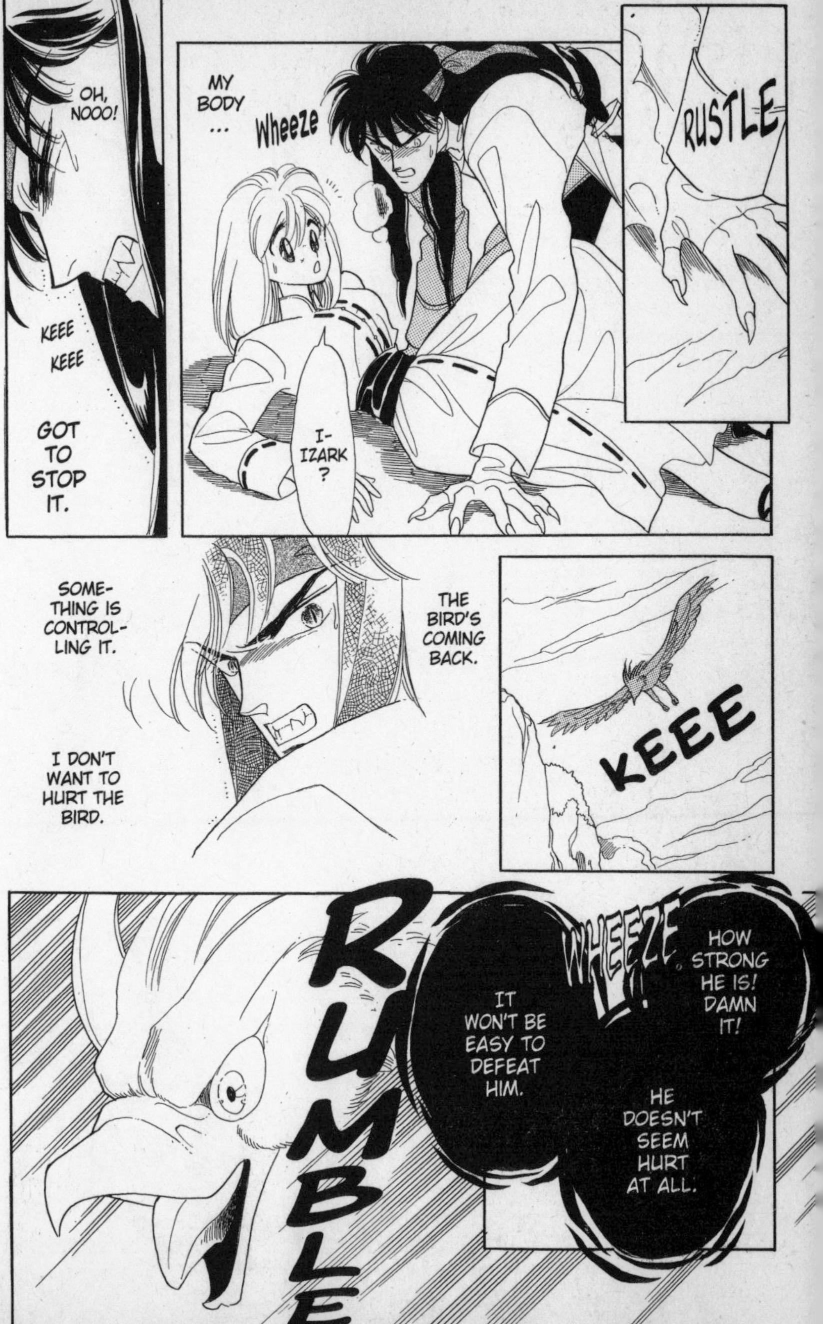
RUSTLE
MY BODY ...
Wheeze
I- IZARK ?
OH, NOOO!
KEEE KEEE
GOT TO STOP IT.
KEEE
THE BIRD'S COMING BACK.
SOME- THING IS CONTROL- LING IT.
I DON'T WANT TO HURT THE BIRD.
HOW STRONG HE IS! DAMN IT!
WHEEZE
IT WON'T BE EASY TO DEFEAT HIM.
HE DOESN'T SEEM HURT AT ALL.
RUMBLE

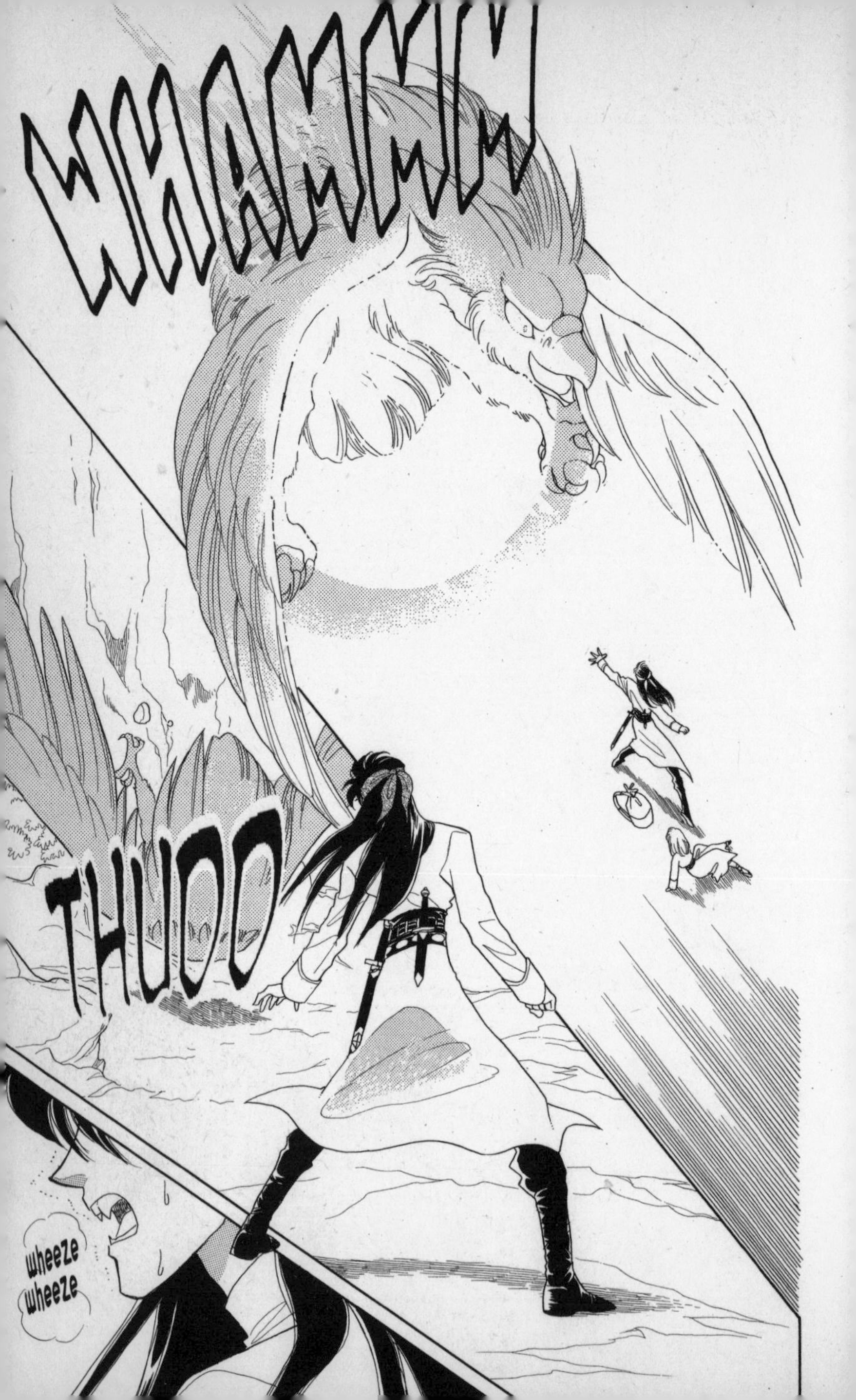
WHAMMM
THUDD
wheeze wheeze

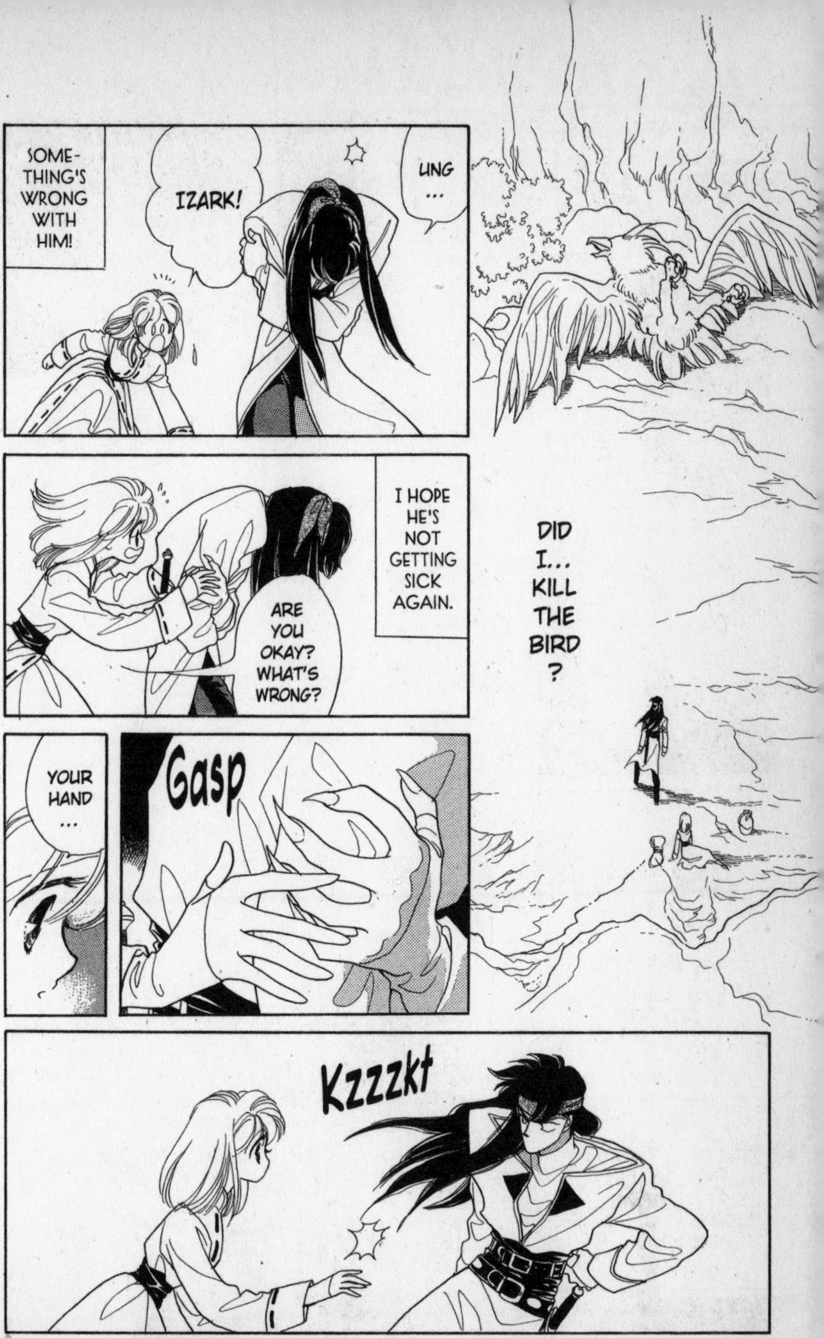
DID I... KILL THE BIRD ?
UNG ...
IZARK!
SOME-THING'S WRONG WITH HIM!
I HOPE HE'S NOT GETTING SICK AGAIN.
ARE YOU OKAY? WHAT'S WRONG?
Gasp
YOUR HAND ...
Kzzzkt

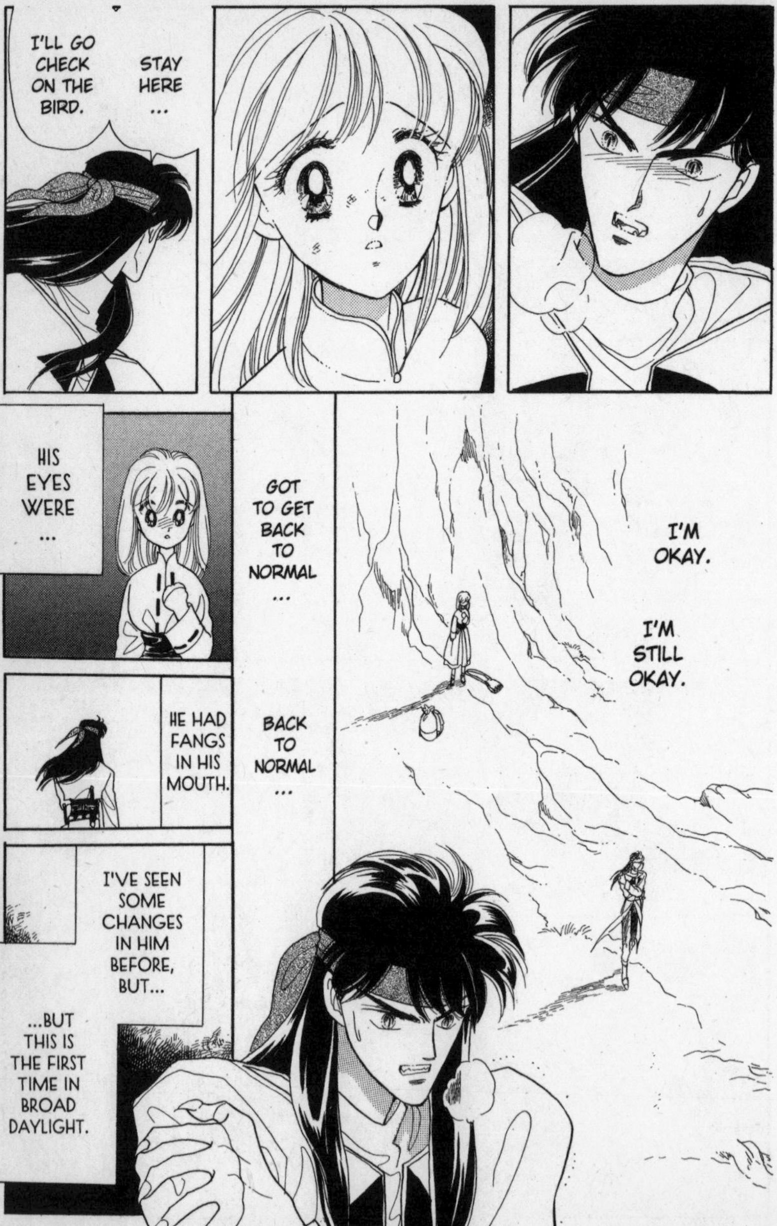
I'LL GO CHECK ON THE BIRD.
STAY HERE...
I'M OKAY.
I'M STILL OKAY.
GOT TO GET BACK TO NORMAL...
BACK TO NORMAL...
HIS EYES WERE...
HE HAD FANGS IN HIS MOUTH.
I'VE SEEN SOME CHANGES IN HIM BEFORE, BUT...
...BUT THIS IS THE FIRST TIME IN BROAD DAYLIGHT.

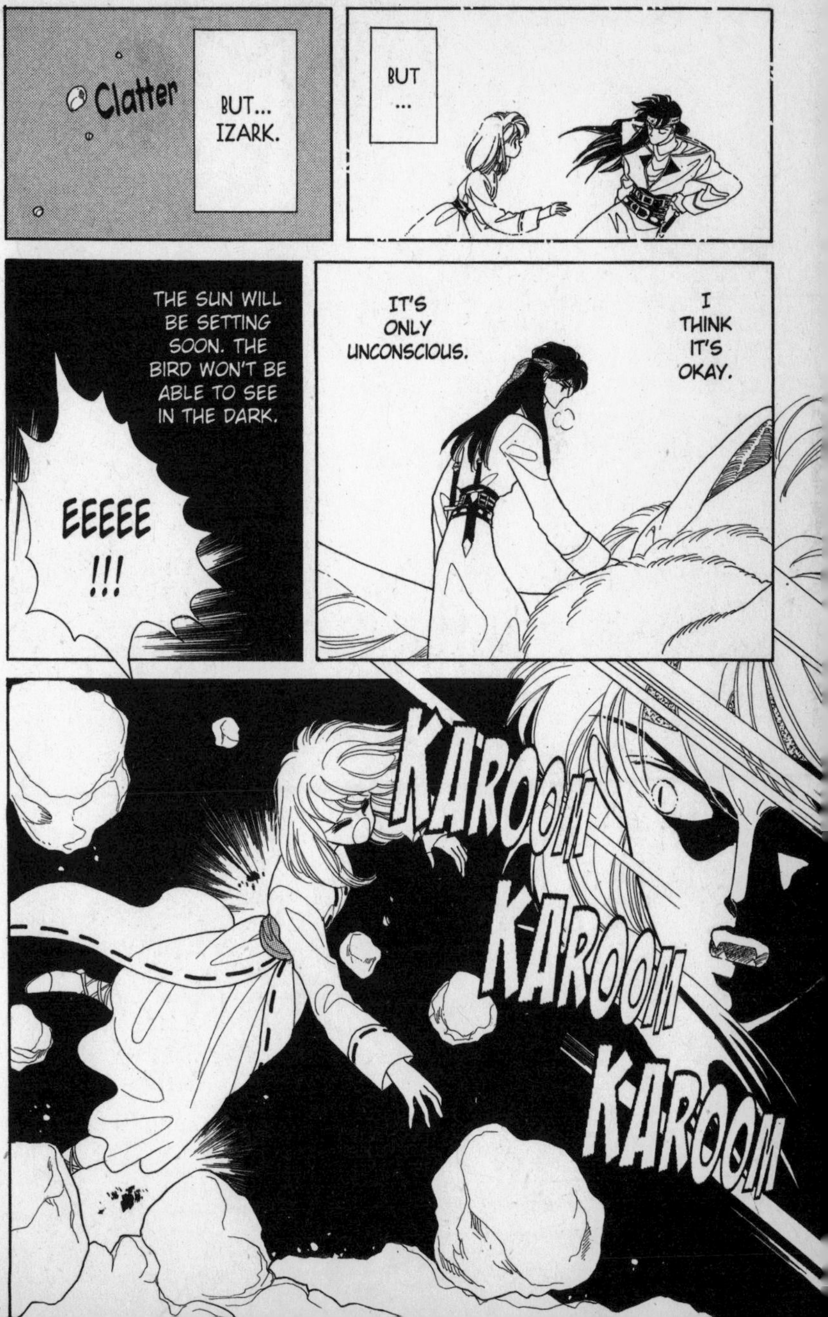
BUT ...
BUT... IZARK.
Clatter
I THINK IT'S OKAY.
IT'S ONLY UNCONSCIOUS.
THE SUN WILL BE SETTING SOON. THE BIRD WON'T BE ABLE TO SEE IN THE DARK.
EEEEE !!!
KAROOM
KAROOM
KAROOM

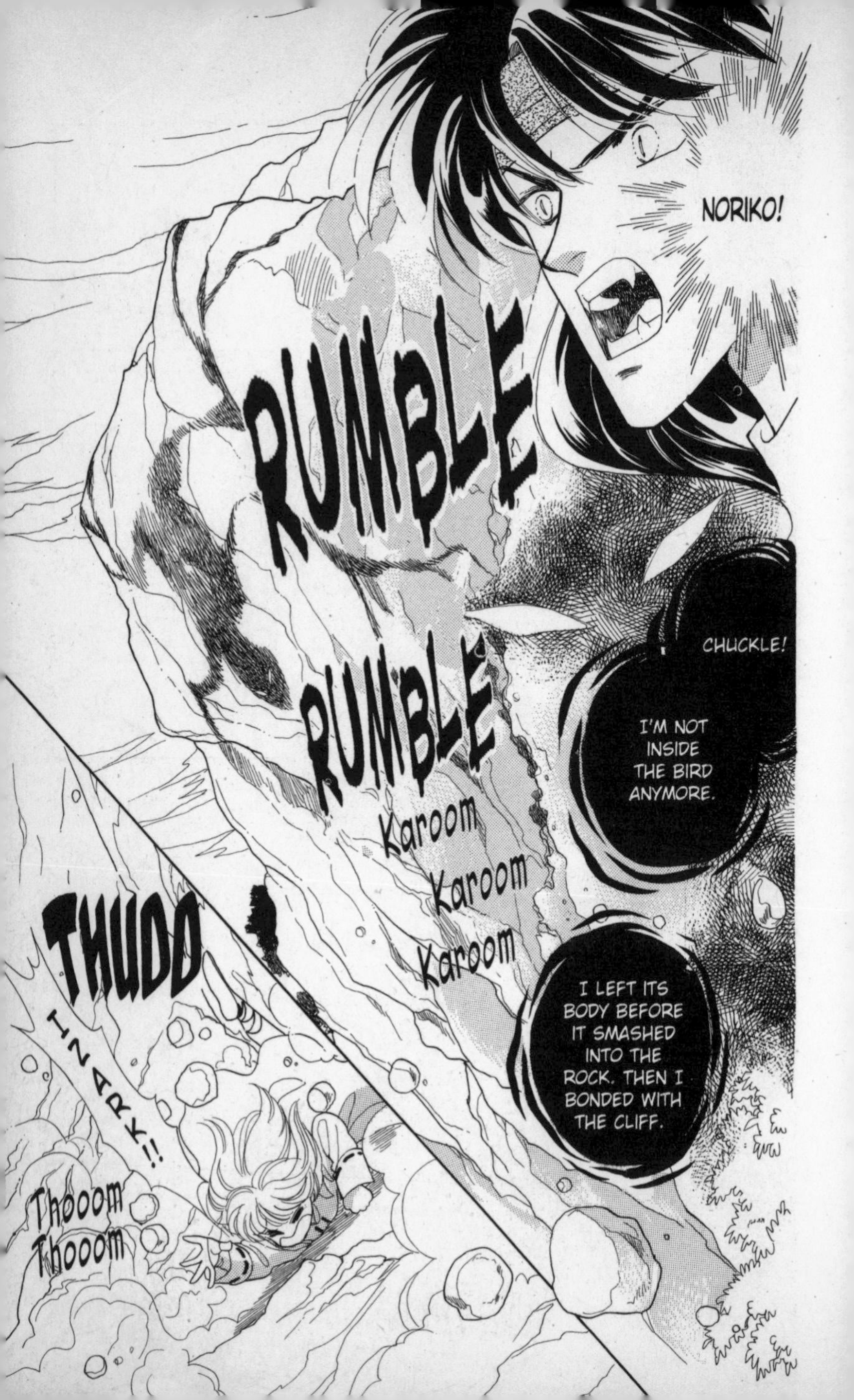
NORIKO!
RUMBLE
RUMBLE
CHUCKLE!
I'M NOT INSIDE THE BIRD ANYMORE.
Karoom
Karoom
Karoom
I LEFT ITS BODY BEFORE IT SMASHED INTO THE ROCK. THEN I BONDED WITH THE CLIFF.
THUDD
INARK!!
Thooom
Thooom

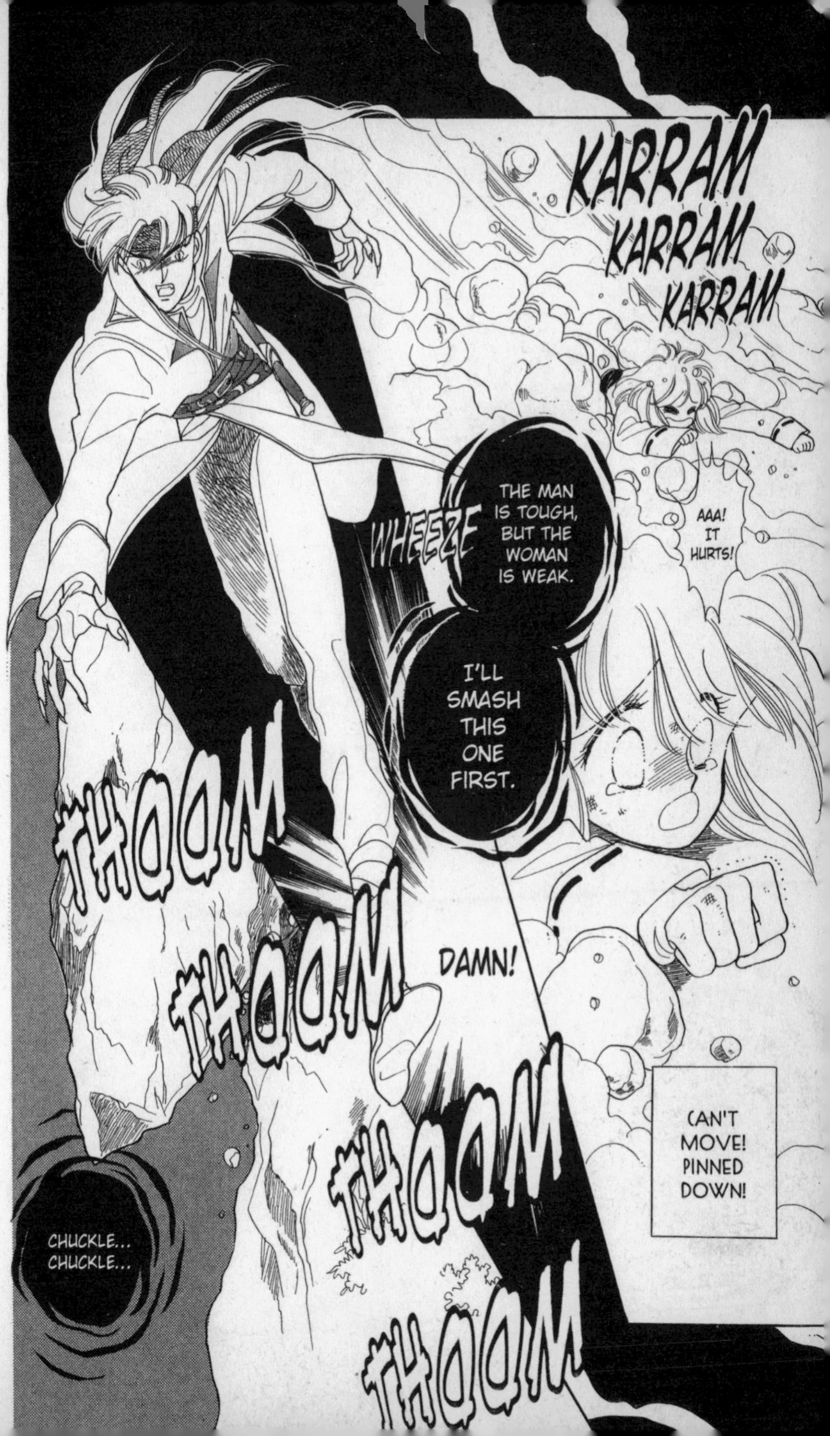
KARRAM
KARRAM
KARRAM
AAA! IT HURTS!
WHEEZE
THE MAN IS TOUGH, BUT THE WOMAN IS WEAK.
I'LL SMASH THIS ONE FIRST.
CAN'T MOVE! PINNED DOWN!
DAMN!
THOOM
THOOM
THOOM
THOOM
CHUCKLE... CHUCKLE...

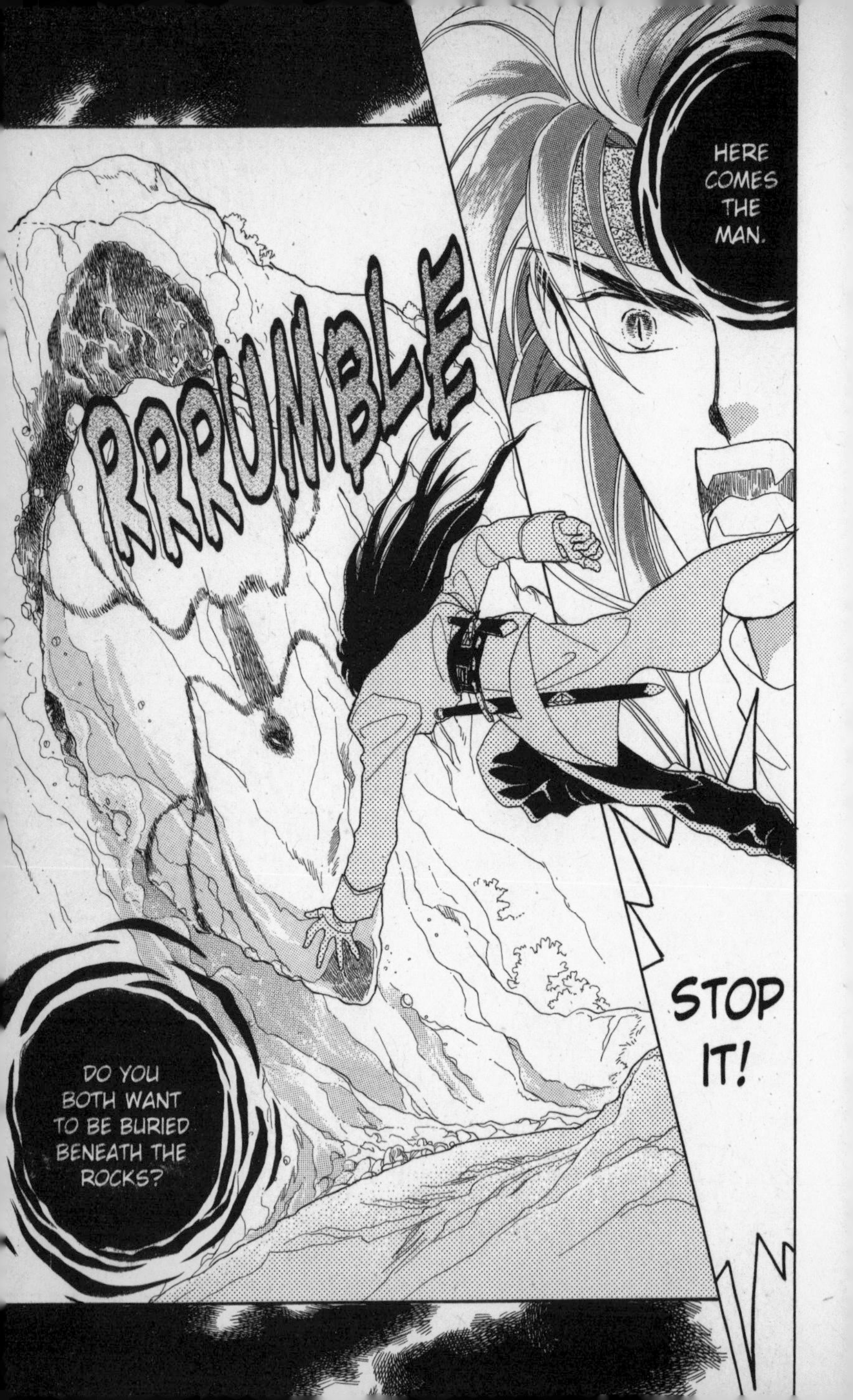
HERE COMES THE MAN.
STOP IT!
RRRUMBLE
DO YOU BOTH WANT TO BE BURIED BENEATH THE ROCKS?

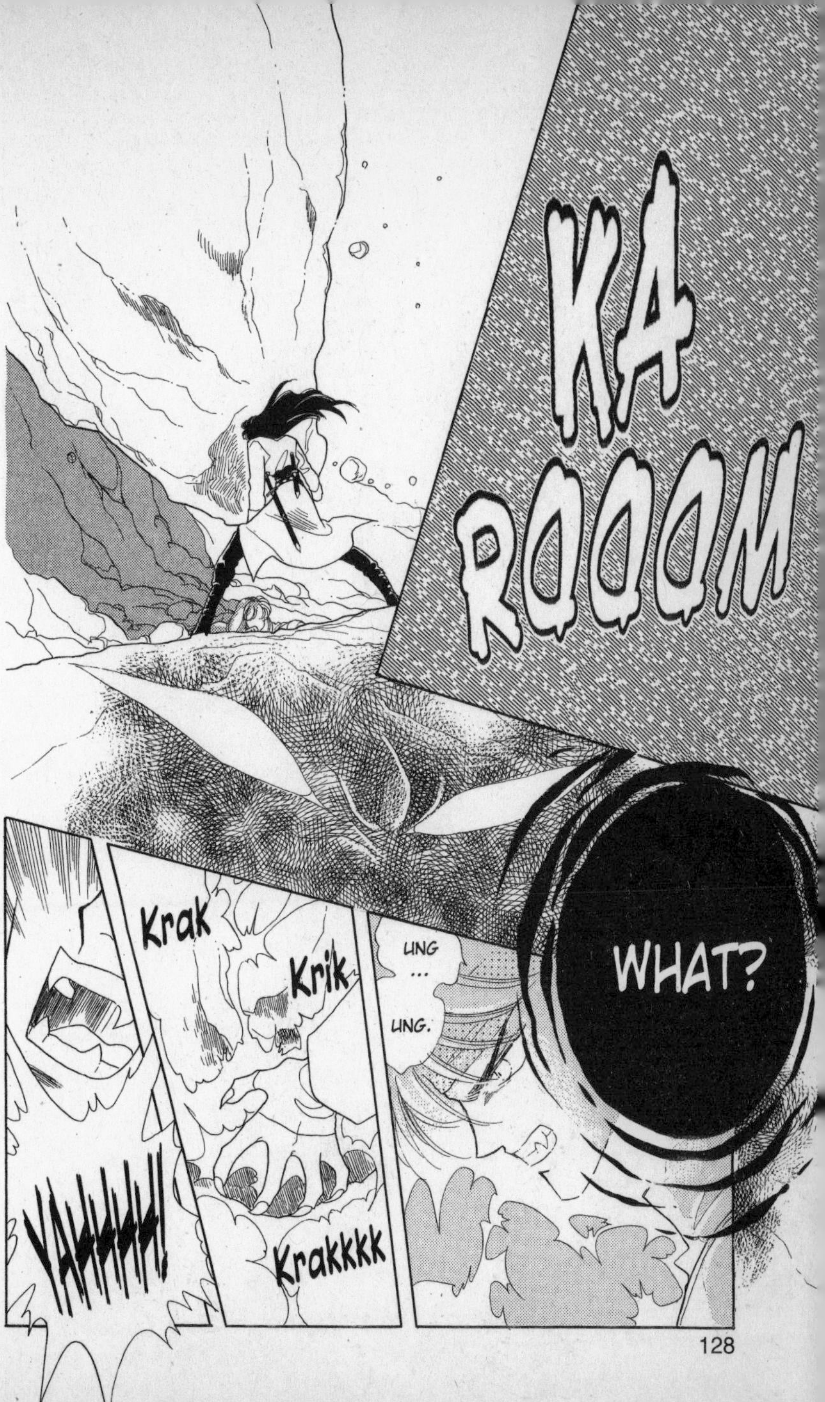
KA ROOOM
WHAT?
UNG ... UNG.
Krak
Krik
Krakkkk
YAHHHH!

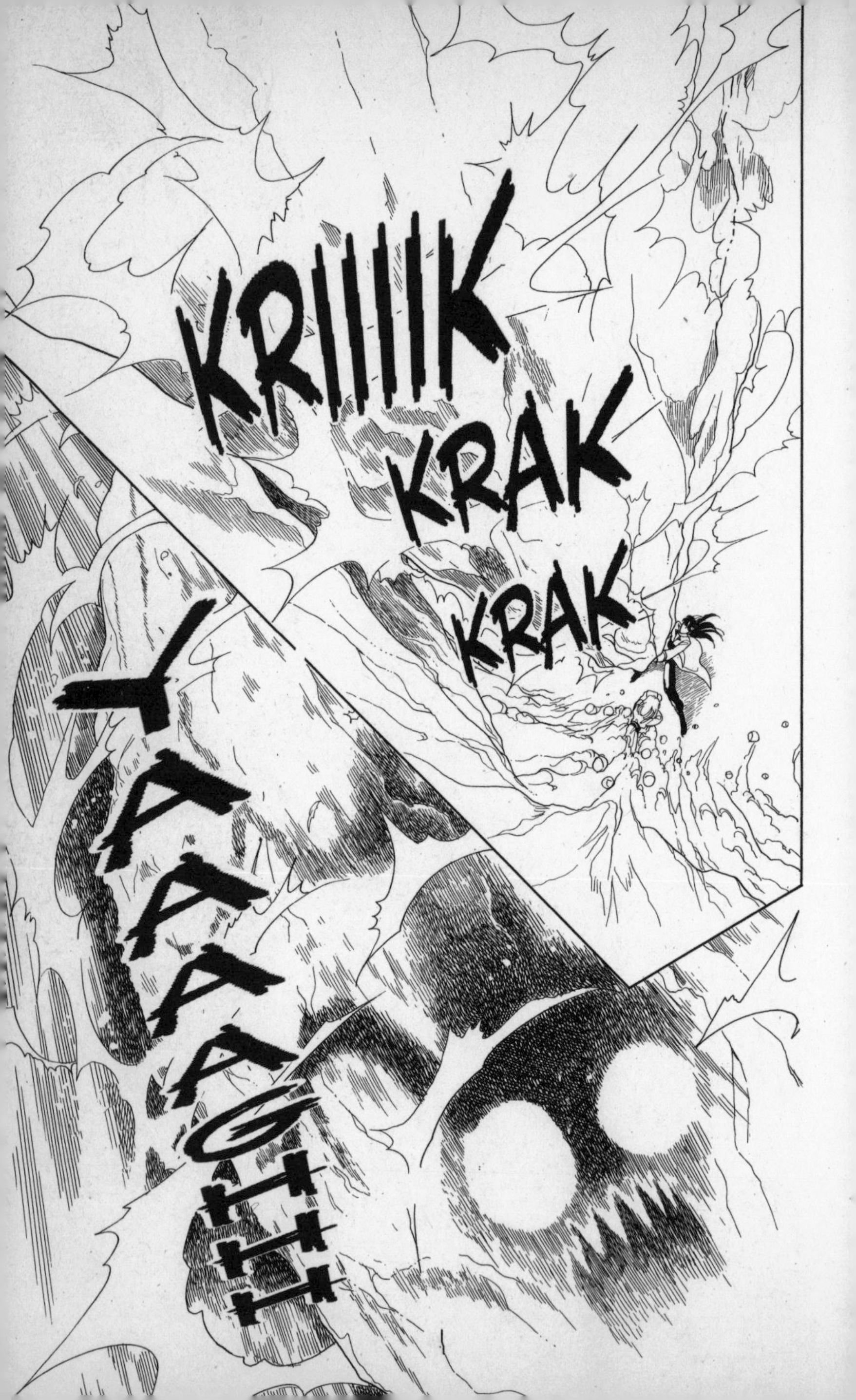
KRIIIIK
KRAK
KRAK
YAAAAGIII

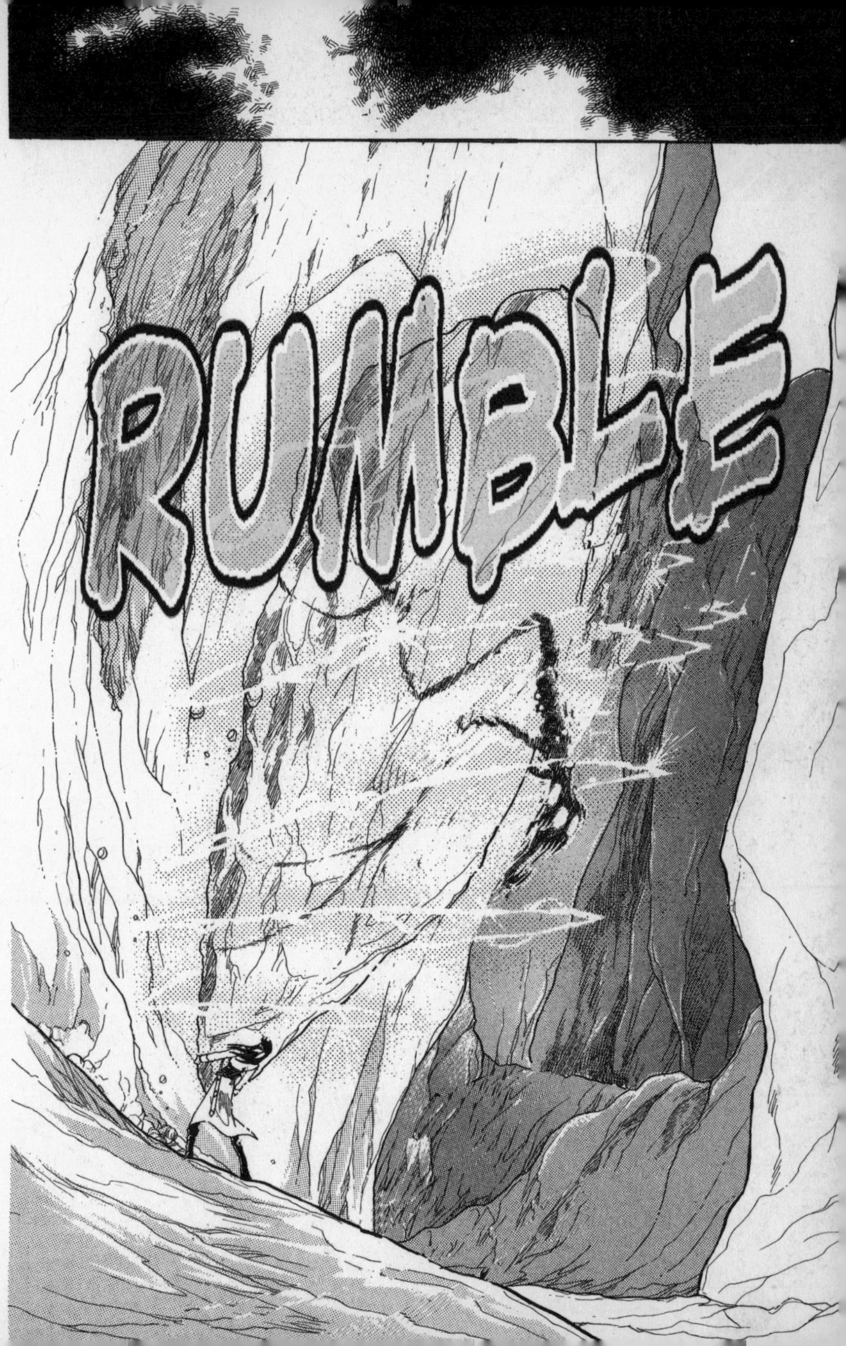
RUMBLE

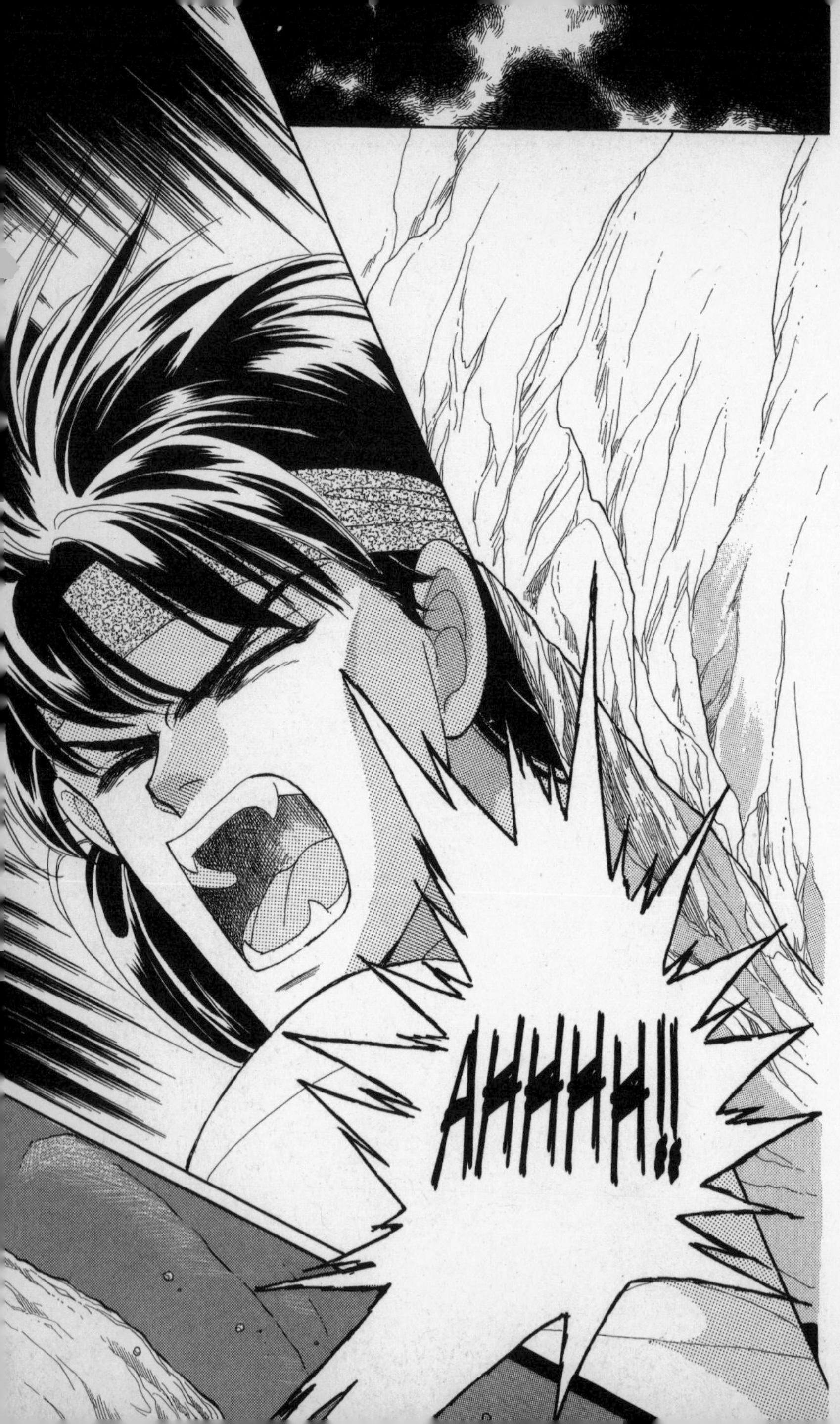
AHHHH!!

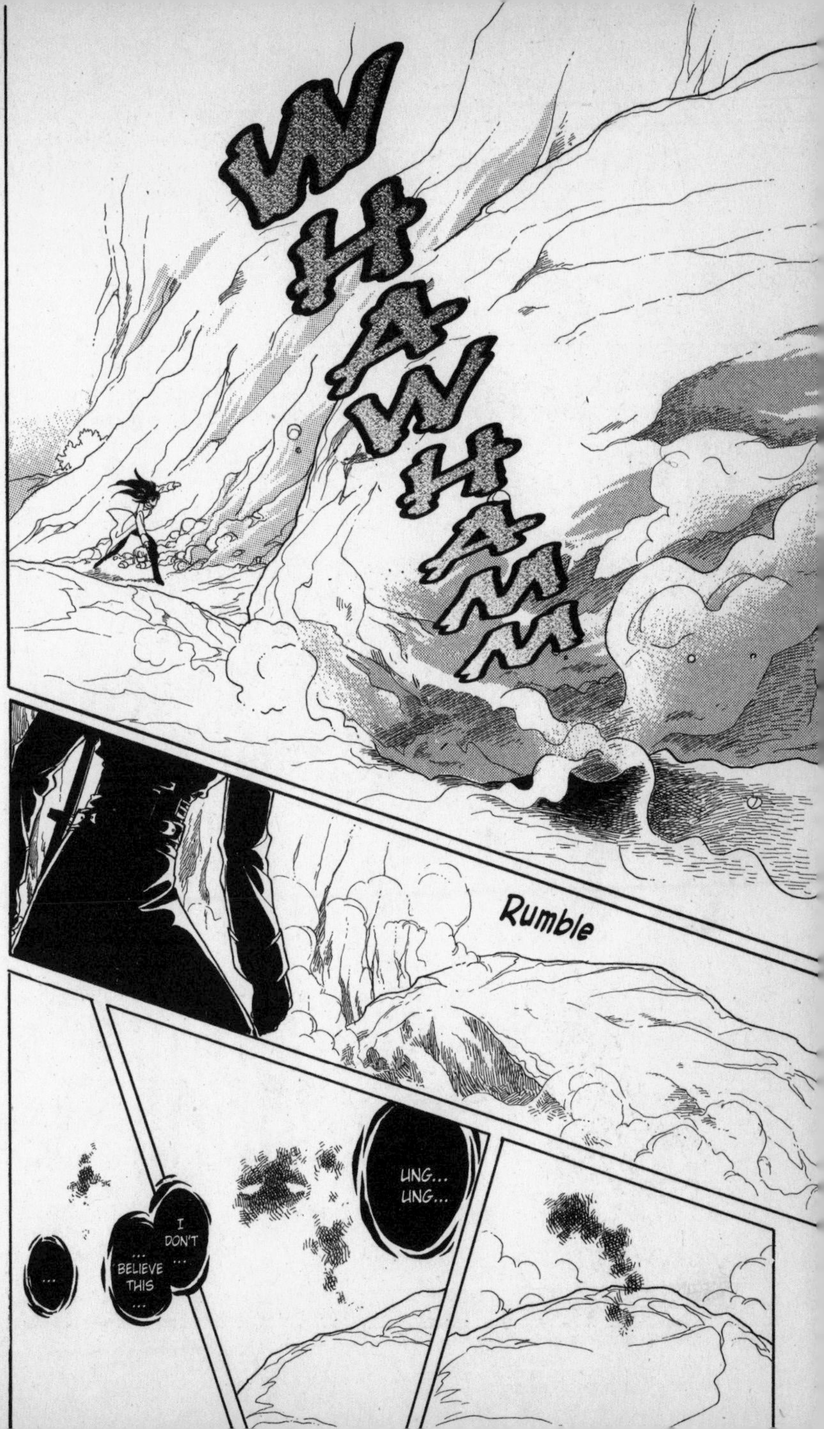
WHAWHAMM
Rumble
UNG... UNG...
I DON'T... ...BELIEVE THIS...
...

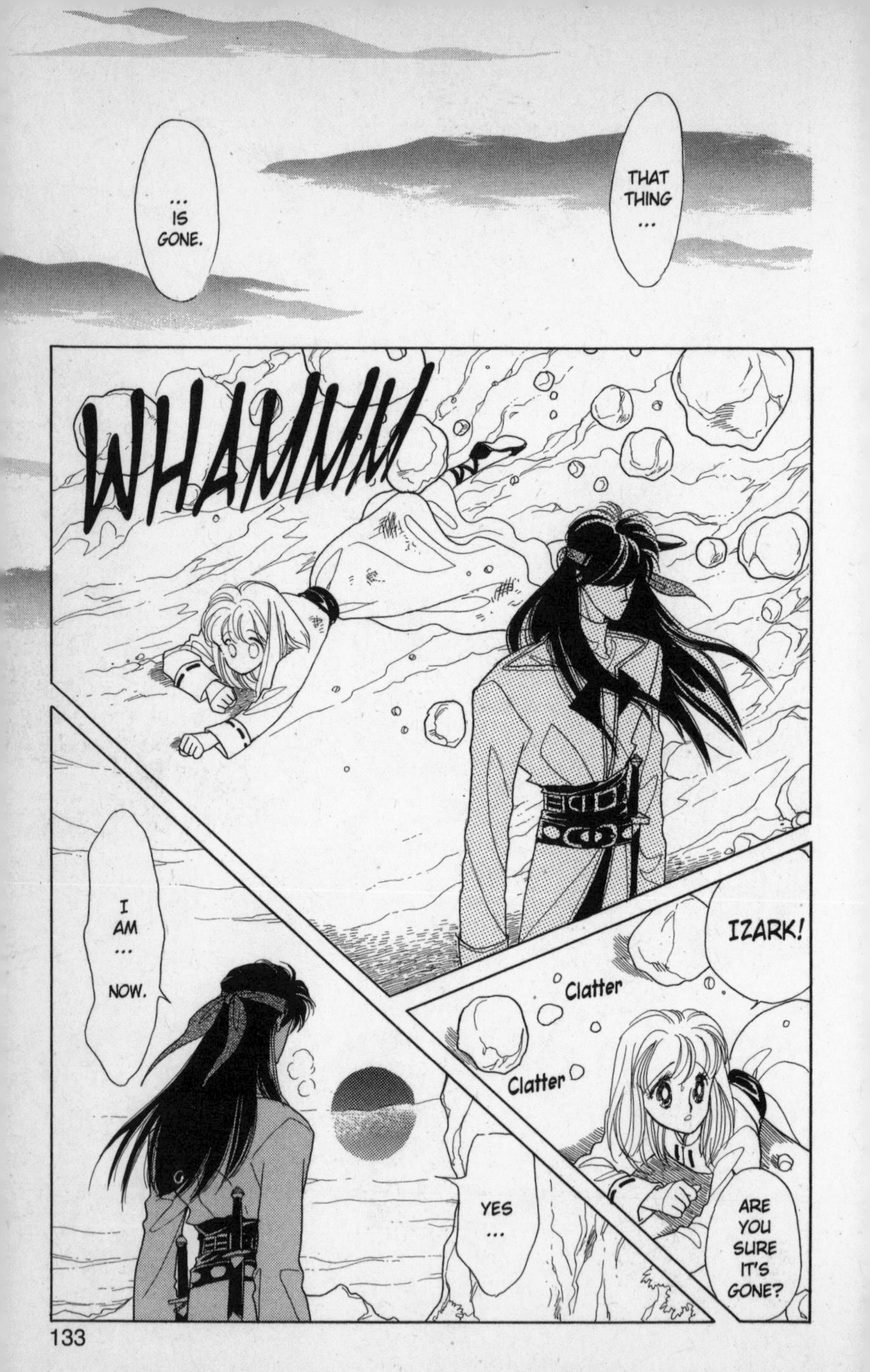
THAT THING ...
... IS GONE.
WHAMMM
IZARK!
Clatter
Clatter
ARE YOU SURE IT'S GONE?
YES ...
I AM ... NOW.

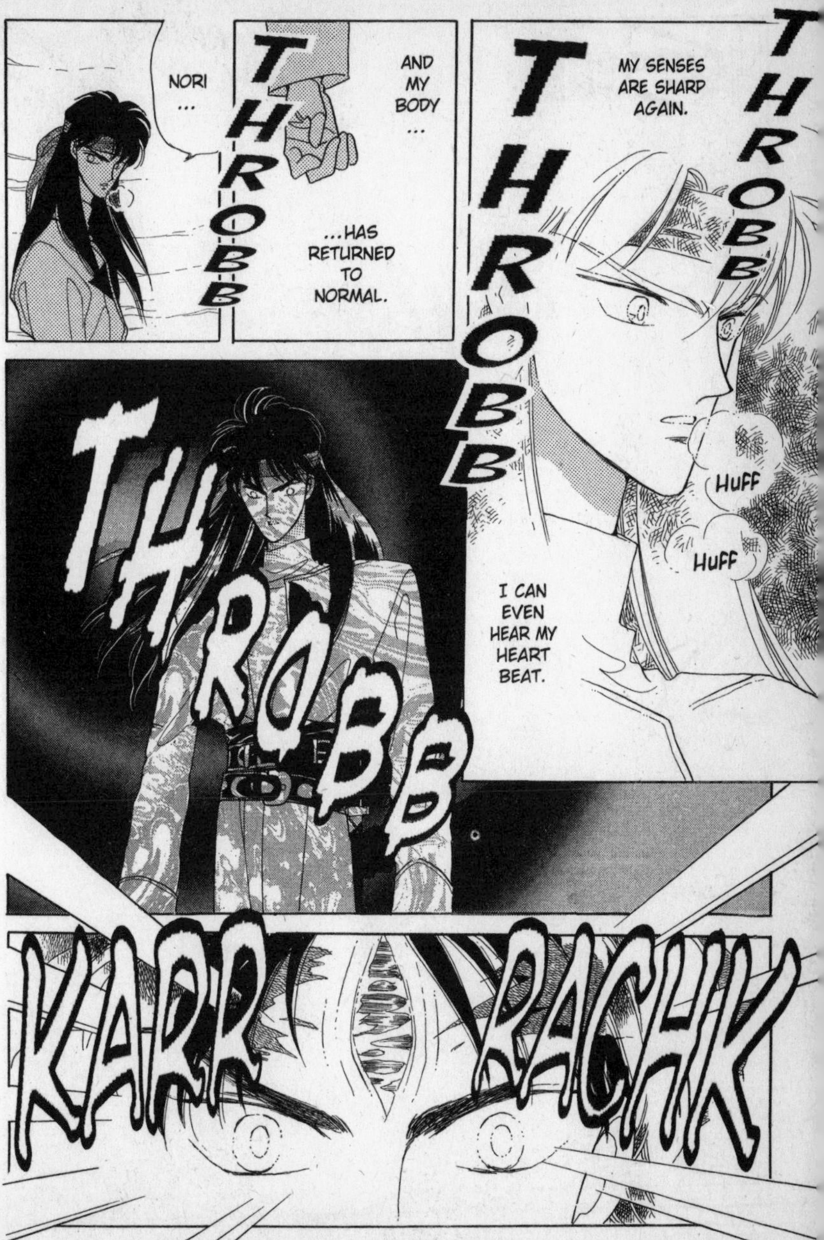
THROBB
MY SENSES ARE SHARP AGAIN.
THROBB
Huff
Huff
I CAN EVEN HEAR MY HEART BEAT.
AND MY BODY ...
...HAS RETURNED TO NORMAL.
THROBB
NORI ...
THROBB
KARR RACHK

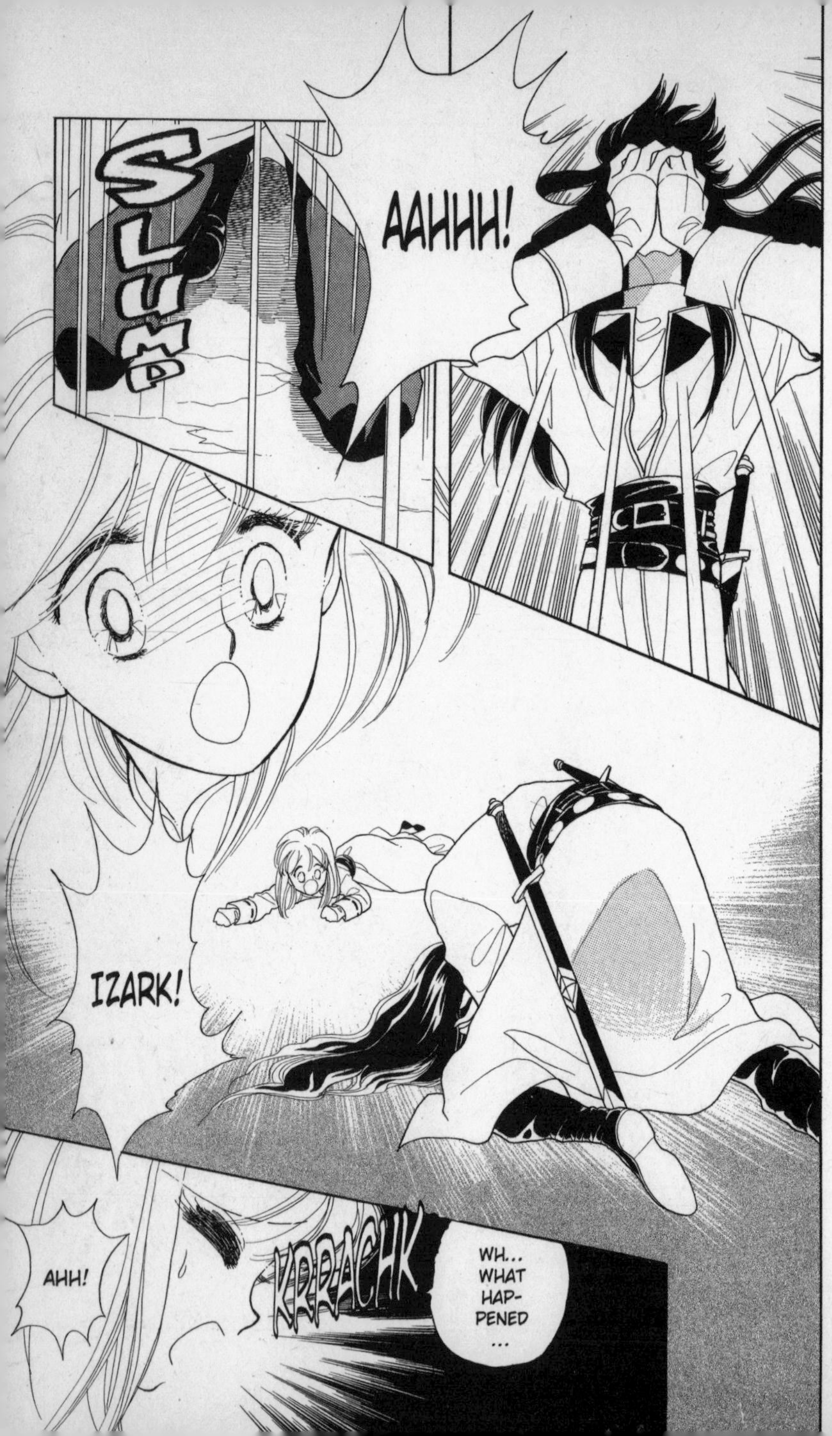
AAHHH!
SLUMP
IZARK!
WH... WHAT HAP-PENED ...
KRRACHK
AHH!

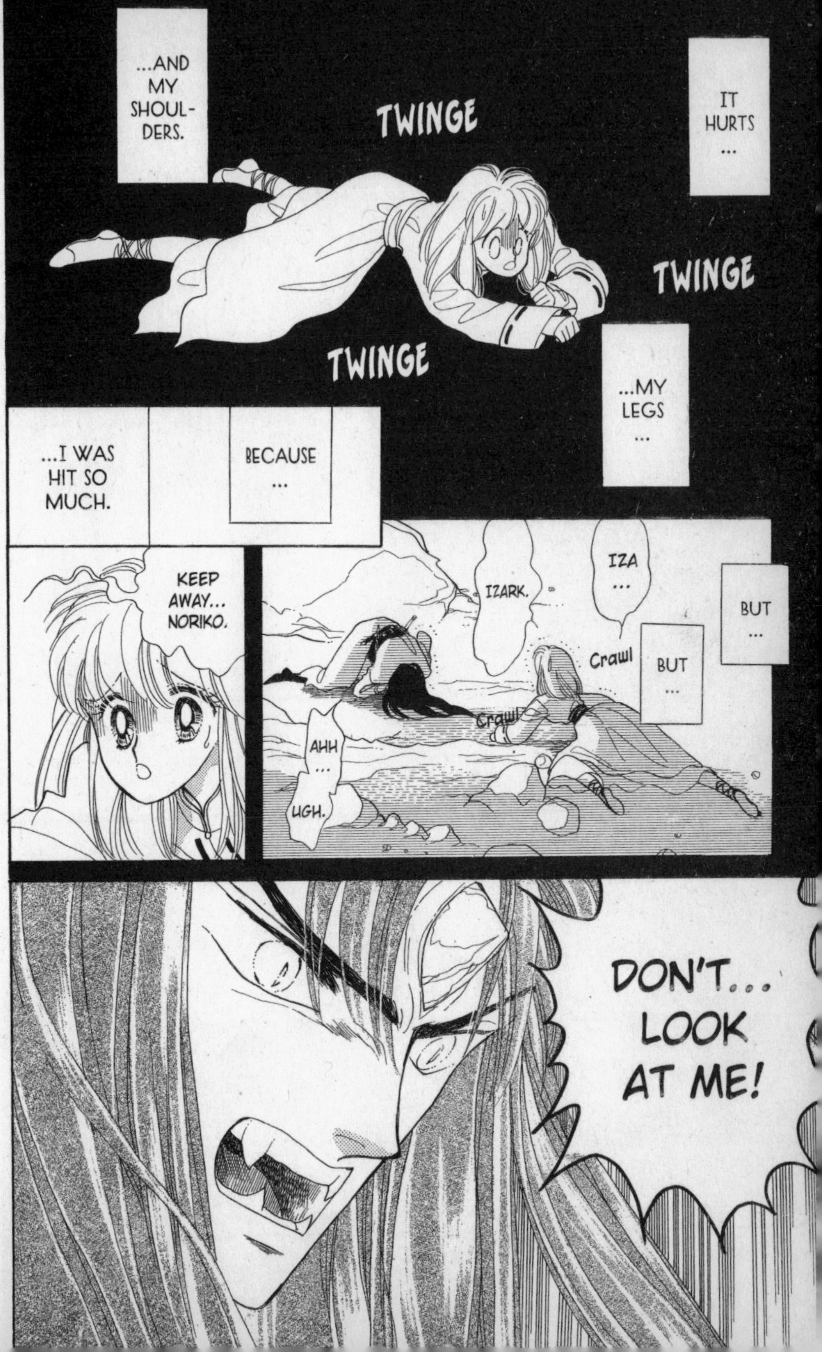
IT HURTS ...
TWINGE
...MY LEGS ...
TWINGE
...AND MY SHOUL-DERS.
TWINGE
BECAUSE ...
...I WAS HIT SO MUCH.
BUT ...
BUT ...
IZA ...
IZARK.
Crawl
Crawl
AHH ...
UGH.
KEEP AWAY... NORIKO.
DON'T... LOOK AT ME!

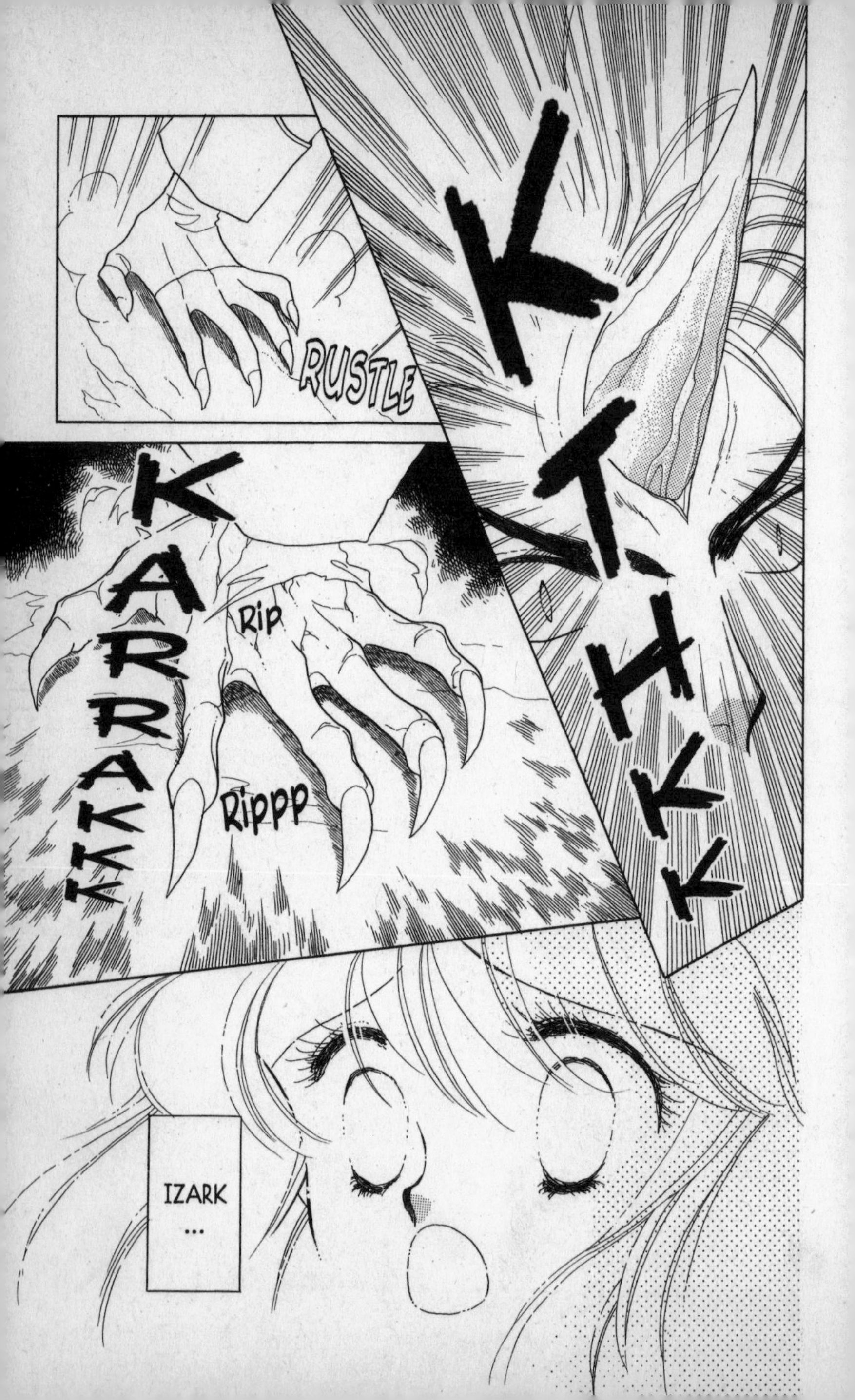
KTHKK
RUSTLE
KARRAKK
Rip
Rippp
IZARK
...

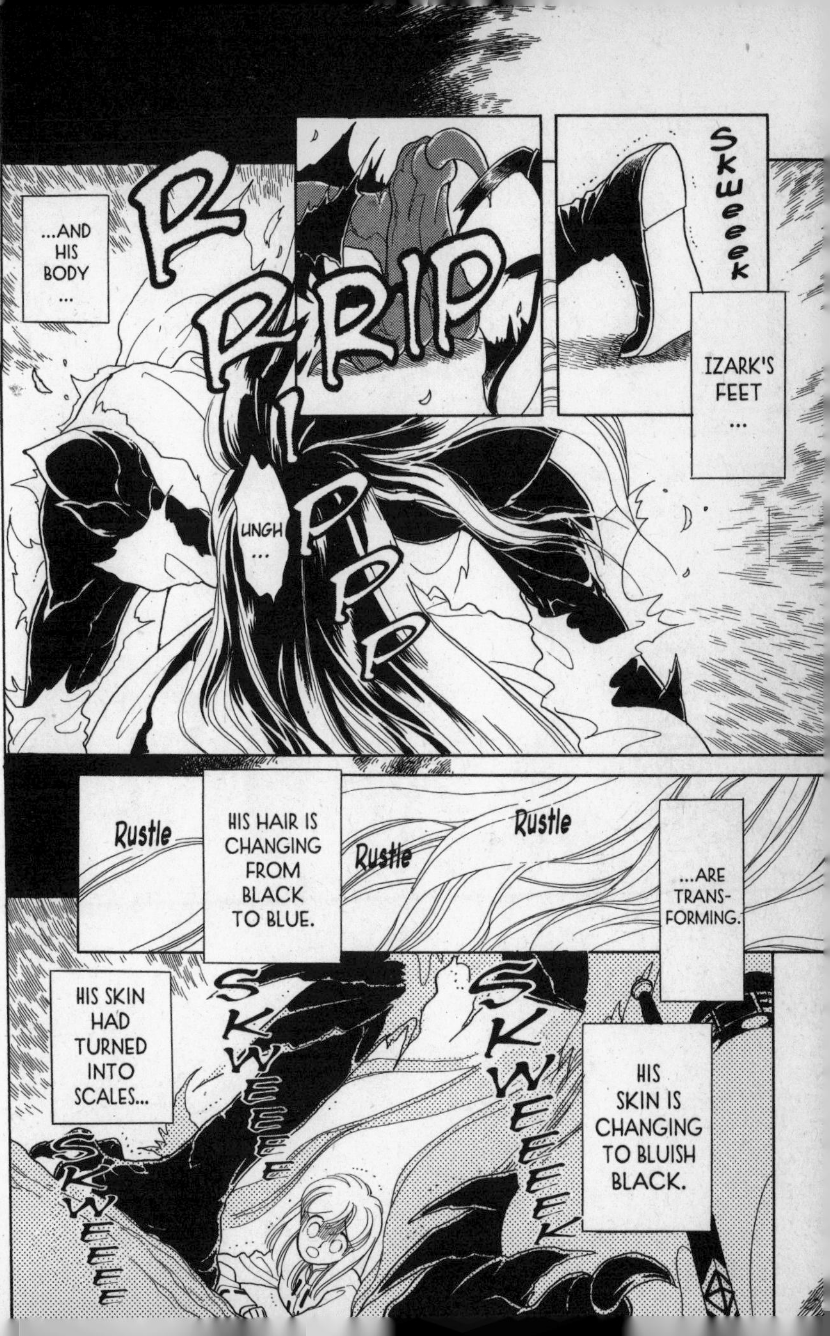
Skweeek
IZARK'S FEET ...
R
RRIP
...AND HIS BODY ...
UNGH ...
IPPPP
...ARE TRANS-FORMING.
Rustle
Rustle
HIS HAIR IS CHANGING FROM BLACK TO BLUE.
Rustle
HIS SKIN IS CHANGING TO BLUISH BLACK.
SKWEEEEK
SKWEEEE
HIS SKIN HAD TURNED INTO SCALES...
SKWEEEEE

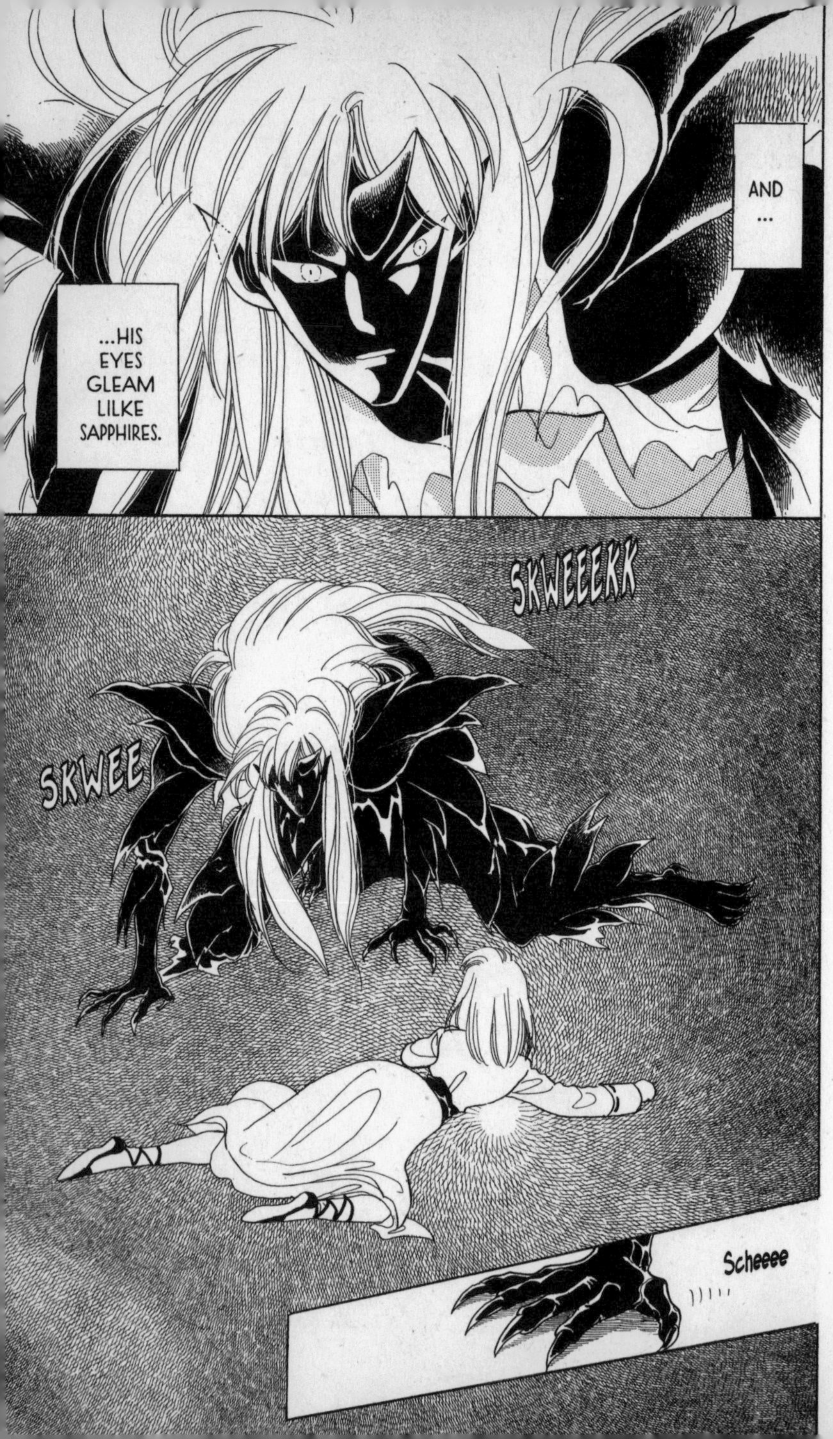
AND ...
...HIS EYES GLEAM LILKE SAPPHIRES.
SKWEEEKK
SKWEE
Scheeee

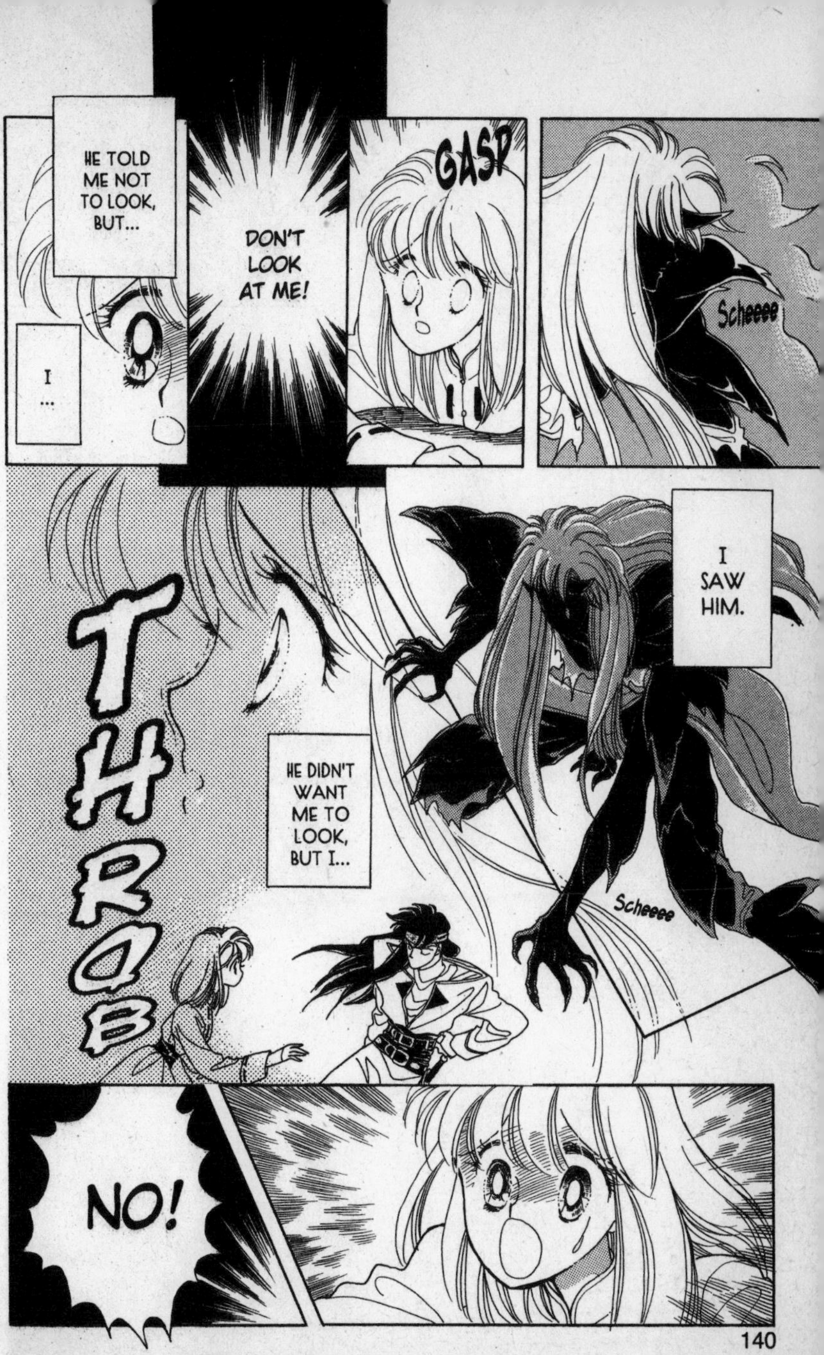
Scheeee
GASP
DON'T LOOK AT ME!
HE TOLD ME NOT TO LOOK, BUT...
I ...
I SAW HIM.
HE DIDN'T WANT ME TO LOOK, BUT I...
Scheeee
THROB
NO!

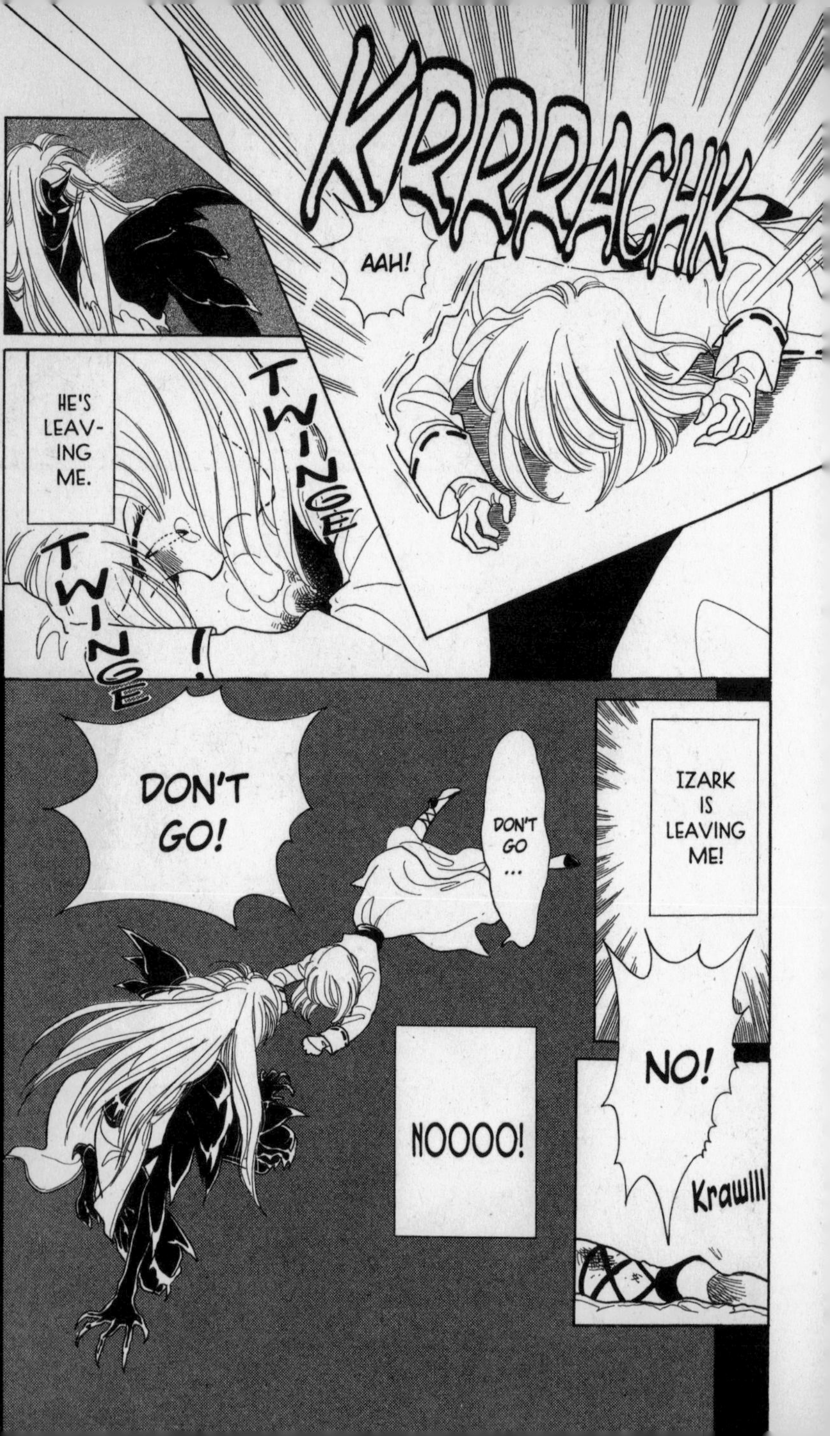
KRRRACHK
AAH!
HE'S LEAV-ING ME.
TWINGE
TWINGE
IZARK IS LEAVING ME!
NO!
Krawlll
DON'T GO ...
DON'T GO!
NOOOO!

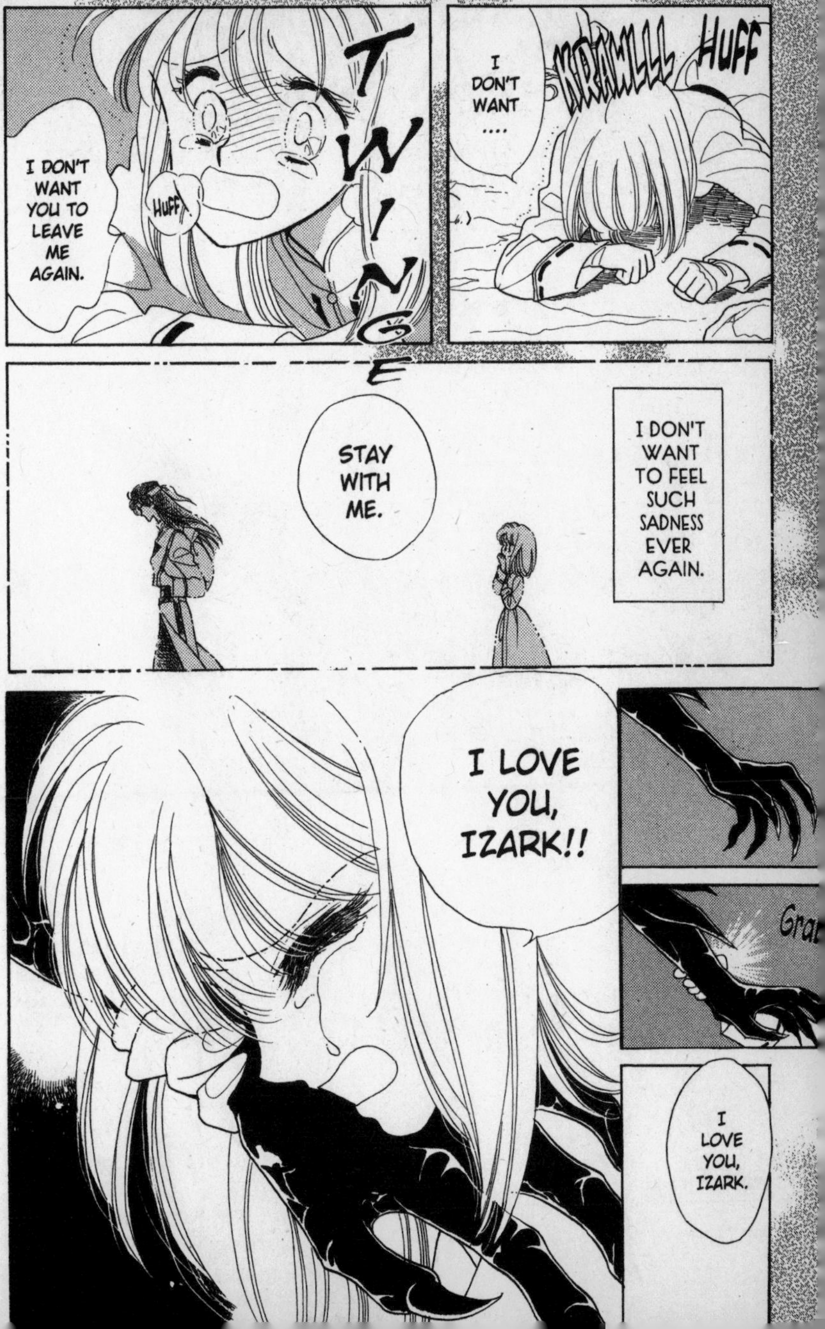
I DON'T WANT ....
KRAWLLL
HUFF
TWINGE
I DON'T WANT YOU TO LEAVE ME AGAIN.
HUFF
I DON'T WANT TO FEEL SUCH SADNESS EVER AGAIN.
STAY WITH ME.
I LOVE YOU, IZARK.
I LOVE YOU, IZARK!!

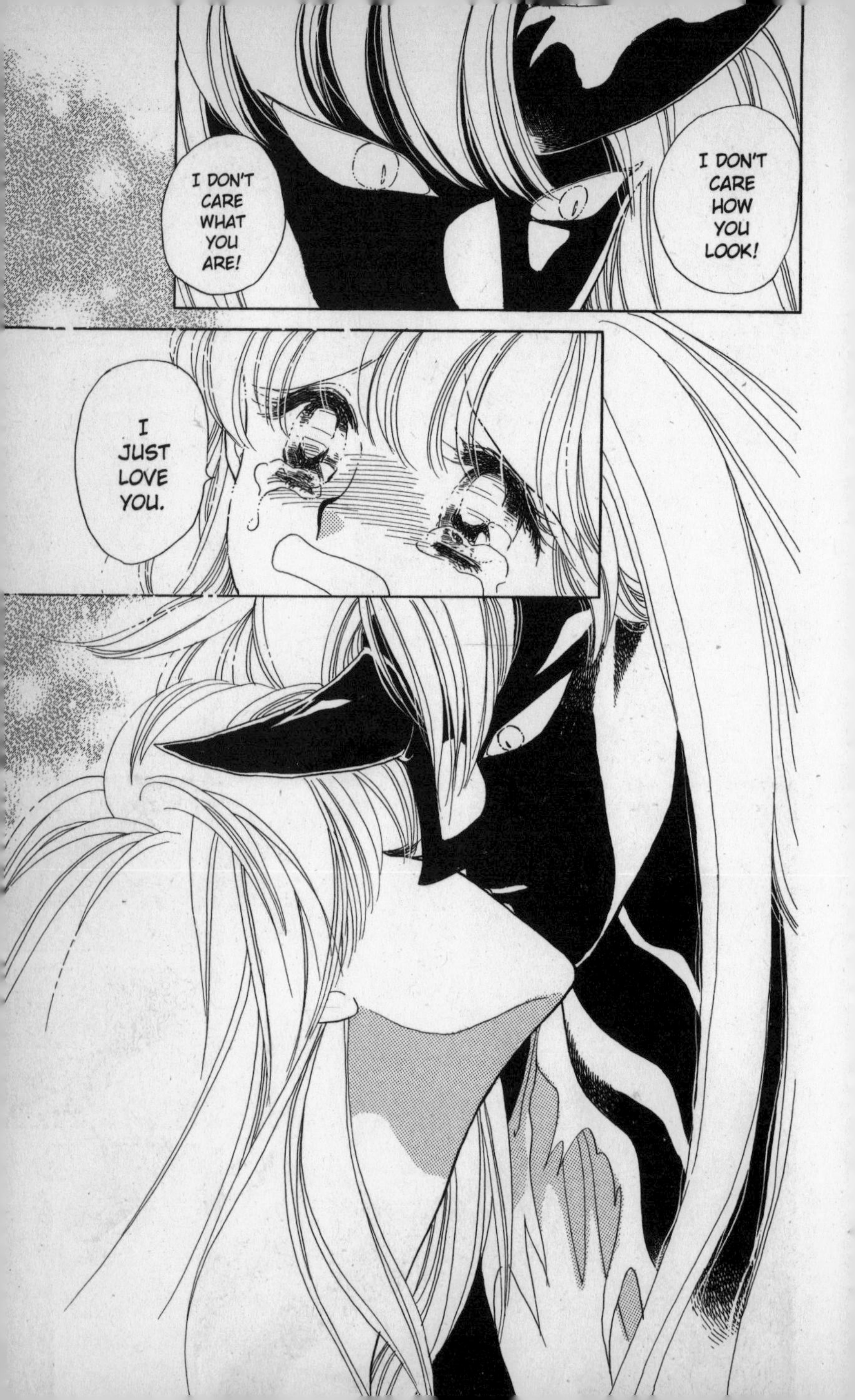
I DON'T CARE HOW YOU LOOK!
I DON'T CARE WHAT YOU ARE!
I JUST LOVE YOU.

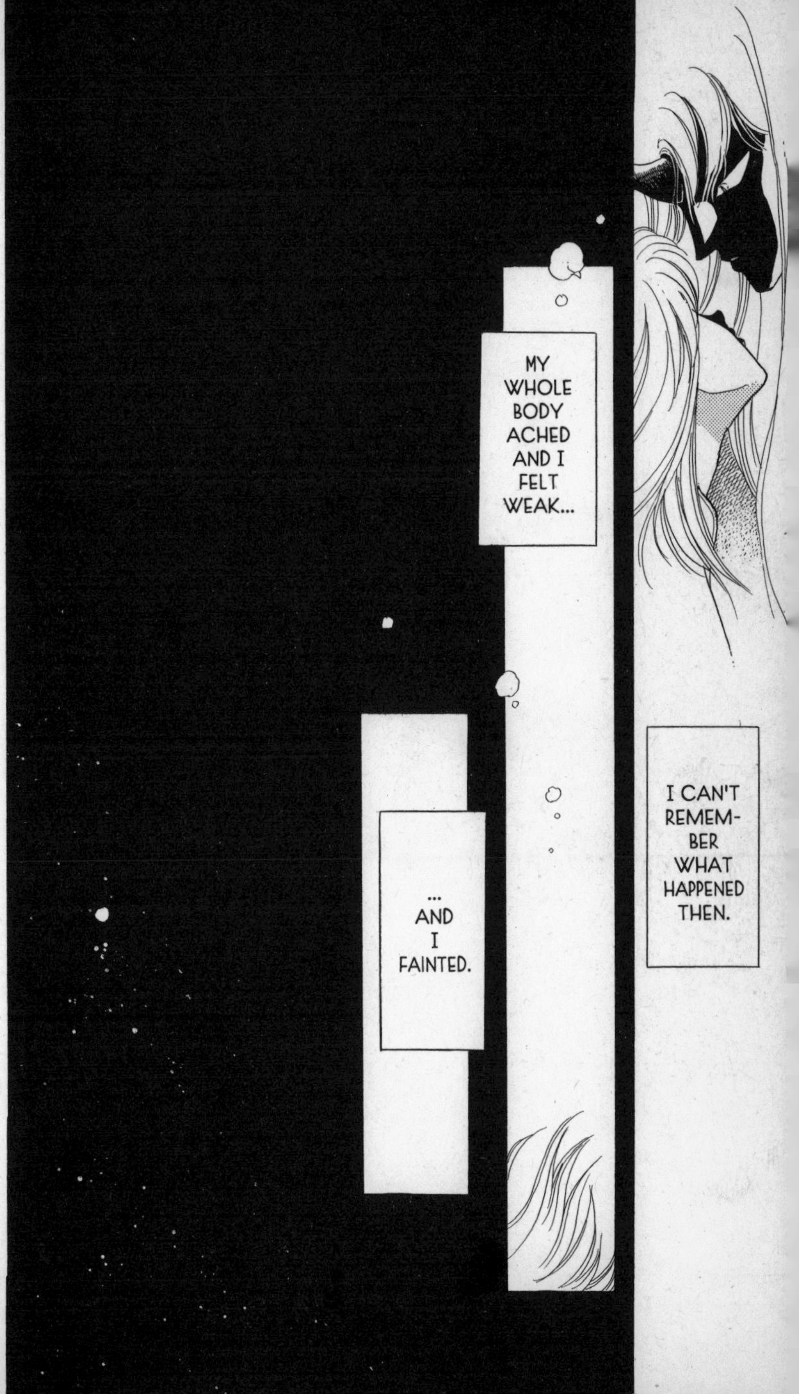
I CAN'T REMEM-BER WHAT HAPPENED THEN.
MY WHOLE BODY ACHED AND I FELT WEAK...
... AND I FAINTED.

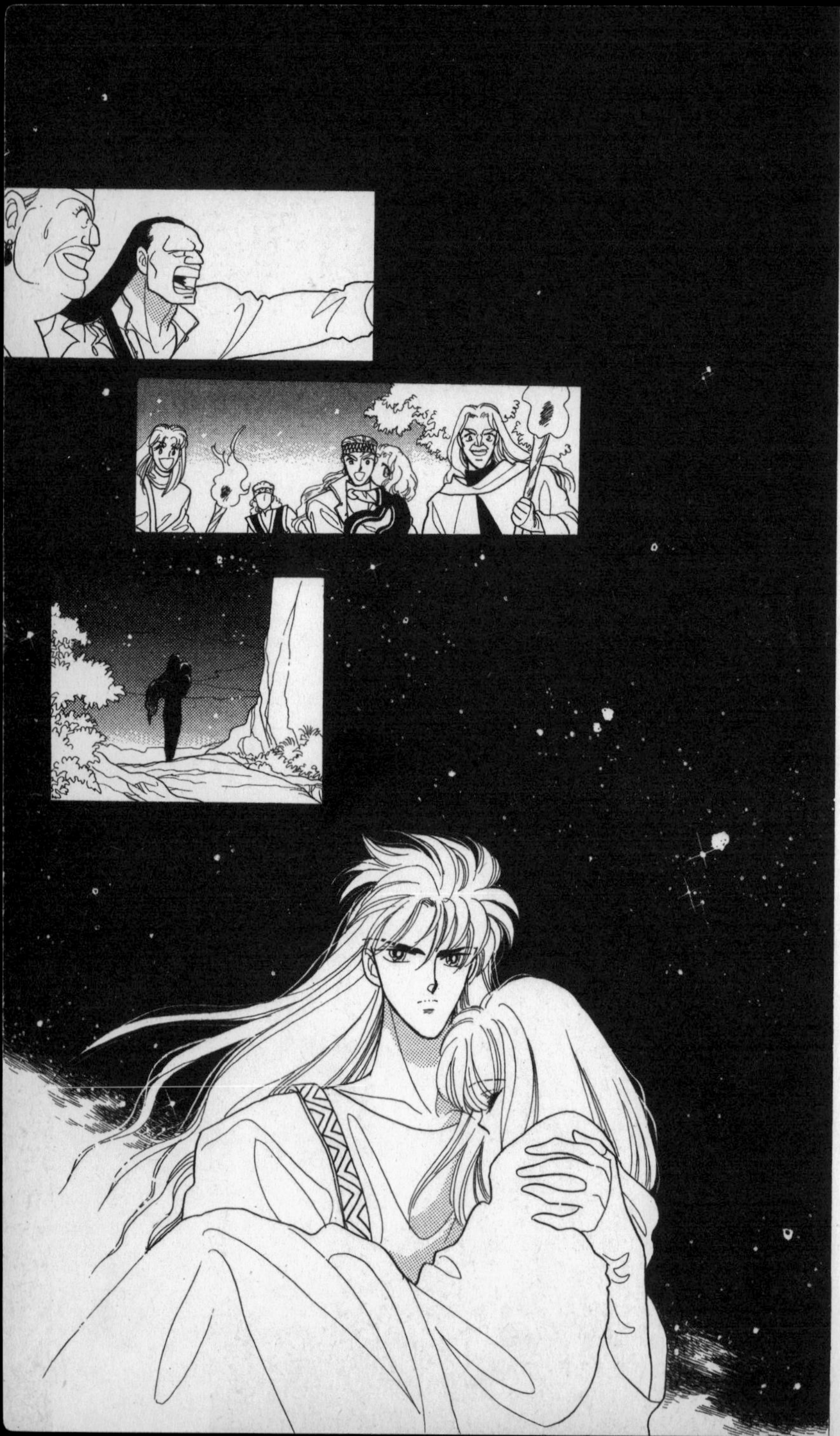

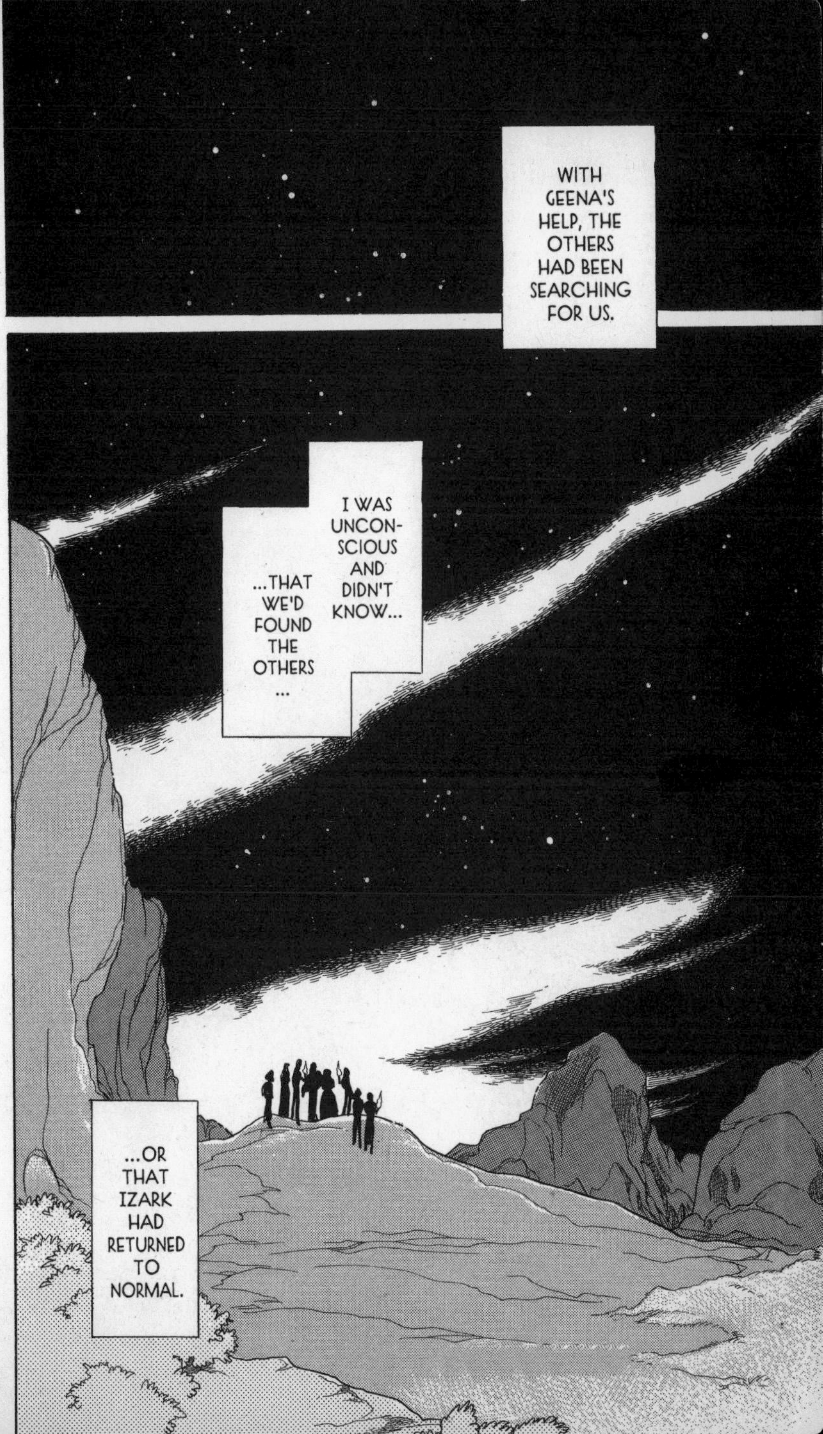
WITH GEENA'S HELP, THE OTHERS HAD BEEN SEARCHING FOR US.
I WAS UNCONSCIOUS AND DIDN'T KNOW...
...THAT WE'D FOUND THE OTHERS ...
...OR THAT IZARK HAD RETURNED TO NORMAL.

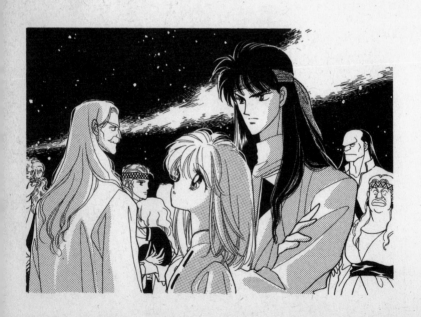

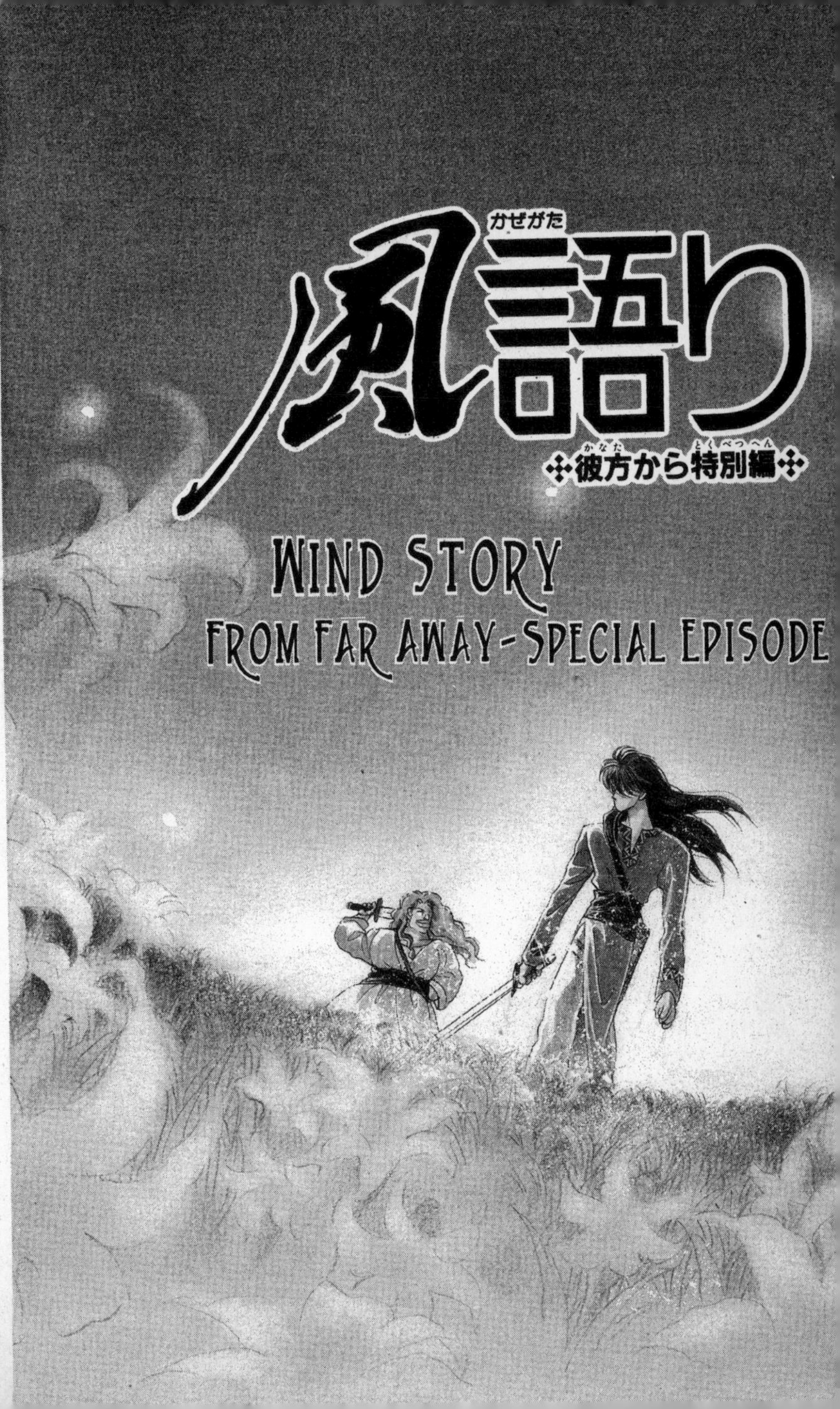
かぜがた
風語り
彼方から特別編
WIND STORY
FROM FAR AWAY-SPECIAL EPISODE

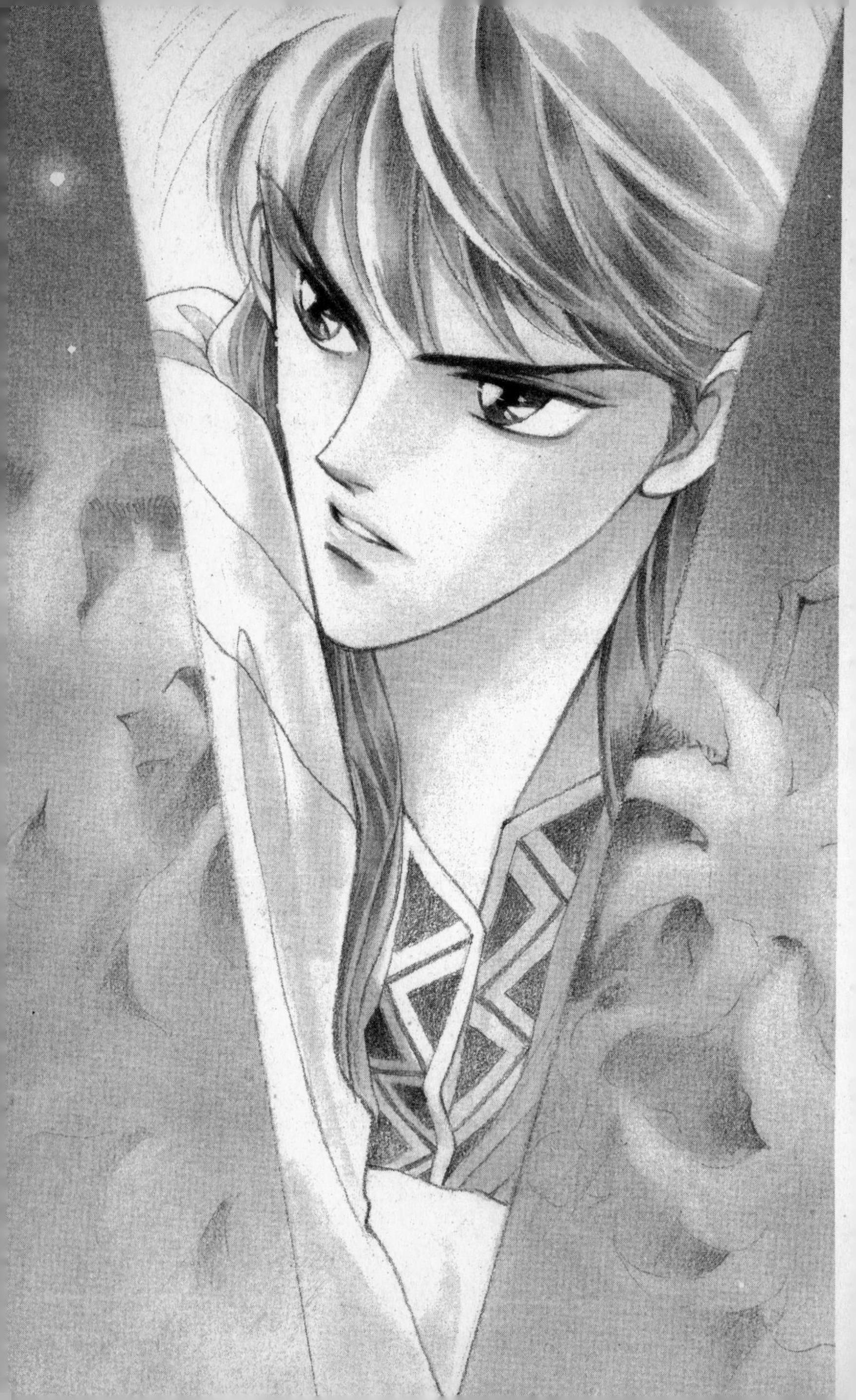

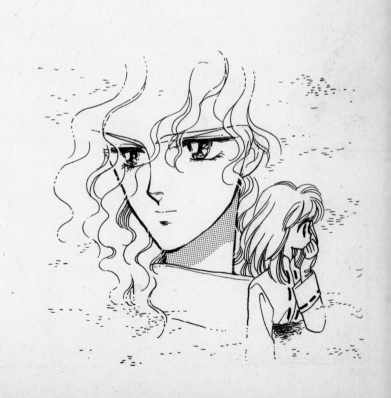

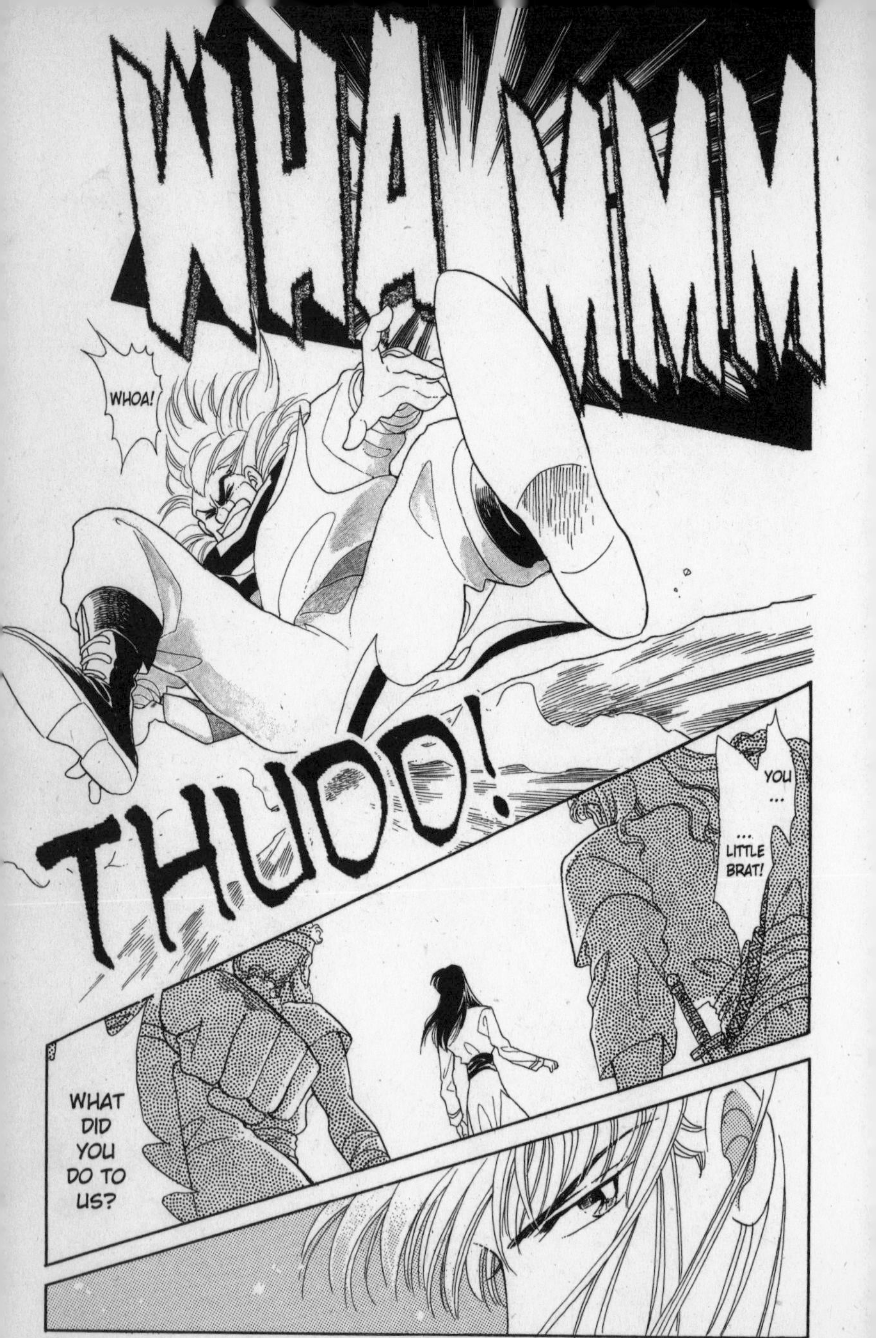
WHAMMM
WHOA!
THUDD!
YOU ... ... LITTLE BRAT!
WHAT DID YOU DO TO US?

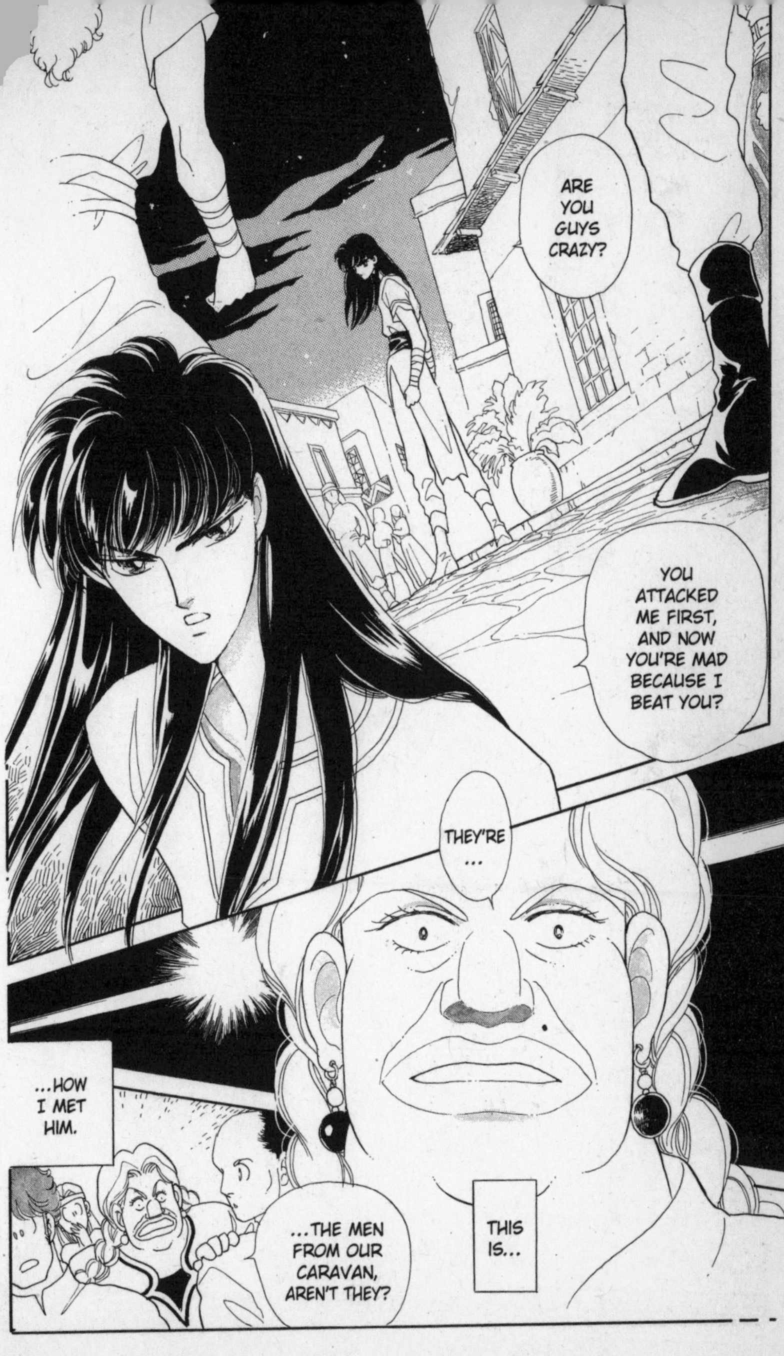
ARE YOU GUYS CRAZY?
YOU ATTACKED ME FIRST, AND NOW YOU'RE MAD BECAUSE I BEAT YOU?
THEY'RE ...
...THE MEN FROM OUR CARAVAN, AREN'T THEY?
THIS IS...
...HOW I MET HIM.

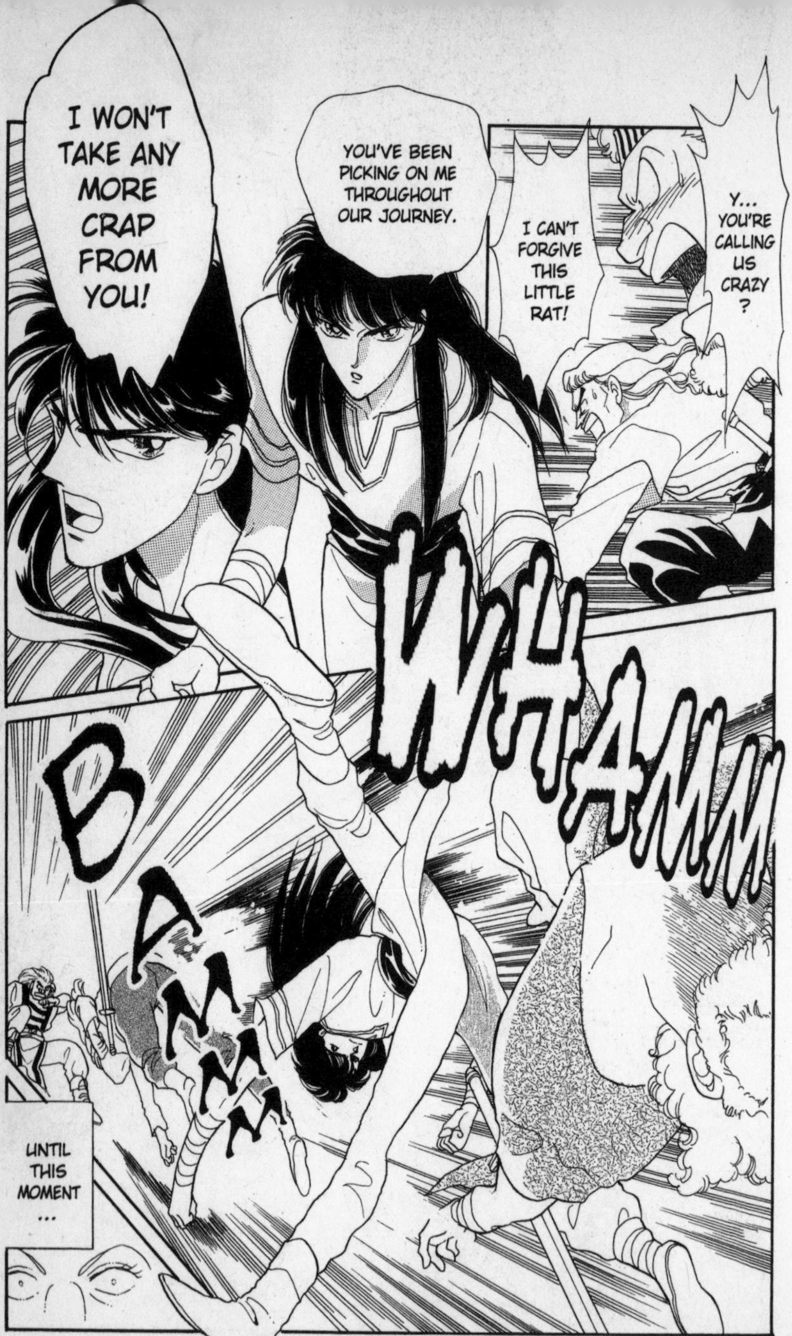
Y... YOU'RE CALLING US CRAZY?
I CAN'T FORGIVE THIS LITTLE RAT!
YOU'VE BEEN PICKING ON ME THROUGHOUT OUR JOURNEY.
I WON'T TAKE ANY MORE CRAP FROM YOU!
WHAMM
BAMMM
UNTIL THIS MOMENT ...

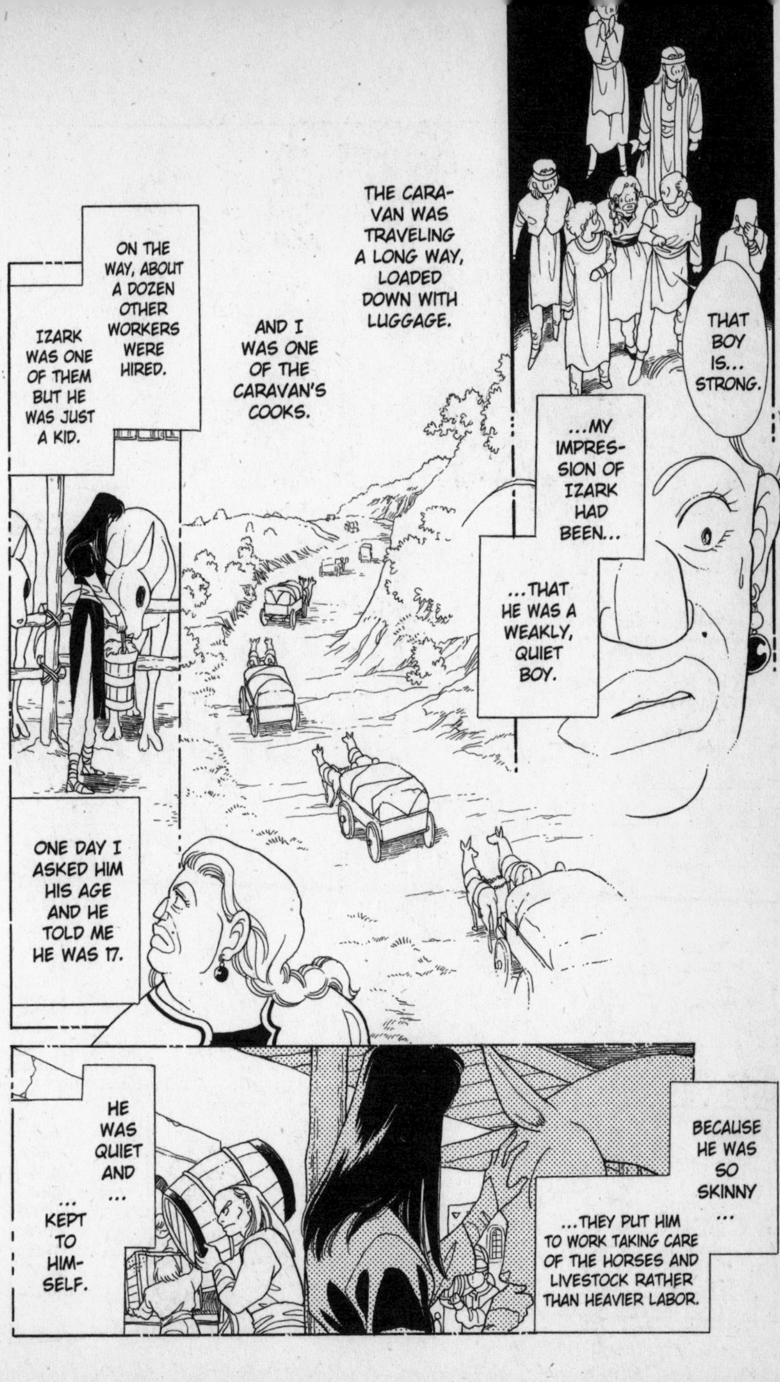
THAT BOY IS... STRONG.
...MY IMPRESSION OF IZARK HAD BEEN...
...THAT HE WAS A WEAKLY, QUIET BOY.
THE CARAVAN WAS TRAVELING A LONG WAY, LOADED DOWN WITH LUGGAGE.
AND I WAS ONE OF THE CARAVAN'S COOKS.
ON THE WAY, ABOUT A DOZEN OTHER WORKERS WERE HIRED.
IZARK WAS ONE OF THEM BUT HE WAS JUST A KID.
ONE DAY I ASKED HIM HIS AGE AND HE TOLD ME HE WAS 17.
BECAUSE HE WAS SO SKINNY ...
...THEY PUT HIM TO WORK TAKING CARE OF THE HORSES AND LIVESTOCK RATHER THAN HEAVIER LABOR.
HE WAS QUIET AND ...
... KEPT TO HIMSELF.

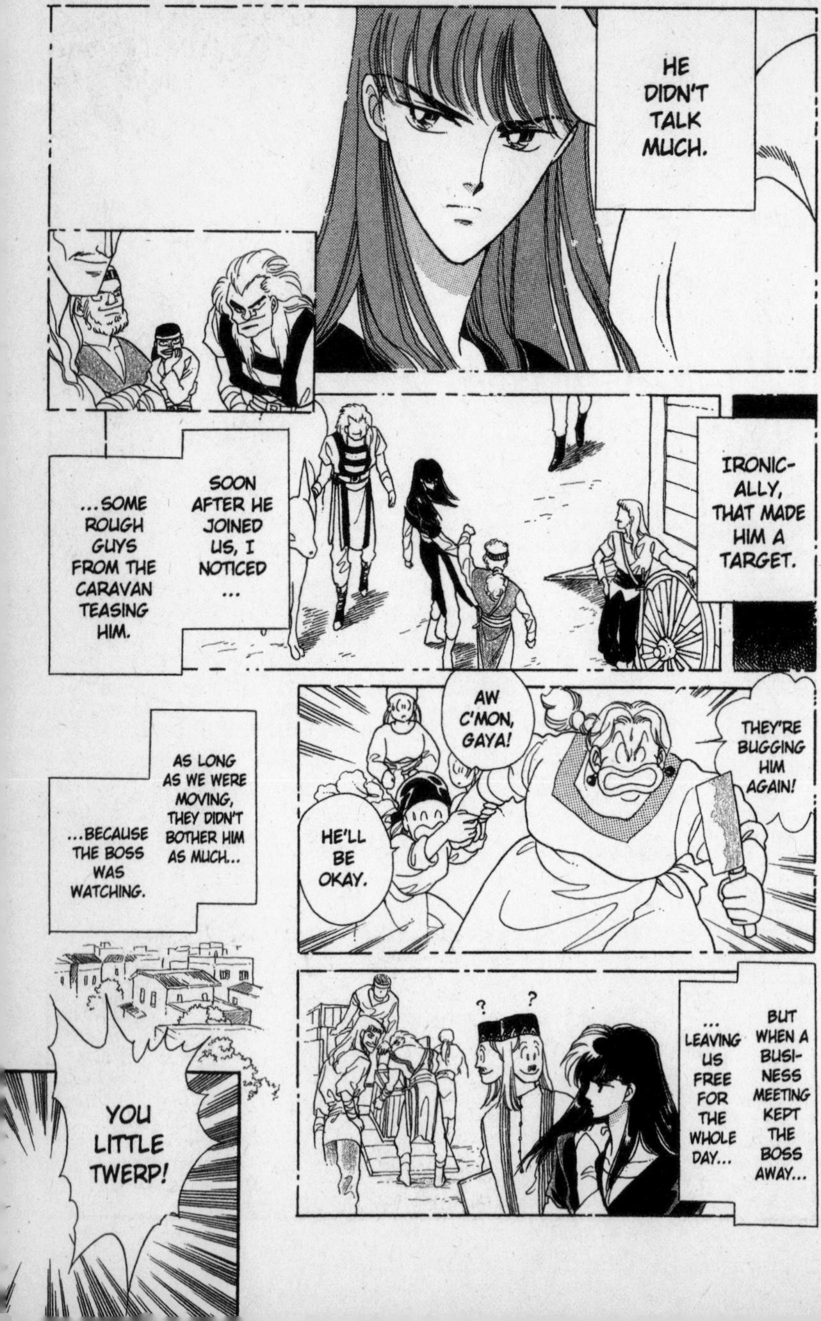
HE DIDN'T TALK MUCH.
IRONIC-ALLY, THAT MADE HIM A TARGET.
SOON AFTER HE JOINED US, I NOTICED ...
...SOME ROUGH GUYS FROM THE CARAVAN TEASING HIM.
THEY'RE BUGGING HIM AGAIN!
AW C'MON, GAYA!
HE'LL BE OKAY.
AS LONG AS WE WERE MOVING, THEY DIDN'T BOTHER HIM AS MUCH...
...BECAUSE THE BOSS WAS WATCHING.
BUT WHEN A BUSI-NESS MEETING KEPT THE BOSS AWAY...
...LEAVING US FREE FOR THE WHOLE DAY...
YOU LITTLE TWERP!

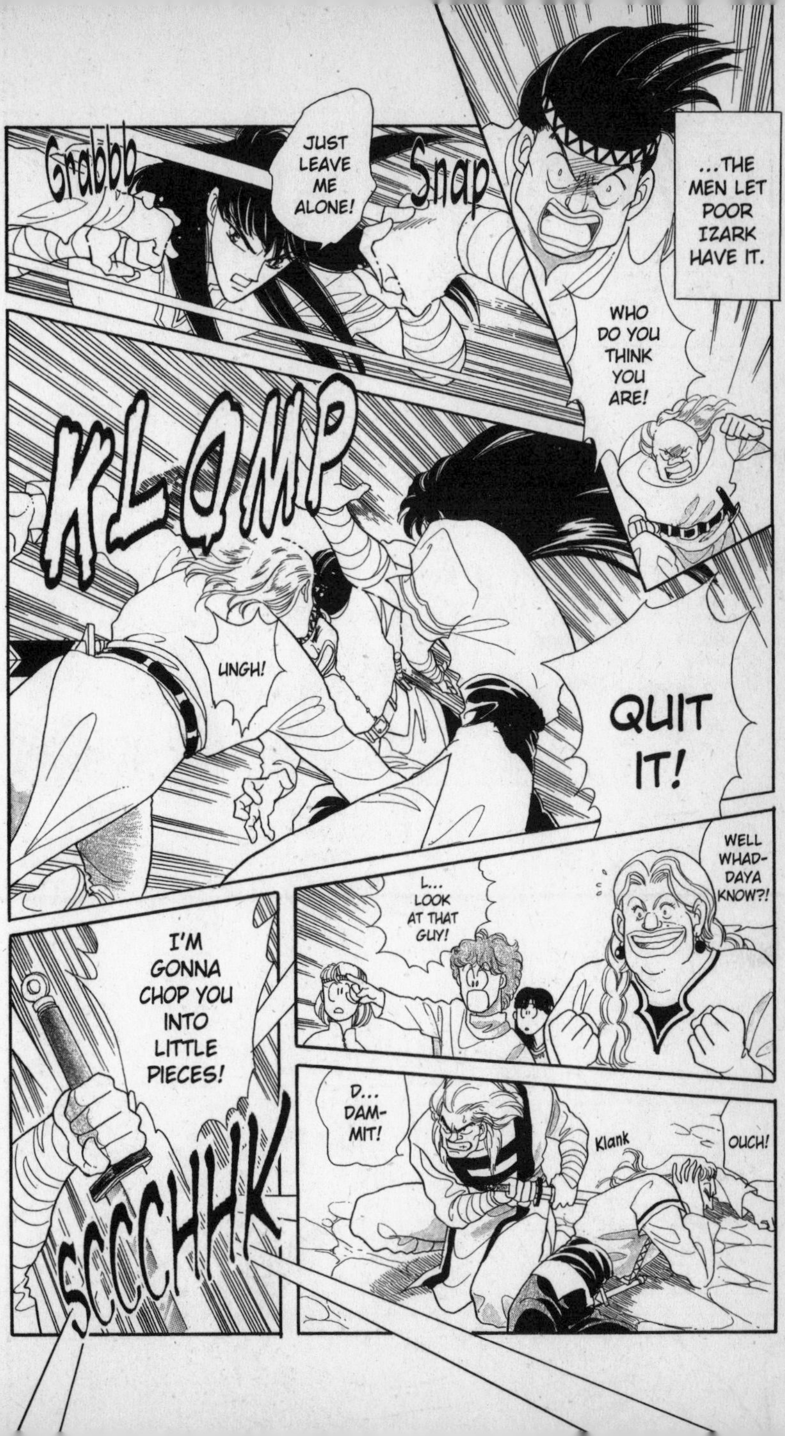
...THE MEN LET POOR IZARK HAVE IT.
Snap
WHO DO YOU THINK YOU ARE!
JUST LEAVE ME ALONE!
Grabbb
QUIT IT!
KLOMP
UNGH!
WELL WHAD-DAYA KNOW?!
L... LOOK AT THAT GUY!
OUCH!
Klank
D... DAM-MIT!
I'M GONNA CHOP YOU INTO LITTLE PIECES!
SCCCHHK

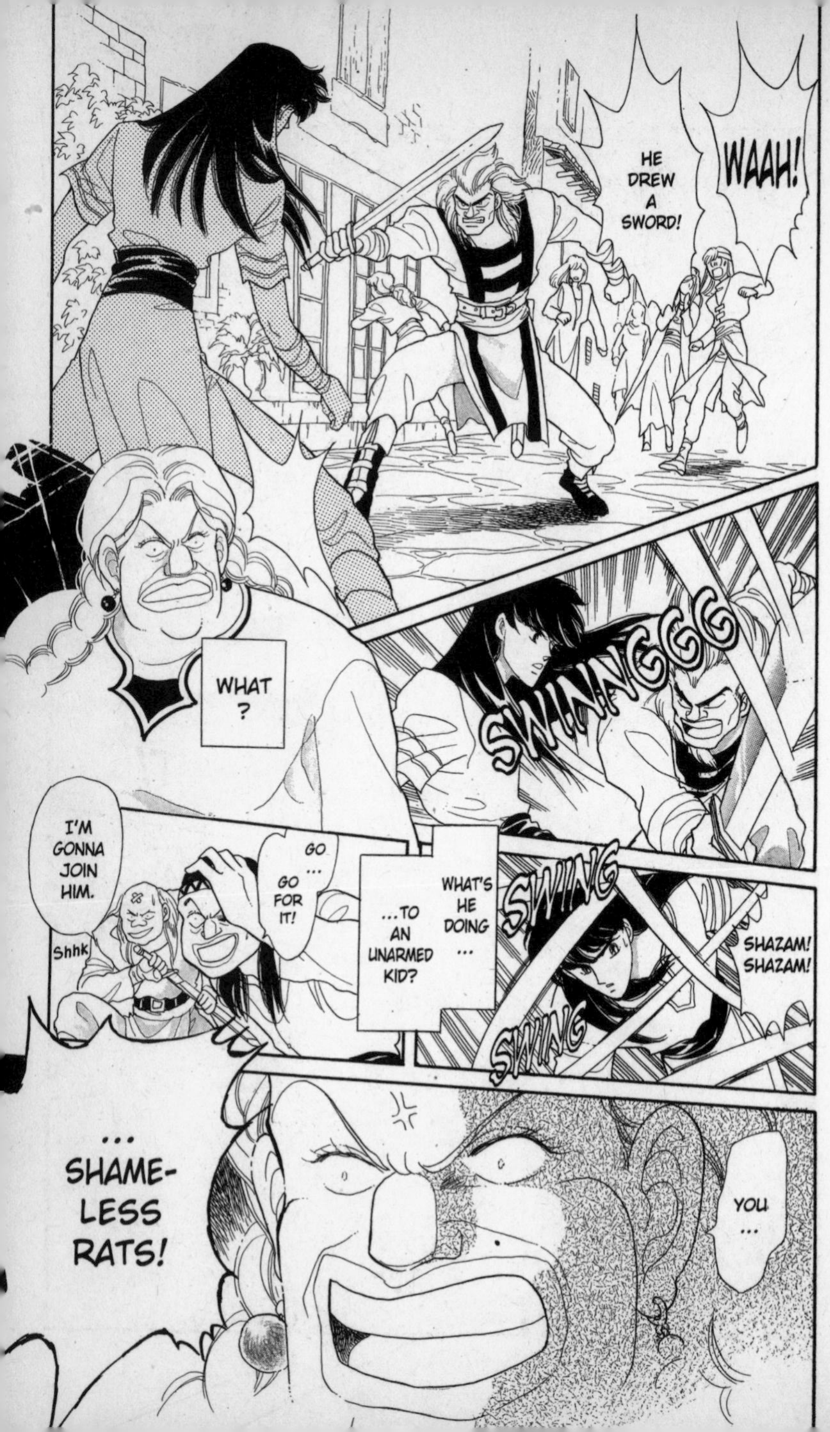
WAAH!
HE DREW A SWORD!
SWINNGGG
WHAT ?
SWING
SHAZAM! SHAZAM!
SWING
WHAT'S HE DOING ...
...TO AN UNARMED KID?
GO ... GO FOR IT!
I'M GONNA JOIN HIM.
Shhk
YOU ...
... SHAME-LESS RATS!

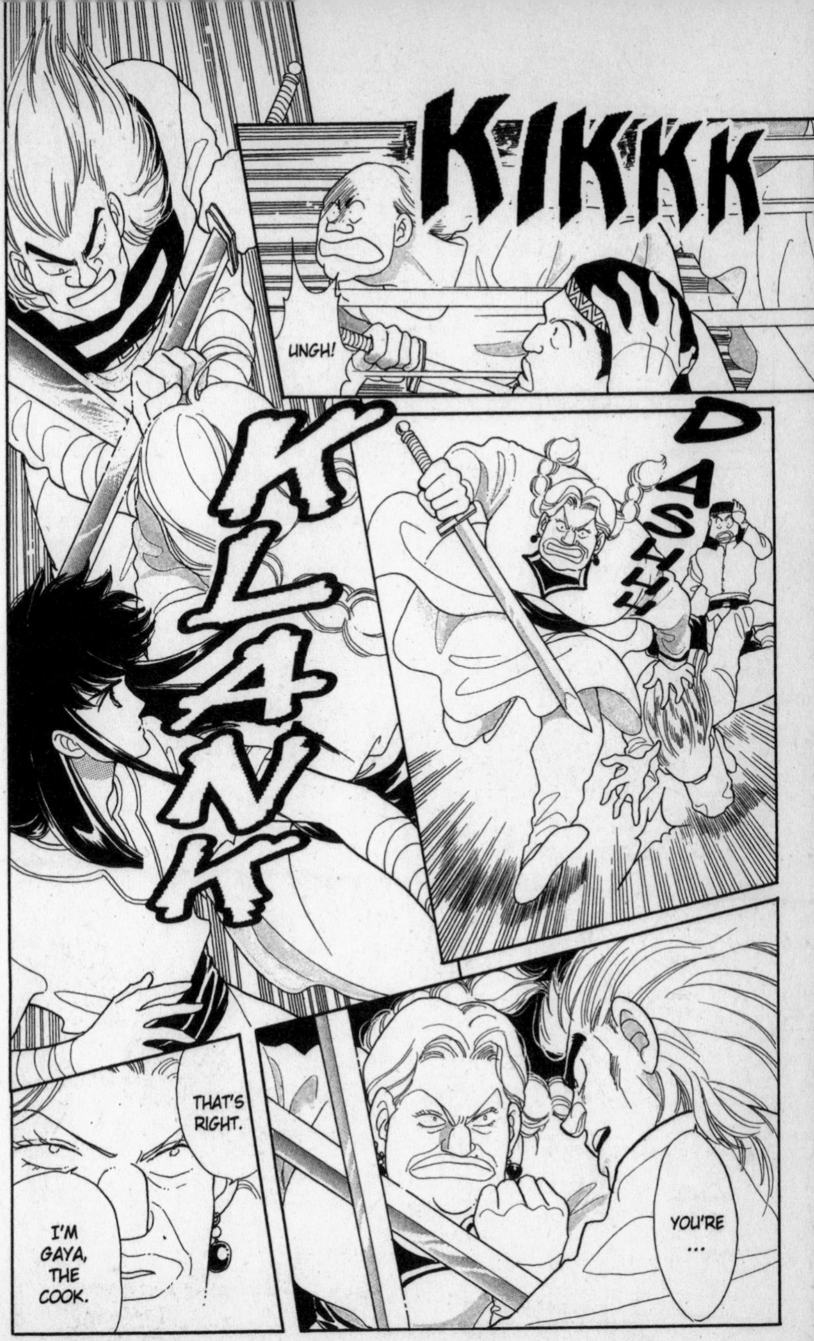
KIKKK
UNGH!
DASHHH
KLANK
YOU'RE ...
THAT'S RIGHT.
I'M GAYA, THE COOK.

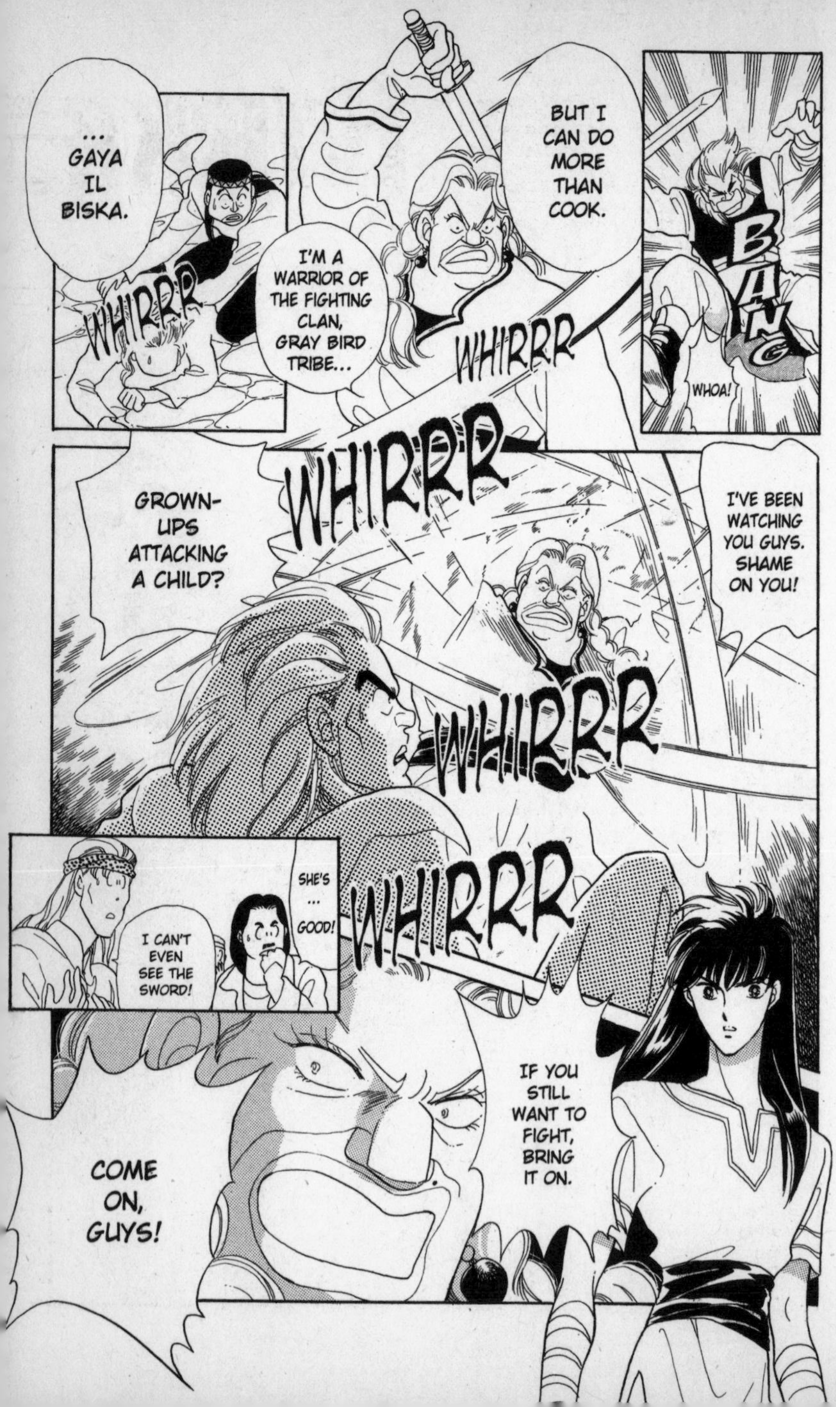
BANG
WHOA!
BUT I CAN DO MORE THAN COOK.
I'M A WARRIOR OF THE FIGHTING CLAN, GRAY BIRD TRIBE...
WHIRRR
... GAYA IL BISKA.
WHIRRR
I'VE BEEN WATCHING YOU GUYS. SHAME ON YOU!
WHIRRR
GROWN-UPS ATTACKING A CHILD?
WHIRRR
WHIRRR
SHE'S ... GOOD!
I CAN'T EVEN SEE THE SWORD!
IF YOU STILL WANT TO FIGHT, BRING IT ON.
COME ON, GUYS!

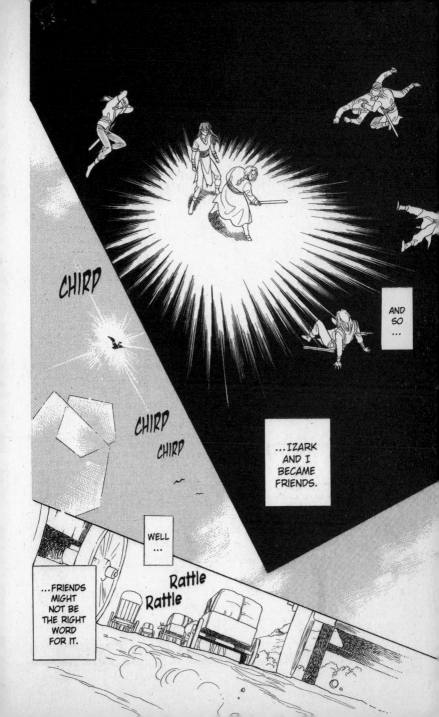

CHIRP

AND SO ...

CHIRP

CHIRP

...IZARK AND I BECAME FRIENDS.

WELL ...

Rattle
Rattle

...FRIENDS MIGHT NOT BE THE RIGHT WORD FOR IT.

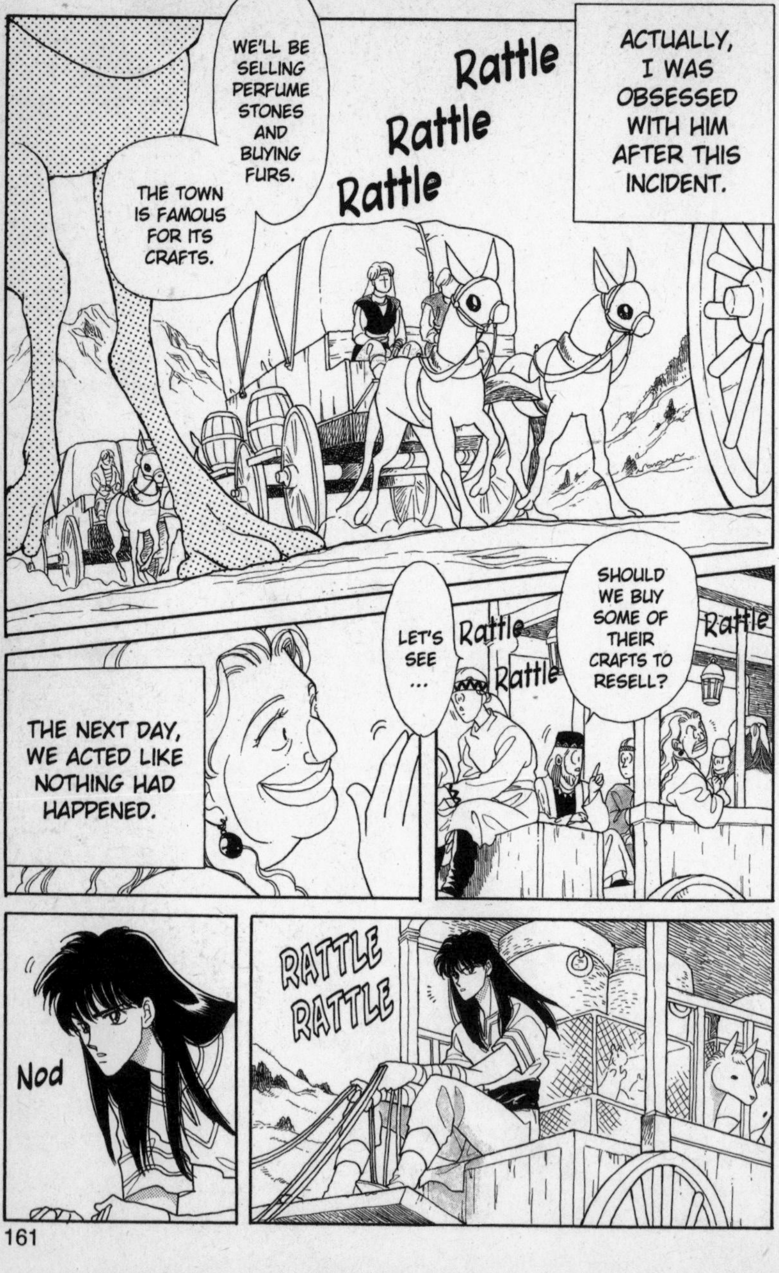
ACTUALLY, I WAS OBSESSED WITH HIM AFTER THIS INCIDENT.
Rattle
Rattle
Rattle
WE'LL BE SELLING PERFUME STONES AND BUYING FURS.
THE TOWN IS FAMOUS FOR ITS CRAFTS.
SHOULD WE BUY SOME OF THEIR CRAFTS TO RESELL?
Rattle
Rattle
Rattle
LET'S SEE ...
THE NEXT DAY, WE ACTED LIKE NOTHING HAD HAPPENED.
RATTLE RATTLE
Nod

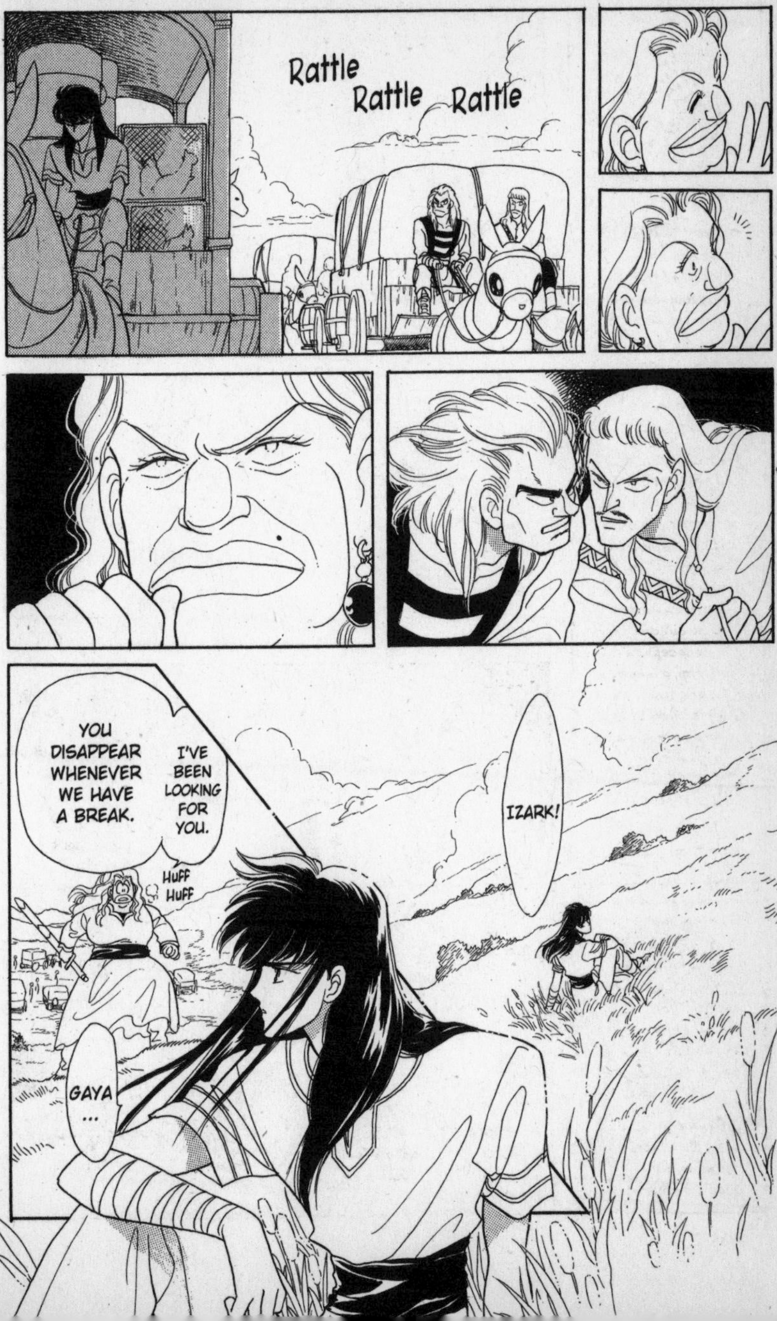
Rattle Rattle Rattle
IZARK!
I'VE BEEN LOOKING FOR YOU.
YOU DISAPPEAR WHENEVER WE HAVE A BREAK.
HUFF HUFF
GAYA ...

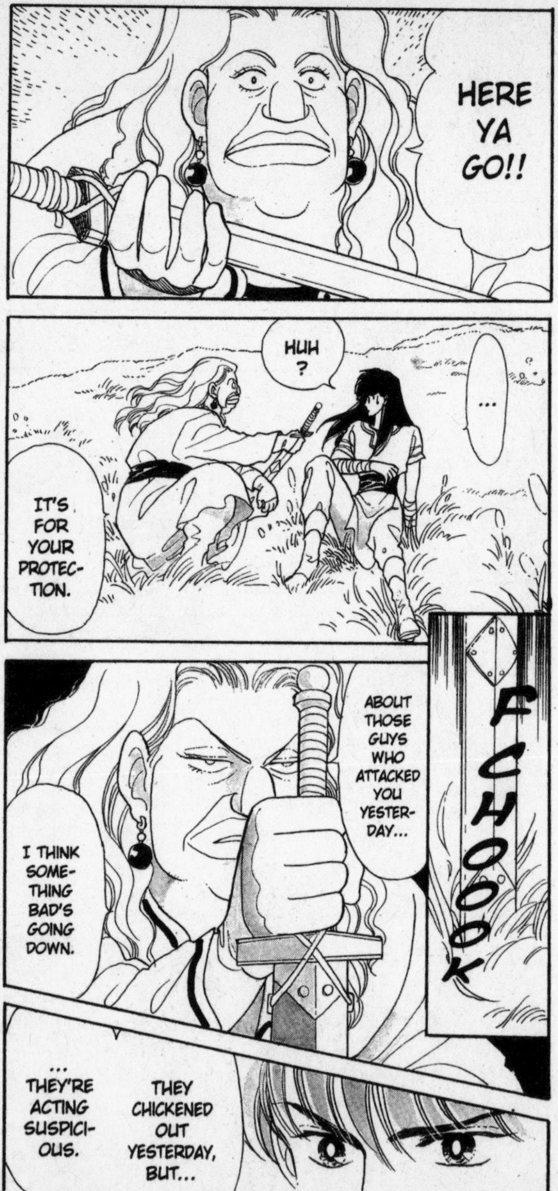
HERE YA GO!!
...
HUH?
IT'S FOR YOUR PROTECTION.
FCHOOOOK
ABOUT THOSE GUYS WHO ATTACKED YOU YESTERDAY...
I THINK SOMETHING BAD'S GOING DOWN.
THEY CHICKENED OUT YESTERDAY, BUT...
... THEY'RE ACTING SUSPICIOUS.

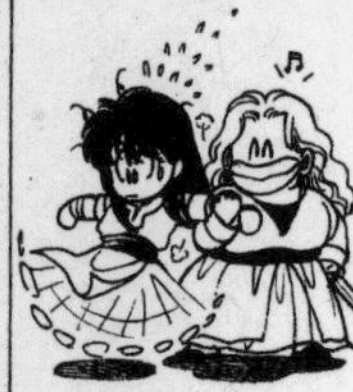

Remember we sort of decided that the buzzing sound I discussed in Vol. 3 was from mole crickets? Someone wrote to me with a new theory about the buzz.

She claims that, if it had been before the '60s, the buzz was definitely mole crickets. However, the sound I heard more recently could have been that of "neck-cut grig" or Euconocephalus thunbergi, a member or the grig family, that migrated from North America to Japan.

The name, "neck-cut grig" comes from the fact that, if you catch the insect while it's eating grass, the head will come off. Creepy!

She also cited a newspaper article that said that mole crickets live underground and their buzz isn't loud enough to be heard above ground. So the insects I heard couldn't have been mole crickets.

Anyway, I never knew that there are so many different insects on this earth.

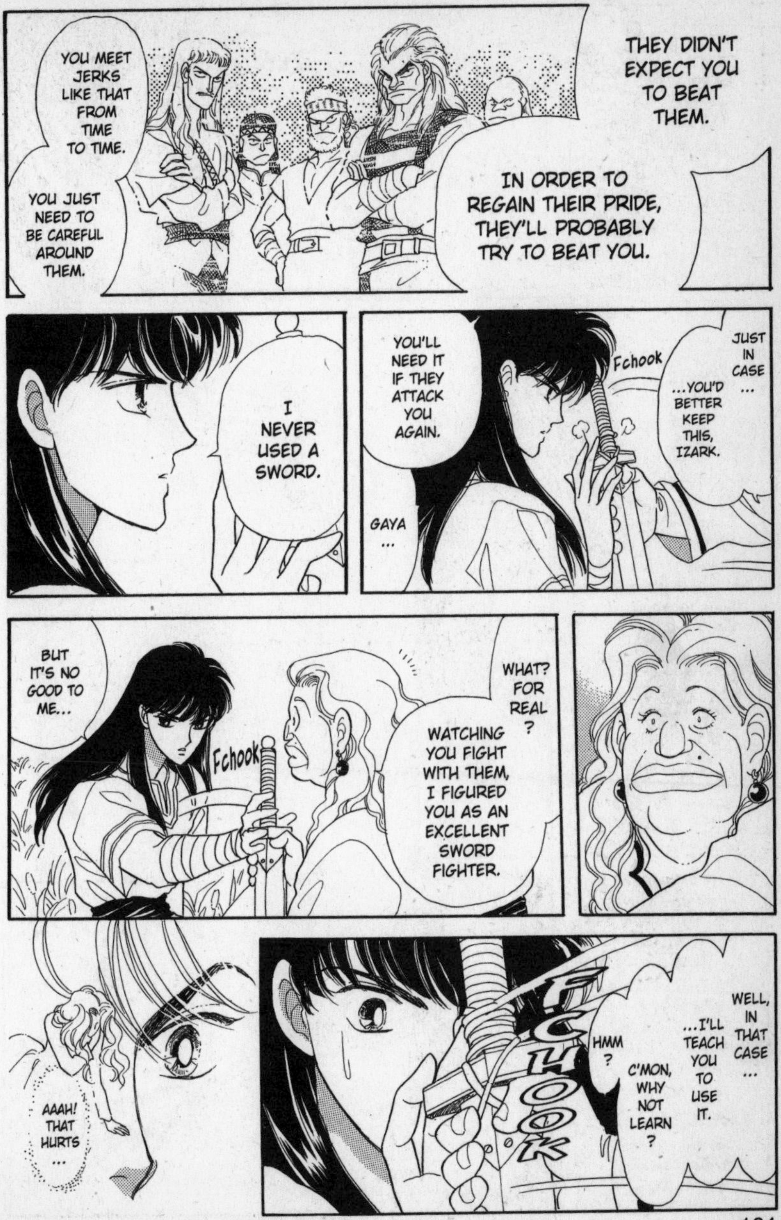
THEY DIDN'T EXPECT YOU TO BEAT THEM.
IN ORDER TO REGAIN THEIR PRIDE, THEY'LL PROBABLY TRY TO BEAT YOU.
YOU MEET JERKS LIKE THAT FROM TIME TO TIME.
YOU JUST NEED TO BE CAREFUL AROUND THEM.
JUST IN CASE ...
...YOU'D BETTER KEEP THIS, IZARK.
Fchook
YOU'LL NEED IT IF THEY ATTACK YOU AGAIN.
GAYA ...
I NEVER USED A SWORD.
WHAT? FOR REAL?
BUT IT'S NO GOOD TO ME...
Fchook
WATCHING YOU FIGHT WITH THEM, I FIGURED YOU AS AN EXCELLENT SWORD FIGHTER.
WELL, IN THAT CASE ...
...I'LL TEACH YOU TO USE IT.
C'MON, WHY NOT LEARN?
HMM?
FCHOOOOK
AAAH! THAT HURTS ...

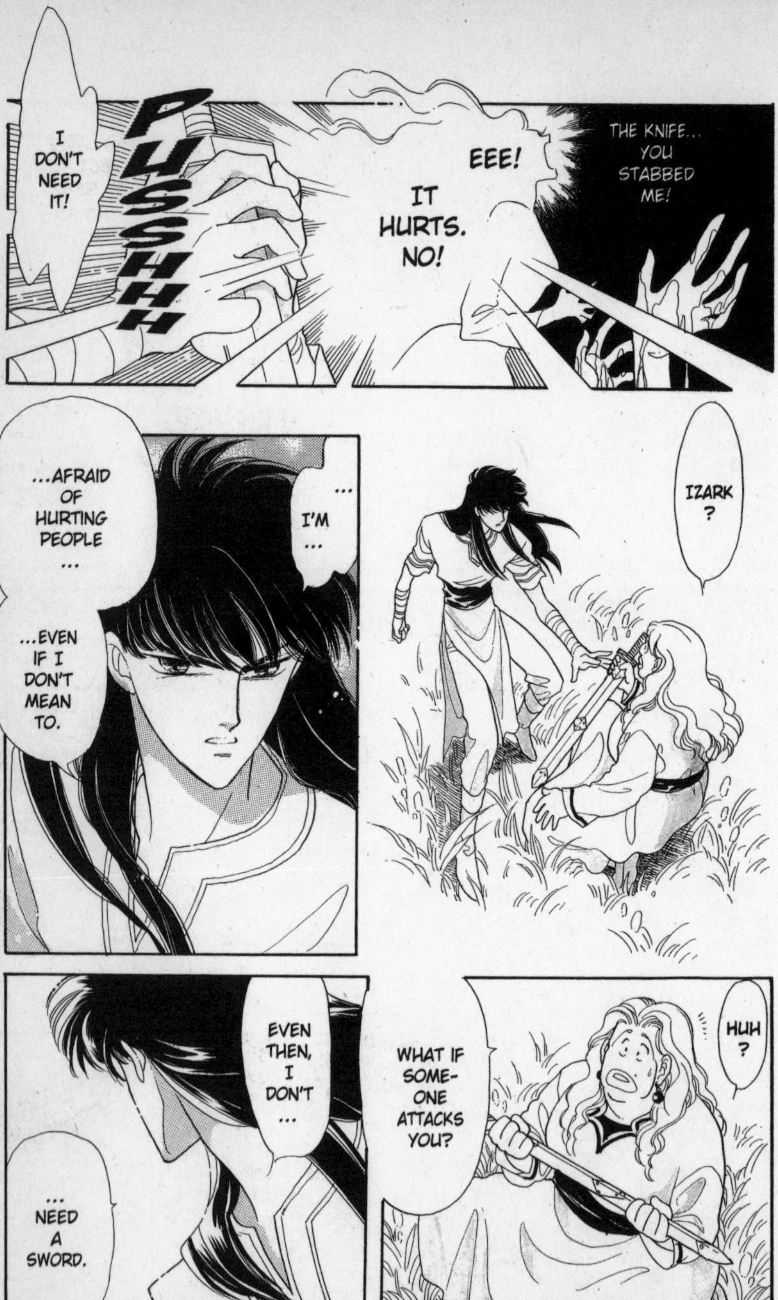
THE KNIFE... YOU STABBED ME!
EEE!
IT HURTS. NO!
PUSSHHH
I DON'T NEED IT!
IZARK?
... I'M ...
...AFRAID OF HURTING PEOPLE ...
...EVEN IF I DON'T MEAN TO.
HUH?
WHAT IF SOME-ONE ATTACKS YOU?
EVEN THEN, I DON'T ...
... NEED A SWORD.

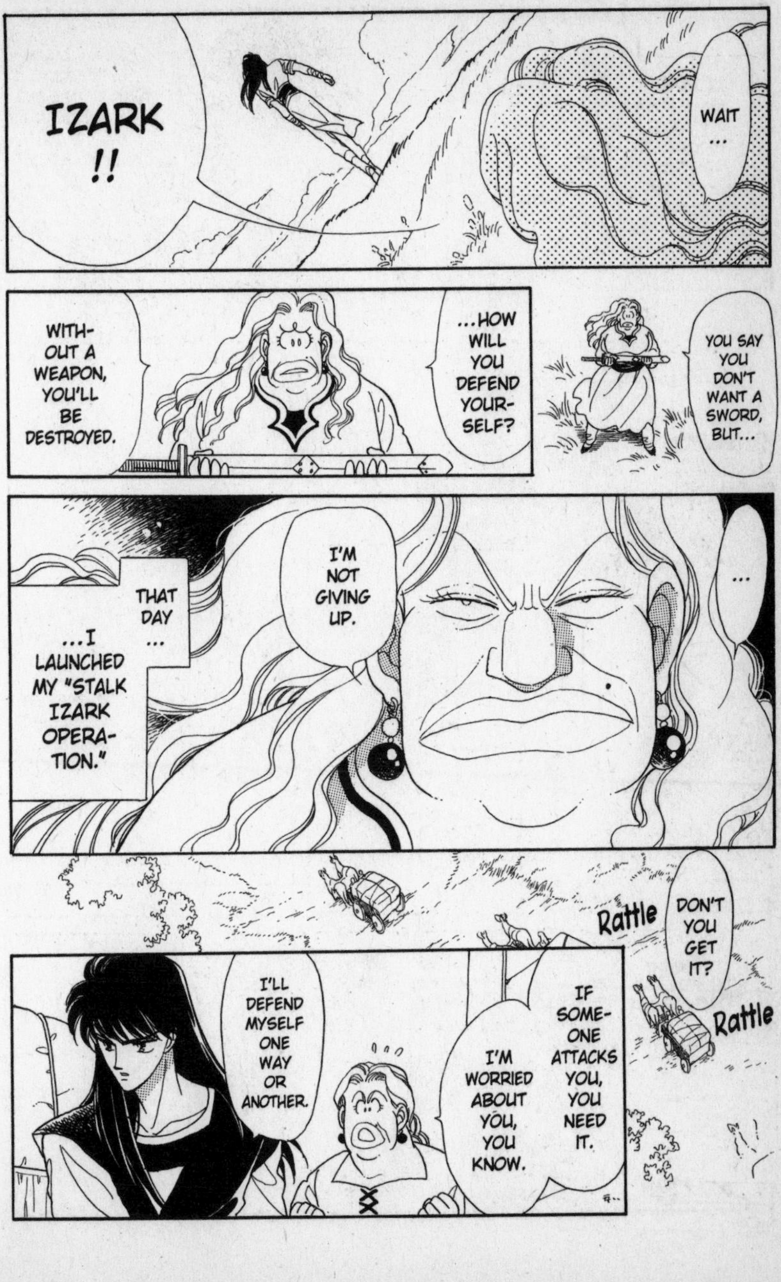
WAIT ...
IZARK !!
YOU SAY YOU DON'T WANT A SWORD, BUT...
...HOW WILL YOU DEFEND YOUR-SELF?
WITH-OUT A WEAPON, YOU'LL BE DESTROYED.
...
I'M NOT GIVING UP.
THAT DAY ... ...I LAUNCHED MY "STALK IZARK OPERA-TION."
Rattle
DON'T YOU GET IT?
Rattle
IF SOME-ONE ATTACKS YOU, YOU NEED IT.
I'M WORRIED ABOUT YOU, YOU KNOW.
I'LL DEFEND MYSELF ONE WAY OR ANOTHER.

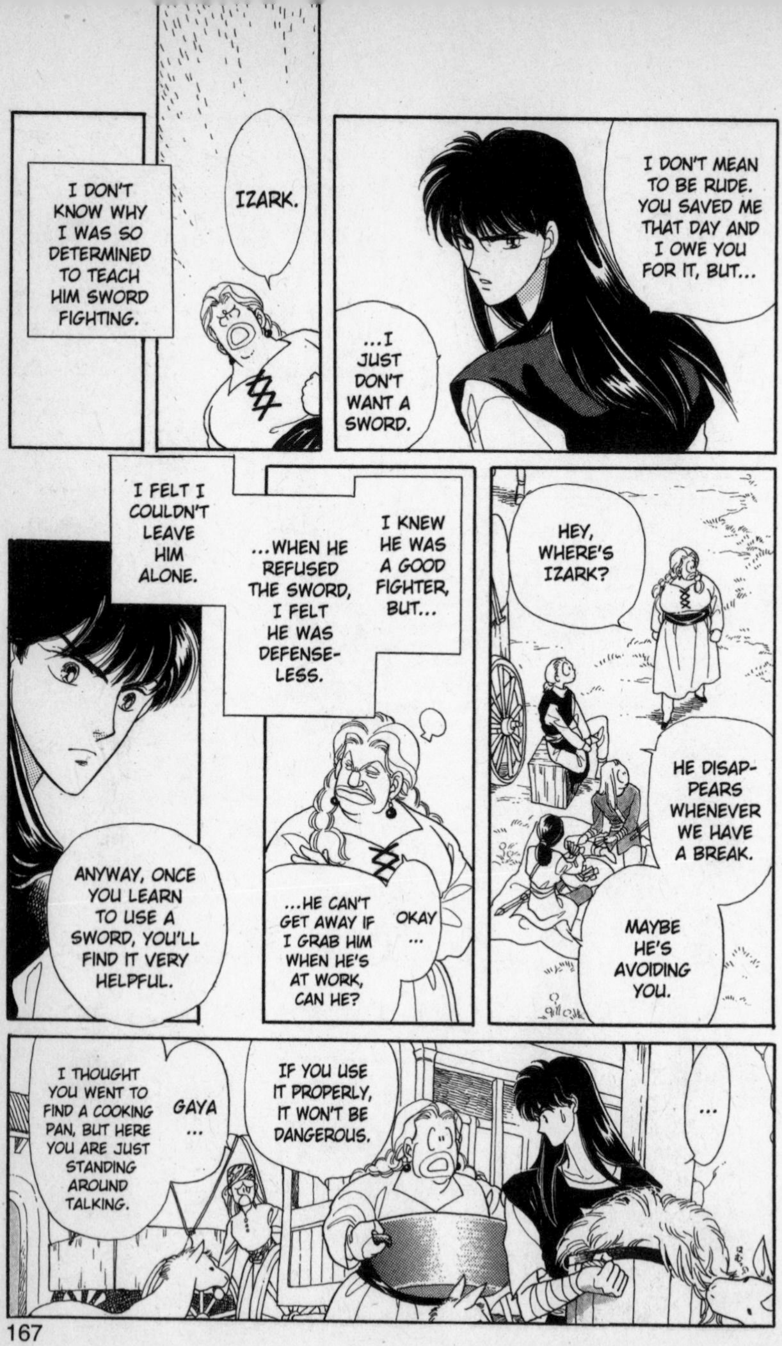
I DON'T MEAN TO BE RUDE. YOU SAVED ME THAT DAY AND I OWE YOU FOR IT, BUT...
...I JUST DON'T WANT A SWORD.
IZARK.
I DON'T KNOW WHY I WAS SO DETERMINED TO TEACH HIM SWORD FIGHTING.
HEY, WHERE'S IZARK?
HE DISAPPEARS WHENEVER WE HAVE A BREAK.
MAYBE HE'S AVOIDING YOU.
I KNEW HE WAS A GOOD FIGHTER, BUT...
...WHEN HE REFUSED THE SWORD, I FELT HE WAS DEFENSELESS.
OKAY ...
...HE CAN'T GET AWAY IF I GRAB HIM WHEN HE'S AT WORK, CAN HE?
I FELT I COULDN'T LEAVE HIM ALONE.
ANYWAY, ONCE YOU LEARN TO USE A SWORD, YOU'LL FIND IT VERY HELPFUL.
...
IF YOU USE IT PROPERLY, IT WON'T BE DANGEROUS.
GAYA ...
I THOUGHT YOU WENT TO FIND A COOKING PAN, BUT HERE YOU ARE JUST STANDING AROUND TALKING.

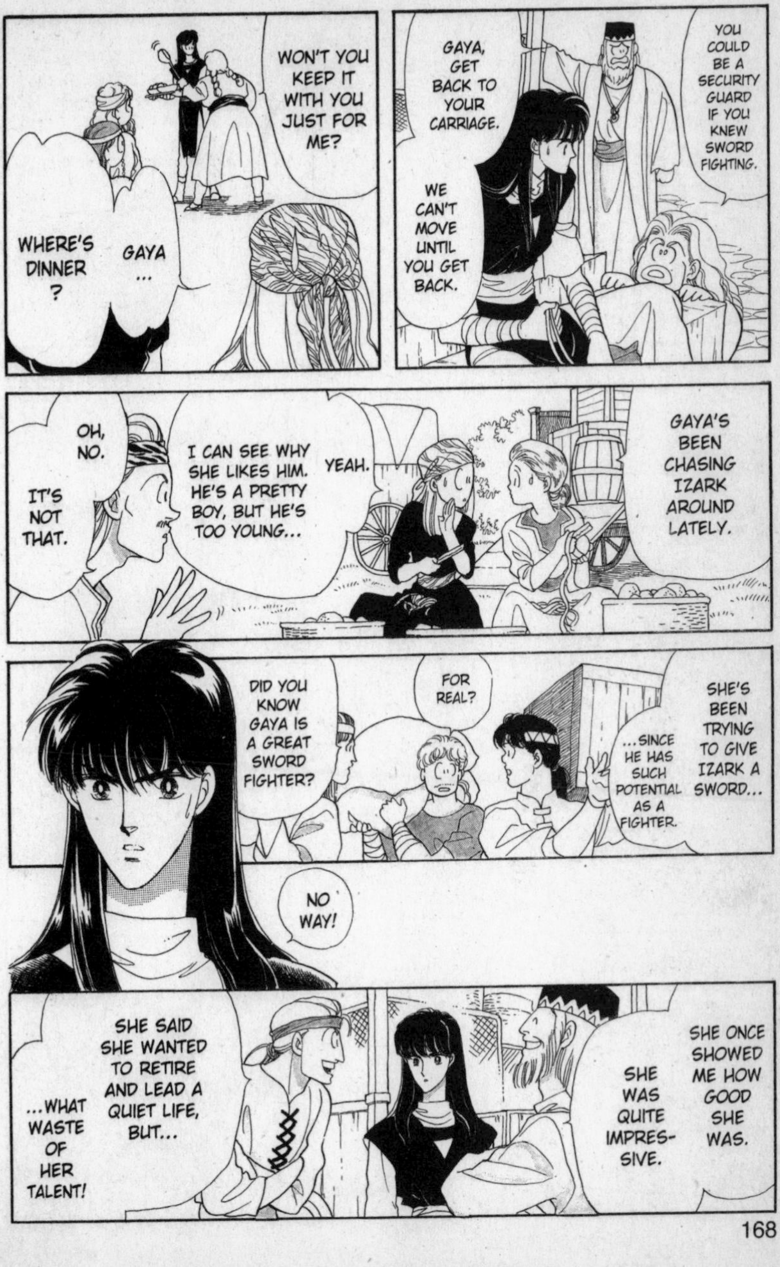
YOU COULD BE A SECURITY GUARD IF YOU KNEW SWORD FIGHTING.
GAYA, GET BACK TO YOUR CARRIAGE.
WE CAN'T MOVE UNTIL YOU GET BACK.
WON'T YOU KEEP IT WITH YOU JUST FOR ME?
GAYA ...
WHERE'S DINNER ?
GAYA'S BEEN CHASING IZARK AROUND LATELY.
YEAH.
I CAN SEE WHY SHE LIKES HIM. HE'S A PRETTY BOY, BUT HE'S TOO YOUNG...
OH, NO.
IT'S NOT THAT.
SHE'S BEEN TRYING TO GIVE IZARK A SWORD...
...SINCE HE HAS SUCH POTENTIAL AS A FIGHTER.
FOR REAL?
DID YOU KNOW GAYA IS A GREAT SWORD FIGHTER?
NO WAY!
SHE ONCE SHOWED ME HOW GOOD SHE WAS.
SHE WAS QUITE IMPRES-SIVE.
SHE SAID SHE WANTED TO RETIRE AND LEAD A QUIET LIFE, BUT...
...WHAT WASTE OF HER TALENT!

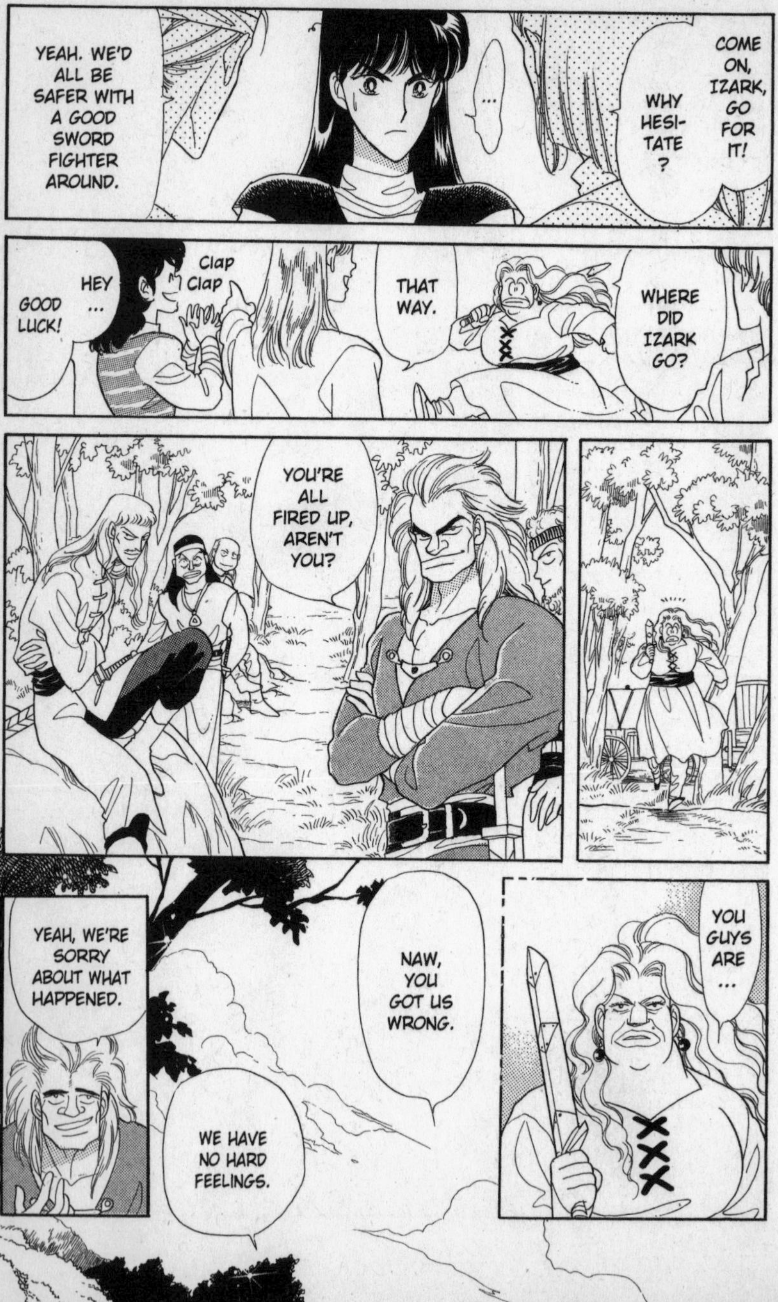
COME ON, IZARK, GO FOR IT!
WHY HESI-TATE?
...
YEAH. WE'D ALL BE SAFER WITH A GOOD SWORD FIGHTER AROUND.
WHERE DID IZARK GO?
THAT WAY.
Clap Clap
HEY ...
GOOD LUCK!
YOU'RE ALL FIRED UP, AREN'T YOU?
YOU GUYS ARE ...
NAW, YOU GOT US WRONG.
YEAH, WE'RE SORRY ABOUT WHAT HAPPENED.
WE HAVE NO HARD FEELINGS.

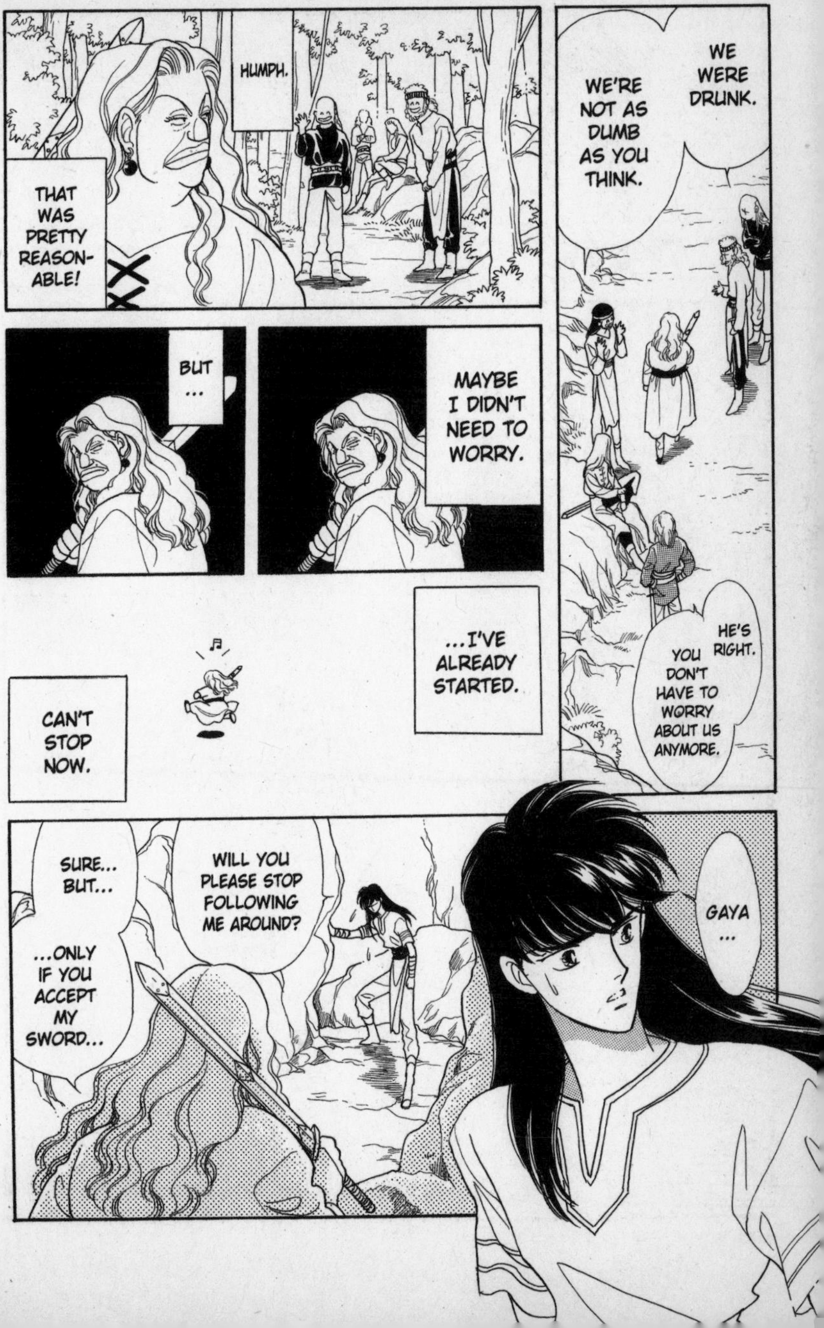
WE WERE DRUNK.
WE'RE NOT AS DUMB AS YOU THINK.
HE'S RIGHT.
YOU DON'T HAVE TO WORRY ABOUT US ANYMORE.
HUMPH.
THAT WAS PRETTY REASONABLE!
MAYBE I DIDN'T NEED TO WORRY.
BUT ...
...I'VE ALREADY STARTED.
CAN'T STOP NOW.
GAYA ...
WILL YOU PLEASE STOP FOLLOWING ME AROUND?
SURE... BUT...
...ONLY IF YOU ACCEPT MY SWORD...

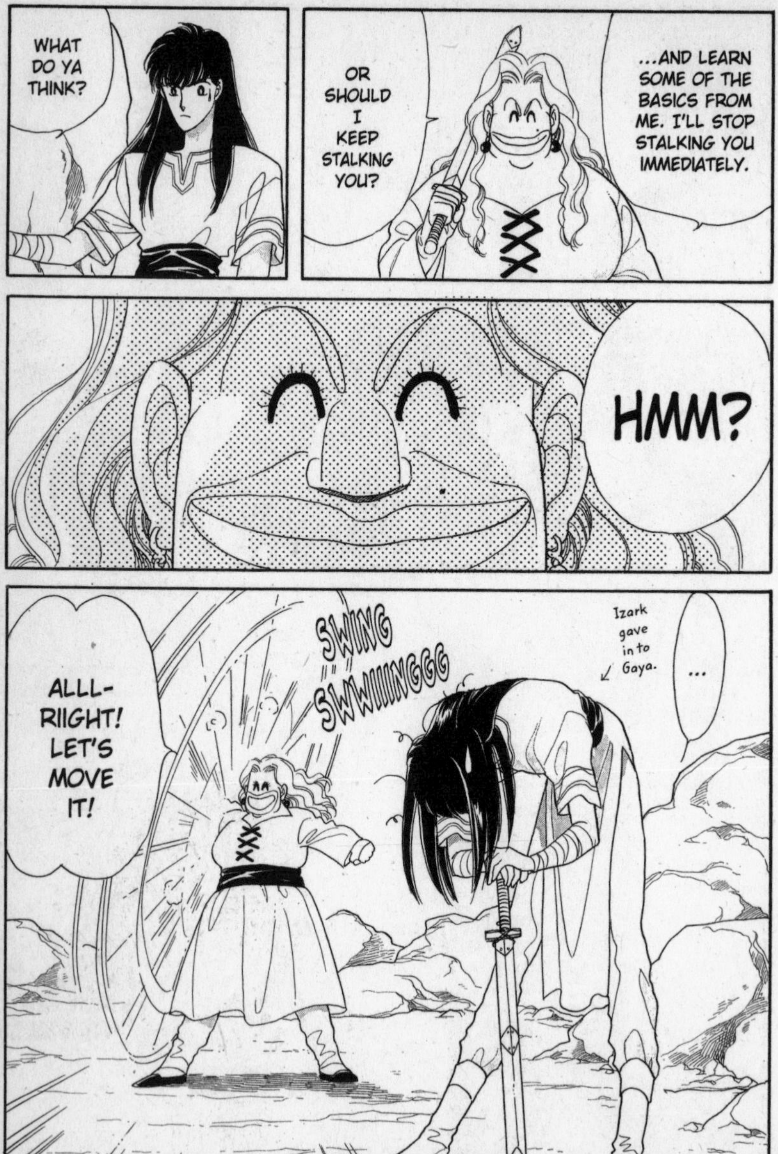

...AND LEARN SOME OF THE BASICS FROM ME. I'LL STOP STALKING YOU IMMEDIATELY.
OR SHOULD I KEEP STALKING YOU?
WHAT DO YA THINK?
HMM?
...
Izark gave in to Gaya.
SWING SWWIIINGGG
ALLL-RIIGHT! LET'S MOVE IT!

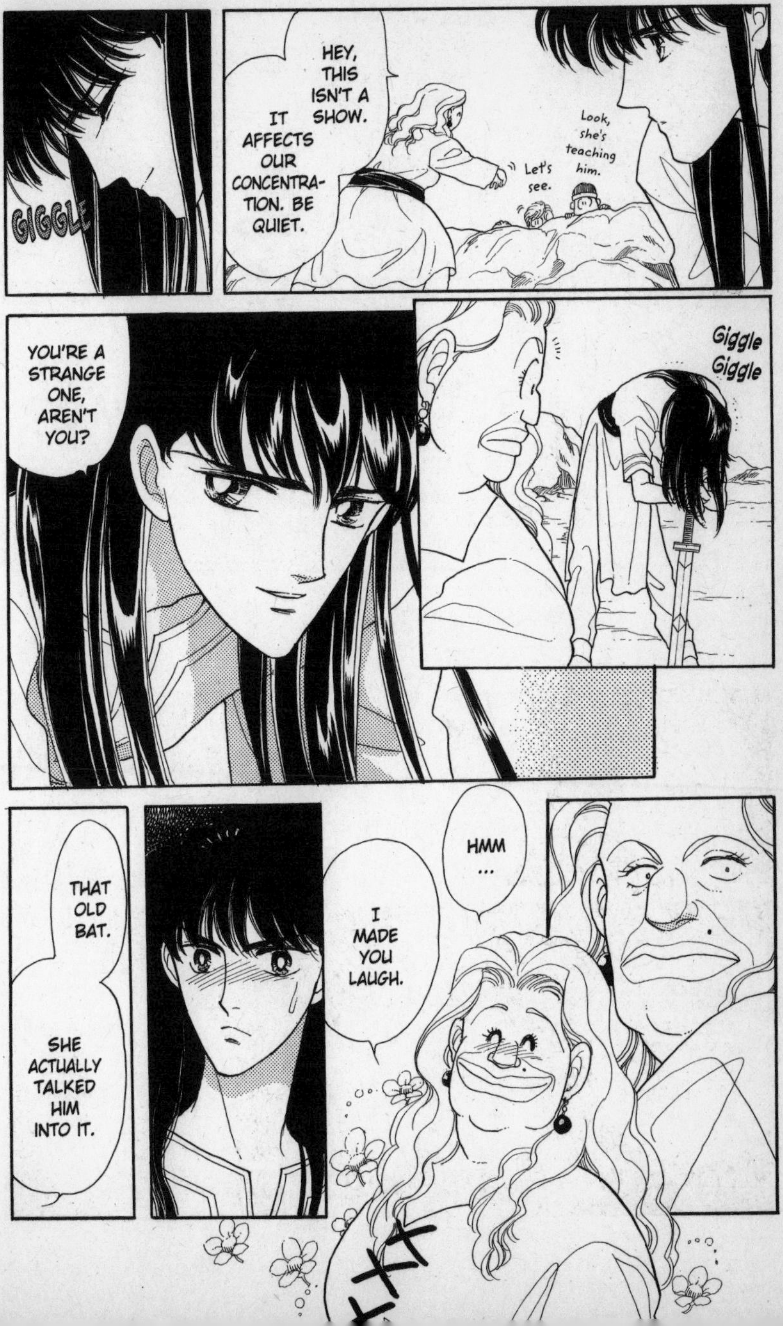
Look, she's teaching him.
Let's see.
HEY, THIS ISN'T A SHOW.
IT AFFECTS OUR CONCENTRATION. BE QUIET.
GIGGLE
Giggle Giggle
YOU'RE A STRANGE ONE, AREN'T YOU?
HMM ...
I MADE YOU LAUGH.
THAT OLD BAT.
SHE ACTUALLY TALKED HIM INTO IT.

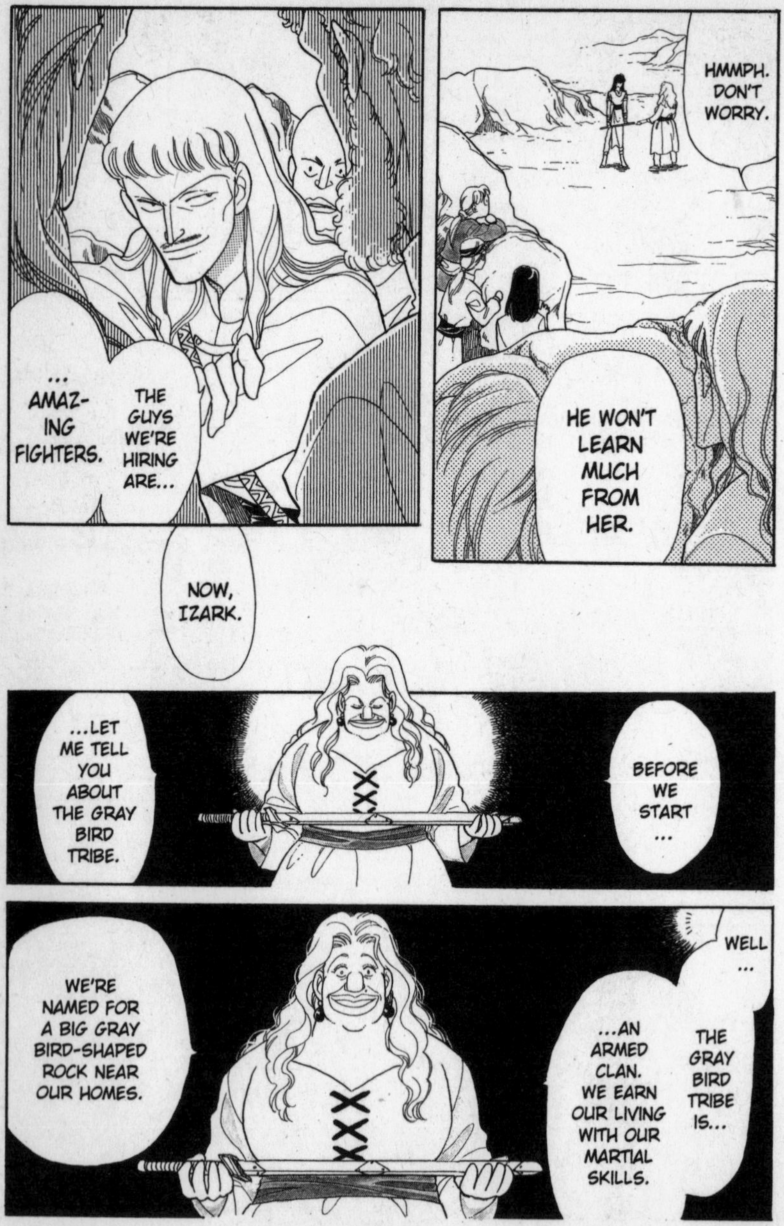
HMMPH. DON'T WORRY.
HE WON'T LEARN MUCH FROM HER.
THE GUYS WE'RE HIRING ARE...
... AMAZ-ING FIGHTERS.
NOW, IZARK.
BEFORE WE START ...
...LET ME TELL YOU ABOUT THE GRAY BIRD TRIBE.
WELL ...
THE GRAY BIRD TRIBE IS...
...AN ARMED CLAN. WE EARN OUR LIVING WITH OUR MARTIAL SKILLS.
WE'RE NAMED FOR A BIG GRAY BIRD-SHAPED ROCK NEAR OUR HOMES.

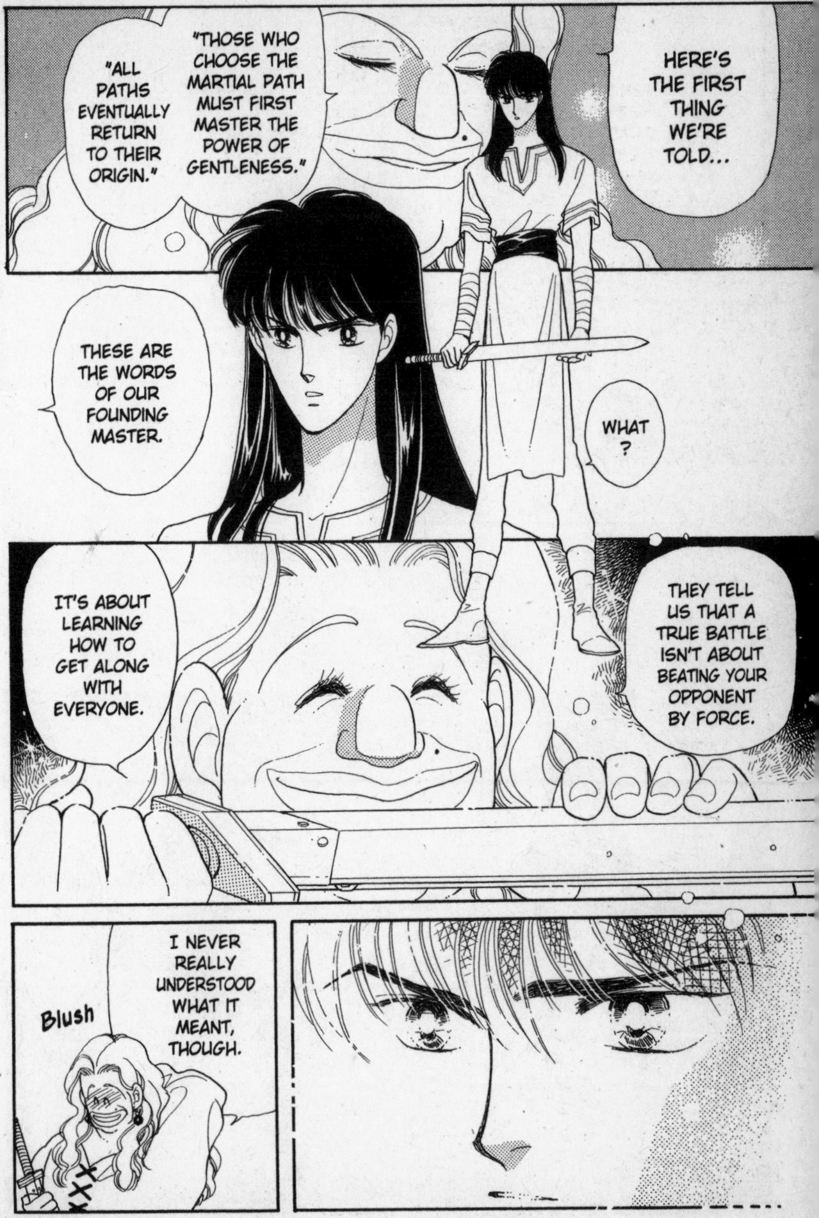
HERE'S THE FIRST THING WE'RE TOLD...
"THOSE WHO CHOOSE THE MARTIAL PATH MUST FIRST MASTER THE POWER OF GENTLENESS."
"ALL PATHS EVENTUALLY RETURN TO THEIR ORIGIN."
WHAT?
THESE ARE THE WORDS OF OUR FOUNDING MASTER.
THEY TELL US THAT A TRUE BATTLE ISN'T ABOUT BEATING YOUR OPPONENT BY FORCE.
IT'S ABOUT LEARNING HOW TO GET ALONG WITH EVERYONE.
I NEVER REALLY UNDERSTOOD WHAT IT MEANT, THOUGH.
Blush

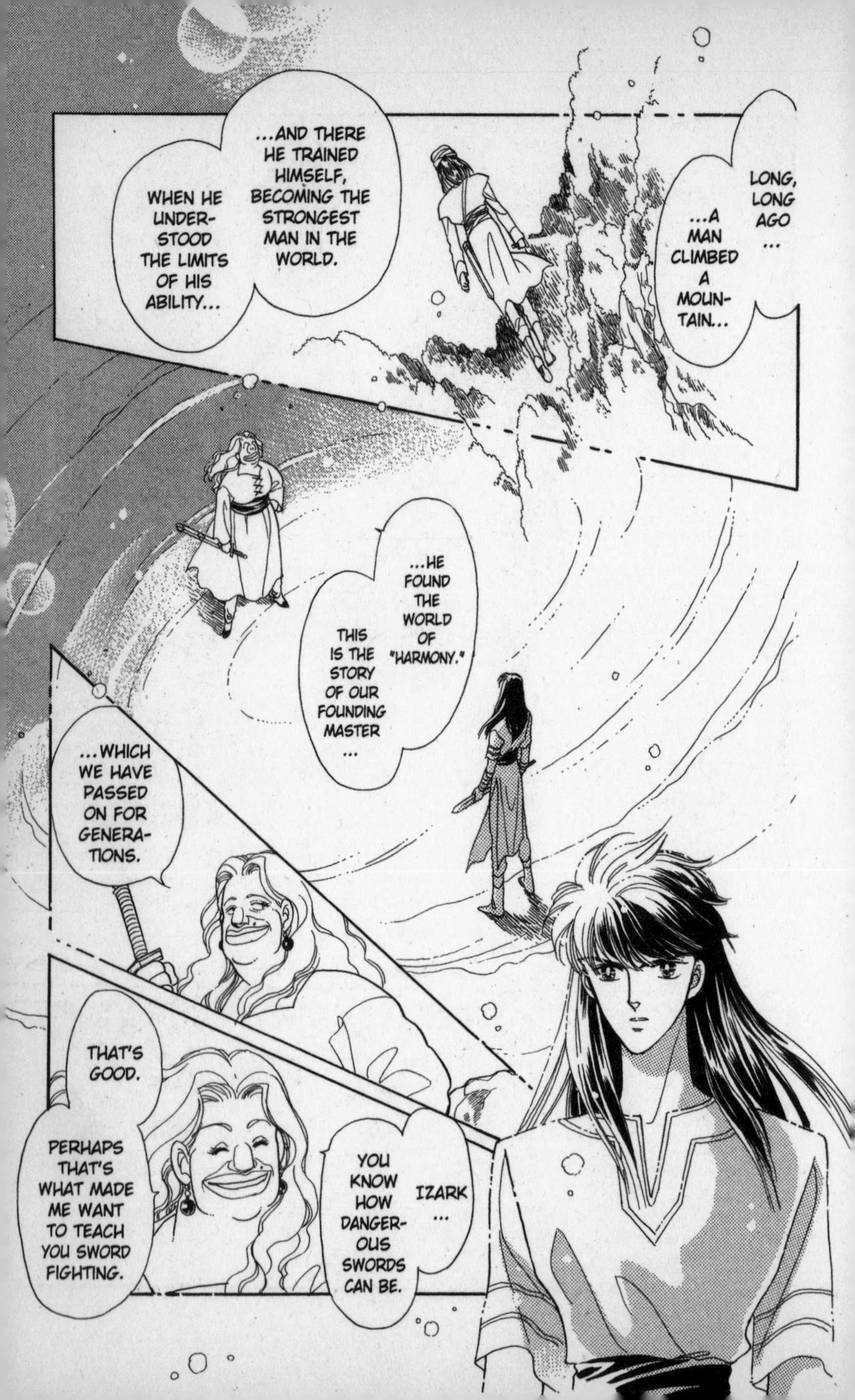
LONG, LONG AGO...
...A MAN CLIMBED A MOUNTAIN...
...AND THERE HE TRAINED HIMSELF, BECOMING THE STRONGEST MAN IN THE WORLD.
WHEN HE UNDERSTOOD THE LIMITS OF HIS ABILITY...
...HE FOUND THE WORLD OF "HARMONY."
THIS IS THE STORY OF OUR FOUNDING MASTER...
...WHICH WE HAVE PASSED ON FOR GENERATIONS.
IZARK...
YOU KNOW HOW DANGEROUS SWORDS CAN BE.
THAT'S GOOD.
PERHAPS THAT'S WHAT MADE ME WANT TO TEACH YOU SWORD FIGHTING.

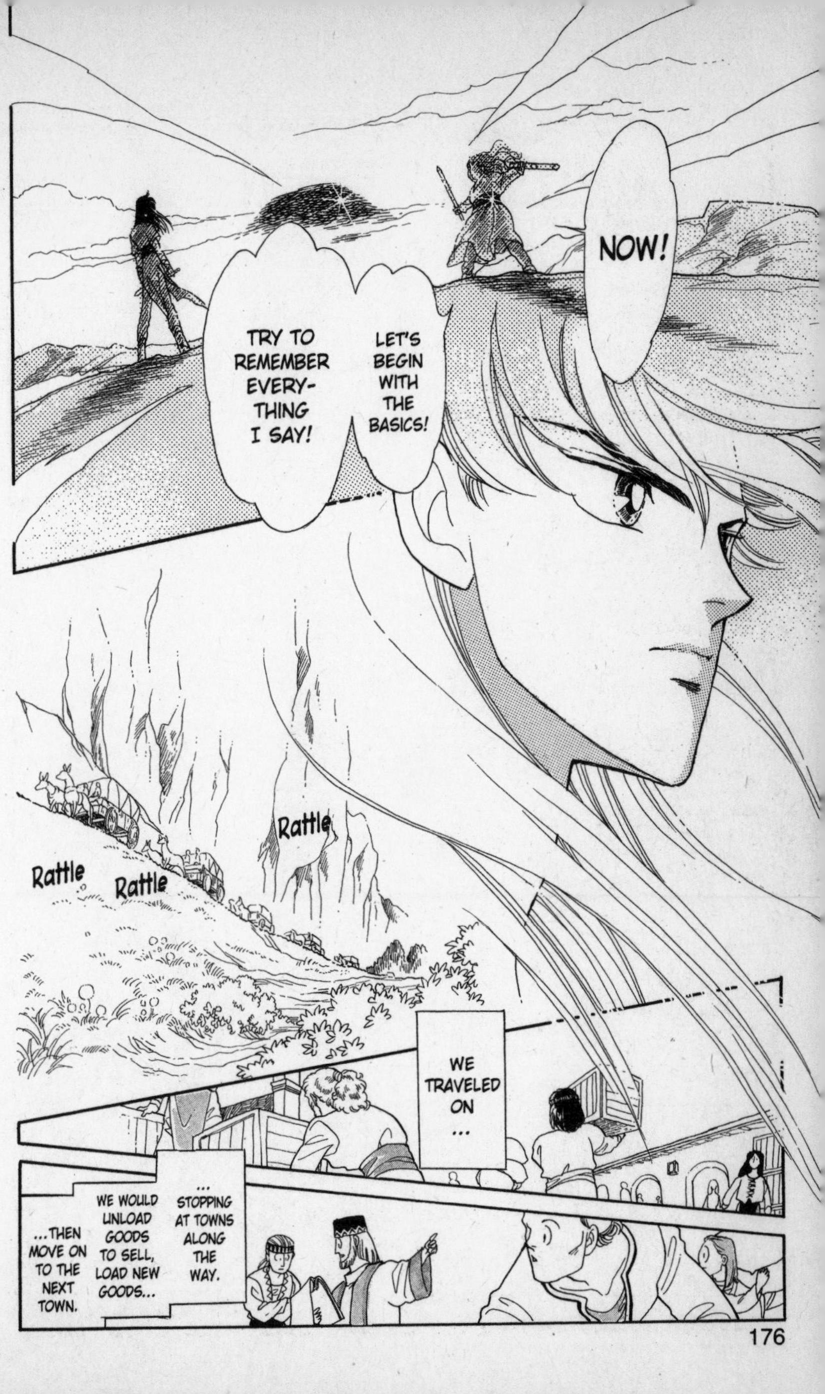
NOW!
LET'S BEGIN WITH THE BASICS!
TRY TO REMEMBER EVERY-THING I SAY!
Rattle
Rattle
Rattle
WE TRAVELED ON ...
... STOPPING AT TOWNS ALONG THE WAY.
WE WOULD UNLOAD GOODS TO SELL, LOAD NEW GOODS...
...THEN MOVE ON TO THE NEXT TOWN.

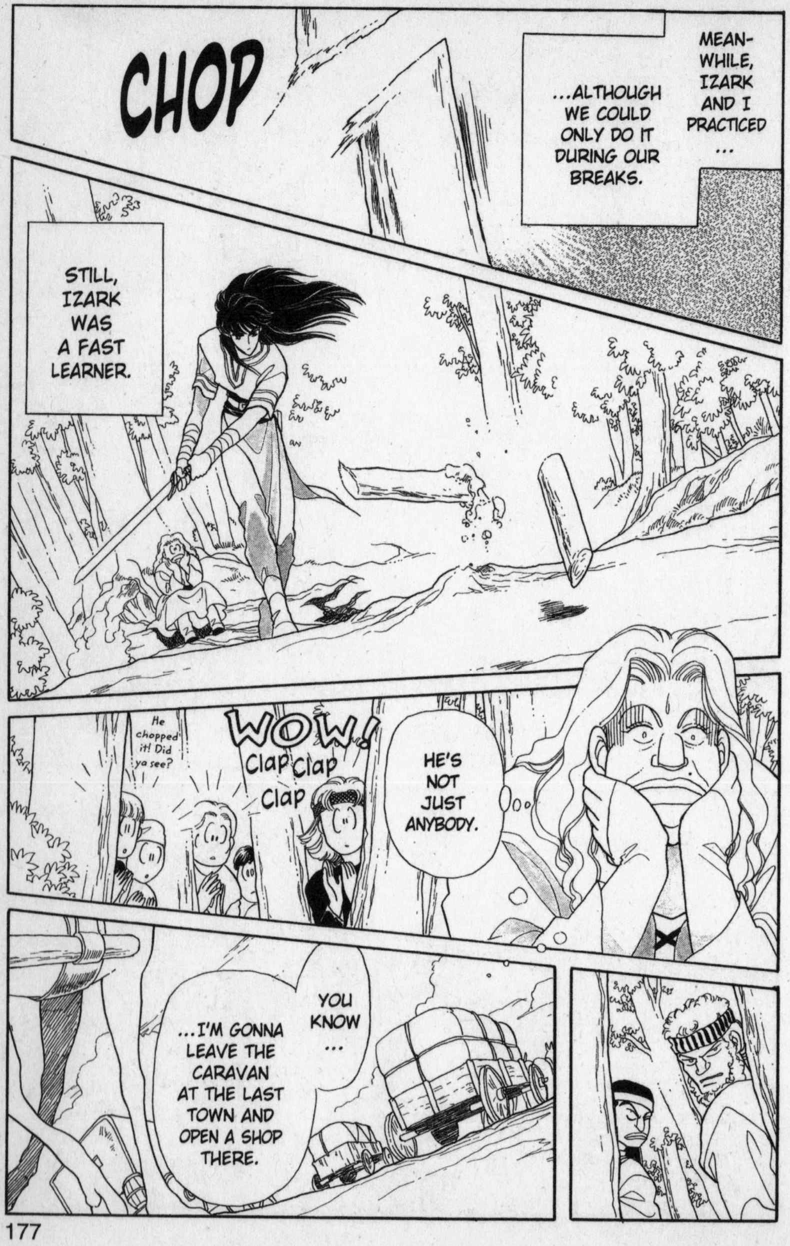
MEAN-WHILE, IZARK AND I PRACTICED ...
...ALTHOUGH WE COULD ONLY DO IT DURING OUR BREAKS.
CHOP
STILL, IZARK WAS A FAST LEARNER.
HE'S NOT JUST ANYBODY.
WOW!
Clap Clap Clap
He chopped it! Did ya see?
YOU KNOW ...
...I'M GONNA LEAVE THE CARAVAN AT THE LAST TOWN AND OPEN A SHOP THERE.

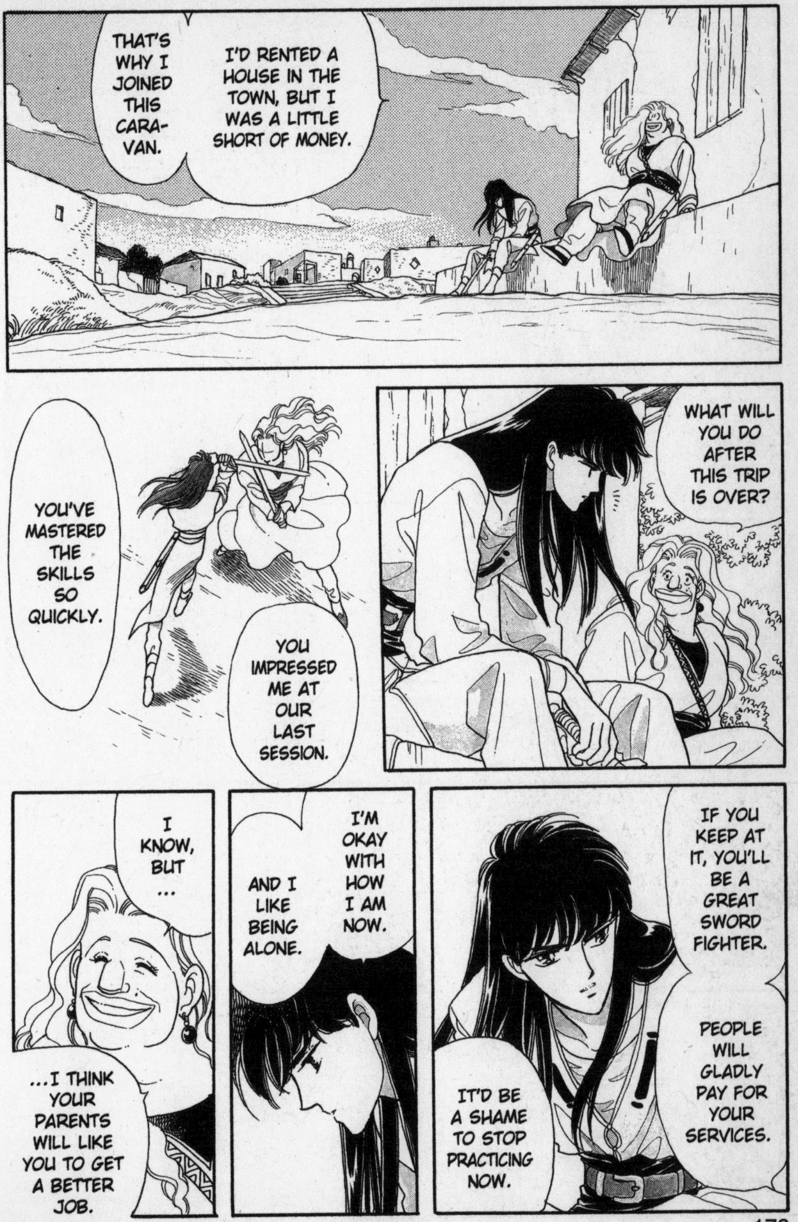
I'D RENTED A HOUSE IN THE TOWN, BUT I WAS A LITTLE SHORT OF MONEY.
THAT'S WHY I JOINED THIS CARA-VAN.
WHAT WILL YOU DO AFTER THIS TRIP IS OVER?
YOU IMPRESSED ME AT OUR LAST SESSION.
YOU'VE MASTERED THE SKILLS SO QUICKLY.
IF YOU KEEP AT IT, YOU'LL BE A GREAT SWORD FIGHTER.
PEOPLE WILL GLADLY PAY FOR YOUR SERVICES.
IT'D BE A SHAME TO STOP PRACTICING NOW.
I'M OKAY WITH HOW I AM NOW.
AND I LIKE BEING ALONE.
I KNOW, BUT ...
...I THINK YOUR PARENTS WILL LIKE YOU TO GET A BETTER JOB.

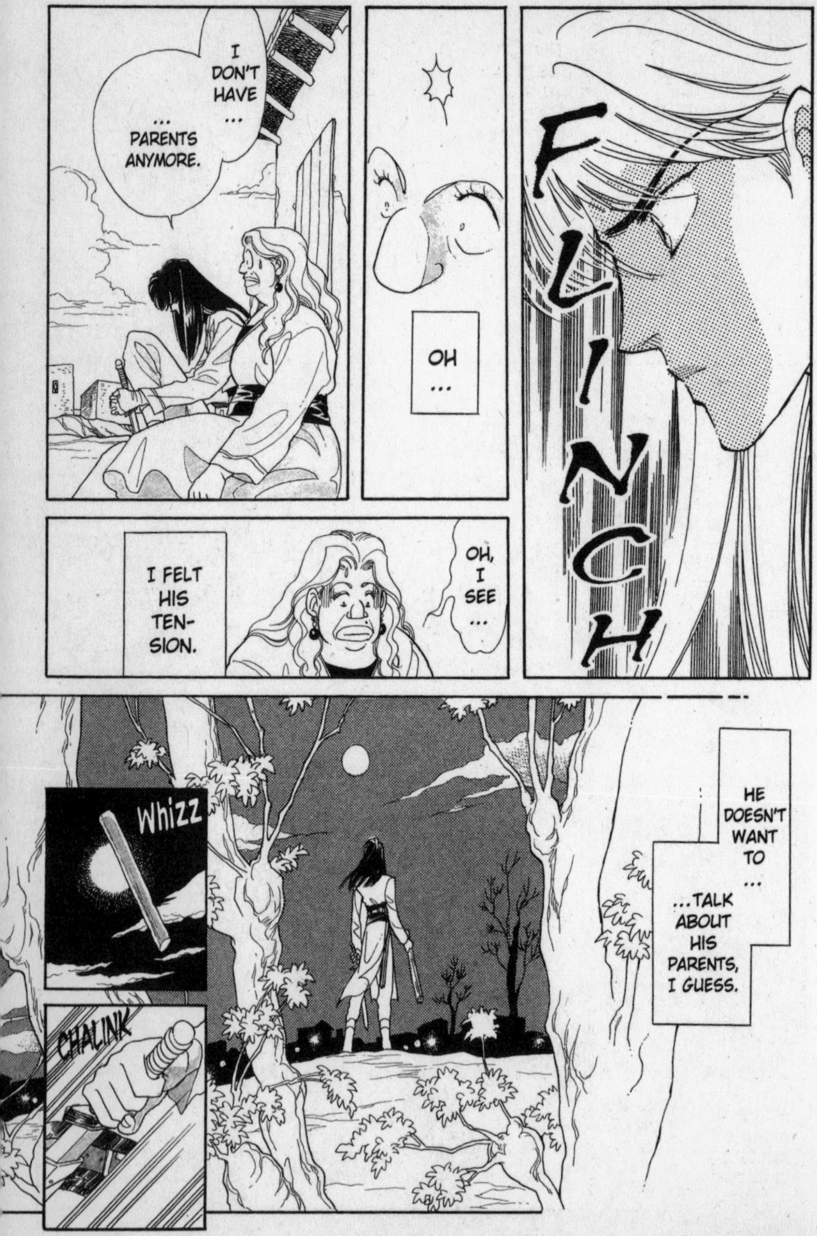
FLINCH
OH ...
I DON'T HAVE ...
... PARENTS ANYMORE.
OH, I SEE ...
I FELT HIS TENSION.
HE DOESN'T WANT TO ...
...TALK ABOUT HIS PARENTS, I GUESS.
Whizz
CHALINK

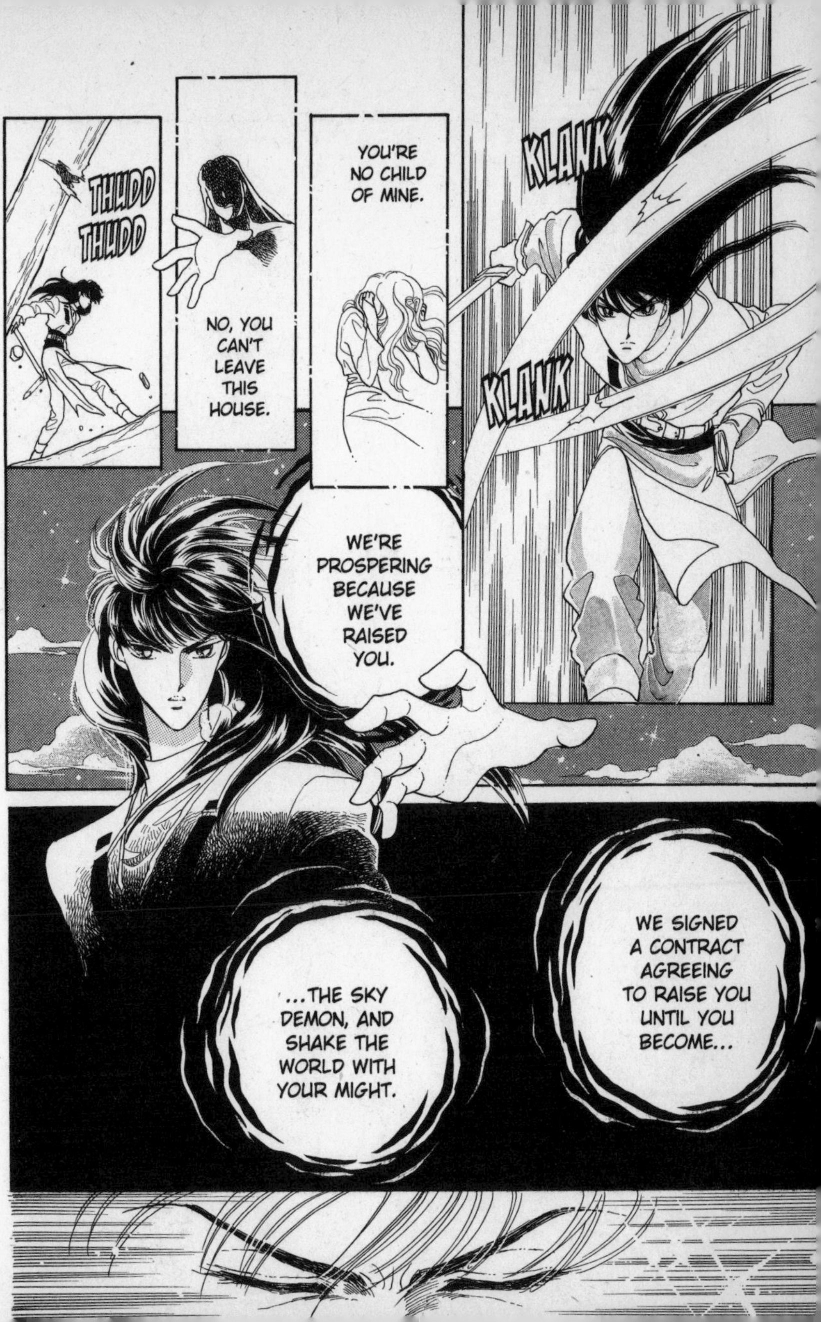
KLANK
KLANK
YOU'RE NO CHILD OF MINE.
NO, YOU CAN'T LEAVE THIS HOUSE.
THUDD THUDD
WE'RE PROSPERING BECAUSE WE'VE RAISED YOU.
WE SIGNED A CONTRACT AGREEING TO RAISE YOU UNTIL YOU BECOME...
...THE SKY DEMON, AND SHAKE THE WORLD WITH YOUR MIGHT.

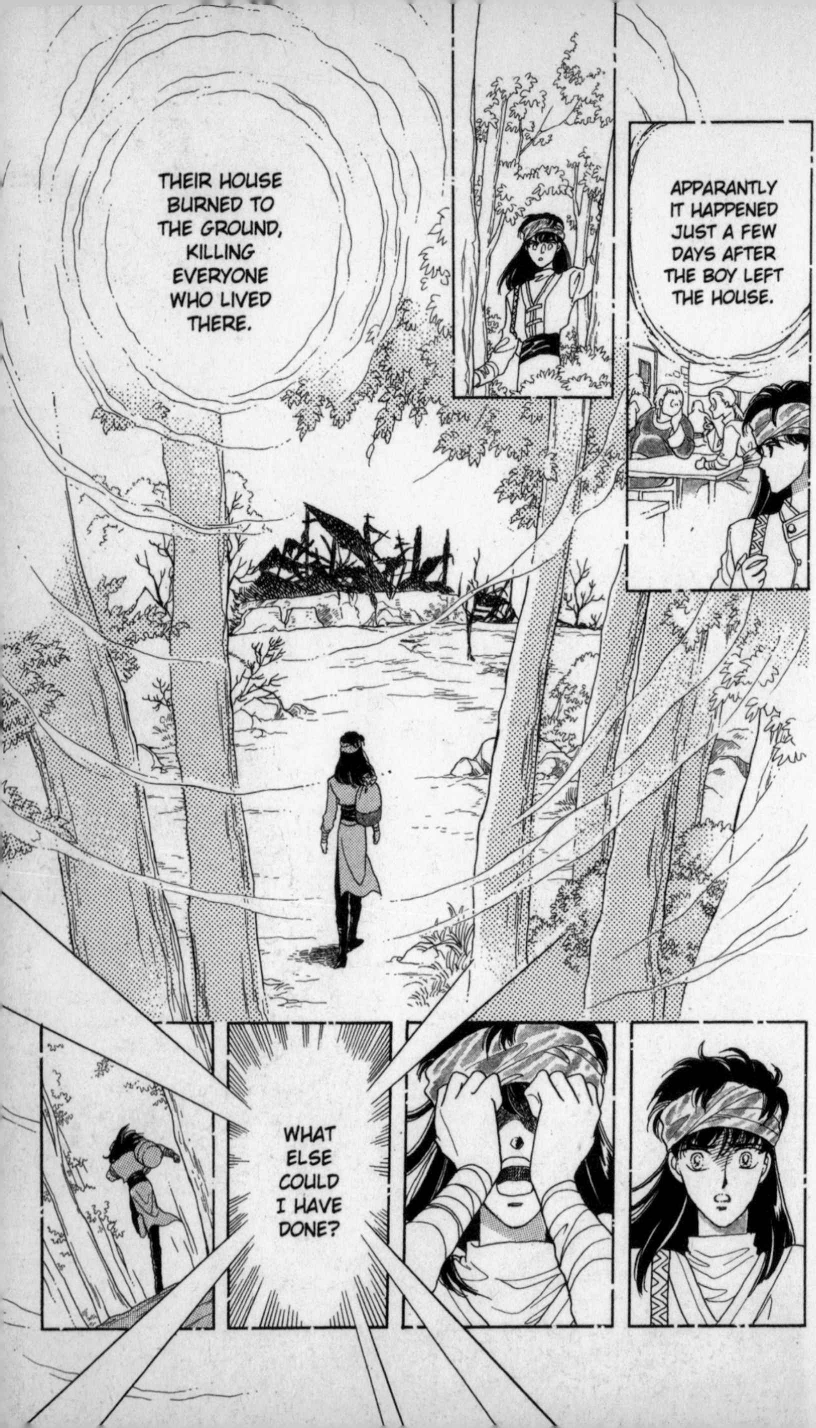
APPARENTLY IT HAPPENED JUST A FEW DAYS AFTER THE BOY LEFT THE HOUSE.
THEIR HOUSE BURNED TO THE GROUND, KILLING EVERYONE WHO LIVED THERE.
WHAT ELSE COULD I HAVE DONE?

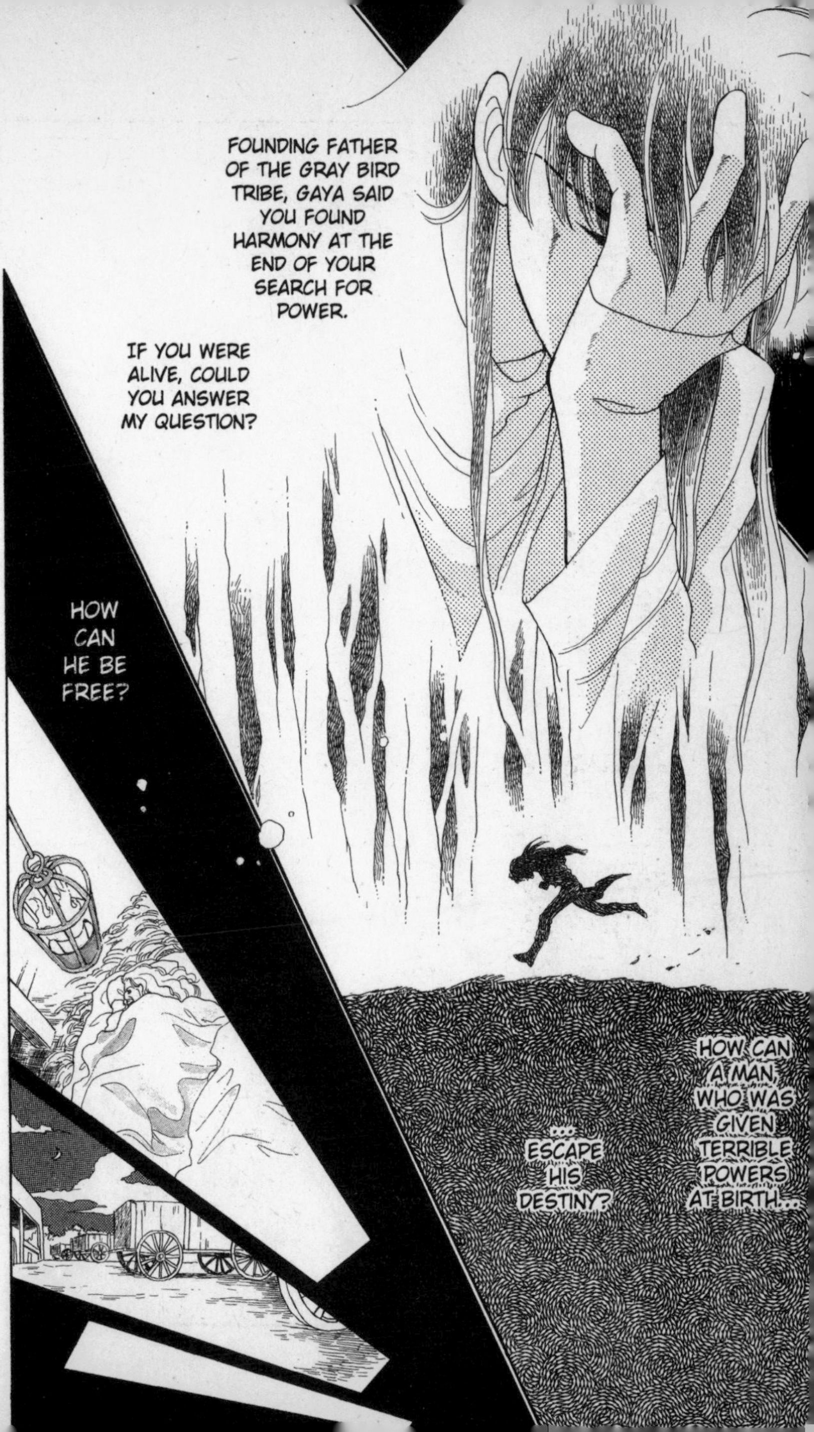
FOUNDING FATHER OF THE GRAY BIRD TRIBE, GAYA SAID YOU FOUND HARMONY AT THE END OF YOUR SEARCH FOR POWER.
IF YOU WERE ALIVE, COULD YOU ANSWER MY QUESTION?
HOW CAN HE BE FREE?
HOW CAN A MAN, WHO WAS GIVEN TERRIBLE POWERS AT BIRTH...
...ESCAPE HIS DESTINY?

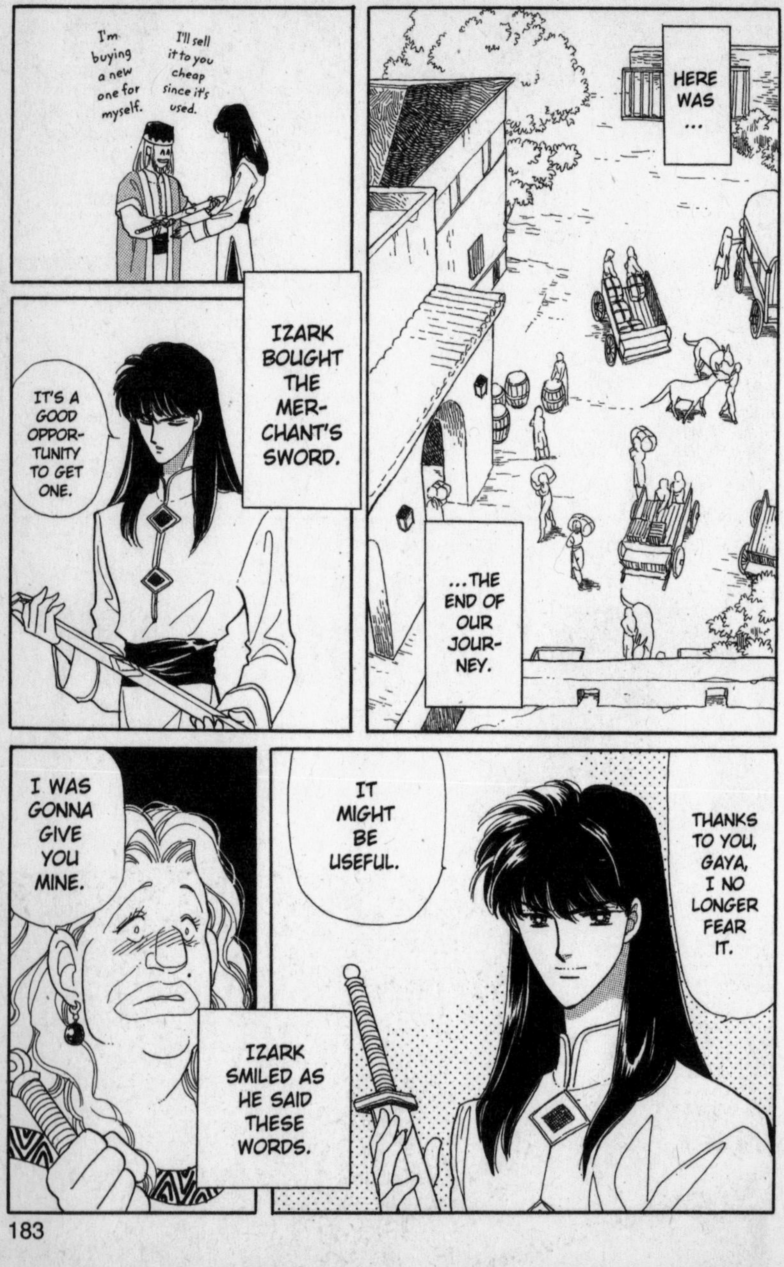
HERE WAS ...
...THE END OF OUR JOUR-NEY.
I'll sell it to you cheap since it's used.
I'm buying a new one for myself.
IZARK BOUGHT THE MER-CHANT'S SWORD.
IT'S A GOOD OPPOR-TUNITY TO GET ONE.
THANKS TO YOU, GAYA, I NO LONGER FEAR IT.
IT MIGHT BE USEFUL.
I WAS GONNA GIVE YOU MINE.
IZARK SMILED AS HE SAID THESE WORDS.

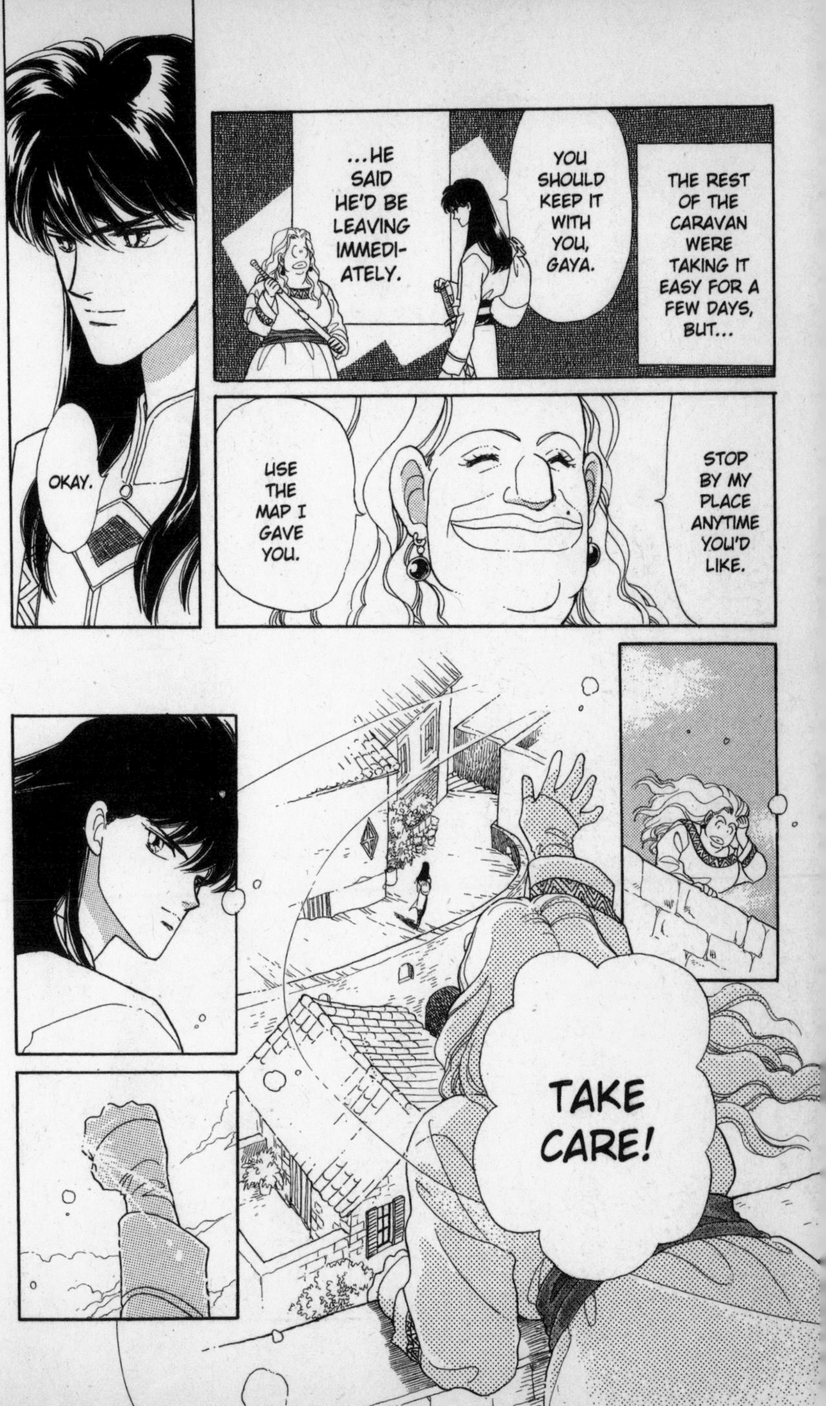
THE REST OF THE CARAVAN WERE TAKING IT EASY FOR A FEW DAYS, BUT...
YOU SHOULD KEEP IT WITH YOU, GAYA.
...HE SAID HE'D BE LEAVING IMMEDI-ATELY.
STOP BY MY PLACE ANYTIME YOU'D LIKE.
USE THE MAP I GAVE YOU.
OKAY.
TAKE CARE!

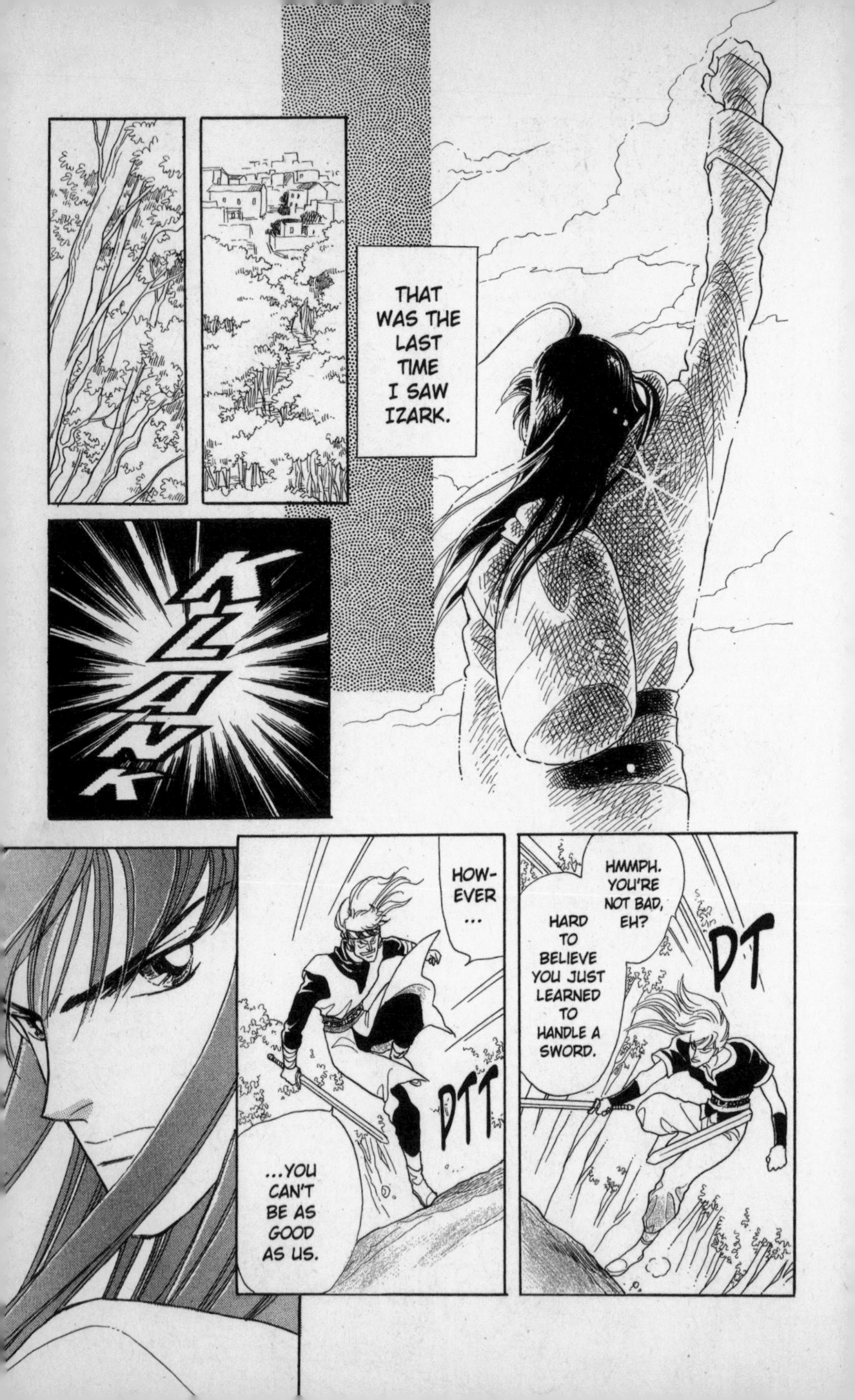
THAT WAS THE LAST TIME I SAW IZARK.
KLANK
HMMPH. YOU'RE NOT BAD, EH?
HARD TO BELIEVE YOU JUST LEARNED TO HANDLE A SWORD.
DT
HOW-EVER ...
DTT
...YOU CAN'T BE AS GOOD AS US.

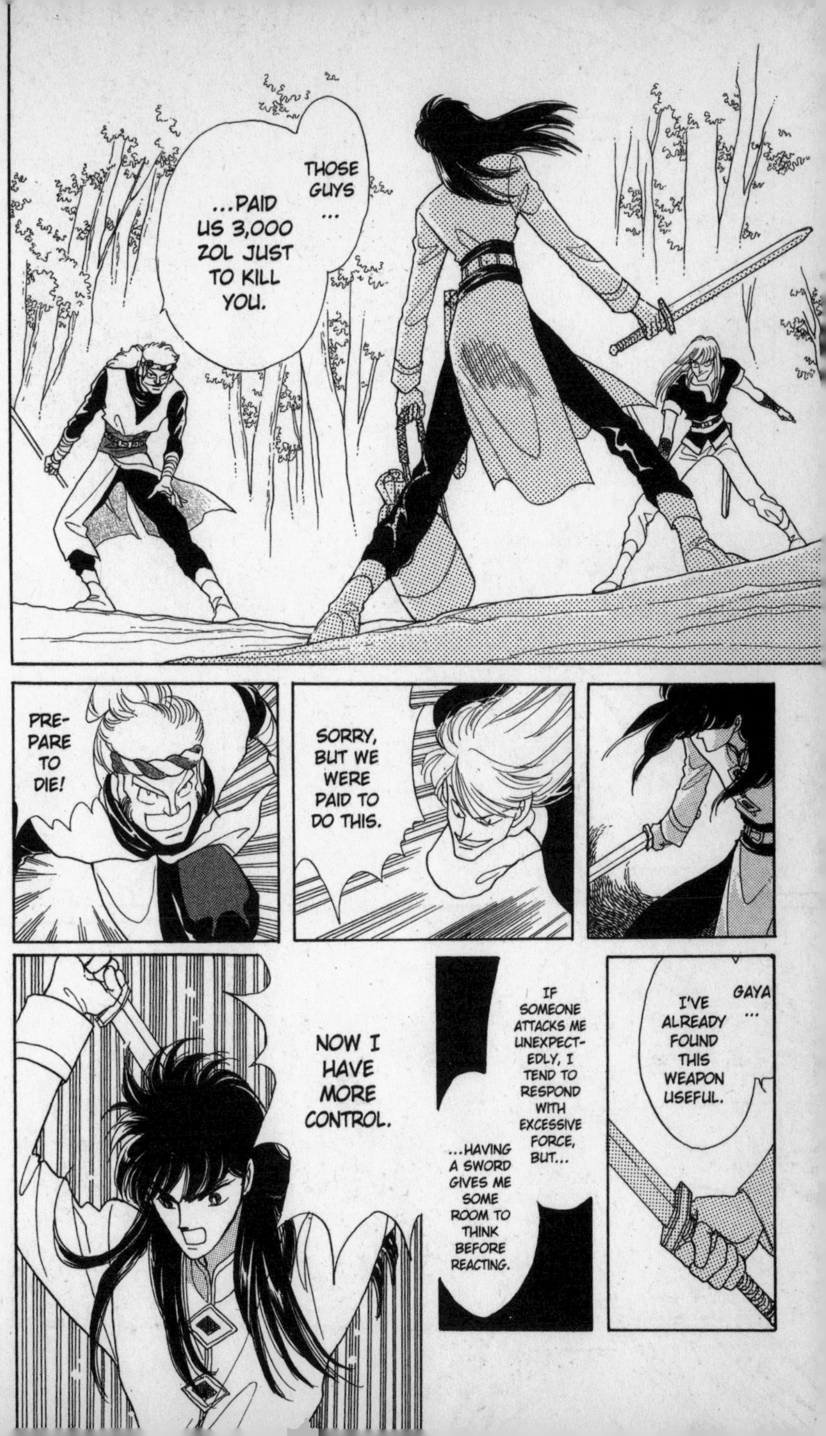
THOSE GUYS ...
...PAID US 3,000 ZOL JUST TO KILL YOU.
SORRY, BUT WE WERE PAID TO DO THIS.
PRE-PARE TO DIE!
GAYA ...
I'VE ALREADY FOUND THIS WEAPON USEFUL.
IF SOMEONE ATTACKS ME UNEXPECT-EDLY, I TEND TO RESPOND WITH EXCESSIVE FORCE, BUT...
...HAVING A SWORD GIVES ME SOME ROOM TO THINK BEFORE REACTING.
NOW I HAVE MORE CONTROL.

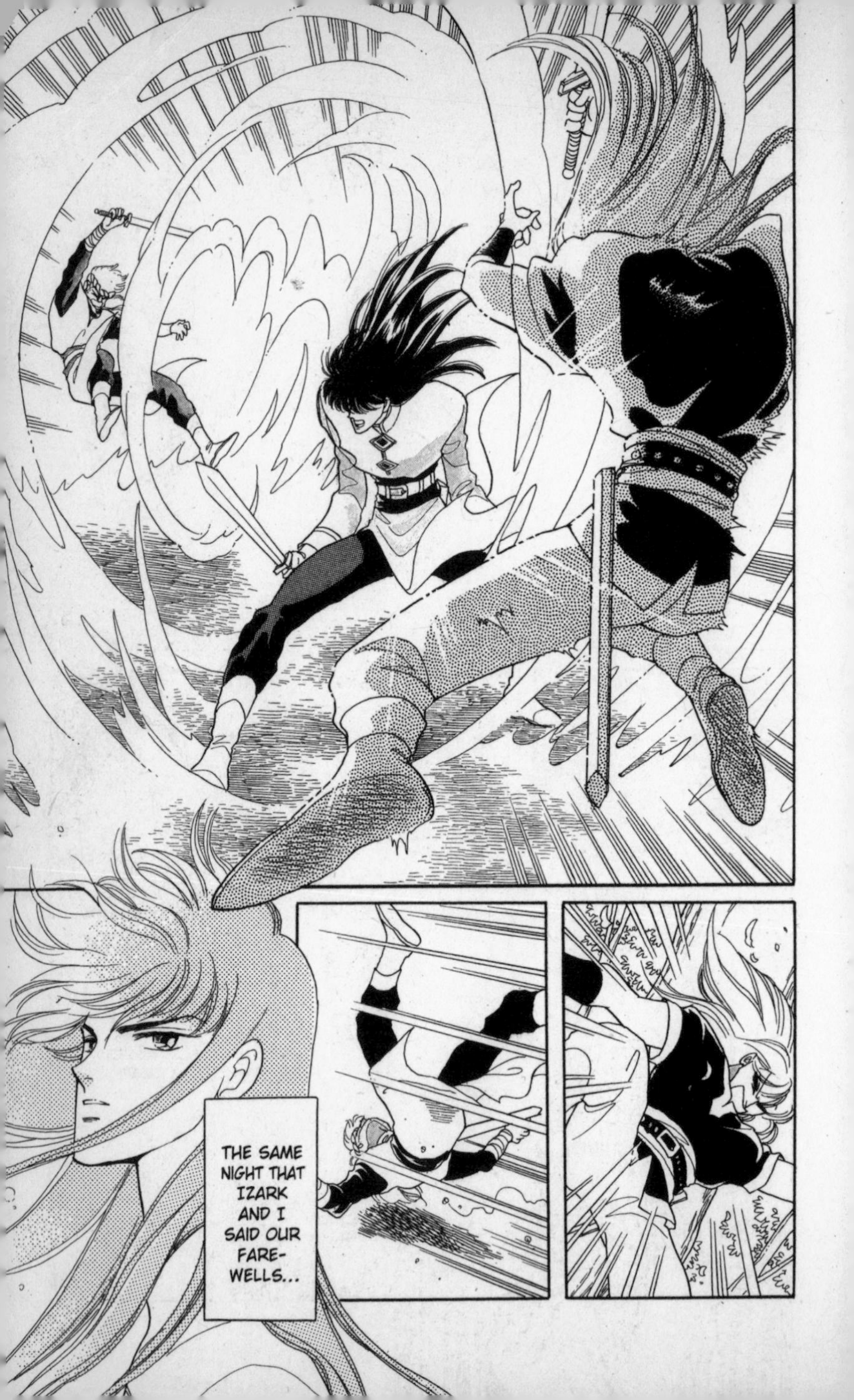
THE SAME NIGHT THAT IZARK AND I SAID OUR FARE-WELLS...

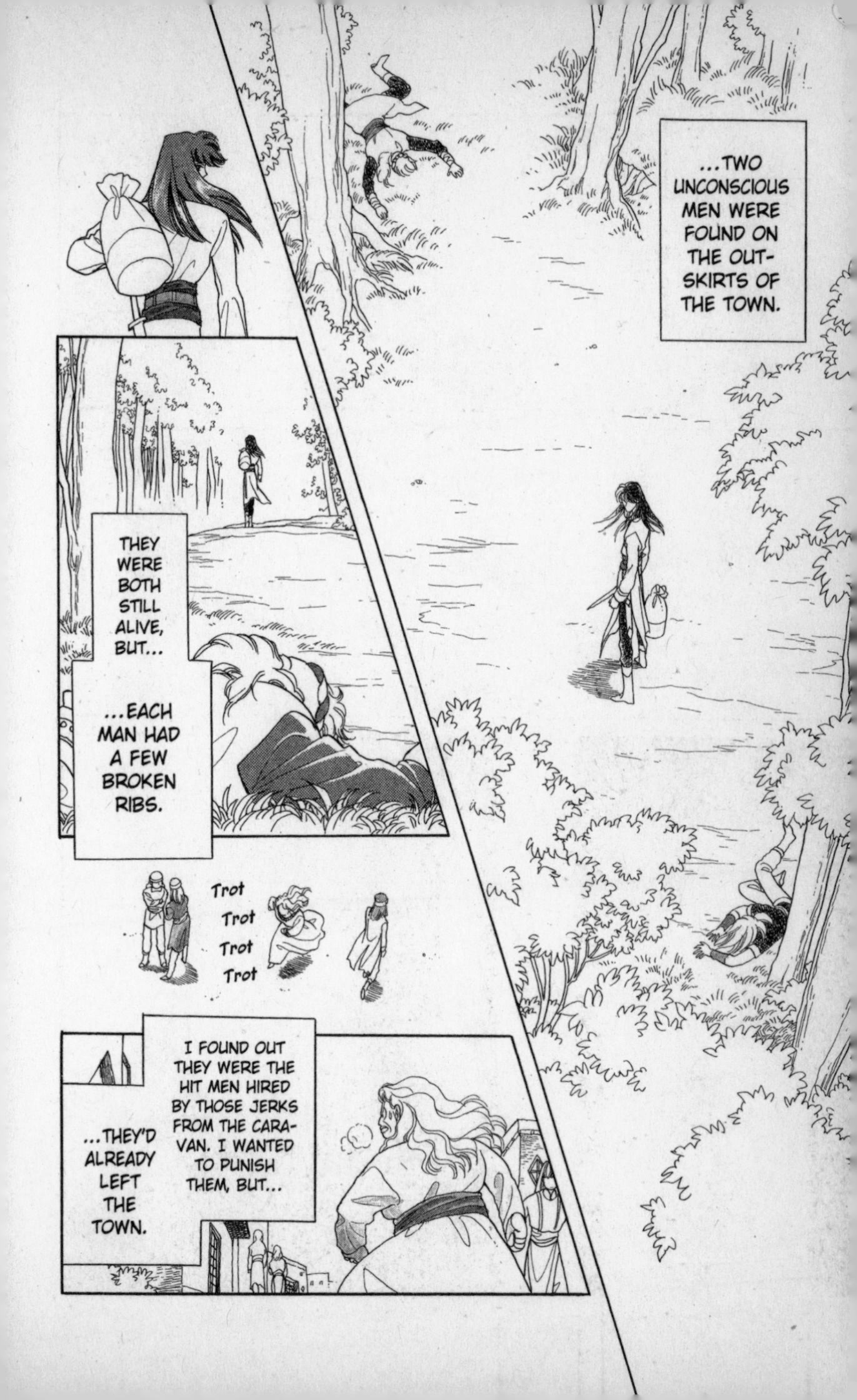
...TWO UNCONSCIOUS MEN WERE FOUND ON THE OUT-SKIRTS OF THE TOWN.
THEY WERE BOTH STILL ALIVE, BUT...
...EACH MAN HAD A FEW BROKEN RIBS.
Trot Trot Trot Trot
I FOUND OUT THEY WERE THE HIT MEN HIRED BY THOSE JERKS FROM THE CARA-VAN. I WANTED TO PUNISH THEM, BUT...
...THEY'D ALREADY LEFT THE TOWN.

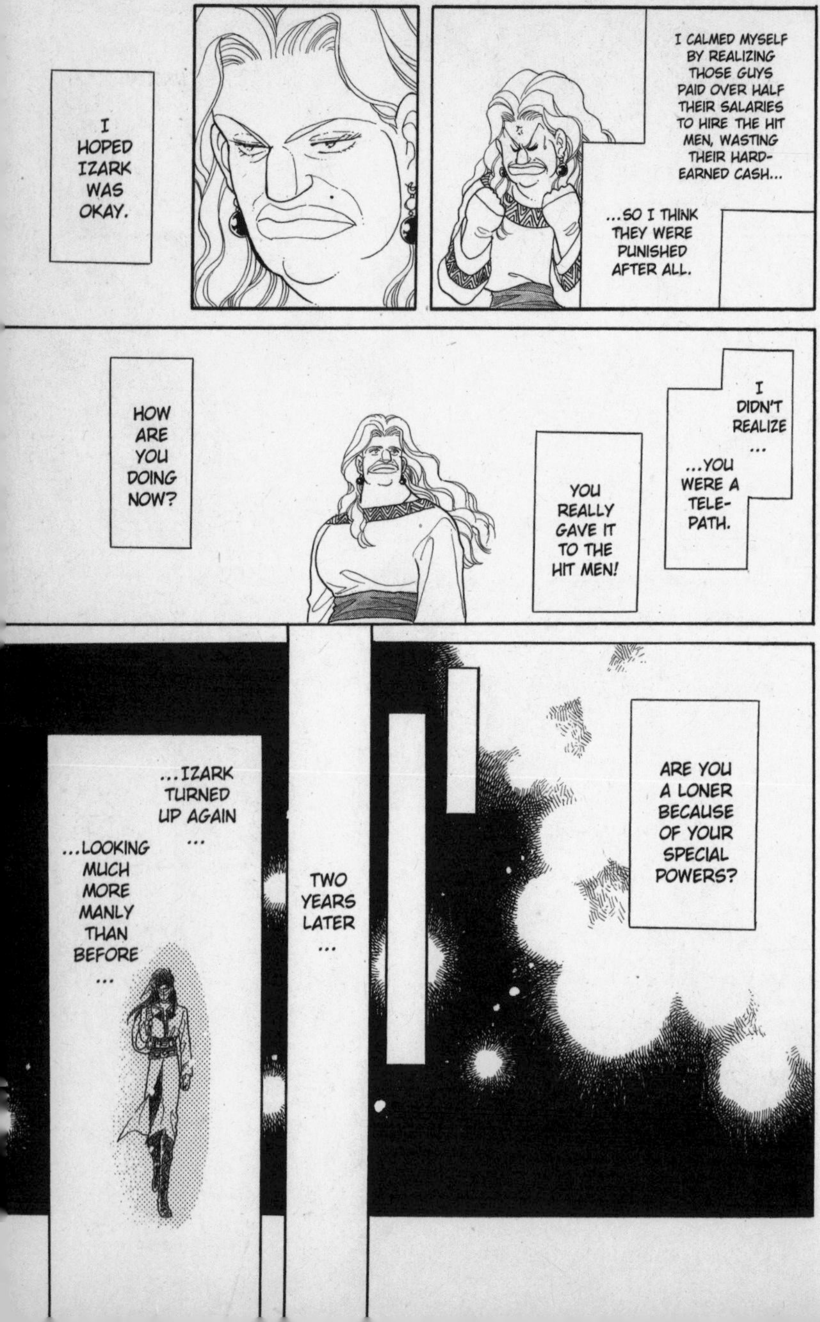
I CALMED MYSELF BY REALIZING THOSE GUYS PAID OVER HALF THEIR SALARIES TO HIRE THE HIT MEN, WASTING THEIR HARD-EARNED CASH...
...SO I THINK THEY WERE PUNISHED AFTER ALL.
I HOPED IZARK WAS OKAY.
I DIDN'T REALIZE ...
...YOU WERE A TELE-PATH.
YOU REALLY GAVE IT TO THE HIT MEN!
HOW ARE YOU DOING NOW?
ARE YOU A LONER BECAUSE OF YOUR SPECIAL POWERS?
TWO YEARS LATER ...
...IZARK TURNED UP AGAIN ...
...LOOKING MUCH MORE MANLY THAN BEFORE ...

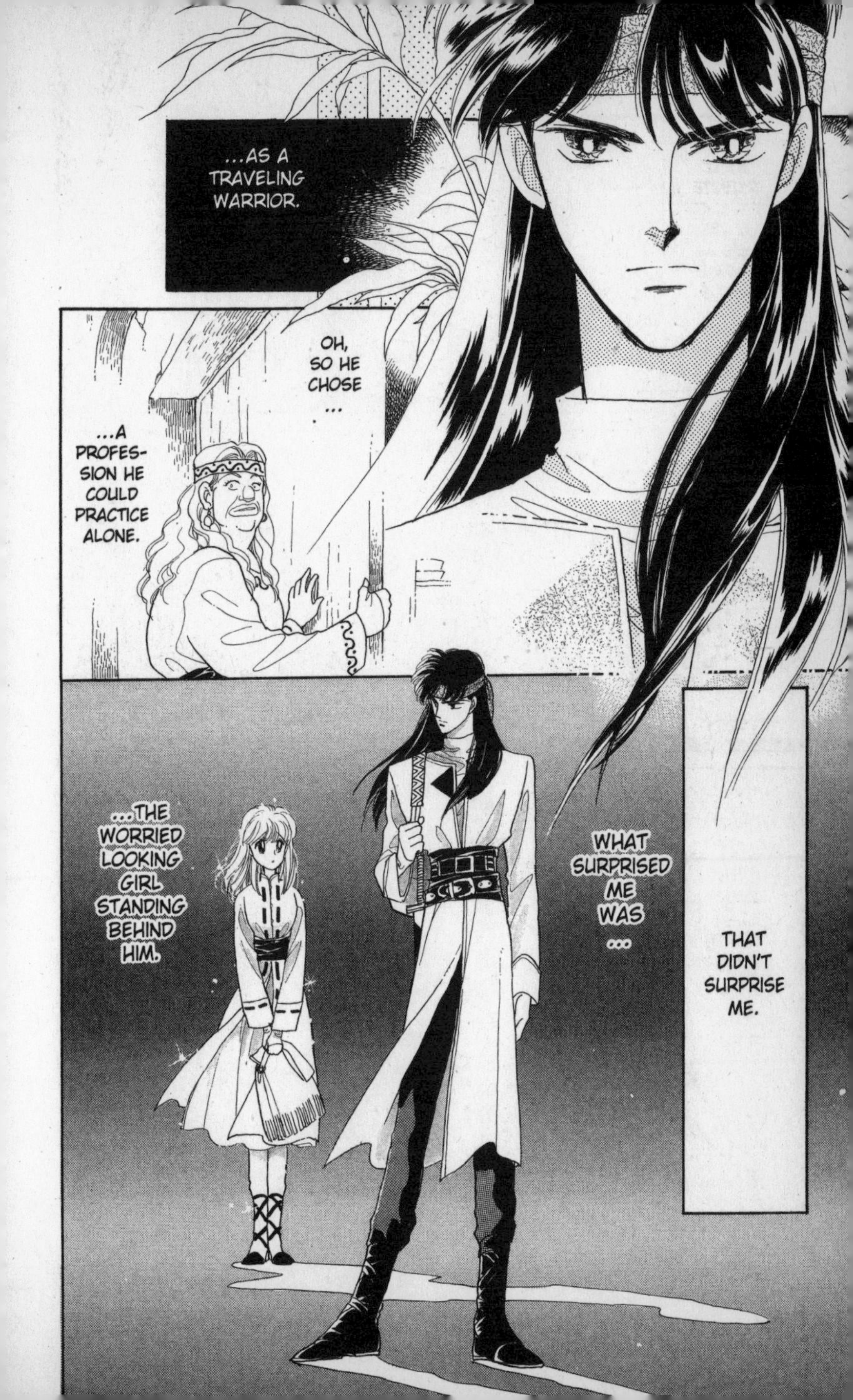
...AS A TRAVELING WARRIOR.
OH, SO HE CHOSE ...
...A PROFESSION HE COULD PRACTICE ALONE.
THAT DIDN'T SURPRISE ME.
WHAT SURPRISED ME WAS ...
...THE WORRIED LOOKING GIRL STANDING BEHIND HIM.

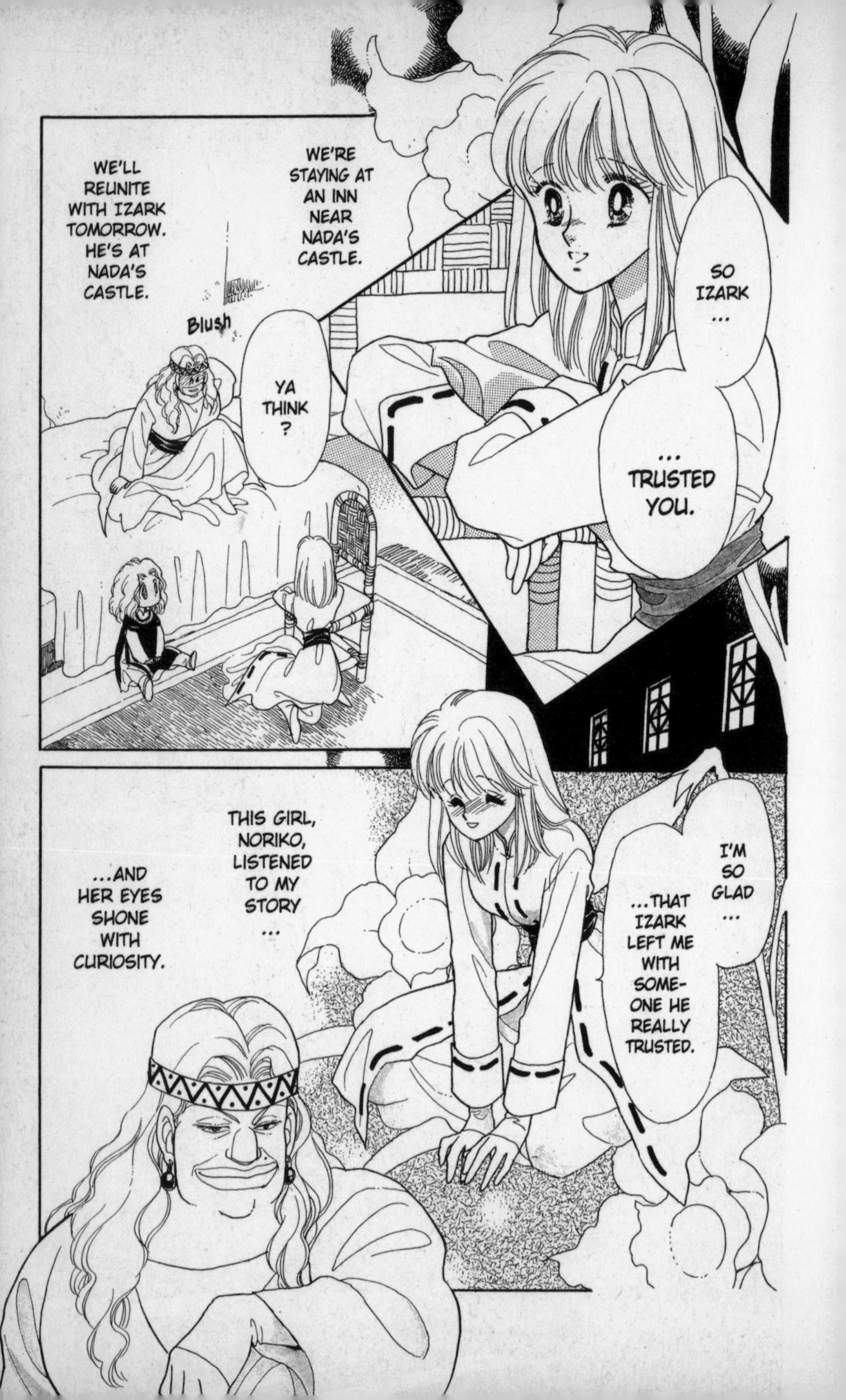
SO IZARK ...
... TRUSTED YOU.
WE'RE STAYING AT AN INN NEAR NADA'S CASTLE.
WE'LL REUNITE WITH IZARK TOMORROW. HE'S AT NADA'S CASTLE.
Blush
YA THINK?
I'M SO GLAD ...
...THAT IZARK LEFT ME WITH SOME-ONE HE REALLY TRUSTED.
THIS GIRL, NORIKO, LISTENED TO MY STORY ...
...AND HER EYES SHONE WITH CURIOSITY.

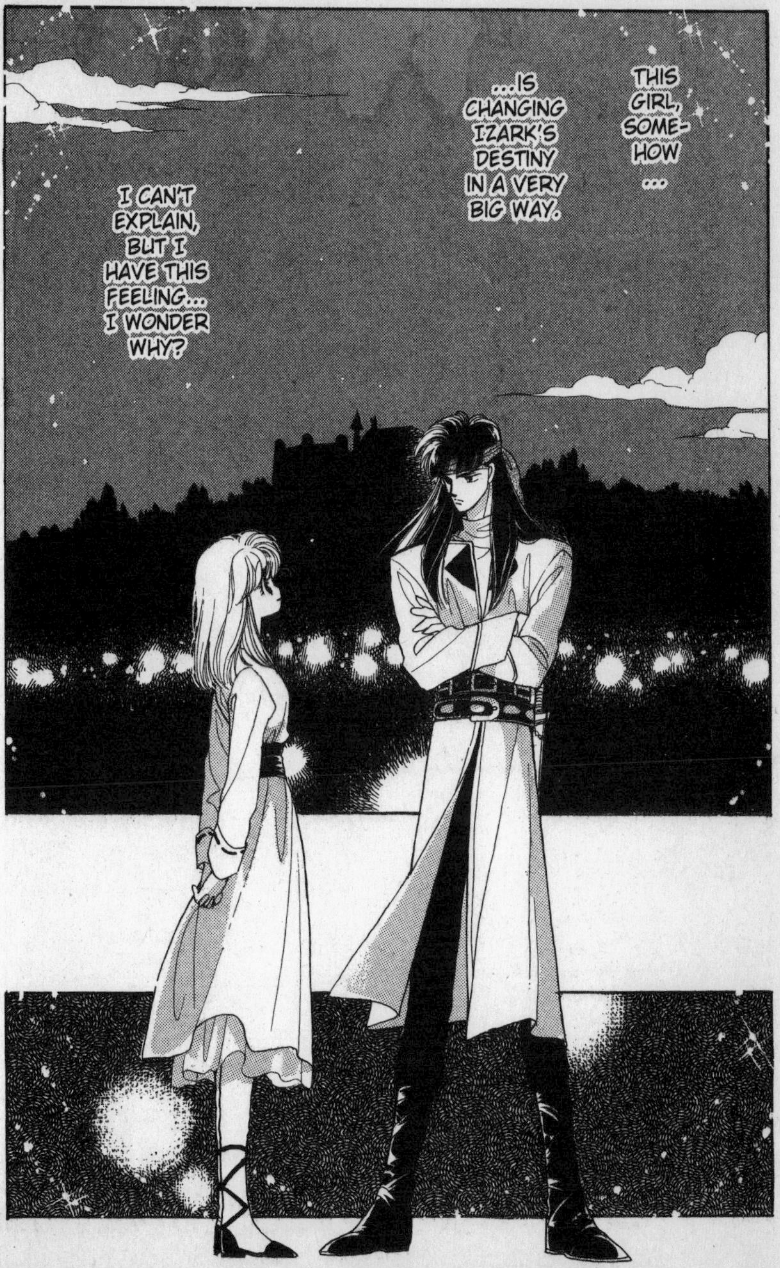
THIS GIRL, SOME-HOW ...
...IS CHANGING IZARK'S DESTINY IN A VERY BIG WAY.
I CAN'T EXPLAIN, BUT I HAVE THIS FEELING... I WONDER WHY?

From Far Away
Vol. 5
Shôjo Edition

Story and Art by
Kyoko Hikawa

English Adaptation/Trina Robbins
Translation/Yuko Sawada
Touch-Up Art & Lettering/Walden Wong
Cover & Graphic Design/Andrea Rice
Editor/Eric Searleman

Managing Editor/Annette Roman
Director of Production/Noboru Watanabe
Vice President of Publishing/Alvin Lu
Sr. Director of Acquisitions/Rika Inouye
Vice President of Sales & Marketing/Liza Coppola
Publisher/Hyoe Narita

Printed in the U.S.A.

Published by VIZ, LLC
P.O. Box 77010
San Francisco, CA 94107

Shôjo Edition
10 9 8 7 6 5 4 3 2 1
First printing, June 2005

www.viz.com

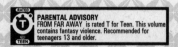

store.viz.com

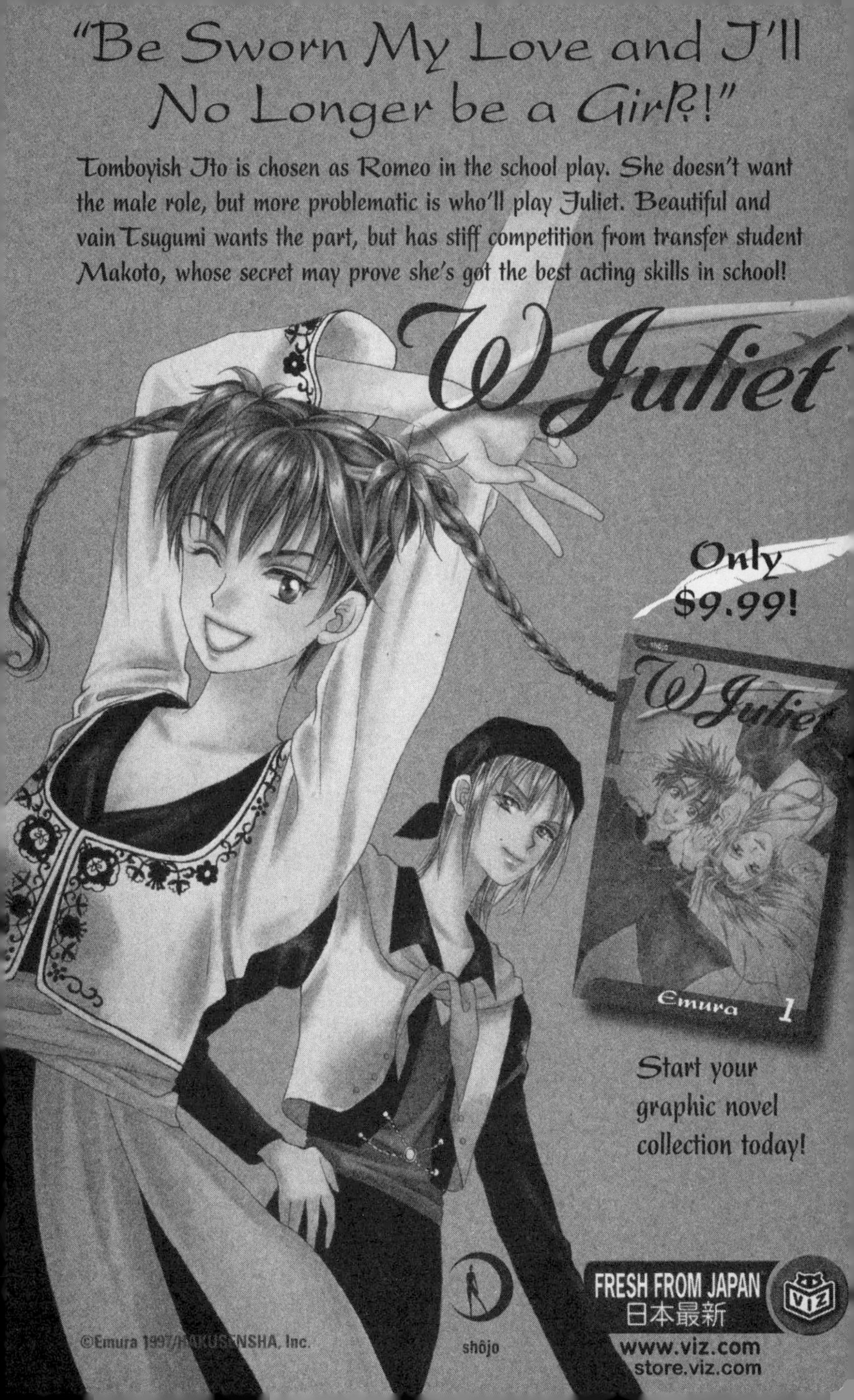
"Be Sworn My Love and I'll No Longer be a Girl?!"
Tomboyish Ito is chosen as Romeo in the school play. She doesn't want the male role, but more problematic is who'll play Juliet. Beautiful and vain Tsugumi wants the part, but has stiff competition from transfer student Makoto, whose secret may prove she's got the best acting skills in school!
W Juliet
Only $9.99!
W Juliet
Emura 1
Start your graphic novel collection today!
FRESH FROM JAPAN
日本最新
VIZ
shôjo
©Emura 1997/HAKUSENSHA, Inc.
www.viz.com
store.viz.com

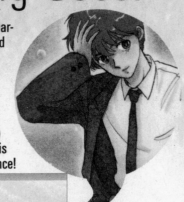

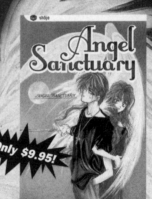

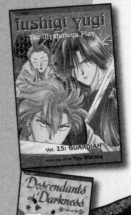

COMPLETE OUR SURVEY AND LET US KNOW WHAT YOU THINK!

☐ Please do NOT send me information about VIZ products, news and events, special offers, or other information.

☐ Please do NOT send me information from VIZ's trusted business partners.

Name: _____

Address: _____

City: _____ **State:** _____ **Zip:** _____

E-mail: _____

☐ Male ☐ Female   Date of Birth (mm/dd/yyyy): ___/___/___   (Under 13? Parental consent required)

What race/ethnicity do you consider yourself? (please check one)

☐ Asian/Pacific Islander ☐ Black/African American ☐ Hispanic/Latino

☐ Native American/Alaskan Native ☐ White/Caucasian ☐ Other: _____

What VIZ product did you purchase? (check all that apply and indicate title purchased)

☐ DVD/VHS _____

☐ Graphic Novel _____

☐ Magazines _____

☐ Merchandise _____

Reason for purchase: (check all that apply)

☐ Special offer ☐ Favorite title ☐ Gift

☐ Recommendation ☐ Other _____

Where did you make your purchase? (please check one)

☐ Comic store ☐ Bookstore ☐ Mass/Grocery Store

☐ Newsstand ☐ Video/Video Game Store ☐ Other: _____

☐ Online (site: _____)

What other VIZ properties have you purchased/own? _____

_____

How many anime and/or manga titles have you [...] VIZ titles? (please check one from each column)

ANIME	MANGA	
☐ None	☐ None	☐ None
☐ 1-4	☐ 1-4	☐ 1-4
☐ 5-10	☐ 5-10	☐ 5-10
☐ 11+	☐ 11+	☐ 11+

I find the pricing of VIZ products to be: (please check one)

☐ Cheap   ☐ Reasonable   ☐ Expensive

What genre of manga and anime would you like to see from VIZ? (please check two)

☐ Adventure   ☐ Comic Strip   ☐ Science Fiction   ☐ Fighting

☐ Horror   ☐ Romance   ☐ Fantasy   ☐ Sports

What do you think of VIZ's new look?

☐ Love It   ☐ It's OK   ☐ Hate It   ☐ Didn't Notice   ☐ No Opinion

Which do you prefer? (please check one)

☐ Reading right-to-left

☐ Reading left-to-right

Which do you prefer? (please check one)

☐ Sound effects in English

☐ Sound effects in Japanese with English captions

☐ Sound effects in Japanese only with a glossary at the back

THANK YOU! Please send the completed form to:

NJW Research
42 Catharine St.
Poughkeepsie, NY 12601

All information provided will be used for internal purposes only. We promise not to sell or otherwise divulge your information.